SEARCH FOR FOOD SECURITY IN ASIA

SEARCH FOR FOOD SECURITY IN ASIA

Edited by
Narottam Gaan
Sandhya Rani Das
Aruna Kumar Nishanka

KALPAZ

First Published 2017

Published by

Kalpaz Publications
C-30, Satyawati Nagar,
Delhi - 110052
E-mail: kalpaz@hotmail.com
Ph.: 9212142040

Printed at: G. Print Process, Delhi

Cataloging in Publication Data—DK
Courtesy: D.K. Agencies (P) Ltd. <docinfo@dkagencies.com>

Search for food security in Asia / edited by Narottam Gaan, Sandhya Rani Das, Aruna Kumar Nishanka.
pages cm
Contributed articles.
Includes bibliographical references.
ISBN 9789351282860

1. Food security—Asia. I. Gaan, Narottam, editor. II. Das, Sandhya Rani, editor. III. Nishanka, Aruna Kumar, editor.

HD9016.A2S43 2017 DDC 338.195 23

Preface

Life is sustained, nourished and shaped with food. Every living being starting from plants, trees, animals to even tiny insects requires food to make its existence on this earth peaceful, healthy and comfortable. In Indian scriptures it is said: "sarirmadyam khaludharma sadhanam".Body is first then all kinds of activities begin. Without sound and healthy body devoid of any ailments human beings cannot be wise and intellectually, physically and spiritually helpful to humankind. This is the reason God brought creation with appetite for food in every living being otherwise His dream created universe will carry no meaning. Without food the creation will be decimated within a moment. This is imbibed in human beings to strive for not only food but delicious and nutritious without which life force cannot be sustained on this earth.Food sustains a civilization and lack of it buries it. In Srimad Bhagvad GitaLord Krishna narrates the types and nature of food that a human being should take for his/her all round development, physical, intellectual, moral, and spiritual. It shapes the character and moral being of a person. The United Nations, WHO and FAO have put stress on the imperatives of states to implement right to food a fundamental human right so that nobody on this earth goes without food. In spite of these international covenants and resolutions the nations have not been able to ensure4 food security to their people. As estimates show majority of the people on this earth have remained without food and many of them particularly women, children and old people have been succumbed to lack of food. Availability of food, agriculture and climate change are closely connected. As is now seen climate change has adversely affected food production denying many the right to food.

Clearly, food production, prices, and food security will all be significantly affected by climate change's impact on temperatures, rainfall, and aquatic species, as outlined by Working Group II of the Intergovernmental Panel on Climate Change in its 5th Assessment report. A report released by International Food Policy Research Institute during the Paris COP predicts that climate change will have an adverse effect on food security in vulnerable countries. It cites the example of the Philippines, where it notes that climate change may increase the number of people at risk of hunger by 1.4 million in 2030 and 2.5 million by 2050. The COP21 agreement includes explicit language on the connections between food and climate, stating it "recognizes the fundamental priority of safeguarding food security and ending hunger, and the particular vulnerabilities of food production systems to the adverse impacts of climate change." In a nod to developing country concerns that any agreement would restrain agriculture, the agreement also states that climate adaptation and mitigation efforts would be done "in a manner that does not threaten food production." Climate change is highly likely to disrupt food production in many regions, raising prices and disrupting markets, and increasing the risk of protests, riots, and civil conflict, as exemplified by the 2007-9 food riots that took place in more than 40 countries. Released in late September 2016, the U.S. Intelligence Community Assessment on "Global Food Security", predicts that "in some countries, declining food security will almost certainly contribute to social disruptions or large-scale political instability or conflict, amplifying global concerns about the availability of food."

Keeping this worldwide phenomenon of food insecurity in the context of climate change and the vulnerabilities of the poor developing countries the present book is an attempt to analyze the prospectus of food security in Asia from various perspectives inviting papers from a host of scholars in India and abroad.

The paper entitled "Nutri-Agriculture: Pathway to a Zero Hunger India"byProf. Dr. M.S. Swaminathan, theIndian renownedagriculture Scientistand thefatherof green revolution in India, enunciated on dynamic form offood security in the context of and acquaintedwiththe current stage of developmentrelatedto thebiotechnological organicfarming with apt module ofirrigationand technologyon prospectiveofworldorder.

The paper written by Sudhansubala Das and Narottam Gaan on "climate change and food security in South Asia" highlights on how climate change will severely hamper agricultural production in South Asia. With frequency of cyclone, flood, drought and fluctuations in monsoon patterns by climate change food production in South Asia will be plummeted.

Thepaperby Dr. Sandhya Rani Das on "Food Security in Odisha" isbasedon the three pillars of food security in Odisha like food availability, food access andfood utilisation.

The next broad based paper is on ". House holdfood Securityin Developingcountries" by Dr. Nkiru Nwamaka Ezeama, asheis from the Department of Medicinehe hasanalysed the data related to the fooditems focusing on their nutritional aspects indevelopingcountries, which home to 80% of the people of the world suffering severely from malnutrition.

The paper on "Community Involvement in Public Goods Provision: Evidence from a Field Experiment in Ghana" by Thomas F. Walker is based on the willingness of individuals in rural communities to contribute to the financing of local public projects. Individuals were asked five mes during 2009 to donate to a public good for their community.His study was based on statistical methods like regression , co-relation anddescriptive statisticsin his paper.

The paper on "Farmers perception on rainfall and its impacts on investment, output, and food security in Switzerland" by Sipho Felix Mamba,University of the Western Cape, RSA, arguedabout the psychologyand perception of the farmers and their fertilizing capacity to produce food with the nationalmeteorological data particularly in South Africa by using chi-square test with special reference to Switzerland.

The next paper is on "Achieving Nutritional Food Security Raising Pulses Output and Arresting Price-rise in India" by Dr.Gopal Kalkoti who discussed about the growing food price specially on pulse items of the food system. He analyzed how national food policy is getting paralysed by this inflationary situation as India is the largest producer, consumer and importer of pulse items in the world.

"Food Security in india: Issues and Strategies" byDr. Parveen Kumar, an agricultural expert is premised on the occupation of farming and the trend analysisof the different professions to farming in India and its impact on different sector of the economy. His paper is based on the growing debtedness of the farmers in Indian agricultural market.

Another micro- nutrient topic " HouseholdFoodSecurityin developingcountries"based on Conceptual framework on Determinants of Child Nutrition and factorsforfood securitywith policy framework on different nationalities is authoredby Dr. Nkiru Nwamaka Ezeam, a doctor by profession.

The topic "Ending 'Malnutrition - Food security and far beyond!" by Dr. Pavan Pandey and his co author Dr. SushrutSharma, based onmulti factorial causation focuses on the issue of eliminating malnutrition which is a complicated issue relating to defecation problem. His argument is that to eliminate malnutrition needs to traverse beyond 'food' security.

Both the authors Dr. Maniklal Adhikary and Khokon Sarkar of the topic"Calorie Availability to Realize Food Security Some Evidences in the District of Burdwan"focus on food security , calorie deprivationand householdin India using lin-log method and some econometric model in their analysis.

Milan Banik's article on "Food Security: Concept, Determinants And Initiatives in India" emphasises on the policy and programmes and theirimplications in theworld onfood securityand thehunger indexand food index, rationing systemand itsanalytical way ofnutrition inthe world beyond it.

Andrew Fraker, Neil Buddy Shah and Ronald Abraham in their topicon "Quantitative assessment: Beneficiary nutritional status and performance of ICDS Supplementary Nutrition Programme in Bihar" argued about the working sphere of both the government and the Anganwadi workers in relation to food security in the state.

Reetika Khera, One of the eminent food security expert contributed a paper entitled "Children's Development Baby Steps in Odisha"which isveryreal andinteresting. Her paper is specially focused on the Anganwadiworkersand the food securityand their nutritional status.

"The Goal and Realities of Food Security: The Way Forward" authored by K. Baby focuses on how environmental degradation and vulnerability to weather-related disasters poses challenges to the country as a whole.

Another important topic is on "Seeds, Soil, and Survival: Towards a Saner Agricultural Future" authored by Ashish Kothari deals with the consequences of soil and the nutritional focus of the different policy relating to it.

Aruna Kumar Nishanka, a co editor of this book has contributed a paper entitled "Food Security, FTA and trade protectionism in Asian Countries" in the world of freeTrade agreements where is perceivedsome nagging problems like protectionism in theinternational trading market which some countries are very slow to realise it.

Two authorsBhabani Mohapatra and Bhagabat Patra deal with food securitywith an insight which is innovative andnew way of thinkingin their paper entitled "Various Approaches for Sustainable Food and Nutritional Security"and adopted various approaches for ensuringfood and nutritional security from international perspective and suggested some good measures for it.

Another paper on "Technologies for Enhancement of Agriculture Production and Sustainability of Rural Livelihoods" by Rekha Dhanai and R.S. Negi, is based on inclusive growthand the environmental degradation or sustainable development.

Dipti Paridhi Kindo in her article on "Aadhaar enabled Public Distribution System (AEPDS) in Jharkhand" is suggestive of various measures to be implemented by the government for making AEPDs more effective in Jharakhanda.

"Feeding the Hungry Assessing the Imperative of FSA"by Samit Karhas analyzed how hunger has been the main obstacle standing in the way of economic development.

Authors Bijaya Laxmi Mahanta andAmit Jena in their paper entitled"Impact of climate change on food security: a conceptual analysis" argued how climate changewill seriously affect and exacerbate food security.

"Empowering Small Farmers for Their Food Security Accelerating Flow of Institutional Credit" byMahendra Patel is verybroad basedidea onsmall and marginal farmer and their life.

P. Srivatsav, an anthropologist focused on agriculture, climate, food security, and globalization, the topic in this book "Food Security in India – Challenges and New Initiatives

All these ideas encapsulated into a book form collected from various eminent scholars will play a meaningful role in guiding the policy makers, planners, researchers and persons engaged in various activities for the well being of the common people. This book we hope maythrow some insight into new vistas of research that will be carried onby researchers in this field not taken up by this book.

Prof. Dr. Narottam Gaan
Dr. Sandhyarani Das
Aruna Kumar Nishanka

Contents

List of Contributors

Amit Kumar Jena, Doctoral Scholar, XLRI, Jamshedpur.

Andrew Fraker, Neil Buddy Shah, and Ronald Abraham.

Aruna Kumar Nishanka, Asst. Professor of Economics, Narasinghpur College, Cuttack, Odisha.

Ashish Kothari Kalpavriksh, Pune, Coordinator the VikalpSangam process, Pune.

B.P. Mahapatra

B. Patra, HOD, Dept. of Economics Berhampur University, Odisha.

Bijayalaxmi Mohanta, Scientist, Agricultural Engineering, Krishi Vigyan Kendra, Jajpur.

Dipti Paridhi Kindo, Doctoral Student, Public Policy and Management at Indian Institute of Management Calcutta (IIM C), India,Prime Minister's Rural Development Fellow (PMRDF) 2012-2015, Jharkhand, Ministry of Rural Development, Govt. of India.

Gopal Kalkoti, Associate Professor and Head, Dept. of Economics, Nagindas Khandwala College, Malad (West), Mumbai-400 064, Maharashtra, India.

K. Baby, Head, Department of Economics, Govt. College, Chittur, Palakkad. Kerala. PIN 678104.

Khokon Sarkar, Asst. Professor of Economics, MUC Women's College, Rajbati, Burdwan-713104.

M S Swaminathan, Founder, Swaminathan Foundation, Father of Green Revolution in India, Chennai.

Sudhansubal Das, Associate Professor in Political Science, P.P. Dev Mahavidyalaya, Tigiria, Cuttack.

Narottam Gaan, Professor and Head, Indira Gandhi National Tribal University, Amarakantak.

Mahendra Patel

Maniklal Adhikary, Professor of Economics,University of Burdwan, Glopbag-713104.

Milan Banik, Asstt. Professor of Economics, Rukasen College, Bakalia, Karbi Anglong, Assam-782482.

Nkiru Nwamaka Ezeama MBBS, MPH, FWACP, Department of Community Medicine, Nnamdi Azikiwe University Teaching Hospital, Nnewi, Nigeria.

Nkiru Nwamaka Ezeama, MBBS, MPH, FWACP, Department of Community Medicine, Nnamdi Azikiwe University Teaching Hospital, Nnewi, Nigeria.

P. Srivatsa, Social Anthropologist, psrv87@gmail.com

Parveen Kumar, Senior Research Fellow; National Innovations on Climate Resilient Agriculture (NICRA), Advance Center for Rainfed Agriculture (ACRA), Sher-e-Kashmir, University of Agriculture Sciences and Technology of Jammu.

Pavan Pandey, MD Affiliation: Programme Officer.

Reetika Khera, The Indian Institute of Technology, Delhi.

Rekha Dhanai, Department of Rural Technology, H.N.B. Garhwal (A Central) University Rekha. dhanai@rediffmail.com

R.S. Negi, Department of Rural Technology, H.N.B. Garhwal (A Central) University Rekha. dhanai@rediffmail.com

Sushrut Sharma, MBBS, Indian Information Services (IIS) Affiliation: Deputy Director, DD News, India.

Samit Kar, The Author is a renowned Sociologist and Former Sociology Faculty in Presidency University.

Sandhya Rani Das, Professor, Dept. of Economics, Berhampur University, Odisha.

Sipho Felix Mamba, Ph.D. Scholar, University of the Western Cape, RSA, Switzerland.

Subhash Sharma

Thomas F. Walker

1

Nutri-Agriculture: Pathway to a Zero Hunger India

M S Swaminathan

Introduction

Our agriculture is now facing three kinds of problems. First, monsoon behaviour is erratic probably because of events associated with climate change. Secondly, the international and national markets are very volatile thereby endangering the stability of farmers' income. Thirdly, we face serious problems of malnutrition caused by both protein hunger and hidden hunger. Therefore, in the further development of our agriculture we should give attention to these challenges. There are also challenges beyond our control like the regulations of the World Trade Organisations. All these problems can be dealt with only by the application of science and technology supported by appropriate public policies. I would like to deal with them briefly.

India is described as the country with the largest number of hungry people by most international agencies. Therefore, our government is told by foreign experts that we must give the highest priority to ending hunger and malnutrition. Both agrarian prosperity and national food security depend on the economics of farming. We have now come to the stage of giving legal right to food through the National Food Security Act, 2013. Thus, our country has evolved from a "ship to mouth existence to a right to food commitment." To fulfil this commitment, we have to give concurrent attention to production, procurement, and public distribution. The difference between agriculture as a commercial occupation and agriculture as a means of abolishing hunger and malnutrition will have to be clearly understood at the Tenth Ministerial Meeting of WTO scheduled to be held in Nairobi this December. It is a matter of pride and satisfaction that the Union Minister for Commerce and Industry Smt Nirmala Sitaraman has clearly tried to convey the message that support policies for food security and abolition of malnutrition are non-negotiable. The industrialised countries should understand and acknowledge the human dimensions of trade in food grains. Developed countries have safeguarded the extensive financial support they are giving to their farmers through the green box provision. It is high time that there is also a Food Security Box which can help countries to adopt farm support policies which can help them to achieve the zero hunger challenge launched by the UN Secretary General.

World Trade and National Food Security

The World Trade Organisation (WTO) is an inter-governmental body to promote free and fair trade. In developing principles for assessing what is fair and what is unfair in trade, a global view is normally taken. This is where the problem arises. Agriculture is essentially a commercial occupation in developed countries where hardly five per cent of the population depend on agriculture for their livelihood. On the other hand, agriculture in many development countries including our own is the principal occupation of a majority of rural families who depend upon crop and animal husbandry, fisheries, forestry and agro-processing for both their livelihood and household food security. Also, the farm size is small and the marketable surplus is low. As a result, farm families require social protection. It is wrong to designate the limited support given to them as subsidy. It will be more appropriate to refer to the assistance given as support to sustainable farming.

Sustainable Water Security

It is therefore appropriate that we develop a sustainable water security system for agriculture, industry, domestic needs and ecosystem preservation. In my view our national water security system should consist of the following six essential action points: first, is the augmentation of supply through mandatory rainwater harvesting, and politically, ecologically and economically feasible inter-basin transfer. Second, the efficiency of water use through appropriate land use planning which involves the choice of crops suited to the local water availability conditions. Third, there is need for involving local communities and panchayats in the co-governance of land, water and energy, the efficacy of which has been demonstrated by several grassroots workers including Salunke in Maharashtra, who promoted pani panchayats, and Rajendra Singh in Rajasthan, who showed the power of community water harvesting. Fourth, the popularisation of technologies like sprinkler and drip irrigation on a large scale particularly for perennial horticultural crops. Fifth, sea water constitutes 97 per cent of the world's water resource. Nearly 25 per cent of our population live near the coast. There are ample opportunities now for bio-saline farming using sea water and available fresh water. Finally, public policies should aim at the sustainable use of groundwater resources since nearly 60 per cent of the irrigation water now comes from tubewells. Demand management is even more important than increasing supply.

Smart Villages

The late Dr Abdul Kalam stimulated widespread interest in rural development by emphasising that our villages should also have access to urban amenities like energy, water, sanitation, healthcare, education etc. Of late, there have been several initiatives both in India and abroad on methods of achieving this goal. A recent one is the initiative of a group in Cambridge, UK, in the form of organisation of 'Smart Villages'. Smart Villages under this programme consider "access to sustainable energy services as a catalyst for development, enabling the provision of good education and healthcare, access to clean water, sanitation and nutrition, the growth of productive enterprises to boost incomes and enhanced security, gender equality and democratic engagement". Sir Brian Heap of Cambridge University, a prime mover of this concept, wishes to extend the Smart Village movement in India. Since the government is now actively promoting Smart Cities, it is important to also promote Smart Villages.

Agriculture as the engine of job-led growth

Recent media reports suggest that increasing demands for reservation in the public sector may be linked to the stagnation of agriculture and growing agrarian distress. Agriculture promotes job-led growth, if there is integrated attention to on-farm and non-farm employment in rural areas. In the Sixth Five Year Plan (1980-85), I had introduced a sub-chapter on 'A New Deal for the Self Employed'. Unless opportunities are created for economically rewarding and intellectually satisfying self-employment for youth, competition for jobs in the organised sector will grow, as will the clamour for reservation. At the national level, the share of agriculture to GDP has come down to 13 per cent. However, the onus of providing employment rests with the farm sector which caters to the livelihood security of nearly 75 per cent of population in rural India. The National Commission on Farmers has made detailed recommendation on how to serve farmers and thereby save farming. Even in the Punjab nearly 80 per cent of farmers do not want their sons to be agriculturists. The immediate implementation of NCF recommendations in their totality will help. Meanwhile, to minimise the incidence of farmers' suicides, there is need for establishing of Agrarian Distress Counselling Centres wherever feasible in Krishi Vigyan Kendras. I hope that the responsibility of safeguarding farmers' welfare given to the Union Ministry of Agriculture will help to improve the livelihood security of rural families and thereby save their lives and livelihoods.

Saving livestock under extreme drought conditions

Shri Sharad Pawar, former Union Agriculture Minister, has drawn attention to the severe drought conditions prevailing in the Marathwada and Nashik-Sangli regions of Maharashtra. He has pointed out that there is extreme water and fodder shortage and that the livestock wealth may be lost. Since livestock and livelihoods are closely related, particularly in the case of small farm families, immediate action is needed to save the livestock. Fortunately, there is very good opportunity today for ensuring adequate nutrition to the livestock. What is needed is the organisation of cattle camps near water sources, and feed the animals with straw enriched with urea and molasses. The paddy harvesting season is starting in Punjab, Haryana and Rajasthan, where the paddy straw is not usually used to feed animals, but is burnt. Therefore, the Government of Maharashtra should make immediate arrangements with the Governments of Punjab, Haryana and Rajasthan for sending the rice straw, to the severely drought affected areas of Maharashtra. Other biomass (cellulosic material) can also be used. Maharashtra has adequate quantities of molasses because of the cultivation of sugarcane. The detailed biomass enrichment technology can be obtained from the Indian Veterinary Research Institute (IVRI), Izatnagar, UP. The Agriculture and Veterinary Universities and Krishi Vigyan Kendras can organise the cattle camps for feeding the animals with the enriched straw. This is based on my personal experience during the recurrent droughts of the 1970s.

Nutri-farms: An idea whose time has come

Experts from India, Pakistan, Bangladesh and Afghanistan are discussing ways to mobilise the agricultural pathway for overcoming the widespread malnutrition in the region. This work is being done under a multi-country consortium supported by DFID. The strategy consists of three main components: mainstreaming nutrition in crop-livestock farming systems (nutri-farms), organising genetic gardens of naturally occurring biofortified plants like moringa to demonstrate the options available to local communities, and creating a cadre of community hunger fighters, well-versed in leveraging agriculture for overcoming nutritional maladies. Bringing agriculture, nutrition and health together will make a major contribution to achieving the goal of freedom from malnutrition.

Need for a Kisan Security Bill

In my view, there is need for legislation to protect the security of farmers' livelihoods in order to ensure that food for all and forever becomes a reality. The Kisan Security Bill can be modelled on the Private Members Bill I had earlier introduced in the Rajya Sabha on the empowerment of women farmers. Such legislation will consist of five components viz. soil healthcare; water security; availability of appropriate technology and inputs; credit and insurance, and assured and remunerative marketing. In addition, small farmers should be provided with opportunities to tap the power of scale through producer companies.

Culinary diversity and agro-biodiversity

Among the methods of protecting community knowledge and technologies under WTO, Geographic Indication (GI) is an important one. UNESCO's World Heritage Site and FAO's Globally Important Agricultural Heritage System (GIAHS) are other forms of recognition of the conservation ethos of local communities. In this context, the Government of Paschim Bangla has done well in seeking GI protection for *Rasagulla*. Odisha feels that it has also a claim on *Rasagulla* from the point of view of GI. Similarly, there is need for according recognition to communities which have conserved agro-biodiversity, i.e., biodiversity used for various human needs. Such diversity can take the form of cultural, culinary and curative (i.e. medicinal plants) diversity. Thanks to the work of MSSRF, the agro-biodiversity based farming systems in the Koraput region of Odisha and the below sea level rice cultivation of Kuttanad in Kerala have both received GIAHS recognition from FAO. We should make similar efforts to get global recognition for the work of rural and tribal communities in areas of significance to human quality of life.

Do Ecology for achieving the UN Sustainable Development Goals (SDG)

Recently Members of the UN adopted 17 Sustainable Development Goals. These goals can be achieved if we integrate the principles of ecology in all development and social protection measures. "Do ecology" involves education, social mobilisation and essential regulation. Sustainable development also involves concurrent attention to environmental, economic and social sustainability. In agriculture, evergreen revolution is the means to achieve sustainability. In the area of ending hunger, achieving food security and improved nutrition, adopting the farming system for nutrition (FSN) approach together with the establishment of genetic gardens of biofortified crops and training of a cadre of community hunger fighters will help. Since the 17 goals are at the moment in the form of generalised objectives, every Panchayat in our country should develop its own operational plan for achieving the goals relevant to their socio-economic and socio-cultural conditions.

Biotechnology and UN Sustainable Development Goals

Two important SDGs are "End hunger, achieve food security and improved nutrition, and promote sustainable agriculture" and "Take urgent action to combat climate change and its impacts". Several scientists are of the view that the use of genetic engineering techniques will be important to develop crop varieties which can help to achieve these goals. There are however difference of opinion on the value and safety of such biotechnological tools. I would suggest the following steps for coming to a consensus on this question.

1. Develop scientific guidelines for the choice of the problem to be taken up for genetic modification. Is there an alternative to recombinant DNA technology like marker assisted selection, genome editing etc?
2. Develop procedures for field testing of the GM material in the breeders' assembly line based on the principles contained in the Cartegena protocol on biosafety. The field testing should be done in full consultation with State Governments and in the fields of public good institutions such as Agricultural Universities.
3. Develop science based methods of assessing risks and benefits. Such procedures coupled with the results of field trials can help to decide whether the GMO pathway is the safe way for achieving the desired end result.

4. Promote biotechnology literacy and establish resource centres for the mass media. Such media resource centres should help to promote public information and education and not become propaganda agencies.
5. Develop a suitable insurance policy to small farmers, so as to insulate them from risks beyond their control, such as drought.
6. State Governments and State Agricultural Universities should be involved at all stages, both in field testing and approval for cultivation.
7. Introduce a Parliament approved National Biosafety Act.

Eternal vigilance is the price of stable agriculture

Recent reports indicate that a devastating whitefly attack on cotton is reducing yields drastically, in Punjab and Haryana. The introduction of Bt cotton helped to overcome the problems of bollworms which are also serious pests. Today the cotton farmers are suffering from the twin problems of whitefly attack and low prices. Adopting measures for effective plant protection against all the important pests and reducing price volatility are essential for the cotton farmers to get a steady income and the textile trade to get a steady supply of raw material.

The whitefly attack should not come as a surprise since whenever one dominant pest is controlled, the pest which was not important earlier becomes serious. For example, when dwarf wheats were introduced in the early 1960s, the wheat rust problem became less serious since the new varieties were resistant to the prevailing races of stem, stripe and leaf rusts. However, soon 'loose smut' in wheat may became a dominant disease. I have pointed out that if the average temperature goes up by 2°C as a result of global warming and climate change, we will have to cultivate potato through true sexual seeds and not through tubers as is the case, now. This is because aphids which are vectors of virus diseases will multiply fast with a higher temperature and cause severe viral infection. If we want to insulate our agriculture from violent undulations in production and prices, we should adopt the principle of eternal vigilance and undertake continuously an action-reaction analysis and appropriate proactive action.

Funding "public good" National laboratories

Scientific research is increasingly becoming oriented towards immediate commercial profit than on short and long-term public good. A recent report suggests that CSIR laboratories have been asked to find funds for their research. This approach can help to promote research on topics of current market interest but research dealing, with issues requiring sustained long-term commitment will suffer. In agriculture for example, public good research institutions are essential for developing technologies relevant to resource poor farmers operating small holdings. Such farmers constitute the majority of our farming population. Public good research involves more investment on long-term basic and strategic research. For example, National laboratories can cooperate with private sector laboratories in the area of translational research, i.e. converting scientific findings into field level applications taking into account considerations of ecology, economics and social and gender equity. The Science Advisory Committee to the Cabinet should go carefully into this question and recommend to government a long-term funding strategy, which will help to achieve a balance between public good and private profit.

Insurance coverage to save farmers from loss arising from the breakdown of resistance to pests

A recent report refers to the collapse of resistance to the pink bollworm in the cotton variety Bollgard II. Bollgard II was released after the breakdown of resistance in Bollgard I. Both Bollgard I and II have been developed by Monsanto through genetic modification. The Genetic Engineering Appraisal Committee (GEAC) of the Ministry of Environment approved the commercial release of Bollgard II in 2006. Because of the breakdown of resistance, Gujarat farmers have suffered seriously both in production and income. The company has pointed out that it is imperative to stay ahead of insect resistance through the periodic replacement of cotton varieties. While this is company's research strategy, farmers are left to bear the loss.

Resource poor farmers with small holdings borrow money for buying seeds every year. In a report submitted to the Ministry of Agriculture, Government of India in 2004, a Committee chaired by me had emphasised the need for seed companies providing insurance cover to farmers in order to insulate them from loss caused by the breakdown of resistance to pests and diseases in the varieties. Unfortunately no steps have been taken and the attack on Bollgard II by the pink bollworm has caused immense hardship to the cotton growers of Gujarat. The need for providing low risk technologies protected by adequate insurance coverage to farmers has become urgent particularly in the context of the growing agrarian distress. Until such arrangements are made, high risk technologies should not be recommended to farmers.

Towards a Pulses Revolution Symphony

A study by Assocham Chamber has indicated that India may have to import 10 million tonnes of pulses to achieve a balance between demand and supply. This reminds me of the situation in 1966 when we had to import 10 million tonnes of wheat largely under the PL480 programme of USA. Internationally we were then described as a "ship to mouth nation". We were determined to change this situation and before the end of the 60s, the country witnessed the Wheat Revolution and the more general Green Revolution. Such a change in our food situation came about through a combination of scientific skill, political will and farmers' toil.

The same symphony approach could bring about similar results in the case of pulses. In all our major pulse crops namely, chickpea, pigeonpea, lentils, urad and moong bean, our average yield is less than one tonne per hectare. The average yields can be easily doubled with technologies on the shelf. This will require attention to improving soil health enhancement, seed conservation and supply, appropriate mechanisation, improved post-harvest technology, community management of plant health and disease control, and appropriate import-export policies. There are also opportunities for expanding the area under pulses in rice fallows and through inter- and multiple cropping.

2016 is the International Year of Pulses

We should try to make 2016 a significant landmark in our efforts to achieve self-sufficiency in pulse production, just as we did in the case of wheat in 1966. MSSRF has initiated a programme of promoting the concept of Pulse Panchayats where all the farmers in the Panchayat cooperate in areas like rain water harvesting and efficient use, crop health management and safe storage and value addition to primary products. The first such Panchayat is in the Edaiyappatti village of Tamil Nadu. I hope such Panchayats will result in the origin and growth of pulse revolution symphonies, just as Seed Villages and national demonstration did, in the case of wheat fifty years ago.

Generating Synergy among Central Universities and in University – Industry Partnerships

The President of India in his capacity as Visitor of Central Universities and Institutions had convened a meeting of Vice Chancellors at Rashtrapati Bhavan from 4-5 Nov 2015. I was invited to speak on the engagement of institutes of higher learning with community and society for sustainable and inclusive development. This is a timely conference since among the 17 sustainable development goals, the fourth goal relates to ensuring inclusive and equitable quality education and promotion of lifelong learning and opportunities for all. In my address, I requested the VCs to organise courses in the field of sustainability science which involves a multidisciplinary approach including social sciences. I also reminded the VCs that lifelong learning has to be an integral part of the academic culture as emphasised by Gurudev Rabindranath Tagore in Gitanjali

"A candle which is not lit, cannot light others

A teacher who is also not learning, cannot teach others"

The course in the field of sustainability science prepared for IGNOU by the MSSRF may now be adopted by other universities and will provide the scientific basis for developing the work plans for achieving the SDGs.

Public good research to the rescue of resource poor cotton farmers

In the absence of alternative choices, cotton farmers have been taking to Bt hybrids which recently have also been affected by white fly. Fortunately, the Central Institute for Cotton Research (CICR) of ICAR, Nagpur which I established in the 1970s has come out with a cotton variety which is ideally suited for small farmers with limited coping capacity in case of crop failure. The new cotton variety has triple strengths namely, crop duration is reduced to 150 days from 200 days, secondly, there will be increased yield because of the opportunity for growing more plants per square meter and thirdly, farmers can keep their own seeds unlike in the case of hybrids where they have to buy seeds every year. The CICR has in the breeders' assembly line about 21 high yielding pest resistant cotton varieties suitable for cultivation in Maharashtra and Telangana. Our gratitude goes to Dr K R Kranti, Director, CICR and his colleagues for orienting the scientific strategy to suit the needs of resource poor farmers who normally have to buy seeds every year by taking loan from either banks or money lenders.

Rice–Saviour of Food Security in an era of Climate Change

World requires 50 per cent more rice in 2030 than in 2004 with approximately 30 per cent less arable land of today. Rice was one of the early green revolution crops because of the changes made in plant architecture and water and nutrient use ability, first through the indica – japonica hybridisation programme and later through the use of dwarfing genes. Rice has a wide adaptation as evident from its cultivation below sea level in Kuttanad in Kerala and in the high Himalayas. More recently, rice has also been enriched with micronutrients like zinc and iron as well as Vitamin A. There are over 150,000 varieties of rice with varying degrees of adaptation to temperature, precipitation, sea level and grain quality. India has the largest area under rice and since long, tribal families like those cultivating rice in Koraput in Odisha have preserved for posterity a wide range of rice germplasm. Wheat is very sensitive to night temperature and has more limited adaptation than rice. We should develop research and extension strategies for producing 150 million tonnes of rice from 30 million hectare by 2030.

Water security in an era of climate change

We need to develop a strategy for mobilising the available water resources of the country in a most economical and effective manner. I emphasised that those involved in developing programmes for river linking should ensure that the projects take into the account the following five E's

- **Economics** – Economic viability is essential for investment.
- **Ecology** – Environmental impact of river linking has to be carefully considered so that the programme is in conformity with the sustainable development goals and does not lead to deforestation.
- **Equity** – both social and gender equity should guide the development of the project so that a win-win situation is created for all participating in such a programme.
- **Energy** – The project should generate additional renewable energy.
- **Employment** – the project should so designed as to generate more employment in all the sectors of the economy, namely agriculture, industry and services sector.

In addition to river linking, the country needs to develop local level *pani panchayats* for harvesting and using effectively the major sources of water, namely rain, ground water, rivers and lakes, snow, treated effluents and sea water. Such action will help us to enhance our coping capacity in relation to the weather abnormalities associated with global warming.

Social Protection against hunger

India occupies a low position in relation to the elimination of widespread hunger. We however know that undernutrition has multiple adverse impacts on human development and economic growth.

Therefore, it is good news that the Union Food Minister has asked all States and Union Territories to implement the National Food Security Act by 31 March 2016. Tamil Nadu already operates a universal PDS and is hence ahead of other states in the matter of extending social protection to the hungry. The effective implementation of the provisions of the National Food Security Act will help to eliminate calorie deprivation in nearly two-thirds of the population. What is now important is also to integrate this programme with attacking protein hunger through pulses and hidden hunger through biofortified crops and multiple fortified salts. If all this is done, India's position in the Global Hunger Index will show a marked improvement and the goal of providing every child, woman and man an opportunity for a productive and healthy life, can be realised.

Management of the Northeast Monsoon

The recent unprecedented rains in coastal Tamil Nadu including Chennai have highlighted the need for an urgent mapping of hotspots in terms of human suffering. The problem has to be viewed in a decentralised manner with the involvement of the local communities. The major cause of flash floods is the lack of proper drainage arrangements. Naturally occurring drains have become clogged and there is no way for the water to recede. Infiltration into the soil is also poor due to a variety of reasons including the hardening of the top soil. Also the surplus water should be saved in aquifer, wells, ponds, reservoirs and other storage structure to overcome water scarcity in later months, thereby making heavy rainfall a blessing, instead of a curse.

Green Revolution : 50 Years Later

The green revolution helped us to move from a ship to mouth existence to being able to make a right to food commitment to nearly 75 per cent of our population. The major problems associated with the green revolution related to environmental factors like depletion and pollution of groundwater, soil erosion and loss of biodiversity. It is these deficiencies that can be remedied through the evergreen revolution pathway developed by me over 30 years ago. Therefore, 50 years later we should work for a transition from the green to an evergreen revolution leading to an enhancement in productivity in perpetuity without ecological harm. The evergreen revolution technology involves the mainstreaming of ecological factors in technology development and dissemination.

Human Development is the foundation for a healthy and happy country

UNDP's 2015 Human Development Report indicates that India ranks 130 out of 188 countries with reference to the Human Development Index. Although we have shown a little progress, we are still occupying a low position which is inexcusable considering our resources and capability. We should revisit our strategy for improving human development. There is need to pay greater attention to education, gender equality and poverty. In my view, the time has come for making every Panchayat calculate its own human development index. Unless action is decentralised, the present situation may continue with only marginal improvement. In education we should use the latest technology to achieve rapid progress. In the area of gender equality the time has come to revisit my private members' bill titled "The Women Farmers' Entitlements Bill, 2011" which I introduced in Rajya Sabha in 2012. Empowerment of rural women will make a great impact on gender justice and equity and thereby on Human Development Index.

Kerala takes an important step in post Paris action

A major consequence of global warming will be a rise in sea level. Fortunately, the Paris agreement calls for limiting the rise in mean temperature to less than two degrees centigrade and preferably 1.5 degree centigrade. Nevertheless, some degree of rise in sea level seems inevitable. The Kerala Government is to be complimented for establishing an International Research and Training Centre for Below Sea Level Farming at Moncompu in Kuttanad. Kuttanad is both a Ramsar site as well as a Globally Important Agriculture Heritage System (GIAHS). The Institute will undertake national and international capacity building programmes in both adaptation and mitigation. It was formally inaugurated on February 6th by the Chief Minister of Kerala at Moncompu. The first International Training Programme will be for Maldives, Sri Lanka, Bangladesh, Sunderbans of both India and Bangladesh and coastal regions of India. The International Centre will specialise in biosaline farming and in developing Biobunds to keep saline water away. The management of water salinity will be a priority task, with rice being grown during the monsoon season and fish during the winter season. Semi-dwarf coconut varieties will be planted in the bunds. Thus, the establishment of this new institution is a major contribution to the management of sea level rise and for avoiding the exodus of climate refugees from the sea coast.

Combating Tsunamis of the Future

The following three steps taken by MSSRF are designed to safeguard coastal communities from the adverse impact of the tsunamis of the future. First, the advance warning system has been very much improved and a "fisher friend" technology for giving information on wave heights at different distances from the shoreline has been introduced. The area under mangrove forests which serve as bioshields has been further enlarged. Finally, methods have been developed for promoting silvi-aquaculture farms and biosaline farming along the coast. A Genetic Garden of Halophytes has been developed at Vedaranyam for ensuring that adequate genetic material is available for breeding varieties of rice and other crops possessing tolerance to salinity. Thus, we will be in a better position to safeguard the lives of fisher and other coastal families and at the same time, strengthen their livelihood security.

International Year of Pulses and Ending Protein Hunger

In recent years, each year is devoted to a particular cause of global importance. Thus, the year 2013 was designated as the International Year of Quinoa (*Chenopodium quinoa*). Rich in protein, quinoa has played an important role in food and nutrition security among the Andean people. The diversification of dietary components has become urgent since recent reports suggest that climate change may result in crops like wheat and rice becoming less nutritive, with particular reference to iron and zinc. The year 2014 was commemorated as the International Year of Family Farming, while 2015 was the year of the Soil. All these years have helped to focus global attention on specific issues like soil healthcare and enhancement and strengthening family farming, with special attention to the role of women.

Organic Agriculture : Pathways to Success

Our Prime Minister in his recent address in Sikkim has advocated the adoption of organic farming methods throughout the country. This will ensure the environmental sustainability of agriculture and thereby help to achieve Goal 2 of the UN Sustainable Development Goals ("End hunger, achieve food security and improved nutrition and promote sustainable agriculture"). Several steps are needed to make organic farming economically viable particularly for small and marginal farmers. These are : The replenishment of soil fertility by giving back to the soil what we take out of it through measures like green manuring, introduction of both grain and fodder legumes in the crop rotation and mobilisation and application of all available organic sources of manure including animal waste and compost. It is also necessary to provide the soil with bio-fertilizss of our country have small holdings and may have only one or two farm animals like cows and buffaloes. Therefore, it is essential they have an integrated nutrient supply strategy based on the available organic sources of manure and biological nitrogen fixation. The other aspect of organic farming is plant protection using biological control methods and the use of pesticides of plant origin. Finally, there is need for providing a premium price taking into account the long-term benefits to the nation. Integrated nutrient supply, integrated pest management and remunerative pricing and marketing are the three pillars of successful organic farming. Farmers should become familiar with organic certification procedures, thereby spreading knowledge of successful marketing strategies.

Education for the UN SDG in the field of Sustainable Agriculture

The initiative of the Avittam Thirunal Government Vocational Higher Secondary School, Moncompu is a path-breaking adventure in education for sustainable agriculture. This school is initiating on February 6th, courses in different areas of agriculture which are designed to promote training which will help to achieve Goal No. 2. A sustainable agriculture course will be introduced at the 10 +2 level. The school is located at the Kuttanad region of Kerala which has been designated by FAO as a Globally Important Agricultural Heritage Site. The additional facilities including new laboratories for soil and plant health were constructed at a cost of Rs 57 lakhs provided from my MPLAD funds. I hope this will be an example for other schools located in agriculturally important areas, so that sustainable agriculture becomes the norm in Rural India. Dr Bruce Alberts, one of world's leading biological scientists and former President of the US National Academy of Sciences, has emphasised the urgency of empowering great teachers' in order to improve the quality of education. I quote from his editorial in *Science* (15 Jan 2016) *"Unless the United States can make dramatic advances in empowering its teachers, the nation will never have public school systems that make the best decisions for their students. Nor will it be able to attract and retain the highly talented teacher corps that every nation needs"*. This is what an old Chinese Proverb stresses, *"If you are thinking one year ahead, plant rice; if you are thinking ten years ahead, plant trees; if you are thinking a hundred years ahead, educate the people"*.

We recently organised the Make in India week (13-18 February 2016). This is a welcome revival of the Swadeshi Approach of Mahatma Gandhi of which the Charka and Khadi became the most powerful symbols. Hence these soil enriching, climate resilient, and nutrition enhancing crops should lead the way in the programmes for Make in India in Agriculture.

Forestry and Agriculture

The critical role played by forests in climate regulation, protection of hydrologic cycles, conservation of biodiversity and provision of a wide range of minor forest produce which protect the lives and livelihoods of tribal and other forest dwellers is now well known. On this day, I wish to recall the farsighted step taken by the Government of Guyana (formerly British Guyana) for promoting the Iwokrama International Centre for Rainforest Conservation and Development (IIC). In 1989, the Government of Guyana offered to the Commonwealth one million acres of prime rainforest for demonstrating how a rainforest can be managed in an environmentally sustainable manner, while at the same time, providing livelihoods to the large number of Amerindians who depend on the forest for their basic needs. I was asked to lead a team to design the project and take charge of the land. My proposal was accepted by both the Government of Guyana and the Common Wealth and the International Centre came into existence in 1996 with support from the Global Environment Facility and the UK government. I am happy that this centre is functioning well and has become a source of technologies for sustainable rainforest management. Also it has demonstrated the wisdom of my decision to involve the Amerindians very intimately with the management of the forest since the Amerindians have very deep knowledge of the flora and fauna of the Iwokrama forest and also of ecosystem. I made an Amerindian Chief, Mr Fred Allicock, the Head of the Campus although he did not have any formal education. I was impressed with the following song with which Ameridians greeted me on my arrival

"The sky is held up by trees, if the forest disappears, the sky which is the roof of the world collapses. Nature and man then perish together"

On this International Day of Forests, we should renew our commitment not only to the conservation of forest but also to the protection of livelihoods of forest dwellers. The best way will be to respect their knowledge and involve them actively in the development of the biosphere reserve. Iwokrama is a standing monument to the effectiveness of participatory conservation involving all stakeholders. After helping this project for 10 years as the Chairman of the Board of Trustees, I entrusted the position of chairmanship to the late Dr Angela Cropper, who nurtured the project with great care and took it forward in achieving its mission of forest conservation as a tool for sustainable livelihoods as well as sustainable water, food and climate security.

Building Sustainable Water Security System

Today (22 March 2016) is observed as the World Water Day. The importance of water in all aspects of human life needs hardly any elaboration. In our country, inter-state water conflicts are growing. There is urgent need for both augmenting supplies and managing demand. In the area of demand management, our Prime Minister has already emphasised the need for more crop per drop of water. The conjunctive use of water involving ground and surface water sources is equally important. One neglected area which I hope will receive attention during this World Water Day is utilisation of sea water which constitutes 97 per cent of world water resource. Sea water farming for coastal area prosperity should become more widespread. Below sea level farming is now possible through sylvi-aquaculture practices. The Kerala Government has already established a Research and Training Centre for Below Sea Level Farming. We also need to establish Farm Schools in the fields of outstanding farmers who are showing the way for using the available water in the most effective and economical manner. Rainwater harvesting both in farms and homes must become mandatory. Inter-linking of rivers on a win-win situation among states is another opportunity. I hope during this World Water Day, conflicts for water will give way to cooperation in water saving and sharing through a pan-political commitment to national water security.

Zero Hunger India

Dr Jose Graziano Da Silva, DG of FAO has recently warned that achieving the zero hunger target is a challenging task and that the battle for eliminating hunger is far from over. This is a timely warning since there is complacency in the food production and consumption areas. FAO estimates that 490 million people across Asia and the Pacific are suffering from undernutrition. This is why I wish to reiterate the three point strategy I have been advocating. First, we should implement effectively the provisions of the National Food Security Act in order to overcome undernutrition. Second, we should eliminate protein hunger through the greater production and consumption of pulses starting from 2016 which is the International Year of Pulses. Third, we should eradicate hidden hunger caused by micronutrient deficiencies in the diet through leveraging agriculture for nutrition. This will involve the cultivation and consumption of biofortified crops which provide agricultural/ horticultural remedies to the nutritional maladies prevailing in the area. Mainstreaming of nutritional consideration in the design of farming systems will help to achieve the goal of freedom from malnutrition speedily and economically. Nutrition literacy can be spread through Community Hunger Fighters.

2

Climate Change and Food Security in South Asia

Sudhansubala Das and Narottam Gaan

Introduction

Climate change is no longer an apocalypse waiting its turn to wreak havoc upon humankind. It has already become a reality playing its ruinous part in various aspects of human living in the globe imperatively urging upon the states of the world to review their way of life, pattern of development and established rapacious outlook about the nature in order to find out a way. Climate change is one of the defining issues of our time. It is now more certain than ever, based on many lines of evidence, that humans are changing Earth's climate. The atmosphere and oceans have warmed, accompanied by sea-level rise, a strong decline in Arctic sea ice, and other climate-related changes. The consequences of climate change in terms of water scarcity, land degradation, food insecurity, recrudescence of environmental induced conflicts, recurrence of cyclones, storms floods and spread of fatal diseases as predicted by IPCC reports stand a witness to holocaust that lies ahead of the world.

Green House Gases such as carbon dioxide (CO_2) absorb heat (infrared radiation) emitted from Earth's surface. Increases in the atmospheric concentrations of these gases cause Earth to warm by trapping more of this heat. Human activities especially the burning of fossil fuels since the start of the Industrial Revolution have increased atmospheric CO_2 concentrations by about 40 per cent, with more than half the increase occurring since 1970. Since 1900, the global average surface temperature has increased by about 0.8°C (1.4°F). This has been accompanied by warming of the ocean, a rise in sea level, a strong decline in Arctic sea ice, and many other associated climate effects. Much of this warming has occurred in the last four decades. Detailed analyses have shown that the warming during this period is mainly a result of the increased concentrations of CO_2 and other greenhouse gases. Continued emissions of these gases will cause further climate change, including substantial increases in global average surface temperature and important changes in regional climate. The magnitude and timing of these changes will depend on many factors, and slowdowns and accelerations in warming lasting a decade or more will continue to occur. However, long-term climate change over many decades will depend mainly on the total amount of CO_2 and other greenhouse gases emitted as a result of human activities.

Climate Threats and Impacts

Global climate change will affect people and the environment in many ways. Some of these impacts, like stronger hurricanes and severe heat waves, could be life threatening. Others, like spreading weeds, will be less serious. And some effects, like longer growing seasons for crops, might even be good! However, as the Earth keeps getting warmer, the negative effects are expected to outweigh the positive ones. Climate change is already beginning to transform life on Earth. Without action, climate change threatens to catastrophically damage our world.

It is calculated that the Earth's temperatures in 2015 were the hottest ever recorded (*Source*: NASA). Why does this matter? Because a change of even 1° Fahrenheit which may sound small can upset the delicate balance of ecosystems, and affect plants and animals that inhabit them. Rising temperatures and changing patterns of precipitation are changing where plants grow, and in the case of our oceans, encouraging the proliferation of species that impact native ocean habitat. As landscapes and habitats literally shift, wildlife must quickly adjust. Experts predict that one-fourth of Earth's species will be headed for extinction by 2050 if the warming trend continues at its current rate. As ocean waters warm, they expand, causing sea-levels to rise. Melting glaciers compound the problem by dumping even more fresh water into the oceans. Rising seas threaten to inundate low-lying areas and islands, threaten dense coastal populations, erode shorelines, damage property and destroy ecosystems such as mangroves and wetlands that protect coasts against storms. Climate change is intensifying drought, storms, and floods around the world. Where nature has been destroyed by development, communities are at risk from these intensified climate patterns. Scientists around the world are studying how nature can be a buffer for these intensified weather patterns, and TNC is working with leaders and communities to implement solutions that make a difference for nature and people. Worldwide, approximately 100 million people live within three feet of sea level. Sea level rise associated with climate change could displace tens of millions of people in low-lying areas especially in developing countries. Inhabitants of some small island countries that rest barely above the existing sea level are already abandoning their islands, some of the world's first climate change refugees. The true economic impact of climate change is hard to predict. But it's safe to say that many key economic sectors – from fishing to energy to water utilities – will feel long-term impacts of climate change. From warming seas, which encourage proliferation of non-native species that impact fishing industries, to rising temperatures, which impact energy usage around the world, our shifting global climate will force many industries to move quickly to adapt to change. Even recreation and tourism industries are weather-dependent with many planning based on historic weather patterns, which climate change will disrupt. As we move into an era in which climate change impacts are all around us, adapting to these changes quickly will be the key factor for all sectors of the global economy.

Climate Change and Food Security

Mean global temperatures have been increasing since about 1850, mainly owing to the accumulation of greenhouse gases in the atmosphere. The main causes are the burning of fossil fuels (coal, oil and gas) to meet increasing energy demand, and the spread of intensive agriculture to meet increasing food demand, which is often accompanied by deforestation. The process of global warming shows no signs of abating and is expected to bring about long-term changes in weather conditions. These changes will have serious impacts on the four dimensions of food security: food availability, food accessibility, food utilisation and food system stability. Effects are already being felt in global food markets, and are likely to be particularly significant in specific rural locations where crops fail and yields decline. Impacts will be felt in both rural and urban locations where supply chains are disrupted, market prices increase, assets and livelihood opportunities are lost, purchasing power falls, human health is endangered, and affected people are unable to cope.

Until about 200 years ago, climate was a critical determinant for food security. Since the advent of the industrial revolution, however, humanity's ability to control the forces of nature and manage its own environment has grown enormously. As long as the economic returns justify the costs, people can now create artificial microclimates, breed plants and animals with desired characteristics, enhance soil quality, and control the flow of water. Advances in storage, preservation and transport technologies have made food processing and packaging a new area of economic activity. This has allowed food distributors and retailers to develop long-distance marketing chains that move produce and packaged foods throughout the world at high speed and relatively low cost. Where supermarkets with a large variety of standard-quality produce, available year-round, compete with small shops selling high-quality but only seasonally available local produce, the supermarkets generally win out. The consumer demand that has driven the commercialisation and integration of the global food chain derives from the mass conversion of farmers into wage-earning workers and middle-level managers, which is another consequence of the industrial revolution. Currently, food insecurity persists primarily in those parts of the world where industrial agriculture, long-distance marketing chains and diversified non-agricultural livelihood opportunities are not economically significant.

At the global level, therefore, food system performance today depends more on climate than it did 200 years ago; the possible impacts of climate change on food security have tended to be viewed with most concern in locations where rain fed agriculture is still the primary source of food and income. However, this viewpoint is short-sighted. It does not take account of the other potentially significant impacts that climate change could have on the global food system, and particularly on market prices. These impacts include those on the water and energy used in food processing, cold storage, transport and intensive production, and those on food itself, reflecting higher market values for land and water and, possibly, payments to farmers for environmental services. Rising sea levels and increasing incidence of extreme events pose new risks for the assets of people living in affected zones, threatening livelihoods and increasing vulnerability to future food insecurity in all parts of the globe. Such changes could result in a geographic redistribution of vulnerability and a relocalisation of responsibility for food security prospects that need to be considered in the formulation of adaptation strategies for people who are currently vulnerable or could become so within the foreseeable future. The potential impacts of climate change on food security must therefore be viewed within the larger framework of changing earth system dynamics and observable changes in multiple socio-economic and environmental variables.

Agriculture, Climate and Food Security

Agriculture is important for food security in two ways: it produces the food people eat; and (perhaps even more important) it provides the primary source of livelihood for 36 per cent of the world's total workforce. In the heavily populated countries of Asia and the Pacific, this share ranges from 40 to 50 per cent, and in sub-Saharan Africa, two-thirds of the working population still make their living from agriculture (ILO, 2007). If agricultural production in the low-income developing countries of Asia and Africa is adversely affected by climate change, the livelihoods of large numbers of the rural poor will be put at risk and their vulnerability to food insecurity increased.

Agriculture, forestry and fisheries are all sensitive to climate. Their production processes are therefore likely to be affected by climate change. In general, impacts are expected to be positive in temperate regions and negative in tropical ones, but there is still uncertainly about how projected changes will play out at the local level, and potential impacts may be altered by the adoption of risk management measures and adaptation strategies that strengthen preparedness and resilience. The food security implications of changes in agricultural production patterns and performance are of two kinds:

- Impacts on the production of food will affect food supply at the global and local levels. Globally, higher yields in temperate regions could offset lower yields in tropical regions. However, in many low-income countries with limited financial capacity to trade and high dependence on their own production to cover food requirements, it may not be possible to offset declines in local supply without increasing reliance on food aid.
- Impacts on all forms of agricultural production will affect livelihoods and access to food. Producer groups that are less able to deal with climate change, such as the rural poor in developing countries, risk having their safety and welfare compromised.

Other food system processes, such as food processing, distribution, acquisition, preparation and consumption, are as important for food security as food and agricultural production are. Technological advances and the development of long-distance marketing chains that move produce and packaged foods throughout the world at high speed and relatively low cost have made overall food system performance far less dependent on climate than it was 200 years ago. However, as the frequency and intensity of severe weather increase, there is a growing risk of storm damage to transport and distribution infrastructure, with consequent disruption of food supply chains. The rising cost of energy and the need to reduce fossil fuel usage along the food chain have led to a new calculus – "food miles", which should be kept as low as possible to reduce emissions. These factors could result in more local responsibility for food security, which needs to be considered in the formulation of adaptation strategies for people who are currently vulnerable or who could become so within the foreseeable future.

Food Security and Climate Change: A Conceptual Framework

Food systems exist in the biosphere, along with all other manifestations of human activity. Some of the significant changes in the biosphere that are expected to result from global warming will occur in the more distant future, as a consequence of changes in average weather conditions. The most likely scenarios of climate change indicate that increases in weather variability and the incidence of extreme weather events will be particularly significant now and in the immediate future. The projected increases in mean temperatures and precipitation will not manifest through constant gradual changes, but will instead be experienced as increased frequency, duration and intensity of hot spells and precipitation events. Whereas the annual occurrence of hot days and maximum temperatures are expected to increase in all parts of the globe, the mean global increase in precipitation is not expected to be uniformly distributed around the world. In general, it is projected that wet regions will become wetter and dry regions dryer. For this analysis, a conceptual framework on climate change and food security interactions was developed to highlight the variables defining the food and climate systems. The climate change and food security (CCFS) framework shows how climate change affects food security outcomes for the four components of food security food availability, food accessibility, food utilisation and food system stability in various direct and indirect ways.

Climate change variables influence biophysical factors, such as plant and animal growth, water cycles, biodiversity and nutrient cycling, and the ways in which these are managed through agricultural practices and land use for food production. However, climate variables also have an impact on physical/human capital such as roads, storage and marketing infrastructure, houses, productive assets, electricity grids, and human health which indirectly changes the economic and socio-political factors that govern food access and utilisation and can threaten the stability of food systems. All of these impacts manifest themselves in the ways in which food system activities are carried out. The framework illustrates how adaptive adjustments to food system activities will be needed all along the food chain to cope with the impacts of climate change. The climate change variables considered in the CCFS framework are:

- The CO_2 fertilisation effect of increased greenhouse gas concentrations in the atmosphere;
- Increasing mean, maximum and minimum temperatures;
- Gradual changes in precipitation: (i) increase in the frequency, duration and intensity of dry spells and droughts; (ii) changes in the timing, duration, intensity and geographic location of rain and snowfall;
- Increase in the frequency and intensity of storms and floods;
- Greater seasonal weather variability and changes in start/end of growing seasons.

Evidence indicates that more frequent and more intense extreme weather events (droughts, heat and cold waves, heavy storms, floods), rising sea levels and increasing irregularities in seasonal rainfall patterns (including flooding) are already having immediate impacts on not only food production, but also food distribution infrastructure, incidence of food emergencies, livelihood assets and human health in both rural and urban areas. In addition, less immediate impacts are expected to result from gradual changes in mean temperatures and rainfall. These will affect the suitability of land for different types of crops and pasture; the health and productivity of forests; the distribution, productivity and community composition of marine resources; the incidence and vectors of different types of pests and diseases; the biodiversity and ecosystem functioning of natural habitats; and the availability of good-quality water for crop, livestock and inland fish production. Arable land is likely to be lost owing to increased aridity (and associated salinity), groundwater depletion and sea-level rise. Food systems will be affected by internal and international migration, resource-based conflicts and civil unrest triggered by climate change.

Climate Change Impacts on South Asia

South Asia, comprising of eight countries i.e., Afghanistan, Bangladesh, Bhutan, India, the Maldives, Nepal, Pakistan and Sri Lanka, is home to over one-fifth of the world's population and is the most densely populated geographical region in the world. South Asia is known to be the most disaster prone region in the world (UNEP, United Nations Environment Programme 2003). Although agricultural sector in South Asia is continuing to grow, it is declining in relative importance, both in terms of its contribution to GDP and its share of the labour force. Urbanisation is increasing, and farm households are diversifying their sources of income beyond agriculture. This relative decline of agriculture is inevitable in countries that experience economic growth, which has been widespread in the region. Nevertheless, a significant percentage of the economically active population is still involved in agriculture in South Asia, and agricultural employment is especially important for the livelihoods of the poor. South Asia is also home to a majority of the worlds poor. According to FAO (2009), 1.02 billion people are undernourished worldwide in 2009. About 456 million people in South Asia are estimated to be undernourished. In the recent past, climate change emerged as the single most pressing issue facing society on a global basis, with serious implications for the food security of billions of people in the developing countries. The inter-annual, monthly and daily distribution of climate variables (e.g., temperature, radiation, precipitation, water vapour pressure in the air and wind speed) affects a number of physical, chemical and biological processes that drive the productivity of agricultural, forestry and fisheries systems. The high rates of population growth, and natural resource degradation, with continuing high rates of poverty and food insecurity make South Asia one of the most vulnerable regions to the impact of climate change. Land use, land degradation, urbanisation and pollution, affect the ecosystems in this region directly and indirectly through their effects on climate. These drivers can operate either independently or in association with one another. Complex feedbacks and interactions occur on all scales from local to global. It has been emphasise that climate change will add to the dual challenge of meeting food (cereal) demand while at the same time protecting natural resources and improving environmental quality in these regions. In the long run, climate change impacts, such as changes in temperature, shifts in growing seasons, storms, floods, droughts, and changed rainfall patterns, risk the livelihood of drylands populations. Therefore, adaptation to the adverse effects of climate change through sustainable land management is a crucial, though simultaneously challenging task.

The current IPCC Assessment Report (May, 2016) states that climate change, in particular increased risk of floods and droughts, is expected to have severe impact on South Asian countries, which economies rely mainly on agriculture, natural resources, forestry and fisheries sectors. In fact, although South Asia has low GHG emissions, climate change has already deeply affected the economic growth and development of the region. About 70 per cent of South Asians live in rural area and account for about 75 per cent of the poor, who are the most impacted by climate change.

Projections indicate that climate variations in South Asia will be varied and heterogeneous, with some regions experiencing more intense precipitation and increased flood risks, while others encounter sparser rainfall and prolonged droughts. The impacts will vary across sectors, locations and populations. Temperature rise will negatively impact rice and wheat yields in tropical parts of South Asia where these crops are already being grown close to their temperature tolerance threshold. While direct impacts are associated with rise in temperatures, indirect impacts due to water availability and changing soil moisture status and pest and disease incidence are likely to be felt. The most significant impacts are likely to be borne by small-holder rain fed farmers who constitute the majority of farmers in this region and possess low financial and technical capacity to adapt to climate variability and change.

Some of the projected impacts of climate change on main sectors that specifically apply to the South Asia are listed below.

Impacts of Enhanced Temperatures

While plant response to elevated CO_2 is positive, recent studies confirm that the effects of elevated CO_2 on plant growth and yield will depend on photosynthetic pathway, species, growth stage and management regime, such as water and nitrogen (N) applications. Increased temperatures may also reduce CO_2 effects indirectly, by increasing water demand. Rain-fed wheat grown at 450 ppm CO_2 demonstrated yield increases with temperature increases of up to 0.8°C, but declines with temperature increases beyond 1.5°C; additional irrigation was needed to counterbalance these negative effects.

Temperature rise will negatively impact rice and wheat yields in tropical parts of South Asia where these crops are already being grown close to their temperature tolerance threshold (Kelkar and Bhadwal, 2007). Kumar and Parikh (2001) show that even after accounting for farm level adaptation, a 2°C rise in mean temperature and a 7 per cent increase in mean precipitation will reduce net revenues by 8.4 per cent in India. Wheat yields are predicted to decline by 6–9 per cent in sub-humid, semiarid, and arid areas with 1°C increase in temperature (Sultana and Ali, 2006), while even a 0.3°C decadal rise could have a severe impact on important cash crops like cotton, mango, and sugarcane (MoE, 2003). In Sri Lanka, half a degree temperature rise is predicted to reduce rice output by six per cent, and increased dryness will adversely affect yields of key products like tea, rubber, and coconut (MENR, Ministry of Environment and Natural Resources, 2000). In the hot climate of Pakistan, cereal crops are already at the margin of stress. An increase of 2.5°C in average temperature would translate into much higher ambient temperatures in the wheat planting and growing stages. Higher temperatures are likely to result in decline in yields, mainly due to the shortening of the crop life cycle especially the grain filling period. The National Communication (MoE, 2003) highlighted that crops like wheat, cotton, mango, and sugarcane would be more sensitive to increase in temperatures compared to rice. Drylands and mountain regions are likely to be more vulnerable than others (Gitay *et al.,* 2001) and ecosystem degradation is largest in these regions (Hassan *et al.,* 2005). Climate change is likely to cause additional inequities, as its impacts are unevenly distributed over space and time and disproportionately affect the poor (Tol, 2001; Stern, 2007).

Impacts of Precipitation Variability and Water Resources

Current vulnerabilities to climate are strongly correlated with climate variability, in particular precipitation variability. These vulnerabilities are largest in the semi-arid and arid low-income countries with large tracts of dry lands, where precipitation and stream flow are concentrated over a few months, and where year-to-year variations are high (Lenton, 2004). In such regions a lack of deep groundwater wells or reservoirs (i.e., storage) leads to a high level of vulnerability to climate variability, and to the climate changes that are likely to further increase climate variability in future. Water resources are inextricably linked with climate, so the prospect of global climate change has serious implications for water resources and regional development (Riebsame *et al.,* 1995). Tendencies of increase in intense rainfall with the potential for heavy rainfall events spread over few days are likely to impact water recharge rates and soil moisture conditions. A warmer climate, with its increased climate variability, will increase the risk of both floods and droughts (Wetherald and Manabe, 2002).

South Asia is endowed with great rivers, which are the lifelines of the regional economy. The ice mass covering the Himalayan-Hindu Kush mountain range is the source of the nine largest rivers of Asia, including the Ganges, Brahmaputra, and Indus. These rivers provide water to more than half of the world's population. Many people in Asia are dependent on glacial melt water during dry season. Accelerated glacial melt questions the very perennial nature of many of the Himalayan flowing rivers. This is likely to have huge implications on those dependent on the resource affecting water availability for agricultural purposes (Kelkar and Bhadwal, 2007). In Nepal and Bhutan, melting glaciers are filling glacial lakes beyond their capacities contributing to Galcial Lake Outburst Floods (GLOFs) (UNEP, United Nations Environment Programme, 2007). Of 2,323 glacial lakes in Nepal, 20 have been found to be potentially dangerous with respect to GLOFs. The most significant such event occurred in 1985, when a glacial lake outburst flood caused a 10–15 m high surge of water and debris to flood down the Bhote Koshi and Dudh Koshi rivers for 90 km, destroying the Namche Small Hydro Project (Raut, 2006).

Semi-arid and arid areas are particularly exposed to the impacts of climate change on freshwater. In semi-arid areas, climate change may extend the dry season of no or very low flows, which particularly affects water users unable to rely on reservoirs or deep groundwater wells (Giertz *et al.,* 2006). Kundzewicz *et al.* (2007) explain that many of these areas will suffer a decrease in water resources due to climate change. The population of Maldives mainly depends on groundwater and rainwater as a source of freshwater. Both of these sources of water are vulnerable to changes in the climate and sea level rise. With the islands of the Maldives being low-lying, the rise in sea levels is likely to force saltwater into the freshwater lens. The groundwater is recharged through rainfall. Although the amount of rainfall is predicted to increase under an enhanced climatic regime, the spatial and temporal distribution in rainfall pattern is not clear (Ministry of Environment and Construction, 2005). Agricultural irrigation demand in arid and semi-arid regions of Asia is estimated to increase by at least 10 per cent for an increase in temperature of 1°C (Fischer *et al.,* 2002; Liu, 2002). Efforts to offset declining surface water availability due to increasing precipitation variability will be hampered by the fact that groundwater recharge will decrease considerably in some already water-stressed regions, where vulnerability is often exacerbated by the rapid increase in population and water demand.

The greatest impact will continue to be felt by the poor, who have the most limited access to water resources. Rapid depletion of water resource is already a cause for concern in many countries in South Asia. About 2.5 billion people will be affected with water stress and scarcity by the year 2050 in South Asia (HDR, 2006). In the dry lands, farmers and pastoralists also have to contend with other extreme natural resource challenges and constraints such as poor soil fertility, pests, crop diseases, and a lack of access to inputs and improved seeds. These challenges are usually aggravated by periods of prolonged droughts and/or floods and are often particularly severe during El Nino events (Vogel, 2005; Stige *et al.,* 2006). The impact of changes in precipitation and enhanced evaporation could have profound effects in some lakes and reservoirs.

Impacts of Increased Frequency of Extreme Events and Natural Disasters

South Asia suffers an exceptionally high number of natural disasters. Between 1990 and 2008, more than 750 million people 50 per cent of the region's population were affected by a natural disaster, leaving almost 60,000 dead and resulting in about US $45 billion in damages. Several studies showed that generally, the frequency of occurrence of more intense rainfall events in many parts of South Asia has increased, causing severe floods, landslides, and debris and mud flows, while the number of rainy days and total annual amount of precipitation has decreased (Mirza, 2002; Lal, 2003). Increasing frequency and intensity of droughts in many parts of South Asia are attributed largely to a rise in temperature, particularly during the summer and normally drier months, and during ENSO events (Lal, 2003). An increase in the frequency of droughts and extreme rainfall events could result in a decline in tea yield, which would be the greatest in regions below 600 m (Wijeratne, 1996). With the tea industry in Sri Lanka being a major source of foreign exchange and a significant source of income for labourers the impacts are likely to be grave. On an average during the period 1962–1988, Bangladesh lost about 0.5 million tonnes of rice annually as a result of floods that accounts for nearly 30 per cent of the country's average annual food grain imports (Paul and Rashid, 1993).

Short-term natural extremes, such as storms and floods, inter-annual and decadal climate variations, as well as large-scale circulation changes, such as the El Niño Southern Oscillation (ENSO), all have important effects on crop, pasture and forest production (Tubiello, 2005). Increased climate extremes may promote plant disease and pest outbreaks (Gan, 2004). There is growing evidence that the frequency and extent of drought has increased as a result of global warming. A global analysis has shown that abrupt changes in rainfall are more likely to occur in the arid and semi-arid regions, and that this susceptibility is possibly linked to strong positive feedbacks between vegetation and climate interactions (Narisma *et al.,* 2007). The socio-economic impacts of droughts may arise from the interaction between natural conditions and human factors, such as changes in land use and land cover, water demand and use. Excessive water withdrawals can exacerbate the impact of drought. Changes in the frequencies of extreme events will have an impact on land degradation processes such as floods and mass movements, soil erosion by both water and wind, and on soil salinisation.

Impacts on Crop, Pasture and Forest Productivity

Agriculture is the mainstay of several economies in South Asia. It is also the largest source of employment. The sector continues to be the single largest contributor to the GDP in the region. As three-fifth of the cropped area is rain fed, the economy of South Asia hinges critically on the annual success of the monsoons (Kelkar and Bhadwal, 2007). In the event of a failure, the worst affected are the landless and the poor whose sole source of income is from agriculture and its allied activities. Cruz *et al.* (2007) concluded that the crop yield in many countries of Asia has declined, partly due to rising temperatures and extreme weather events and that future climate change is likely to affect agriculture, risk of hunger and water resource scarcity with enhanced climate variability and more rapid melting of glaciers.

For Asia, the results of recent studies suggest that substantial decreases in cereal production potential could be likely by the end of this century as a consequence of climate change. Cruz *et al.* (2007) stressed, however, that regional differences in the response of wheat, maize and rice yields to projected climate change could likely be significant. Results of crop yield projections, using the HadCM2 climate model, indicate that crop yields could likely increase up to 20 per cent in East and South-East Asia while likely decrease up to 30 per cent in Central and South Asia even if the direct positive physiological effects of CO_2 are taken into account. In South Asia, there could be a significant decrease in non-irrigated wheat and rice yields for a temperature increase of greater than 2.5°C which could incur a loss in farm-level net revenue of between nine per cent and 25 per cent. One study points out that in Bangladesh, production of rice and wheat might drop by eight per cent and 32 per cent, respectively, by the year 2050. Studies show that a 0.5°C rise in winter temperature could reduce wheat yield by 0.45 tonnes per hectare in India. Other studies suggest that 2–5 per cent decrease in Indian wheat and maize yield potentials for temperature increases of 0.5–1.5°C could occur.

For countries in South Asia, the net cereal production is projected to decline at least between four per cent and ten per cent by the end of this century under the most conservative climate change scenario. The changes in cereal crop production potential suggest increasing stress on resources induced by climate change in many of the developing countries of Asia. Climate change could affect not only the crop production per unit area but also the area of production. More than 28 Mha in South and East Asia will require a substantial increase in irrigation for sustained productivity and the demand for agricultural irrigation in arid and semi-arid regions of Asia is estimated to increase by at least 10 per cent for an increase in temperature of 1°C.

Grasslands in the dry lands of South Asia consisting of fast-growing, often short lived species are sensitive to CO_2 and climate change, with the impacts related to the stability and resilience of plant communities (Mitchell and Csillag, 2001). Experiments support the concept of rapid changes in species composition and diversity under climate change. In dry regions, there are risks that severe vegetation degeneration leads to positive feedbacks between soil degradation and reduced vegetation and rainfall, with corresponding loss of pastoral areas and farmlands (Zheng *et al.*, 2002). The natural grassland coverage and the grass yield in Asia, in general, are projected to decline with a rise in temperature and higher evaporation (Lu and Lu, 2003). Thermal stress reduces productivity, conception rates and is potentially life-threatening to livestock (Easterling *et al.*, 2007).

Although climate change will impact the availability of forest resources, the anthropogenic impact, particularly land-use change and deforestation in tropical zones, is likely to be extremely important (Zhao *et al.*, 2005). The mangrove forests along the Indus Delta in Pakistan are an especially diverse ecosystem. They provide fuel wood and fodder to local inhabitants and are breeding grounds for an estimated 90 per cent of shrimps that are exported. Pakistan's national communication report states that detrimental impacts of climate change on rural livelihoods would result in more people being forced to seek employment in urban areas (MoE, 2003). In Sri Lanka, Somaratne and Dhanapala (1996) estimate a decrease in tropical rain forest of 2–11 per cent and an increase in tropical dry forest of 7–8 per cent. This study also indicates that increased temperature and rainfall would result in a northward shift of tropical wet forest into areas currently occupied by tropical dry forest. Droughts combined with deforestation increase fire danger (Laurance and Williamson, 2001).

Impacts on Crop Pests and Diseases

According to Cruz *et al.* (2007), some studies have shown that higher temperatures and longer growing seasons could result in increased pest populations in temperate regions of Asia. Warmer winter temperatures would reduce winter kill and increase insect populations. Overall temperature increases may influence crop pest and disease interactions by increasing pest and disease growth rates which would then increase the number of reproductive generations per season and by decreasing pest and disease mortality due to warmer winter temperatures, would make the crop more vulnerable. The report stated that climate change along with changing pest and disease patterns will affect how crop production systems react in the future.

Impacts on Fisheries

For fisheries, an increased frequency of El Niño events could likely lead to measurable declines in fish larvae abundance in the coastal waters of South and South-East Asia (Cruz *et al.,* 2007). This and other factors are expected to contribute to a general decline in fishery production in the coastal waters of East, South and South-East Asia. There is a potential to substantially alter fish breeding habitats and fish food supply and therefore the abundance of fish populations in Asian waters due to the response to future climate change to the following factors: ocean currents; sea level; sea-water temperature; salinity; wind speed and direction; strength of upwelling; the mixing layer thickness; and predator response.

Impacts of Sea Level Rise

Low-lying coastal cities will be at the forefront of impacts; vulnerable to the risks of sea level rise and storms. These cities include Karachi, Mumbai, and Dhaka – all of which have also witnessed significant environmental stresses in recent years. Higher seawater levels would also increase the risk of flooding due to rainstorms, by reducing coastal drainage. A rise in sea level would raise the water table, further reducing drainage in coastal areas. All these effects could have possibly devastating socioeconomic implications, particularly for infrastructure in low lying deltaic areas. Noronha *et al.* (2003) provided a coastal district level ranking of vulnerability to one metre sea level rise in India by constructing a weighted index as an average of the share of land area affected in the total area of district; the share of population affected in the total population of the district; and the index of relative infrastructure development. The most vulnerable districts were found to be the metropolises of Chennai and Mumbai. The population of Maldives mainly depends on groundwater and rainwater as a source of freshwater. Both of these sources of water are vulnerable to changes in the climate and sea level rise. With the islands of the Maldives being low-lying, the rise in sea levels is likely to force saltwater into the freshwater lens (Ministry of Environment and Construction, 2005).

Food security challenges conventional understanding of security

The traditional understanding of security on realist and neo-realist parlance revolves around state and its military apparatus. Increasing state military capability will ensure security of the state and it is coeval with that of the people. A state perceives the other states as threats to its own survival and security unless strongly guarded by uncontested military power. The problems plaguing the entire humanity in terms of grinding poverty, burgeoning population growth, spread of diseases, scarcity of resources and environmental degradation could not be comprehended within the realist framework based on state centric military capability. Thus, the dominant realist paradigm to understand the current realities seems to be inadequate. It has "become an anachronism that has lost much of its explanatory and prescriptive power" (Holsti O.R., 1991: 94).

Inadequacy of the conventional approach hovering round state and its military apparatus as found prominent in realist parlance to meet the non-military and non-conventional threats stemming from environmental degradation led to a reschedule of security agenda. The illusion of a hermetically sealed and self reliant security founded on the dominant realist paradigm is felt to be naïve and dangerous. The question remains persistently nagging the arrogant security paradigm:

How can a nation launch fighter planes to resist global warming?

How can a nation dispatch tanks to counter advancing deserts?

How can a nation fire the smartest missiles against rising sea levels?

Non-military threats to security could not be perceived as concrete and tangible as the conventional threats find a central place in the security agenda of the states. But the climate change has changed this archetypal security thinking saying the wrong end of a smokestack can be as much of a security concern to humans as the barrel of a gun. The growing number of people vulnerable to environmental hazards makes it clear that the security of a state well impregnated with modern and nuclear weapons is not coeval with that of individuals or human beings. America, representing the metaphor of the unipolar moment in the world at present demonstrated its utter inability to forestall the orgy of Katrina or Gustav, which wreaked havoc on its citizens recently. Food insecurity induced by climate change stands as a non-traditional security threats to human beings. The approach to the crisis of food insecurity needs a non-military approach in the sense that it is multilateral as it involves water, land, and climate, use of chemicals and fertilisers and myriad interconnected factors. It is not confined to a particular nation, but it is regional and global at the same time. The connections between climate change, food insecurity, conflict and instability have become spectacularly present in many of the recent crises in various parts of the globe. Arab Spring has been the result of climate change and its impact on China as the latter suffered a heavy decline in wheat production which happens to be the largest exporter of wheat to Egypt. The heavy price rise in wheat in Egypt with a mediation of other factors led to such a crisis. Syria is also another example of embroiled conflict and war induced by climate change.

Climate Change and Food Security in South Asia

Climate change has the potential to be the most significant challenge to human development in the near future, it is not only an environmental issue but also one that affect our very existence because of its direct links with agriculture and food security. The most painful reality of climate change is that it is the poorer countries that stand to suffer most, and it is the poorest in the poor countries that have the least capacity to withstand the effects of climate change. At a time when South Asia is seized with the problem of poverty and inflation, it stands to be further aggravated by climate change. Therefore, the action ought to be on the most vulnerable sector that climate change will affect i.e. food and agriculture. Across South Asia (Bangladesh, Bhutan, India, Maldives, Nepal, Pakistan and Sri Lanka), large proportion of the population depend on agriculture for their livelihoods. Most of the South Asia receives Monsoons every year, but rainfall in the semi-arid and sub-humid regions of South Asia is highly variable and unpredictable and influences agricultural productivity accordingly. Over the centuries, farming practices in the South Asia has developed as a response to local climatic conditions. The greatest challenge that South Asia faces is lifting some 500 million people out of poverty, but this already-formidable challenge is made all the more difficult because along with local environmental repercussions of intensive agriculture, global warming has also started to affect food production, raising food deficit over the last two decades, showing stagnation in productivity curve of the Green Revolution agricultural miracle of South Asia. The environmental challenges due to climate change, such as water shortages and storms resulting in soil erosion threaten future social upheavals, climate change migrants and political conflicts in the region.

What Climate Change Means for Food Security in South Asia

Agriculture in South Asia is dependent on the ecosystem that is synchronised with the monsoon rain system. Any unexpected change in the climatic conditions could bring devastation to millions of farming families in South Asia. To prepare for change in precipitation or timing of monsoon rains is no easy task for the farming communities. Systematic analysis is required of any signs that show deviation from the long-term trends in precipitation and temperatures. Meanwhile, disaster preparedness for devastation caused by climate change; floods, storms, cyclones, avalanches and landslides needs to be accelerated in climatically vulnerable areas. The cropping and livestock systems will need to be made more flexible in case of climate change related prolonged droughts or regular flooding. The farm to market infrastructure and transport system will need to be in sync with these changing crops and livestock breeds.

The fourth assessment report of the Intergovernmental Panel on Climate Change (IPCC) lists the consequences of climate change for the South Asian region. The melting of the Himalayan glaciers will lead to increased flooding and affect water resources within the next two to three decades. Crop yields could decrease by up to 30 per cent in South Asia by the mid-twenty-first century. This could hamper the achievement of many of the Millennium Development Goals (MDGs), including that of poverty eradication. Climate change is expected to have severe socio-economic implications for South Asia. As three-fifth of the cropped area is rain fed, the economy of South Asia hinges critically on the annual success of the monsoons. In the event of a failure, the worst affected are the landless and the poor whose sole source of income is from agriculture and allied activities.

The HDR, 2006, had pointed out that in South Asia alone; 2.5 billion people will be affected by water stress and scarcity by the year 2050. A rise in temperature will negatively impact rice and wheat yields in the tropical parts of South Asia where these crops are already being grown close to their temperature tolerance threshold. While the direct consequences of climate change are associated with rise in temperatures, the indirect impact will be felt in terms of water availability, changing status of soil moisture, and pest and disease incidence. The worst hit by these changes are likely to be farmers with small holdings in rain fed areas who constitute a majority of the farmers in this region and whose financial and technical capacity to adapt to climate variability and change is low. Landholdings are already very small due to large family sizes in this region. In the region's hilly parts, holdings are also fragmented, preventing farmers from reaping economies of scale.

Safety-net Programmes - Country Policies

Household food security in many instances is more about income security than just the availability of food. It is the inability of the households to purchase food or have access to the physical storage of food, which leads to the household's food insecurity. In order to increase food availability, various macro policies and safety-net programmes such as building buffer stocks and controlling prices have been implemented in the countries of South Asia. Since food-based safety-net programmes are effective only if individuals have access to these facilities and many households do not have the income to buy food, some countries have introduced income based or employment generating programmes along with price control and distributive measures. Many South Asian countries have direct cash transfers too. The number of programmes, their magnitude, reaches and target population vary from country to country and also within the country. Some of the major safety nets of the South Asian countries that are directly or indirectly linked to the goal of food security are discussed below.

Afghanistan

The state of political and economic affairs is highly complicated in Afghanistan. Population is extremely vulnerable to food insecurity; the social, physical and political infrastructure does not provide bankable support to food security interventions and investments by the international community. The country's agricultural sector is also under extreme pressure. Farmers receive little professional guidance and limited opportunities for development of farming activities. Furthermore, employment opportunities are not increasing which could provide secure livelihood to a large segment of population especially in the rural areas. In this regard, there is a need for taking concrete steps to solve the problem of food insecurity. The National Risk and Vulnerability Assessment conducted in 2005 (NRVA, 2005) by the Ministry of Rural Rehabilitation and Development together with the Central Statistic Office, Government of Afghanistan found that approximately 61 per cent of the Afghan population experienced low dietary diversity and poor to very poor food consumption. Around 30 per cent of the population does not get the minimum food requirements and is food insecure. Twenty per cent of the population suffers from chronic food insecurity. NRVA, 2005 summarises food insecurity in Afghanistan as follows: "At the household level, food insecurity in Afghanistan is largely caused by inadequate access to food resulting from low household incomes." The 2006 drought affected rain-fed wheat and resulted in a reduction of yield in most regions, further increasing food insecurity. In 2007, 6.5 million people faced food insecurity in Afghanistan according to the FAO.

Afghanistan used to be a major exporter of fresh and dry fruits, but conflict and political disturbances destroyed orchards. Although international development agencies are helping the Afghans rebuild their orchards, both time and resources are needed for production to become sustainable. One of the necessary conditions for rebuilding public and private assets for food security is to improve the security situation across Afghanistan. Various international development agencies have been working to achieve food security in the country. This includes a substantial amount of food aid. A bulk of the relief assistance that reached households in Afghanistan has been in the form of food. Where food aid commodities reached, they saved lives, discouraged migration and protected families from further indebtedness. Most of the aid was distributed in areas identified by the World Food Programme's Vulnerability Assessment.

Apart from the aid from the World Food Programme, the European Commission Humanitarian Aid Office has also arranged various food aid programmes in Afghanistan, beginning with a food aid programme valued at six million Euros per year in October, 2007. The Government of Afghanistan was provided with 8,700 tonnes of vegetable oil in 2006 and 8,200 tonnes in 2007 under a US Department of Agriculture (USDA)-

supported Title I-funded Food for Progress Programme. USDA is also providing technical assistance for the reconstruction of Afghanistan's agricultural sector. Mercy Corps has monetised Food for Progress vegetable oil, including 2,000 tonnes of vegetable oil in 2005 and 10,000 tonnes of soybean oil in 2006. The proceeds from the sale of the commodities are being used to finance agribusiness, horticulture, and animal husbandry projects besides health activities in six provinces of Afghanistan. World Vision is implementing a USDA-supported multi-year McGovern-Dole International Child Nutrition (Food for Education) Programme in the province of Hirat.

Bangladesh

The Government of Bangladesh has, over the past three and a half decades, introduced reform measures and policies for agricultural development in its quest for food security for all. In the 1970s and early 1980s, Bangladesh pursued a policy of agricultural modernisation by supplying modern agricultural inputs (seed, fertiliser and irrigation) and technology (HYVs and machinery) through government agencies and parastatal organisations like the Bangladesh Agricultural Development Corporation (BADC), and Bangladesh Water Development Board (BWDB). The government liberalised the seed market, allowed import of improved germplasm for research and development and developed its own facilities for producing foundation seeds (except for five notified crops - rice, wheat, sugarcane, potato and jute) through the Seed Policy Act of 1992 and 1998. It also encouraged the involvement of the private sector and NGOs in the seed delivery system. More recently, the newly elected government has decided to extend fertiliser subsidy to fertilisers other than urea in a bid to promote balanced fertiliser use. Earlier, while the government procured and marketed urea at administered prices, the marketing of phosphoric, potassium and other fertilisers was left to the private sector. This resulted in a disproportionate rise in the prices of these, leading to imbalanced use of fertilisers. During this period, the Bangladesh government also took a series of measures to expand its irrigation network. Minor irrigation systems have been developed in the country at a rapid pace. To promote the use of irrigation facilities, electricity for irrigation purposes is subsidised. In the 1970s and early 1980s, irrigation was promoted through public agencies, but, since the mid-1980s, the government began to involve the private sector too.

Bhutan

Bhutan has initiated several agricultural, food and trade policies to increase food production and ensure food security in the country since the initiation of the first five-year plan in 1961. Since Bhutan did not have the resources and technological know-how, several multilateral and bilateral development agencies have supported Bhutan in achieving food self-sufficiency. In 1983, the International Development Research Centre (IDRC) and IRRI supported "Rice Farming Systems Research" to build Bhutan's rice research capabilities and this lead to a remarkable process in rice production. The Bhutan government's policy to increase food production includes the sale of farm inputs such as seeds/seedlings, fertilisers and plant protection chemicals through private commission agents appointed by the concerned ministry. Subsidies on inputs, except those for promotional purposes, do not exist anymore. However, the transportation of inputs is subsidised even today to maintain cost uniformity throughout the country. The government has been investing in the construction of roads to improve rural connectivity, setting up of Renewable Natural Resources (RNR) centres (120), research centres and in the training of ministry officials and farmers to improve food security. Bhutan has also set up the Food Corporation of Bhutan (FCB) to imports food to meet domestic demand. Besides, under the FAO and the Netherlands Partnership Programme (FNNP), the government chose rice, maize, citrus fruits and potatoes for pro-poor commodity chain analysis to both improve food security and increase rural incomes. The key policy directives to enhance food security in Bhutan are to intensify and diversify production, to adopt an integrated approach to nutrient and pest management and to achieve at least 70 per cent self-sufficiency in food grains. Emphasis has been placed on developing and promoting high-value, low-volume cash crops that offer comparative advantages over other crops in capturing the off-season markets in India and neighbouring countries; promoting the use and breeding of superior, healthy breeds of highly productive livestock; placing a higher priority on conservation than on commercial exploitation of forests and maintaining at least 60 per cent of the country's area under forest cover.

India

India's initiatives to ensure food security for its citizens ranges from concerted efforts to boost agricultural production to far-ranging market interventions aimed at both income and price stabilisation. Besides, measures have been introduced to improve the access to food of the really poor through public distribution and income generating schemes. One of the first interventions by the Indian government was the passing of the Essential Commodities Act in 1955 to protect the poor from the vagaries of the market. The act conferred on the government the power to control production, supply and distribution of essential commodities to ensure equitable distribution of food grains at fair prices. In the mid-1960s, the government ushered in what has widely come to be known as the 'green revolution' by encouraging the use of high yielding varieties of seeds, expansion of irrigation networks and active encouragement of the use of chemical fertilisers in a bid to boost the productivity of Indian agriculture. Most of the agricultural subsidies such as those for power and fertilisers were introduced to improve farmers' access to inputs that would help improve farm productivity. One of the oldest initiatives taken by the Indian government was the establishment of a public distribution system (PDS) with the objective of making basic food grains available to all at affordable prices. It set up the Food Corporation of India under an act of Parliament in 1964 to oversee its implementation. The Corporation was entrusted with the task of both procuring food grains at minimum support prices announced for 24 crops by the government and regulating supply to ensure that prices remained stable by building a buffer stock of food grains. In effect, the Corporation has been the main instrument to implement the government's income and price stabilisation policies.

The TDPS has been plagued by poor administration and local resource constraints. Despite this, it has proved largely effective in ensuring food security both at the national and household levels. Several measures have been proposed to make the scheme more effective. One that was mooted in the Tenth Five-Year Plan was the issue of subsidy entitlement cards to eligible households. The subsidy entitlement was to be based on family size and composition. The cards would entitle the household to monthly food stamps from prescribed distribution centres which could be encashed for food from any food store at a subsidised rate. The proposal is now being implemented on a pilot basis. Besides the TPDS, the Indian government has also implemented programmes for the benefit of more targeted groups. In 1975, it launched the Integrated Child Development Scheme (ICDS) to provide nutrition and healthcare services to children and pregnant women. The Antyodaya Anna Yojana (AAY), launched in 2000, sought to provide affordable food to below poverty level (BPL) households. The objective of the scheme was to make the TDPS more focused and targeted an identified 10 million of the poorest of the poor in different states. Wheat and rice at subsidised prices of Rs 2 and Rs 3 per kg respectively are provided to these households under the scheme. State governments are expected to meet the distribution costs of the programme.

Another scheme that addresses the nutritional requirements of a specified target group is the mid-day meal scheme. The scheme was launched in 1995 for the benefit of students in government run and aided primary schools and in schools run by local bodies. Under the scheme, the government supplies free food grains to schools in quantities determined on the basis of specific nutritional requirements for a specified minimum number of days in a year. In 2005, the government passed the National Rural Employment Guarantee Act to improve the livelihood security of rural households by providing them with guaranteed wage employment for a minimum number of days in a year. Semi-skilled and unskilled workers living below the poverty line in rural areas have been specifically targeted under the programme. Works undertaken in the programme aim to create enduring assets in rural areas and include projects such as land-levelling, bush clearing, deep ploughing, building of earthen bunds, flood control works and horticulture. These contribute to improved farm productivity and higher farm incomes. The National Rural Employment Guarantee Scheme was preceded by the National Food for Work Programme (NFFWP) which was implemented in 2004 in 150 of the most backward districts of the country. These were identified by the Planning Commission in consultation with the Ministry of Rural Development and state governments. The objective of the programme was to provide additional resources apart from the resources available under the Sampoorna Grameen Rozgar Yojana (SGRY) to these backward districts to generate supplementary wage employment and provide food-security through the creation of need-based economic, social and community assets.

Recently as National Food Security Act (NFSA), 2013 has been passed by the Parliament, government has notified the National Food Security Act, 2013 on 10th September, 2013 with the objective to provide for food and nutritional security in human life cycle approach, by ensuring access to adequate quantity of quality food at affordable prices to people to live a life with dignity. The Act provides for coverage of upto 75 per cent of the rural population and upto 50 per cent of the urban population for receiving subsidised foodgrains under Targeted Public Distribution System (TPDS), thus covering about two-thirds of the population. The eligible persons will be entitled to receive five Kgs of foodgrains per person per month at subsidised prices of Rs 3/2/1 per Kg for rice/wheat/coarse grains. The existing Antyodaya Anna Yojana (AAY) households, which constitute the poorest of the poor, will continue to receive 35 Kgs of foodgrains per household per month.

The Act also has a special focus on the nutritional support to women and children. Besides meal to pregnant women and lactating mothers during pregnancy and six months after the child birth, such women will also be entitled to receive maternity benefit of not less than Rs 6,000. Children upto 14 years of age will be entitled to nutritious meals as per the prescribed nutritional standards. In case of non-supply of entitled food grains or meals, the beneficiaries will receive food security allowance. The Act also contains provisions for setting up of grievance redressal mechanism at the District and State levels. Separate provisions have also been made in the Act for ensuring transparency and accountability.

Nepal

For the past 13 years, agricultural policy in Nepal has been shaped by the Agricultural Perspective Plan (APP), which covered the period 1995-2010. The APP strategy is to achieve economic growth and poverty reduction objectives through accelerated growth of agriculture. Perhaps reflecting the relative antiquity of the APP, food security receives scant mention, and what discussion does exist is largely confined to the improved access the poor will receive as a result of increased employment opportunities, and the lower prices that are a spin-off of increased production and efficiency.

Other targeted food assistance programmes are implemented by the government with considerable financial and logistical support from donor agencies including the World Food Programme (WFP). The various modes of assistance include the following: provision of rural employment opportunities to the poor through the Rural Community Infrastructure Works Programme (RCIW), a food for education programme directed at improving the nutritional status of and school enrolment and attendance by children, a mother and child health initiative aimed at improving the health and nutritional status of pregnant women, nursing mothers and their young children, and emergency assistance in natural disasters.

Pakistan

Pakistan does not have any national food policy except for a few food security policies at the regional level. There is a plethora of food laws, mainly dealing with quality standards. Standards are also not addressed properly and require a complete overhaul. The Pakistani government neglected the issue of food security and just focused on measures to increase production. Though production did increase, it was not sufficient to meet the country's consumption needs. In Pakistan, procurement, handling, marketing, storage and supplies are handled by the four provincial food departments and the national agency, the Pakistan Agricultural Services and Supplies Corporation (PASSCO). The Corporation was established in 1973 as a public limited company, fully owned by the federal government and six public sector banks. The agency has been entrusted with the tasks of procuring wheat and other agricultural commodities, providing price support to farmers, ensuring adequate supplies in deficit provinces/regions, intervening in the open market to stabilise prices of agricultural commodities and, above all, maintaining strategic reserves to meet any emergent situation. In 2006, the rated storage capacity with these agencies (PASSCO and provincial food departments) was 4.34 million tonnes, of which 2.45 million tonnes was with the Punjab Food department, 0.71 million tonnes with the Sindh Food Department, 0.16 million tonnes with the NWFP, 0.44 million tonnes with the Balochistan Food Department, 0.45 million tonnes with PASSCO and about 0.13 million tonnes with other agencies.

The 2007-08 food crisis pushed the government to revisit food production and food security issues. In 2008, the Planning Commission of Pakistan formulated a task force on food security to provide policy recommendations to ensure food security. It was also asked to look into issues regarding procurement, medium-term research priorities, water resources and climate change. Two major initiatives taken by the Pakistan government to improve food access are the Benazir Income Support Programme (BISP) and the Food Support Programme (FSP). BSP was initiated with an initial allocation of Rs 34 billion (US $ 425 million approximately) for the year 2008-09. The programme was initiated to partially offset the impact of inflation on the purchasing power of the poor. Food prices have seen a sharp rise since 2005. In the years 2005-07, inflation stood at almost 10 per cent with food inflation in the range of 13-15 per cent. In 2007-08, the sharp rise in oil prices and primary products in the international as well as domestic market resulted in double-digit inflation, which almost halved people's purchasing power. The programme aims at covering almost 15 per cent of the entire population, which constitutes 40 per cent of the population below the poverty line. A monthly payment of Rs 1000 per family would increase the income of a family earning Rs 5000 by 20 per cent. BISP will cover all four provinces. The food support programme (FSP) was launched in 2002-2003 targeting the poor to improve their living standard by providing them financial support. A subsidy of Rs 2000 was given to around 1.25 million poor families in two biannual instalments of Rs 1000 through post offices countrywide. The government increased the rate of annual subsidy to

Rs 2400 in 2003-04 and further to Rs 3000 in 2005-06. The programme's annual budget was increased from Rs 4.38 billion to Rs 6 billion in 2007-2008 to cover a larger number of the country's poor.

Sri Lanka

There are three main food security-related programmes in Sri Lanka targeted at special groups and the poor. These are Samurdhi programme, Thriposha Programme and the mid-day meal programme in schools. It is important to note that none of these are aimed specifically at ensuring food security; these are food-based welfare programmes with objectives that go beyond mere food security. Sri Lanka's largest welfare programme, the Samurdhi programme, was launched in 1995 with the twin objectives of ensuring food security and reducing poverty. The programme covers two million households. Eighty per cent of its outlay is accounted for by a food stamp programme. Its biggest drawback has been poor targeting of beneficiaries. Intended to cover a target of 20 per cent of the population which is below the poverty line, the programme actually covers half the total number of households in the country. The Thriposha Programme focuses on the specific group of mothers in low income groups with children below the age of one. It is essentially a programme of food supplementation in which cereals, pulses and micro-nutrients are distributed free among the target group. Despite its sharply defined target population, this programme has also seen a considerable part of the subsidy offered going to ineligible recipients. Apart from problems of execution, the programme suffers from limited reach and inadequate monitoring of the health of recipients. The school mid-day meal programme targets children with the objective of improving school attendance and children's nutrition. The programme covers 500,000 children in 6,440 schools, which have at least 30 per cent malnourished children.

Maldives

The main source of food security in the Maldives is the fisheries sector. The Ministry of Fisheries, Agriculture, and Marine Resources (MOFAMR) is responsible for the sustainable management and development of fisheries, agriculture, and marine resources of the nation. One of the most important initiatives towards achieving food security in Maldives is the Hydroponics Agriculture Pilot Project taken up by MOFAMR in 2006. The project aims to promote the development of hydroponics production systems (it is a technique of growing plants without soil, in water containing nutrients) both by households and on a commercial scale, to help the country achieve food security as well as provide its citizens with an additional avenue of employment and income generation. The project also aims to increase the availability of high-quality horticultural products, which would improve nutritional status. There is considerable emphasis on raising awareness of the benefits of hydroponics among, and imparting training to, the young, especially in rural islands. In addition, following the tsunami in 2004, an assessment of the food safety situation was undertaken to assist the Ministry of Health, Government of Maldives. Various food-safety monitoring guidelines were developed for food-processing units, resorts, hotels and guesthouses, and port health authorities (food imports). These guidelines were basically developed on the lines of "Good Manufacturing Practices" (GMP) and "Good Hygiene Practices" (GHP). Since the quality and safety of processed food products depends on the raw material used, these guidelines lay considerable stress on the assessment of "primary production" along with an assessment of food processing facilities. In order to meet household or individual level food security in the country, the Department of Public Health organises food safety advocacy sessions to create awareness among the population regarding food safety. The government is considering the establishment of a National Food Safety Committee (NFSC) to provide a strong coordinating mechanism for uniform enforcement of food safety norms. NFCS also recommended that food safety education should be initiated in educational institutions in order to lay the foundation of overall good health of the young. This will ensure that the students who work in the hospitality and tourism sector will become role models in safe food practices and thereby strengthen the competitive advantage of Maldives as a tourism destination in all aspects.

Policy Recommendations

Poverty alleviation is vital to securing food security in South Asia. The poor communities are the ones who suffer the most from climate change. These people rely on natural vegetation for sustenance and face limited coping strategies in times of climatic crises. Hence, in order to minimise the impact of climate change on such vulnerable communities, poverty of the region must be addressed first. Initiatives such as land entitlement to poor communities and empowerment of small and marginal farmers through microfinance loans can be some of the effective measures to alleviate poverty. Such initiatives will increase the poor's asset base and limit their reliance on natural vegetation for subsistence.

Developing economies like South Asia must embrace the path of environmentally sustainable economic growth. Growth and poverty are intertwined with each other. In order to eradicate poverty, economic growth is indispensable. However, economic growth at the expense of natural resources is detrimental in the long-run. In South Asia, industrialisation is occurring at the expense of natural resources. Furthermore, industrialisation is degrading the environment rapidly. If economic growth continues in that fashion, then future generations will suffer immensely. Hence, any developmental process must incorporate environmental aspects to achieve a sustainable economic growth in the region.

Furthermore, elimination of intra-regional trade barriers is essential for a sustainable economic development and greater cooperation in the region. Over the recent decades, South Asia has become a food surplus zone.[2] However, despite being a food surplus zone, vast majority of South Asian children and women suffer from malnutrition and anaemia, respectively. So, where does the surplus food of the region end up? While South Asian countries have extensively engaged in overseas trade, the intra-regional trade has been disappointingly low, due to host of trade barriers, protectionism and distrust among member countries. When intra-regional trade alone can address significant aspect of food insecurity, the respective governments of the region must not exhibit pessimism towards intra-regional trade. Let free trade prevail for an overall economic development of the region.

Bilateral Initiatives to Tackle Climate Change and Food Security

- **Food Bank** – Despite being enacted several years ago, the SAARC Food Bank continues to remain at a nascent stage, mainly due to lack of effective initiation from member countries. Although the notion of bank implies profit, the SAARC Food Bank can be established as a non-profit humanitarian aid organisation. If the SAARC Food Bank can be materialised, then this will greatly enhance food security in the region. Most importantly, the region does not have to rely on foreign food assistance in times of natural calamities.
- **Intellectual Property Rights and Sharing of Knowledge and Experience** – While India has been a leader in Intellectual Property Right (IPR) issues in the region, other South Asian economies lag far behind in this field. As such, other South Asian countries can learn from the Indian experience. Furthermore, an increased transfer

and share of SAARC technology is essential for promoting economic growth and regional cooperation in the region.

- **Climate Resilience Agriculture** – In order to better adapt to changing weather patterns, South Asian economies need to invest in research and development of climate resilient agriculture. There is a greater need for improved farming systems, diversification of agricultural products and development of breeds that adapt to climate change. The region can seek foreign technical assistance in this regard.

If greater economic cooperation is sought after in South Asia, then it is imperative that South Asians be aware of the importance of SAARC and its initiatives. Even after decades of SAARC establishment, vast majority of South Asians are practically unaware of SAARC and its declarations. By contrast, in Europe, Europeans are aware of the importance of the EU zone and participate in EU policies by voting in referendums. However, no such activities exist in South Asia. Hence, until and unless the civil society in the region is aware of SAARC and its greater manifestations towards economic development and regional cooperation, SAARC ministerial summits and subsequent declarations will have little significance at all.

Conclusion

Climate change has a profound impact on agriculture and on food security. At the same time agriculture contributes to climate change to a considerable extent. Fortunately, there is also much to gain since the agricultural sector holds significant climate change mitigation potential through reductions of greenhouse gas emissions and enhancement of sequestration: "Agriculture offers a wealth of opportunities to deliver simultaneously on improving agricultural resilience to climate change, increasing food production, and lowering emissions. Many of these opportunities use practices, technologies, and systems that are already available and affordable, but need to be tailored to specific contexts and may require incentives from climate finance to ensure adoption. Some interventions also benefit wider environmental services, farming incomes, and agriculture-based economies." A policy aimed at achieving greenhouse gas emission reductions, adaptation to climate change and an increase in productivity is, therefore, very much needed. "Climate smart agriculture" policies are being proposed, but so far remain underdeveloped.

Unfortunately, the Paris Climate Agreement, 2015 does not provide a powerful stimulus to adopt and implement climate smart agriculture policies. The Paris Climate Agreement, in this respect, does not change the troublesome relationship between agriculture policies and climate policies that we have already witnessed under the United Nations Framework Convention on Climate Change (UNFCCC) and the Kyoto Protocol. Under the UNFCCC, there is little attention to reducing emissions from agriculture. Most attention focuses on adaptation to climate change in rural areas in developing countries, particularly through the various instruments that finance adaptation projects in developing countries. Yet even in that area progress is painfully slow. Much more concrete action is needed to facilitate the transfer of adaptation technologies and adaptation know-how as well as funds to finance adaptation measures in agriculture to developing countries. For the developed countries, the UNFCCC does not make much of a contribution to addressing climate change and food security issues. This is a pity, as the developed country agriculture sector will play an important role in addressing the increasing global demand for food. Fortunately developed countries, including important players such as the EU, do not have to wait for the UNFCCC process. The EU recently announced its intention to implement an ambitious policy aimed at climate friendly and resilient food production, while optimising the agricultural sector's contribution to greenhouse gas mitigation and sequestration. It is of vital importance that this example is followed and implemented across the globe. Hopefully such initiatives will then be picked up by the international community under the UNFCCC process.

South Asia is one of the most vulnerable regions in the world to climate change in view of the huge population, the large number of poor facing food insecurity, inappropriate soil and management practices on marginal lands in the semi-arid regions leading to increasing rates of land degradation and the projected impacts of climate change on the agricultural, forestry and fisheries sectors. The coping capacity of the rural poor, especially in the marginal areas, is poor and there is a need to mainstream the good practices for adaptation to climate change into sustainable development planning in the region. Improved understanding of the climate change impacts, vulnerability and the adaptation practices to cope with climate change could help this process.

The nexus of climate change and food security presents a vital combination of issues and the current effort is far behind what is needed to deal with the challenge. South Asia is among the areas expected to face severe impacts of climate change, for example, melting of glacier will impact Nepal. Devastating flooding in 2007 along the Ganges and

Brahmaputra rivers affected over 13 million people in Bangladesh. Flooding in Pakistan in 2010 severely affected 20 million people. India has suffered a drastic drop in groundwater levels due to overexploitation, heavy rainfall, devastating flooding and severe droughts. Sea level rise is a threat to low lying areas of Bangladesh and Sri Lanka. South Asia is highly vulnerable to the impact of climate change because of its reliance on agriculture and forestry with a concentration of large populations along exposed coastlines and rivers. Millions of South Asians live in fast-growing cities along the coast. There is a need to develop a system of networking and collaboration among relevant research organisations involved in research on the economics of adaptation to climate change in South East Asia. For climate change impacts, adaptation, and policy response in the South Asian countries, the focus is needed on economics and socioeconomics aspects of sustainable development. A set of national policies on adaptation strategies needs to be implemented by the governments of South Asian countries to ensure food security in the region. Ensuring food security to all those who are in most need in South Asian countries remains one of the cornerstones of human security. The climate change as noted above has already exacerbated the food crisis in South Asia. Food production depends on a congeries of interconnected factors which are inextricably connected with climate change. The South Asian countries should give top priority to human security which encompasses food security instead of being moved by the conventional understanding and formulating foreign policies on state centric military terms. Climate change is not confined to a particular nation. It is a global phenomenon. Unless all nations of the world take strong action as was promised in Paris talk in 2015 to stall the temperature of the earth from slipping to more than 1.5 degree Celsius, the people in South Asia will be vulnerable to the devastating impacts of climate change. The South Asian countries must come together to take multilateral action along with unilateral action apart from the global action to mount pressure on developed countries to transfer finance, technology and knowledge based information to them. Clearly, food production, prices, and food security will all be significantly affected by climate change's impact on temperatures, rainfall, and aquatic species, as outlined by Working Group II of the Intergovernmental Panel on Climate Change in its 5th Assessment report. A report released by International Food Policy Research Institute during the Paris COP 21 predicts that climate change will have an adverse effect on food security in vulnerable countries. Climate change is highly likely to disrupt food production in many regions, raising prices and disrupting markets, and increasing the risk of protests, riots, and civil conflict, as amplified by the 2007-09 food riots that took place in more than 40 countries. Syria has been an amplifying example to show how severe drought has resulted in a civil war due to climate change. The South Asian countries before being turned into a burning cauldron of violent conflict because of climate change induced food insecurity must take sufficient measures collectively as a pathway to peace.

References

Abbass, Z. (2009). Climate Change, Poverty and Environmental Crisis in the Disaster Prone Areas of Pakistan, Islamabad, Pakistan.

Ahmed, A.U. (ed.) (2010). Reducing Vulnerability to Climate Change: The pioneering Example of Community-Based Adaptation in Bangladesh, Dhaka, Bangladesh: Centre for Global Change (CGC) and CARE Bangladesh.

Alam, M. and B.R. Regmi (2004). Adverse Impacts of Climate Change on the Development of Nepal: Integrating Adaptation into Policies and Activities, CLACC Nepal Working Paper No. 3, Dhaka, Bangladesh: Bangladesh Centre for Advanced Studies (BCAS).

Available online at: http://www.confluence.org.uk/2008/11/09/ food-balance-sheets-of-south-asia-positive/

Bajracharya, S.R., P.R. Mool, and B.R. Shrestha (2007). Impact of Climate Change on Himalayan Glaciers and Glacial Lakes: Case Studies on GLOF and Associated Hazards in Nepal and Bhutan, International Centre for Integrated Mountain Development (ICIMOD).

CARE International (2009). Climate Vulnerability and Capacity Analysis Handbook.

CARE International (2010a). Toolkit for Integrating Climate Change Adaptation into Development Projects.

Central Department of Hydrology and Meteorology (2008) Integrated Study on Hydrology and Meteorology of Khumbu Region with Climate Change Perspectives, Kathmandu, Nepal: WWF Nepal.

Chaudhary, Sanjay (2005). Report on Capacity Building in Food Safety in Post Tsunami Maldives. Project: MAV EHA 050. WHO, Maldives.

Christian Aid (2009a). 'Module One: Framework and Approach', Adaptation Toolkit: Integrating Adaptation to Climate Change into Secure Livelihoods.

Christian Aid (2009b) 'Module Two: Developing a Climate Change Analysis', Adaptation Toolkit: Integrating Adaptation to Climate Change into Secure Livelihoods.

Colls, A., N. Ash, and N. Ikkala (2009). Ecosystem-based Adaptation: A Natural Response to Climate Change, Gland, Switzerland: IUCN.

Deb, Uttam (2009). Food Security in Bangladesh: Achievements, Challenges and Way Forward. Mimeo, ICRIER.

Department of Census and Statistics, Institute of Policy Studies and Samurdhi Division, Ministry of Nation Building and Estate Infrastructure Development (2009). SAARC Regional Poverty Profile 2006/2007: Infrastructure Development and Poverty Reduction (to be published). Kathmandu: SAARC Secretariat.

Eriksson, M. *et al.* (2009). The Changing Himalayas: Impact of Climate Change on Water Resources and Livelihoods in the Greater Himalayas, Kathmandu, Nepal: ICIMOD.

Food and Agriculture Organisation of The United Nations (2015). Statistics Division. http://faostat.fao.org/default.aspx

Government of India (2008). National Action Plan on Climate Change.

Holsti O.R.1991. "International Systems, Systems Change and Foreign Policy," Diplomatic History 15 : 94.

ICIMOD (2007). Impact of Climate Change on Himalayan Glaciers, Kathmandu, Nepal: ICIMOD.

IPCC (Intergovernmental Panel on Climate Change). 2001. Climate change 2001: Impacts, Adaptation and Vulnerability. Cambridge: Cambridge University Press.

IPCC has published four assessment reports (AR), one each in 1990, 1995, 2001 and 2007. These reports present summarised assessment of the scientific, socio-political and technical information available on climate change.

Karim, Hussain, and Ahmed (1996). Assessing Impacts of Climate Variations on Foodgrain Production in Bangladesh. In Erda L *et al.* (eds) Climate Change Variability and Adaptation in Asia and the Pacific. Dordrecht, The Netherlands: Kluwer Academic Publishers.

Karmacharya, Binod K (2009). Food Security in Nepal. Mimeo, ICRIER.

Kumar, K S K and Parikh J. 2001. Indian Agriculture and Climate Sensitivity. Global Environmental Change 11(2): 147-154.

M. Sajid Raihan, M. S. *et al.* (2010). Understanding Climate Change from Below, Addressing Barriers from Above: Practical Experience and Learning from a Community-Based Adaptation Project in Bangladesh, Dhaka, Bangladesh: ActionAid.

MENR (Ministry of Environment and Natural Resources) (2000). Initial National Communication under the United Nations Framework Convention on Climate Change: Sri Lanka. Colombo: MENR, Government of Sri Lanka.

Mitchell, T. and M. Ibrahim (2010). Climate Smart Disaster Risk Management, Brighton, UK: Strengthening Climate Resilience, Institute of Development Studies.

Mitchell, T. and T. Tanner (2006). Adapting to Climate Change: Challenges and Opportunities for the Development Countries, Tearfund.

Mittal, Surabhi (2009). Food Security in India. Mimeo, ICRIER.

MOF (2008), 'Economic Survey of Pakistan 2007-08', Ministry of Finance, Government of Pakistan, Islamabad.

NEC (National Environment Commission). 2000. Initial National Communication under the United Nations Framework Convention on Climate Change. Thimphu: NEC, Royal.

Oxfam Novib (2010) South Asia Food Security and Climate Change: Afghanistan, Bangladesh and Pakistan 2010-2015.

SAARC Disaster Management Centre, SAARC Action Plan on Climate Change, Available at http://www.nset.org.np/nset/ climatechange/pdf/ SAARC_Action_Plan.pdf

Samaratunga, Parakrama A and Thibbotuwawa, Manoj (2009). Food Security in Sri Lanka. Mimeo, ICRIER.

Sen, A. K. (1976), 'Famines as Failures of Exchange Entitlements', Economic and Political Weekly, Special Number, August.

South Asia Cooperative Environment Programme, Website http:// www.sacep.org/html/about_overview.htm

USAID-India, Partnership Agreement for the Agriculture and Food Security Programme, Available at http:// www.usaid.gov/in/our_work/pa_fs.html

World Development Indicators, 2008.

World Development Report. Agriculture for Development, 2008.

World Food Prices: South Asia's Poor at Risk. World Bank, 2008.

World Food Programme (2008) Food Security Overview, Where We WorkAfghanistan, http://www.wfp.org/country_brief/indexcountry.asp? country=004

WWF India (2010). Sundarbans: Future Imperfect, Climate Adaptation Report.

3

Food Security in Odisha

Sandhya Rani Das

Food is the most important requirement of human beings. World Bank as back as in 1986 has defined food security as "access by all people at all times to enough food for an active and healthy life." This is a most simple definition without specific on any aspect of it. It is a multidimensional concept. In 1996, World Food Summit held in Rome, after elaborate discussion adopted this definition of Food Security as a working definition to tackle the problems of food material. According to food summit, "Food security exists when all people, at all times, have physical and economic access to sufficient safe and nutritious food that meets their dietary needs and food preferences for an active and healthy life." (FAO, 2008)

This definition indicates four dimensions of Food Security: (1) Physical availability of food materials, (2) Economic and physical access to food, (3) Utilisation of food, and (4) Stability of all the three dimensions over time. The food security problem appeared in the economic situation when the world faced food crisis in the several parts of the world.

Food security generally conceived as availability of main food grains of wheat and rice or only cereals for consumption. It is not just cereals but nutritious food is required for a healthy living. Hence only adequate availability of cereals cannot be taken as food security for the people. In food security apart from cereals the following four have to be included under food items, for the purpose of Nutritional Security.

(1) Adequate quantity of pulses has to be included for a balanced nutritious diet for an individual,

(2) Milk and milk products,

(3) Vegetables and fruits, and

(4) For non-vegetarians egg, fish and meat etc.

Dimensions of Food Security

Nutritional security is built on three pillars, which can be taken as dimensions of food security, and each has to be analysed accordingly for the overall nutritional security for the people.

(1) Food Availability: This dimension refers to availability of sufficient quantity of food in the country/world. It must be available consistently. This dimension addresses the supply side of food security and expects sufficient quantities of quality food from domestic agricultural production and imports. This is simply a statistical calculation of availability of food in the country from local agricultural production, level of stock and net availability of food stuff from imports/exports.

(2) Food Access: Food access is another dimension of Food Security which encompasses income, expenditure and buying capacity of individuals and households. This addresses whether the households and individuals have adequate resources to acquire appropriate quantity and quality of food. Some of the indicators of this dimension at different levels of food price, wage rate, per capita food consumption, meal frequency, employment rate have to be assessed for this purpose. The dimensions of these can be assessed by Vulnerability Analysis and Mapping (VAM) investigations and Food Access Surveys helps to tackle the problems of food access and food security.

(3) Food Utilisation: Utilisation of food is equally important for nutritious food security. This addresses not only how much food the people eat but also how and what they eat. It also covers the process of food preparation, intra-household food distribution, problems of water, sanitation and also health-care practices. The nutritional outcome of the food taken by the individuals depends on how food is prepared/cooked properly which is equally important.

The three dimensions of food security are shown in Fig.3.1. Each pillar is equally important in achieving and maintaining food security in the world.

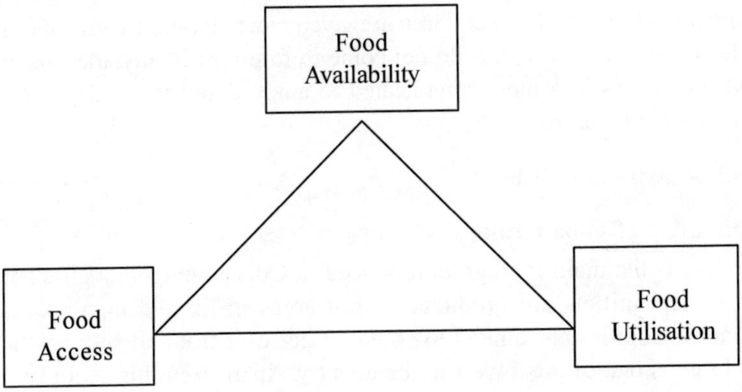

Fig. 3.1: Pillars of Food Security.

Food security is one of the major elements of development and poverty alleviation and has been the goal of an economy now. According to the state of food insecurity estimates of FAO (2012), around 87 crores of people in the world estimated to be undernourished, of which 85.2 crores are from the developing economies of Africa and South East Asia.

Types of Food Security

Food security or Insecurity is divided into two for intensive analysis: (1) Community Food Security and (2) Household Food Security.

Community Food Security: "Community food security exists when all citizens obtain a safe, personally acceptable, nutritious diet through a sustainable food system that maximises healthy choices, community self-reliance and equal access for everyone." (Public Health of British Colombia) According to this definition achieving food security seems Utopian even though it is an ideal one. No country could hope to reach this reality. Hence Food Security has been defined which is measurable and achievable. However, in whatever manner it is defined enough to eat regularly for active and healthy life is the most essential need of the people. Many developing economies of South Asia and Africa have not yet been able to fulfil this need.

Household Food Security: Food need is actually a house-hold problem. But this problem has not been given emphasis whenever food security is being discussed; it is discussed in a general way for the total population. Household food security involves that needs of food for a healthy life for all its members in terms of quality, quantity and culturally acceptable. It is found, especially in developing countries, during the periods of food insecurity in the family parents' diet, both in quality and quantity is diminished and children are given more attention with regards to diets. But these problems do not come to forefront in any analysis of food security as it is most complicated to analyse, but it should be the focus of food security.

Food Security in Odisha

Availability of Food Grains

Rice is the main food grain produced in Odisha, even though other cereals and millets are produced in hill areas in limited manner. As irrigation facilities are limited to about 33 per cent from all sources the yield rate is one of the lowest in the country. Apart from this as a result of frequent climatic changes the production fluctuates from year to year. During the seven years period from the year 2007-08 to 2013-14 the annual cereal production fluctuated from 70.12 lakh tonnes to 97.82 lakh tonnes and average production remained 70 lakh tonnes.

In India, net availability of cereals per capita per day remained at 366.2 grams in 2000-01 which increased to 407 grams in the year 2010-11. There is no change in the estimated grams of food availability per capita in the years 2009-10 and 2010-11.

The trend of growth of per capita per day availability of cereals in India is shown in Fig.3.2.

Production of Food Grains

Total production of cereals in Odisha in 2013-14 according to latest government estimate is 79.41 lakh MTs and per capita per day average availability of cereals comes to 516 grams estimated on projected population of the state at 4.22 crores for the year 2013-14. Imports of cereals into Odisha and the stocks available in the state are not included in this estimate. Accordingly per meal for an Odia person comes to 258 grams. In the year 2009-10, the PDP for Odisha comes to 467 grams as per cereal production of 71.53 lakh tonnes. In comparison to national average of 407 grams PDP Odisha is at a better position with 60 gms higher to national PDP in the year 2009-10. Even though Odisha is at a better position in case of average per day per capita (PDP), higher of 60 grams than national figure, but comparison of these average figures is not providing a real picture.

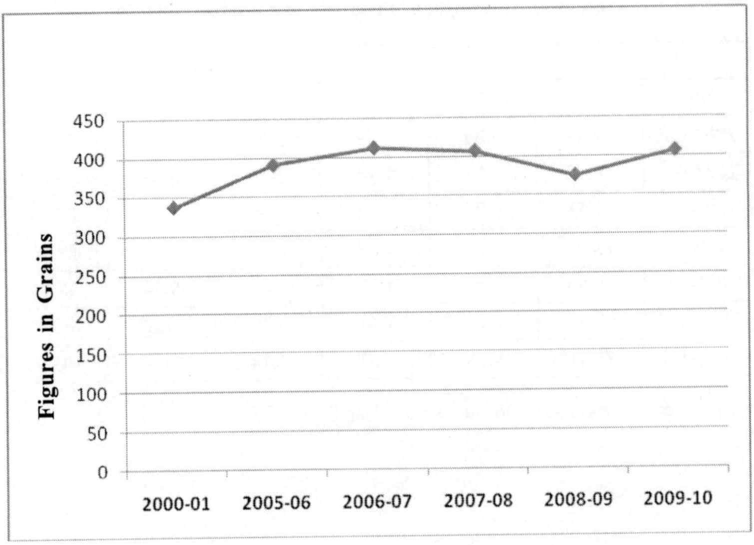

Fig. 3.2: Per Capita Per Day Availability of Food Grains in India.

Source: Economic Survey, India, 2011-12.

An Odia Meal

On the basis of production of cereals and other food material in Odisha an average Odia meal can be compiled. For a nutritious food in Odisha at least pulses, vegetables and non vegetarian items of fish and meat have to be included, even though egg, milk and fruits are important for a nutritious food they are not included as their consumption in Odisha is very low.

Production of these five food items individually and its total is presented in Table 3.1.

Composition of non-cereal items in a meal is now gradually improving. In the year 2007-08, cereals constituted 86 per cent of a meal but now in 2013-14 it came down to 75 per cent. The growth of total food items and growth of cereal are shown in Fig. 3.3, which clearly indicates the position of the non-cereal component of a diet in Odisha. In 2007-08, the non-cereal component was formed 16.23 per cent of a diet, which increased to 33.39 per cent in 2013-14. Even though it is a good improvement, but seeing the low quantity of per capita diet it is not relevant from the point of view of Food Security.

Table 3.1: Agricultural Products in Odisha, 2008-14

					Quantity in Lakh Tonnes	
Year	*Cereals*	*Pulses*	*Meat*	*Fish*	*Veg.*	*Total*
2007-08	77.61	3.84	0.59	3.50	4.64	90.18
2008-09	70.12	3.81	1.15	3.74	4.83	83.65
2009-10	71.53	3.98	1.28	3.71	7.14	87.64
2010-11	71.92	4.27	1.38	3.82	7.37	88.76
2011-12	80.60	2.47	1.38	3.81	9.74	98.00
2012-13	97.86	4.24	1.41	4.10	11.87	119.48
2013-14	76.41	4.18	1.51	4.14	15.69	101.93

Source: Economic Survey, Odisha, 2011-12 and 2014-15.

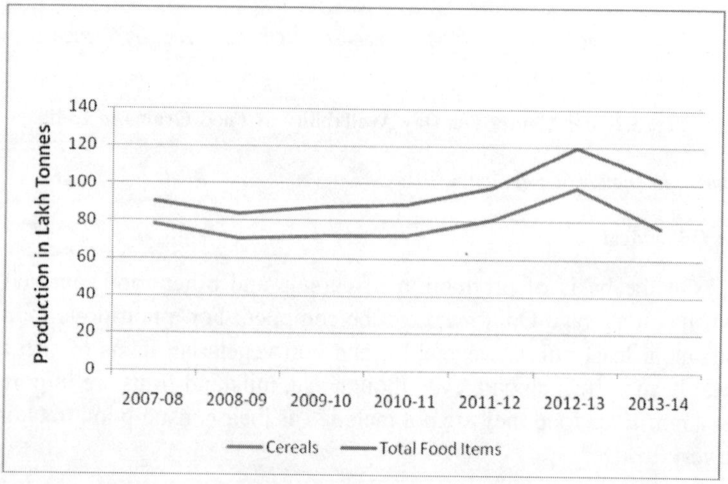

Fig. 3.3: Growth of Cereals and other Food Items in Odisha, 2007-08 – 2013-14.

Fig. 3.3. indicates a comparative growth trend of cereal production and production of other food items in Odisha from 2007-08 to 2013-14. The production of vegetables made good progress only during the last three years of the study.

According to the production figures of different items of food, namely, rice, pulses, fish, meat and vegetables composition of an average Odishan meal can be explained with the help of a pie diagram. With the latest figures of production of five of food items for the years 2007-08 and 2013-14 are presented in Figs. 3.4 and 3.5 in Pie diagrams. The consumption figures as per production figures in Odisha, the cereals form

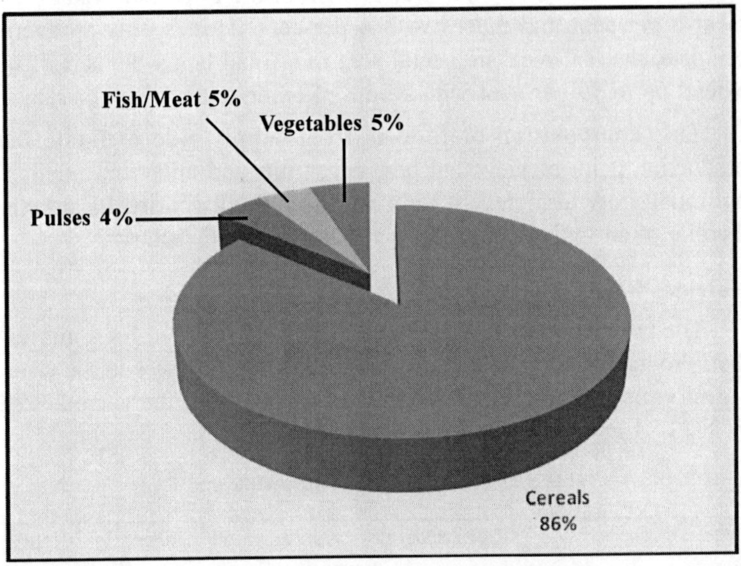

Fig. 3.4: Composition of an Odia meal as per Production of food materials, 2007-08.

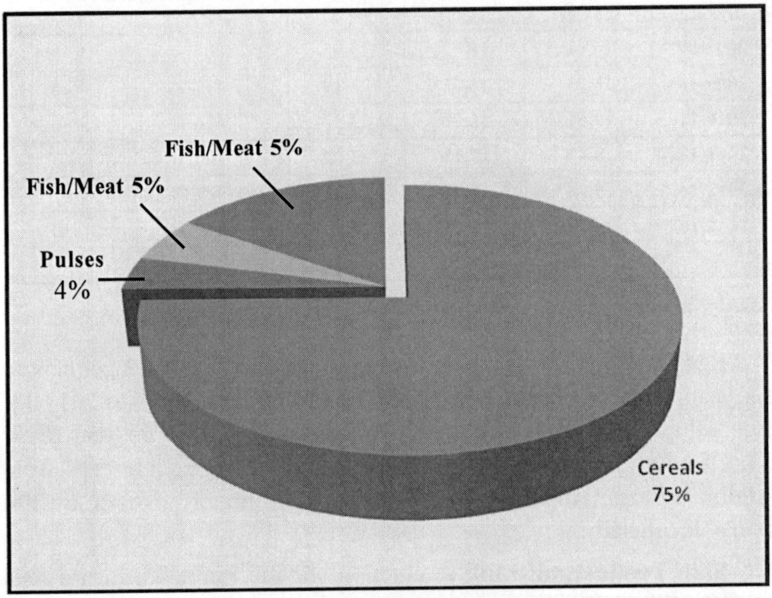

Fig. 3.5: Composition of an Odia meal according to the Production of food materials, 2013-14.

75 per cent of the meal. In the rest of 25 per cent, vegetables are 15 per cent, the highest among non-rice content of the meal followed by fish/meat 6 per cent and pulses with 4 per cent. This is only an average estimate, the real meal in a rural area in a tribal home the cereals may extend up to 99 per cent with a bulb of onion and a pinch of salt.

This composition of food is from supply side estimate from production point of view, but here egg, fruits and milk consumption is not satisfactory to include it for a nutritious food security. Its entry into the diet of an individual in Odisha is far from satisfactory.

Nutrious Food

The production of eggs, milk and fruits are required for a nutritious diet. Production of these three items made good progress in the state in recent years. The production figures in Odisha from the years 2007-08 to 2013-14 are shown in Table 3.2.

Table 3.2: Production of Fruits, Milk and Eggs

2008-09 – 2013-14					
Year	*Fruits Lakh Tonnes*	*Milk Lakh litres*	*Eggs No Crores*	*Population Lakh*	*PDP*
2007-08	12.75	16.25	45.50	400.6	31
PDP	0.87 gr	11 ml	No 31		
2008-09	16.61	16.72	19.93	405.9	13
2009-10	18.73	16.51	23.19	411.2	15
2010-11	19.51	16.70	23.57	416.7	
2011-12	79.42	17.18	23.00	422.2	
2012-13	79.78	17.84	23.22	427.8	
2013-14	79.59	18.61	23.60	439.3	30
	0.49 gm	12 ml	No 30		

Source: Economic Survey, Odisha, 2011-12 and 2014-15.

Eggs Production: Production of eggs declined by 48.13 per cent in six years from 45.50 crore in 2007-08 to 23.60 crore eggs in 2013-14. Accordingly, PDP of 31 eggs in 2007-08 reduced to 30 in the year 2013-14. Of course in recent years Odisha imported large scale eggs from Andhra Pradesh and from West Bengal. The import figures are not available officially.

Milk Production: Milk production slightly improved during this period. Milk production reached 18.61 lakh tonnes in 2013-14 from that of 16.25 lakh tonnes in 2007-08, a growth rate of 14.52 per cent in six years, at the annual growth rate of 2.42 per cent. But because of growth rate of population the PDP of milk consumption increased only one more milli litre in 2013-14.

Fruits Production: Official figures show that the production of fruits in Odisha increased on a large scale during the last three years of study. Between the years 2007-08 and 2013-14 the production of different fruits increased from 12.75 lakh tonnes to 79.59 lakh tonnes a growth of more than six times in six years. But PDP consumption declined to 49 grams by 2013-14.

Access to Food

Simply the production of food materials in an area does not guarantee that the food is actually consumed by the people. Consumption of food depends on the actual income of the family and their nature of spending on food and non-food expenditure. In Table 3.3, monthly per capita expenditure incurred on food and non-food materials are displayed. As it can be observed that the urban people spent more than double of the total expenditure. In food expenditure the rural people spend less than the urban, while in non-food items they consume 2.56 times higher than the rural people.

As per these figures in the Table 3.3, the monthly expenditure per person on food comes to Rs 470.3 15.68 in rural sector and Rs 718.65 23.95 in urban sector of Odisha and accordingly expenditure per day comes to Rs 15.68 and Rs 23.95 respectively. These expenses certainly cannot be taken as fulfilling of food security. These are again averages and not taken as actual situation, even though it helps as comparison with figures of other states and national figures.

Expenditure monthly per capita incurred by people of Odisha and India is shown in Table 3.3.

Table 3.3: Monthly Per capita Expenditure in Odisha and India

Figures in Rs.

Type of Expenditure	*Odisha*		*India*	
	Rural	*Urban*	*Rural*	*Urban*
Food	470.30	718.65	904.79	1830.35
Non-Food	434.49	1111.70	1287.17	24.77.03
Total	**904.79**	**1830.35**	**2191.96**	**1855.15**

Source: NSS 68th Round.

Per capita monthly expenditure computed by NSS 68th Round on individual food items gives some different picture with regards to the consumption pattern in rural and urban sectors of Odisha. The table indicates that in all food items the urban people spend more in comparison to rural spending. In consumption of beverages the gap is widest. The urban people send about 21 per cent of their monthly income on beverages which is second highest after consumption of cereals. In total expenditure the urban consumers spend about 52.43 per cent higher than the rural people.

The urban people are little better than the rural population, but the population of urban population is just 15 per cent of total population of the state, so the rural consumption figures are for the 85 per cent of the people, hence for practical purposes they represent Odisha.

Detailed figures of food consumption for rural and urban people are shown in Table 3.4.

Table 3.4: Food Consumption in Rural and Urban Sectors of Odisha

Figures in Rupees

S.No.	*Items*	*Rural*	*Urban*
1	Cereals	166.55	203.41
2	Vegetables	68.64	88.96
3	Beverages	54.24	138.82
4	Meat/Fish	39.32	63.24
5	Pulses	32.32	43.57
6	Oil	31.56	39.32
7	Milk	27.07	62.07
8	Spices	22.05	27.82
9	Sugar	12.73	17.23
10	Fruits	12.31	28.41
11	Salt	2.93	3.14
	Total	469.72	715.99

Source: NSS 68th Round for Odisha.

The consumption pattern of rural and urban people of Odisha are presented in two pie diagrams, in Figs. 3.6 and Fig. 3.7 respectively. It can be seen that in cereals and vegetables only the rural people are above the urban people.

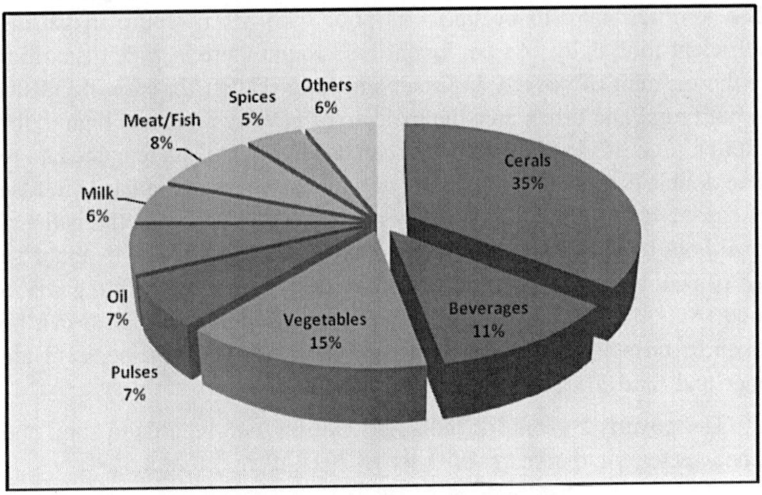

Fig. 3.6: Food Composition of Rural Odisha.

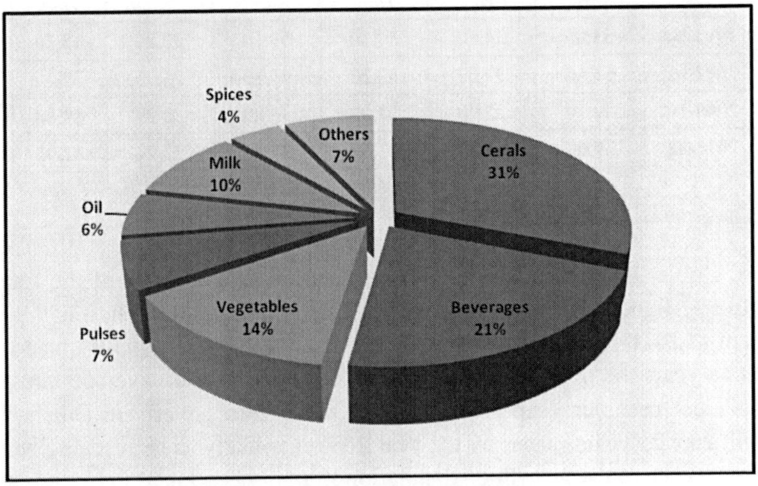

Fig. 3.7: Food Composition of Urban Odisha.

Poverty and Food security

Food security analysis cannot be separated from poverty analysis. The families have to be taken as poor who are insecure in getting sufficient food daily. As per recent NSS round there is wide disparities in the incident of poverty in urban and rural sectors. In case of Odisha in both rural and urban area the incident of poverty remained high to the national figures. In 2009-10, the urban poverty in Odisha remained more than double the incident of poverty of national figures. Peculiarity in case of Odisha is that the urban poverty is t rural poverty, but at the national level both rural and urban poverty remained almost same with about 16 per cent. It is the fact that the poor families are insecure with regards to food. About 33.44 per cent of urban population who are poor can be taken as unsecure in food but in rural areas about 29.06 per cent are poor and food insecurity is less in rural Odisha.

The poverty figures for India and Odisha with regards to rural and urban sector for the years 1993-94 to 2011-12 in Table 3.5.

Table 3.5: Poverty in India and Odisha

1993-94 to 2011-12						
Year	*Odisha*			*India*		
	Rural	*Urban*	*Total*	*Rural*	*Urban*	*Total*
1993-94	63.00	34.50	**59.10**	59.10	30.80	**45.30**
2004-05	63.80	37.60	**57.20**	41.80	25.70	**37.20**
2009-10	39.20	25.90	**37.00**	33.80	20.29	**29.80**
2011-12	39.69	17.29	**32.59**	25.70	13.70	**21.92**

Source: Economic Survey, Odisha, 2014-15

Table 3.5 shows that as per calculation of government the total poverty figures on head-count Tendulkar Method reduced to 32.59 per cent in 2011-12 from that of 59.10 per cent in the year 1993-94, that is, in 18 years the poverty reduced by 26.51 per cent, at an average rate of 1.47 per cent per year. At this rate to reach zero poverty in Odisha it will take 23 years that is by the year 2035 it is likely to be reaching zero poverty. Here the growth of population has not been taken into account. After 2011 the growth of population of Odisha is growing at the rate of 1.3 per cent per annum, the population would reach 450 lakhs by 2035 and 659 lakhs by 2061, that is half century from 2011. What would be the fate of new growth of population of 242 lakhs cannot be predicted now. Presently as per 2013-14 figures 76.41 lakhs tonnes cereals is produced, on this basis by 2060-61; to maintain the present standard Odisha requires 120.73 lakh tonnes that is, more production 44.32 lakh tonnes. This seems impossible.

Conclusion

The analyses of food security, nutrition security and poverty elevation programmes from 2010-11 to 2060-61, shows that Odisha can't reach total food security.

(1) Production of Cereals: Per capita per day availability of cereals in Odisha comes to only 516 grams calculated on the basis of 2011 population and production of cereals for the year 2013-14. To maintain this standard by 2060-61 Odisha has to produce 120.43 lakh tonnes cereals which is a difficult task.

(2) Production of nutritious food items: Production of fruits, milk and eggs which is required for a nutritious diet has to grow fast. The present growth rate of these items shows that it can't be a good proportion of a people's diet by 2060-61.

(3) Reduction of Poverty. Odisha's percentage of poverty at head-count basis is 32.59 per cent. (2011-12) Poverty is being reduced in Odisha at the annual rate of 1.48 per cent. On this basis only by 2035 Odisha is likely to reach zero poverty. Odisha's population, which increases annually 1.3 per cent, will reach 450 lakh by 2035 and 659 lakhs by 2061.

Under these situations providing full food security and nutritional security or reaching zero poverty by 2061 is a Herculean task. An integrated project of food security and poverty elevation may help us to achieve the target.

References

Etienne, O., Food and Poverty, (1988).

Govt. of Odisha, Economic Survey, 2011-12 to 2014-15.

Government of India, Economic Survey, 2013-14 and 2014-15.

Planning Commission, Eleventh Five Year Plan, 2007-12.

4

Household Food Security in Developing Countries

Nkiru Nwamaka Ezeama

1. Introduction

In 1948, the Universal Declaration of Human Rights recognised the right to food as central to adequate living standards where every man, woman and child alone or in community with others, has physical and economic access at all times to adequate food or means for its procurement. (United Nations, 2008). The hunger target of the first millennium development goal (MDG) which required reducing by half the proportion of people who suffer from hunger between 1990 and 2015 was measured by two indicators: the prevalence of undernourishment and the prevalence of underweight children under the age of five years. Although success stories in achieving this target have been reported in 31 developing countries spread across Africa, Asia, Latin America, the Caribbean and Oceania, levels of hunger, undernourishment and other forms of malnutrition still remain unacceptably high in these regions (FAO, 2015).

Globally, the problem of hunger still persists although there has been a gradual reduction over the years. According to estimates from the Food and Agriculture Organisation of the United Nations (FAO), there were 795 million people worldwide suffering from hunger in 2014-16,

780 million (98.1 per cent) of which were in the developing regions. These figures are down from 821 million globally and 805 million in developing countries in 2012-14 and have experienced a decline by 216 million globally and 211 million in developing countries since 1990-92 (FAO, 2015). Table 4.1 presents data on the pattern of undernourishment across Africa, Asia, Latin America and the Caribbean and Oceania. (1991).

Sub-Saharan Africa has the highest prevalence of under-nourished people for any region of the world; the slow progress in reducing hunger relative to 1990-92 estimates have been attributed to a number of factors, for example, rising food prices, droughts and political instability in several countries in the region (FAO, 2015). A closer look at the changing distribution of hunger in the developing regions between 1990-92 and 2014-16 is presented in Figure 4.1.

The prevalence of underweight children in developing regions as a whole also experienced a similar decline from 27.4 per cent in 1990-92 to 16.6 per cent in 2014-16 (FAO, 2015). Compared to the MDGs, the post-2015 sustainable development agenda is broader in scope and draws attention through its second goal to not only ending hunger, but also achieving food security, improving nutrition as well as promoting sustainable agriculture by 2030 (United Nations 2015).

2. The Concept and Definition of Household Food Security

The world food crisis of 1972-74 gave rise to global concern for food security and the concept has since evolved considerably over the years. There was an initial focus in the 1970's on the problems of national food supplies and the capability of nations to provide for their populations' energy and nutrient needs. The green revolution of the 1980's lead to the realisation of need to include both physical and economic access, poverty alleviation and promotion of the role of women in the concept of food security (Gross *et al.,* 2000). The 1990's then arrived with the development of concrete plans to eradicate or drastically reduce hunger and malnutrition. A high point of this period was in 1992, at the World Food Summit, where there was a reaffirmation of the human right to adequate food and nutrition by the international community and national governments made commitments to a more proactive role (FAO, 2006; Gross *et al.,* 2000). The concept of food security has continued to develop since then and the categorical elements of food security are clearly relevant at all levels of social organisation from the macro level (national and global) to the meso level (the community comprising cities, sub-districts, districts, provinces, local government areas, towns, villages) and the micro level (the individual and the household) (Gross *et al.,* 2000).

Table 4.1: Undernourishment in developing countries, 1990-92 to 2014-16

	Number of undernourished children (millions) and prevalence of undernourishment (%)									
	1990 – 92		*2000 - 02*		*2005 - 07*		*2010 – 12*		*2014 - 16*	
	No.	*%*	*No.*	*%*	*No.*	*%*	*No.*	*%*	*No.*	*%*
DEVELOPING REGIONS	**990.7**	**23.3**	**908.4**	**18.2**	**926.9**	**17.3**	**805.0**	**14.1**	**779.9**	**12.9**
Africa	**181.7**	**27.6**	**210.2**	**25.4**	**213.0**	**22.7**	**218.5**	**20.7**	**232.5**	**20.0**
Northern Africa	6.0	<5.0	6.6	<5.0	7.0	<5.0	5.1	<5.0	4.3	<5.0
Sub-Saharan Africa	175.7	33.2	203.6	30.0	206.0	26.5	205.7	24.1	220.0	23.2
Eastern Africa	103.9	47.2	121.6	43.1	122.5	37.8	118.7	33.7	124.2	31.5
Middle Africa	24.2	33.5	42.4	44.2	47.7	43.0	53.0	41.5	58.9	41.3
Southern Africa	3.1	7.2	3.7	7.1	3.5	6.2	3.6	6.1	3.2	5.2
Western Africa	44.6	24.2	35.9	15.0	32.3	11.8	30.4	9.7	33.7	9.6
Asia	**741.9**	**23.6**	**636.5**	**17.6**	**665.5**	**17.3**	**546.9**	**13.5**	**511.7**	**12.1**
Caucasus and Central Asia	9.6	14.1	10.9	15.3	8.4	11.3	7.1	8.9	5.8	7.0
Eastern Asia	295.4	23.2	221.7	16.0	217.6	15.2	174.7	11.8	145.1	9.6
South-Eastern Asia	137.5	30.6	117.6	22.3	103.2	18.3	72.5	12.1	60.5	9.6
Southern Asia	291.2	23.9	272.3	18.5	319.1	20.1	274.2	16.1	281.4	15.7
Western Asia	8.2	6.4	14.0	8.6	17.2	9.3	18.4	8.8	18.9	8.4

contd...

	Number of undernourished children (millions) and prevalence of undernourishment (%)									
	1990 – 92		*2000 - 02*		*2005 - 07*		*2010 – 12*		*2014 - 16*	
	No.	*%*	*No.*	*%*	*No.*	*%*	*No.*	*%*	*No.*	*%*
Latin America and the Caribbean	**66.1**	**14.7**	**60.4**	**11.4**	**47.1**	**8.4**	**38.3**	**6.4**	**34.3**	5.5
Caribbean	8.1	27.0	8.2	24.4	8.3	23.5	7.3	19.8	7.5	19.8
Latin America	58.0	13.9	52.1	10.5	38.8	7.3	31.0	5.5	26.8	<5.0
Central America	12.6	10.7	11.8	8.3	11.6	7.6	11.3	6.9	11.4	6.6
South America	45.4	15.1	40.3	11.4	27.2	7.2	ns	<5.0	ns	<5.0
Oceania	**1.0**	**15.7**	**1.3**	**16.5**	**1.3**	**15.4**	**1.3**	**13.5**	**1.4**	**14.2**

Source: Food and Agriculture Organisation, 2015.

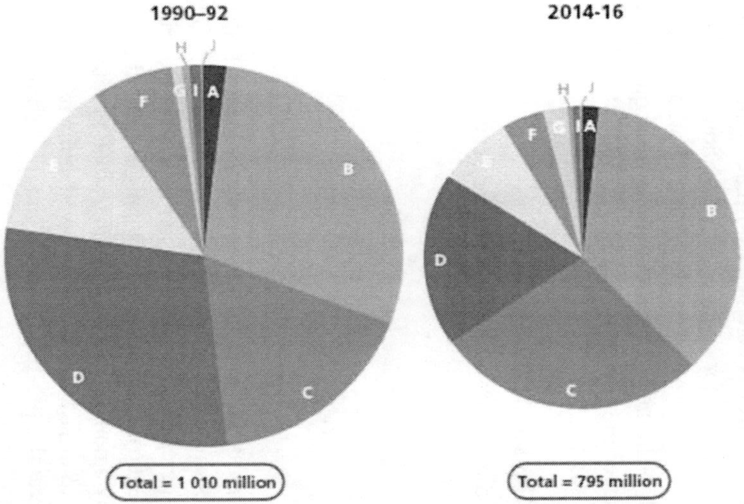

	Number (millions)		Regional share (Per cent)	
	1990–92	2014–16	1990–92	2014–16
A Developed regions	20	15	2.0	1.8
B Southern Asia	291	281	28.8	35.4
C Sub-Saharan Africa	176	220	17.4	27.7
D Eastern Asia	295	145	29.2	18.3
E South-Eastern Asia	138	61	13.6	7.6
F Latin America and the Caribbean	66	34	6.5	4.3
G Western Asia	8	19	0.8	2.4
H Northern Africa	6	4	0.6	0.5
I Caucasus and Central Asia	10	6	0.9	0.7
J Oceania	1	1	0.1	0.2
Total	1 011	795	100	100

Fig. 4.1: The Changing distribution of hunger in the world:number and shares of undernourished people by region, 1990-92 and 2014-16.

Note: The areas of the pie charts are proportional to the total number of undernourished in each period. Data for 2014–16 refer to provisional estimates. All figures are rounded.
Source: FAO.

As is the case in many developing countries, often there is high food sufficiency at national level but food security at the household level leaves much to be desired manifesting as high rates of hunger, malnutrition and micronutrient deficiencies. Global and national food security, though crucial, are not necessarily enough for achieving household food security. Smith *et al.* (2000) demonstrated a very weak correlation between national food availability and food insecurity. In their study of 58 developing countries with high prevalences of food insecurity, groups of countries that showed the most severe levels of food insecurity were those with high poverty and paradoxically high food surpluses underscoring the view that poverty is the most widespread cause of food insecurity.

Household food security can therefore be defined as a situation when all members of a household at all times have physical, social, and economic access to buy, produce, obtain or consume sufficient, safe and nutritious food to meet their dietary needs and food preferences for a healthy and active life (FAO and WHO, 1992; FAO and WHO, 1998; Red Cross, 2006). The term 'household' in this context refers to a group of two or more persons living together who make common provision for food or other essentials for living (United Nations, 2007, p. 114). Households are food insecure when they have "limited or uncertain availability of food, or limited or uncertain ability to acquire acceptable foods in socially acceptable ways" (Red Cross, 2006; Skalicky *et al.*, 2006).

3. Dimensions of Household food security

There are four dimensions to household food security (Gross *et al.*, 2000) namely,

- Availability
- Access
- Utilisation
- Stability

Food availability at the level of the household means that food is physically present because it has been grown, manufactured, imported and/or transported there; in other words, food that is visible and in the home (Red Cross, 2006). It addresses the supply side of food security and is determined by a number of factors such as food production levels, stock levels and net trade (FAO, 2008) Food availability in the household also means that overall, the food supply should be enough for all nutritional needs of all members in terms of quantity (energy needs) and nutritional quality (able to provide all essential nutrients); it should be safe that is, free of toxins and contaminants and of good food quality with regard to taste, texture and so on. Finally the food available to the household should be culturally acceptable (Ruel *et al.*, 1998).

Food access includes economic and physical access to food and refers to the different ways the household obtains the available food often through a combination of home production, purchase, exchange, gifts or borrowing. Also influential is the intra-household distribution of these resources, the income available to the household, the distribution of income within the household and the price of food (Red Cross, 2006). Food supply may be adequate at national or international levels but this does not necessarily guarantee food security at the household level.

Food utilisation is the way the household uses the food and this can include how often meals are eaten and what they consist of (Red Cross, 2006). It depends on several factors such as the quality of the food, its preparation and storage method, dietary diversity, adequate nutritional knowledge and good care and feeding practices, intra-household food distribution as well as culturally prescribed food taboos and the health status of the individuals consuming the food in terms of the ability of the body to make the best use of the various nutrients in the food (biological utilisation) (Red Cross, 2006; FAO, 2008). The combination of all these factors determines the nutritional status of individuals.

Food stability refers to the stability of the other three dimensions over time. A household may have adequate food intake today but will

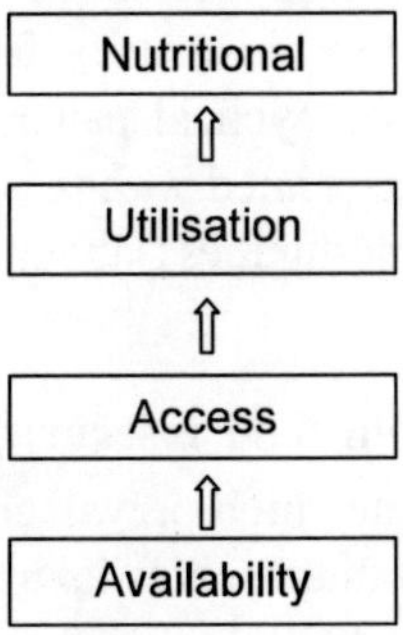

Fig. 4.2: The Relationship between the Dimensions of Food Security and Nutritional Status.

Source: Gross *et al.*, 2000.

still be considered food insecure if it has inadequate access to food on a periodic basis. Food stability is temporal affected by shifting factors such as adverse weather conditions, political instability, economic factors, for example unemployment, rising food prices and so on (FAO, 2008). It connotes the element of time making it necessary to distinguish different types of food insecurity on the basis of the duration. This is described further below. Suffice it to state that for a household to be food secure, all four dimensions must be fulfilled simultaneously. Fig. 4.2 shows the relationship between all four dimensions of food security and nutritional status.

4. Duration of food insecurity

Three types of food insecurity have been described (Gross *et al.*, 2000; FAO, 2008):

- chronic food insecurity
- transitory food insecurity
- seasonal food insecurity

Chronic food insecurity is long-term or persistent and occurs when a household is continually unable to meet the minimum food needs of household members over a sustained period of time. It results from extended periods of poverty, lack of assets and inadequate access to productive or financial resources. Transitory food insecurity on the other hand, is short-term and temporary and occurs as a result of short-term shocks and fluctuations in food availability and access. These include intra- and inter-annual variations in food production, the price of food and income available to the household. Compared to chronic food insecurity, it is relatively unpredictable and often occurs due to unforeseen circumstances. Seasonal food insecurity falls somewhere in between chronic and transitory, has a cyclical pattern of inadequate availability and access to food and is associated with seasonal fluctuations in climate, cropping patterns, work opportunities (labour demand) and disease. (FAO, 2008)

5. Prevalence of household food insecurity

Recent research indicates high prevalence levels of household food insecurity in countries and underscores its importance as a global public health problem. Ajao *et al.* (2010) in their study on the influence of family size, household food security status, and childcare practices on the nutritional status of under-five children in Ile-Ife, Nigeria found an overall prevalence of household food insecurity of 65 per cent. Similarly, high levels of household food insecurity have been observed in other countries in Africa (Omuemu *et al.,* 2012; Nyahurucha *et al.,* 2006; Orewa and Iyanbe, 2009; Oldewage-Theron *et al.,* 2006; Hadley *et al.,* 2001), Asia (Chinnakali *et al.,* 2014; Gopichandran *et al.,* 2010), and in developed countries such as the United States (Oberholser and Tuttle, 2004; Sharkey *et al.,* 2011).

6. Poverty, hunger, nutritional status and household food security

Household food security has long been identified as a chief determinant of an individual's nutritional status and the nutritional status of children in particular (Ruel *et al.,* 1998; UNICEF, 1990). Research has shown that poverty among households in developing countries perpetuates the intergenerational transfer of poor nutritional status among children and prevents social improvement and equity (Victora *et al.,* 2008; Kanjilal *et al.,* 2010). Household socioeconomic conditions directly affect the dietary intake of vulnerable members in different ways such as, through a family's purchasing power affecting food expenditure or gender factors such as intra-household distribution of food favouring adult men and boys even when food is scarce (Torlesse *et al.,* 2003).

Fig. 4.3 shows an adaptation of the conceptual framework for malnutrition developed by the United Nations Children's Fund (UNICEF) (1990, pp.18-23) and the subsequent extended model of care developed by Engle, Menon and Haddad (1999). The framework is comprehensive and is useful in analysing both biological and socioeconomic causes of malnutrition, encompassing factors at both the micro and macro level. Three levels of determinants of nutritional status are recognised: immediate, underlying and basic determinants. The immediate determinants, an individual's dietary intake and health status are influenced by three underlying determinants that manifest at household level: household food security, care for individuals especially mothers and children and health environment and services. It is clear from the framework that household food security occupies a key position as a determinate of nutritional status but it is not a sufficient condition for good nutritional status. Its influence on nutritional status depends on a range of other factors such as the care given to individuals particularly vulnerable members of the household as well as health and environmental factors such as the availability of a safe water supply and sanitation (Maxwell and Smith, 1992). Poverty is a crucial factor that affects all three underlying determinants. These underlying determinants (and poverty) are in turn influenced by basic determinants which include the potential resources available to a community or country and the political,

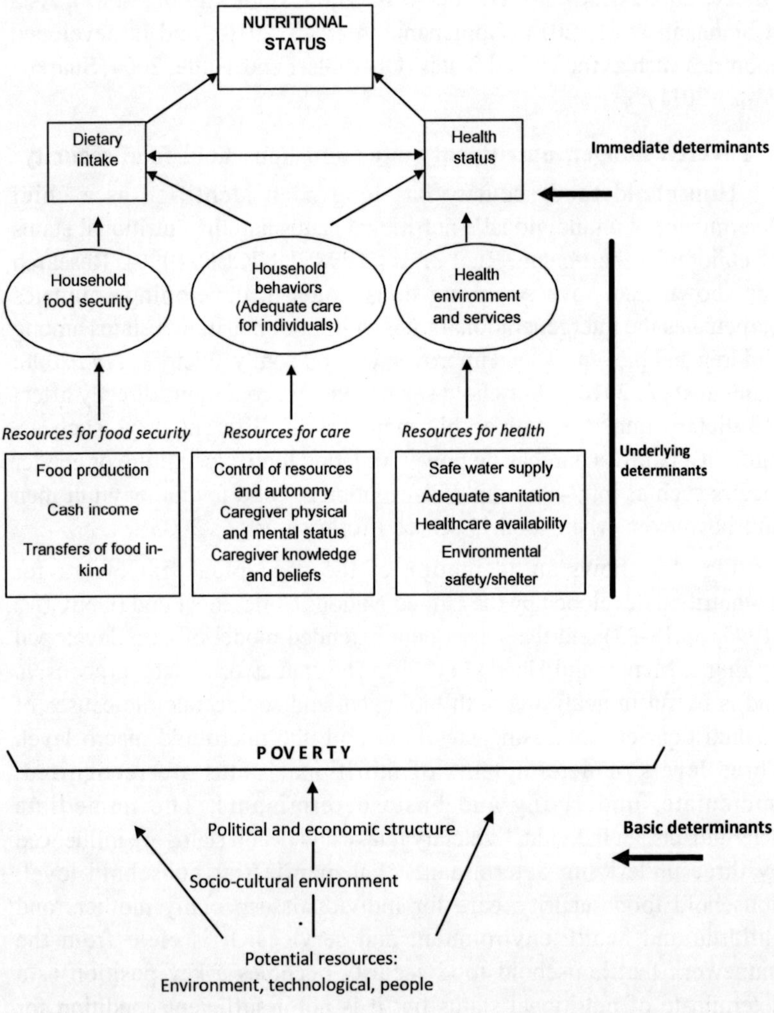

Fig. 4.3: Conceptual framework on Determinants of Child Nutrition Status Adapted from UNICEF, 1990 and Engle *et al.*, 1999.

economic, social and cultural factors that influence their utilisation (Smith and Haddad 2000, pp. 5-8).

7. Factors affecting household food security

Omonona and Agoi (2007) provide insight into the role socioeconomic differences play in the food security status of households. In their study, a positive relationship was observed between the prevalence of household food insecurity and the age of the head of the household, the prevalence being highest when household heads were within the range of 61-70 years; prevalence was also higher in female-headed households than male-headed households (49 per cent and 39 per cent respectively) and increased with a rise in household size and dependency ratio. The proportion of food secure households was highest among households whose heads were professionals (55 per cent) compared with 22 per cent who were traders (Omonona and Agoi 2007). The influence of the interaction of income and gender of the head of household on food security and child nutrition status was also observed in Malawi and Kenya (Kennedy and Peters, 1992). Household food security was found to be influenced not only by total household income but also positively and significantly by the proportion of income controlled by women (Kennedy and Peters, 1992). As shown in a review of different studies on determinants of food security by Endalew *et al.* (2015), family size, low annual production, small farm size, attitude on food aid and poor wealth status significantly affect food security status. Furthermore, the age of household heads, labour and market accessibility were shown to have significant and negative effect on food security; whereas, cultivable land size, fertiliser utilisation, engagement in rain water harvesting have significant and positive influence on food security. Shariff and Khor (2008) in their study among low-income rural communities in Malaysia also observed that more food insecure households lived below the poverty line, had larger household sizes, more children, more school-going children and mothers as housewives. Other demographic and economic characteristics such as having more members, older parents and lower incomes were observed more in food insecure households compared to food secure households in Colombia. In addition, rural residence and female-headed households had higher rates of food insecurity (Hackett *et al.,* 2010).

There are differences in the patterns of food insecurity between the urban poor and rural poor. With regard to food access, people in the rural areas can often produce their own food whereas urban dwellers depend more on food purchases with some households purchasing up to 90 per cent of their food (Ezeama *et al.,* 2015; Ruel *et al.,* 1998, p. 7). Food prices and the ability to earn cash income are therefore important factors affecting urban household food security. Cost of food for the urban poor can be increased by inefficient marketing systems connecting the rural agricultural production areas with the urban areas; for example, large losses may occur during transportation of food as a result of bad roads and poor storage facilities. Macroeconomic and import policies on the price of food may more adversely affect food access for the urban poor than those in the rural areas. (Ruel *et al.,* 1998, p. 7).

It is widely accepted the household food security is influenced by underlying seasonal fluctuations, although research has been mostly in rural areas. Apart from food prices, health status and access to loans and markets, household food security is also affected by factors that include weather and soil quality. All these factors affect food security likely through seasonal fluctuations in rural food availability related to the agricultural calendar. This situation was found among urban households in Dinajpur, Bangladesh; rates of food insecurity were consistently higher during the monsoon season than during the dry season, most likely reflecting changes in food prices and/or food availability (Hillbruner and Egan, 2008). Seasonal food insecurity appears to have lasting effects that are likely to create and reinforce poverty among households (Hadley *et al.,* 2007).

Assessing household food insecurity

The importance of measuring food insecurity and its causes and consequences as a key part of tackling the problem cannot be overemphasised. Measurement of food security allows for estimating its prevalence, identifying its causes as well as improving the targeting of high risk groups and establishing reliable monitoring and evaluation of national food and nutrition programmes (Melgar-Quinonez and Hackett, 2008). Food security is a complex phenomenon affected by a myriad of factors and this poses a challenge to its effective and reliable measurement in populations. At national and regional levels, food production, food availability and other economic indicators are used to assess food security. Unfortunately, besides being very expensive, these methods do not provide a true picture of the situation at household level in terms of availability of and access to food by poor households (Melgar-Quinonez and Hackett, 2008).

The ideal household food security measurement therefore needs to be easy to apply, valid and reliable, inexpensive, easy to evaluate, comparable over time and space, able to capture all the different elements of food security and closely reflect the actual situation at the household and community levels (Melgar-Quinonez and Hackett, 2008; Maxwell *et al.,* 2013). These qualities will encourage regular application through community based networks (Melgar-Quinonez and Hackett, 2008).

Indicators for household food security: There is a myriad of indicators used to measure household food security with different methods of data collection, aggregation and analysis. The lack of consensus is seen in an inefficient multiplicity of survey instruments collecting information on various dimensions of food and nutrition security, with large-scale variation in the content, quality, and quantity of the information collected (Carletto *et al.,* 2013). The multidimensional nature of food security has made it impossible for the development of a single measure that meets the criteria enumerated above despite the development of different indicators in the past decade. Age-adjusted per capita calorie intake was the gold standard for assessing food access at household level but fell short due its narrow focus on quantity of food consumed and its inability to assess other elements of food security such as quality (dietary diversity and micronutrient sufficiency), vulnerability and risks, fluctuations and trends in food consumption over time. It can also be time consuming and expensive to measure (Maxwell *et al.,* 2013). Maxwell and colleagues compared seven different measures that address different elements of the complex phenomenon that is household food security. These are:

1. Coping Strategies Index (CSI).
2. Reduced Coping Strategies Index (RCSI).
3. Household Food Insecurity and Access Scale (HFIAS).
4. The Household Hunger Scale (HHS).
5. Food Consumption Score (FCS).
6. Household Dietary Diversity Scale (HDDS).
7. A self-assessed measure of food security (SAFS).

Nanama and Souli (2007) have described two methods for assessing household food security and vulnerability that have been used in Burkina Faso:

1. The Months of Adequate Household Food Provisioning (MAHFP) developed by Africare, and

2. The FANTA/Cornell questionnaire method developed by the US Agency for International Development (USAID) Title II-funded Food and Nutrition Technical Assistance (FANTA) project and the Cornell University Division of Nutritional Sciences.

A detailed discussion of these measures is however beyond the scope of this paper. Further information on the use of these measures, how they compare with one another and whether they can be used in combination or complementary ways to achieve a multidimensional assessment of household food security can be obtained from the publications by Maxwell *et al.* (2013) and Nanama and Souli (2007).

8. Policy and programmatic issues in tackling household food security

Food security at household, community and national levels is an important focus of many governments of the world. Food insecurity differs in nature and scale among and within countries, between rural and urban areas and these differences must be taken into account in policy formulation. There is no 'one-size-fits-all' approach to improving food security rather interventions need to be country- and region-specific and problem-oriented (ACC/SCN, 1991).

The Federal Government of Nigeria developed the National Programme for Food Security (NPFS) in 2007 in collaboration with the State and Local Governments as a major response to the twin problems of food and nutrition insecurity in the country. The first phase was a five-year programme with emphasis on commercial agriculture, food security and sustainable land management amongst others. The programme is now in its expansion phase and currently supports farmers in 327 sites in crop and non-crop agricultural enterprise such as maize, cassava, yam, poultry, piggery, agro-processing, aquaculture production (Federal Government of Nigeria and African Development Bank, n.d.). Furthermore, the programme finances infrastructural development in the form of construction of rural roads and markets, construction and rehabilitation of dams, sinking of boreholes for potable water supply amongst others. In addition, it also promotes the participation of women and youths as well as enhances women's leadership role in agricultural activities especially in agro-processing, home and school gardening, health and nutrition and other income generating activities that would lead to improvements in food security at household, community and national levels (Federal Government of Nigeria and African Development Bank, n.d.). The NPFS aims to improve national food security and reduce poverty with four specific objectives:

- Improvement of household food security and income through increased productivity, diversification and sustainable use of natural resources,
- Enhancement of food security of beneficiaries through improved access to and availability of food and increased income of producers through marketing,
- Enhancement of farmers and participating communities' access to support services such as agriculture extension, credit and nutrition, and
- Foster participation of poor rural populations in the development of their communities.

Funding for the NPFS has been received from the African Development Bank (AfDB) and the Arab Bank for Economic Development in Africa (BADEA) with technical support from the Food and Agriculture Organisation of the United Nations (FAO). It is also funded by the Federal Government of Nigeria, State governments, Local governments and the participating communities themselves.

In Asia, the World Bank embarked on the South Asia Food and Nutrition Security Initiative (SAFANSI) in 2010 with the goal of addressing the South Asian Enigma – the continued, intractable existence of chronic malnutrition despite high economic growth in the region. By fostering cross-cutting actions, enabling more effective domestic stewardship and increasing commitment of governments and development partners in the South Asia region, SAFANSI is working to translate these into measurable improvements in food and nutrition security (World Bank 2015). To achieve this, the SAFANSI has a four-pronged strategy:

- **Improved evidence and analysis.** Knowledge of what works and why to establish focus areas for programming and policies.
- **Enhanced awareness and commitment.** Increasing awareness of the problems and potential solutions among critical audiences within the region.
- **Building systems and capacity.** Creating the institutions and process that will help countries better address food security and nutritional challenges in a sustainable way.
- **Fostering innovations.** Creating space to try new solutions that can work at the grassroots and beyond.

It is the responsibility of all levels of government including communities and local governments, to ensure that families and communities achieve long-term food security and too provide them with safety nets to prevent destitution. Household food security can be enhanced through development strategies supportive of sustainable agriculture and rapid growth in labour-intensive output. This may require macro-economic adjustment policies which must be cushioned with compensatory measures. The problem of food insecurity is too large for central governments to tackle alone. The capacity of governments to assess, analyse, act and evaluate actions relating to food security needs to be developed and will require community participation and mobilisation for successful capacity building at all levels and phases of implementation. Governments must, in addition to being able to design the right policies, implement them well and monitor their effect and impact on their populace. Integrating all these activities into a continuous process will help to ensure that initial mistakes in policy conception are corrected, and that adjustments are made as circumstances change. The right set of indicators will serve as yardsticks for evaluation of policies and interventions (ACC/SCN, 1991).

References

ACC/SCN. 1991. "Some Options for Improving Nutrition in the 1990s." Supplement to SCN News No. 7 (Mid-1991), United Nations. http://www.unsystem.org/scn/archives/scnnews07supplement/begin.htm#Contents

Ajao, K.O., E.O. Ojofeitimi, A.A. Adebayo, A.O. Fatusi, and O.T. Afolabi. 2010. "Influence of family size, household food security status, and child care practices on the nutritional status of under-five children in Ile-Ife, Nigeria."*African Journal of Reproductive Health*; 14(4): 123-132.

Carletto, Calogero, Alberto Zezza and Raka Banerjee. 2013. "Towards better measurement of household food security: Harmonising Indicators and the Role of Household Surveys." *Global Food Security* 2(1):30-40, doi: 19.1016/j.gfs.2012.11.006

Chinnakali, Palanivel, Ravi P. Upadhyay, Deepa Shokeen, Kavita Singh, Manpreet Kaur, Arvind K. Singh, Anil Goswami, Kapil Yadav and Chandratant S. Pandav. 2014. "Prevalence of Household-level Food Insecurity and Its Determinants in an Urban Resettlement Colony in North India." *Journal of Health, Population, and Nutrition*, 32(2), 227–236.

Endalew, Birara, Menquanent Muche and Samuel Tadasse. 2015. "Assessment of Food Security Situation in Ethiopia: A Review." *Asia Journal of Agricultural Research*, 9(2): 55-68. doi: 10.3923/ajar.2015.55.68.

Engle, Patrice L., Purnima Menon and Lawrence Haddad. 1999. "Care and nutrition: concepts and measurement." *World Development*, 27(8): 1309-1337.

Ezeama, Nkiru N, Christian Ibeh, Echendu Adinma, Obiageli Emelumadu and Prosper Adogu. 2015. "Coping with Household Food Insecurity: Perspectives of Mothers in Anambra State, Nigeria." *Journal of Food Security*, 3(6):145-154, doi: 10.12691/jfs-3-6-2

Federal Government of Nigeria and Africa Development Bank. n.d. "Support to National Program for Food Security." http://npfs-webtrace.org (accessed March 4, 2016).

Food and Agriculture Organisation and World Health Organisation. 1992. "World Declaration and Plan of Action for Nutrition." International Conference on Nutrition, Rome, p. 27.

___________. (1998). "Rome Declaration on World Food Security and World Food Summit Plan of Action." World Food Summit, November 13-17 1996, Rome, Italy: Food and Agriculture Organisation.

Food and Agriculture Organisation, International Fund for Agricultural Development and World Food Programme. 2015. "The State of Food Insecurity in the World 2015. Meeting the 2015 International Hunger Targets: Taking Stock of Uneven Progress." Rome.

Food and Agriculture Organisation. 2006. "The State of Food Insecurity in the World, 2006: Eradicating World Hunger - Taking Stock Ten Years after the World Food Summit." Rome.

___________. 2008. "An introduction to the basic concepts of food security." Food Security Information for action, Practical guides. http://www.fao.org/docrep/013/al936e/al936e00.pdf

Gopichandran, Vijay, P. Claudius, L.S. Baby, A. Felinda and V.R. Mohan. 2010. "Household Food Security in Urban Tamil Nadu: A Survey in Vellore." *The National Medical Journal of India*, 23(5):278-80.

Gross, Rainer, Hans Schoeneberger, Hans Pfeifer and Hans-Joachim A. Preuss. 2000. "The Four Dimensions of Food and Nutrition Security: Definitions and Concepts" In, Nutrition and Food Security, Food and Agriculture Organisation.

Hackett, Michelle, Hugo Melgar-Quinonez, Christopher A.Taylor and Martha Cecilia Alvarez Uribe. 2010. "Factors associated with household food security of the participants of the MANA food supplement programme in Colombia." *Archivos Latinoamericanos de Nutricion*. 60(1):42-7.

Hadley, Craig, Drew A. Linzer, Tefera Belachew, Abebe Gebre Mariam, Fasil Tessema and David Lindstrom. 2011. "Household capabilities, vulnerabilities and food insecurity in rural and urban Ethiopia during the 2008 food crisis." *Social Science and Medicine*; 73(10):1534-42.

Hadley, Craig, Monique Borgerhoff Mulder and Emily Fitzherbert. 2007. "Seasonal food insecurity and perceived social support in rural Tanzania." *Public Health Nutrition,* 10(6): 544-551.

Hillbruner, Chris, and Rebecca Egan. 2008. "Seasonality, household food security, and nutritional status in Dinajpur, Bangladesh." *Food and Nutrition Bulletin*, 29(3):221-31.

International Federation of Red Cross and Red Crescent Societies. 2006. "How to conduct a food security assessment: A step-by-step guide for National Societies in Africa." 2nd ed. Geneva: International Federation of Red Cross and Red Crescent Societies: 7-11.

Kanjilal, Barun, Papiya G. Mazumdar, Moumita Mukherjee and M. Hafizur Rahman. 2010. "Nutritional status of children in India: household socio-economic condition as the contextual determinant." *International Journal for Equity in Health,* 9:19. BioMed Central. doi:10.1186/1475-9276-9-19.

Kennedy, Eileen, and Pauline Peters. 1992. "Household food security and child nutrition: the interaction of income and gender of household head." *World Development*, 20(8):1077-1085.

Maxwell, Daniel, Clement Ahiadeke, Carol Levin, Margaret Armar-Klemesu, Sawudatu Zakariah and Grace Mary Lamptey. 1999. "Alternative food-security indicators: revisiting the frequency and severity of 'coping strategies'." *Food Policy*, 24: 411–429.

Maxwell, Daniel, Jennifer Coates and Bapu Vaitla. 2013. "How Do Different Indicators of Household Food Security Compare? Empirical Evidence from Tigray." Feinstein International Center, Tufts University: Medford, USA.

Maxwell, Simon, and Marisol Smith. 1992. "Household Food Security: A Conceptual Review." Household food security: Concepts, indicators, measurement, International Fund for Agricultural Development. http://www.ifad.org/hfs/tools/hfs/hfspub/hfs_1.pdf

Melgar-Quinonez, Hugo and Hackett, Michelle. 2008. "Measuring household food security: the global experience." *Revista de Nutrição*, 21(Suppl.), 27s-37s. http://www.scielo.br/scielo.php?script=sci_arttextandpid=S1415-52732008000700004&lng=en&tlng=en.

Nanama, Simeon and Karim Souli. 2007. "Comparison of Two Methods for Measuring Household Food Security and Vulnerability- Evidence from the Zondoma Food Security Initiative, Burkina Faso" Brief. *Africare Food Security Review*, September, Washington DC: Africare/Headquarters, http://www.africare.org/at_work/offd/index.html.

Nyaruhucha, C.N.M., J.M. Msuya, P.S. Mamiro and A.J. Kerengi. 2006. "Nutritional Status And Feeding Practices of Under-Five Children in Simanjiro District, Tanzania." *Tanzania Health Research Bulletin*, 8(3): 162-67.

Oberholser, Cheryl A. and Cynthia Reeves Tuttle. 2004. “Assessment of Household Food Security among Food Stamp Recipient Families in Maryland.” *American Journal of Public Health*, 94(5):790–795.

Oldewage-Theron, Wilna H., Emsie G. Dicks and Carin E. Napier. 2006. “Poverty, Household Food Insecurity and Nutrition: Coping Strategies in an Informal Settlement in the Vaal Triangle, South Africa.” *Public Health,* 120: 795–804.

Omonona, Bolarin Titus and Grace Adetokunbo Agoi. “An Analysis of Food Security Situation among Nigerian Urban Households: Evidence from Lagos State, Nigeria.” *Journal of Central European Agriculture*, 8(3): 397-406.

Omuemu, Vivian O., Efosa M. Otasowie, and Ugochukwu Onyiriuka. 2012. “Prevalence of food insecurity in Egor local government area of Edo State, Nigeria.” *Annals of African medicine*, 11(3):139.

Orewa, S.I., and C.O. Iyanbe. 2009. “Household Food Insecurity in Nigeria: An Assessment of the Present Status of Protein – Energy Malnutrition among Rural and Low-Income Urban Households.” *Journal of Applied Sciences Research*, 5(10): 1615-1621.

Ruel, Marie T., James L. Garrett, Saul S. Morris, Daniel Maxwell, Arne Oshaug, Patrice Engle, Purnima Menon, Alison Slack and Lawrence Haddad. 1998. “Urban Challenges to Food and Nutrition Security: A Review of Food Security, Health and Caregiving in the Cities.” FCND Discussion Paper No. 51, Food Consumption and Nutrition Division, International Food Policy Research Institute, Washington, D.C.

Shariff, Zalilah M. and Khor, Geok L. 2008. “Household food insecurity and coping strategies in a poor rural community in Malaysia.” *Nutrition Research and Practice*, 2(1): 26-34.

Sharkey, Joseph R., Wesley R. Dean, and Cassandra M. Johnson. 2011. “Association of Household and Community Characteristics with Adult and Child Food Insecurity among Mexican-Origin Households in Colonias along the Texas-Mexico Border.” *International Journal for Equity in Health*, 10:19. BioMed Central. doi:10.1186/1475-9276-10-19.

Skalicky, Anne, Alan F. Meyers, William G. Adams, Zhaoyan Yang, John T. Cook and Deborah A. Frank. 2006. “Child Food Insecurity and Iron Deficiency Anaemia in Low-Income Infants and Toddlers in the United States.” *Maternal and Child Health Journal*, 10(2):177-185.

Smith, Lisa C. and Lawrence Haddad. 2000. “Conceptual framework: the determinants of child nutritional status.” In: Explaining child malnutrition in developing countries: a cross-country analysis. International Food Policy Research Institute. Report number: 111.

Smith, Lisa C., Amani E. El Obeid and Helen H. Jensen. 2000. “The geography and causes of food insecurity in developing countries.” *Agricultural Economics* 22(2): 199-215.

Torlesse, Harriet, Lynnda Kiess, and Martin W. Bloem. 2003. "Association of Household Rice Expenditure with Child Nutritional Status Indicates a Role for Macroeconomic Food Policy in Combating Malnutrition." *The Journal of nutrition* 133(5): 1320-1325.

United Nations Children Fund. 1990. "Strategy for Improved Nutrition of Children and Women in Developing Countries: A UNICEF Policy Review." Unicef.

United Nations. 2007. "Principles and Recommendations for Population and Housing Censuses." Revision 2, Series M, No. 67.

____________. 2008. "The Universal Declaration of Human Rights: A Living Document." Sixtieth Anniversary Universal Declaration of Human Rights, http://www.un.org/en/events/humanrightsday/udhr60/declaration.shtml

____________. 2015. "Sustainable Development Goals: 17 Goals to Transform Our World." http://www.un.org/sustainabledevelopment/

Victora, Cesar G, Linda Adair, Caroline Fall, Pedro C. Hallal, Reynaldo Martorell, Linda Richter and Harshpal S. Sachdev. 2008. "Maternal and child under-nutrition: consequences for adult health and human capital". *Lancet*, 371: 340–57. doi: 10.1016/S0140-6736(07)61692-4

World Bank. 2015. "South Asia Food and Nutrition Security Initiative (SAFANSI)" www.worldbank.org/en/regon/sar/breif/food-nutirion-security-initiative-safansi (accessed March 3, 2016).

5

Community Involvement in Public Goods Provision: Evidence from a Field Experiment in Ghana

Thomas F. Walker

1. Introduction

During the past two decades, economists have increasingly embraced the concept of community-driven development, a process by which public goods in developing countries are provided in consultation and collaboration with members of the recipient communities.[1] Relative to centralised provision by a government or foreign agency, community-driven development promises greater accountability, increased involvement by minorities, better targeting and quality of projects, and diminished potential for corruption and waste. Community involvement in the development of local infrastructure has become popular in the form of 'social funds', which have been set up and supported by external agencies such as the World Bank. Mansuri and Rao (2004: 15-17) cite evidence from a range of studies suggesting that while community involvement in development projects can be beneficial, it does not always improve their success.

This study is concerned with the process of community fund-raising for local infrastructure projects. Evaluative studies have found that infrastructure is better targeted, lasts longer and works better if community members are required to contribute to its cost (Jimenez and Paqueo, 1996; Kleemeier, 2000). There are a number of arguments in favour of seeking financial contributions from community members. First, community members should be willing to pay something for facilities that they use and value. Provided private contributions approximately reflect individuals' true valuations, a community fund-raising initiative serves as an ex-ante test of the community's need for the proposed infrastructure.[2] This should improve targeting and reduce wastage of funds on facilities that are not wanted by community members. Second, making a financial contribution to infrastructure encourages community members to become involved in other aspects of the project, and supports maintenance of the facility once built.[3] Third, funds raised from community contributions augment those provided by central government and donors, increasing the number of projects that can be completed with a given government or external donor budget. Community contributions thus reinforce the objectives of decentralised public goods provision: promoting local ownership and improving the targeting and mobilisation of resources.

In this paper I report the results of a field experiment in four small communities in southern Ghana that tests the willingness of individuals to contribute to local public goods. The experiment was conducted in five sequential rounds during 2009, in conjunction with a household survey. Before the study began, we held public meetings in each community and asked residents to nominate a small infrastructure project. We then visited participants five times during 2009, gave them a small endowment and invited them to donate to the project. In this paper I focus on two aspects of the contributions behaviour of these individuals: the effectiveness of two commonly used mechanisms to encourage greater donations; and the effect of individual and social network characteristics on the amount contributed.

If individuals were expected to contribute towards the cost of local infrastructure, it would be useful to elicit contributions in a way that reflects their valuation of the project. Projects that are not sufficiently valued by the community might thereby be reconsidered or redesigned. However, because of the free-rider problem, private contributions may understate private demand. Individuals will tend to contribute less to a public good than their expected private benefit, expecting their neighbours to contribute the difference. This implies that the funds raised will fall short of the socially optimal level, leading to underprovision of public goods. Various mechanisms have been proposed which to some extent alleviate the free-rider problem. In the experiment, I test the effectiveness of two of these mechanisms: the matching grant and the provision point mechanism. These mechanisms have been tested experimentally in developed country contexts, but to my knowledge there have been no field experiments testing their performance in a developing country. It is therefore an open question whether they would be as effective in raising funds for community public goods.

Since all of the respondents in the household survey were participants in the experiment, I have detailed data on their individual and household characteristics and their social network. I use these data to describe who in the community donates the most, and whether high-status individuals can be relied on to contribute more. Previous studies have identified social capital as crucial to the success of community-driven development projects (Isham and Käkhönen, 2002). The theoretical literature on social networks and trust suggests that in the confined social setting of a small village, individuals' economic interdependence and susceptibility to social sanction should make them more willing to contribute to public goods (Fehr and Gächter, 2000). Since this interdependence is greater the smaller and more ethnically concentrated the community, we would expect contributions to be greater in such communities. There is suggestive empirical evidence that this is so. In their study of western Kenyan villages, Miguel and Gugerty (2005) found that the quality of public goods was worse in villages with greater ethnic diversity. Akramov and Asante (2009) reach similar conclusions using data from Ghana. In a study of water and sanitation projects in Ghana, Sun *et al.* (2010) find that ethnically diverse communities are less likely to have functioning committees to manage provision at the local level, and accordingly a lower standard of water and sanitation facilities. This suggests the link between ethnic heterogeneity and the success of community-driven development projects may be the effectiveness of the political system. With a sample of four villages I cannot draw conclusions about the effects of ethnic heterogeneity or village size on aggregate behaviour. However, using a unique dataset on the social networks of the study communities I focus on how social attitudes, position in the social network, ethnicity and social status affect individual behaviour.

This paper makes a number of novel contributions. To my knowledge it is the first field experiment to assess the public goods contributions behaviour of individuals in a developing country, and the first to test the match ratio and provision point mechanism in this context. Furthermore, it is the first experiment to compare the two mechanisms, yielding valuable information on their relative effectiveness. This study provides the first experimental evidence on which individuals contribute the most to public goods for their communities, an important factor in understanding the relationship between status, the social network and development in rural communities. More broadly, the results of this study have implications for the design of effective development policy, and our understanding of economic behaviour in general.

The paper is structured as follows. In Section 2, I describe the existing literature on the matching grant and provision point mechanism. I introduce the study communities and discuss their economic circumstances in Section 3. In Section 4, I describe the sampling procedure used to select participants, and the household survey in which they took part. Section 5 presents the design of the public goods experiment, describing the process by which public projects were selected in each community and how individuals were invited to contribute to the projects. In Section 6, I discuss the qualitative results of the experiment. In Section 7, I then look more closely at the results using econometric models. Section 8 presents a discussion of the policy implications stemming from my findings, and Section 9 offers concluding remarks.

2. Previous Research on Incentive Mechanisms

It is well known that public goods provision is hampered by the free-rider problem. Where individuals bear the cost of funding public projects through individual voluntary contributions (a scheme hereafter referred to as a voluntary contributions mechanism, or VCM), individuals' donations typically fall short of their true private valuation of the project (Bagnoli *et al.,* 1992; Fischbacher *et al.,* 2001). Various mechanisms have been proposed in which the Nash equilibrium is for individuals to reveal their true private valuations (Clarke, 1971; Groves and Ledyard, 1977; Smith, 1979). But these mechanisms are too complex to be employed in most real-world applications. Accordingly, a number of second-best mechanisms have been tested experimentally in the laboratory and in the field.[4] The two mechanisms I test in this paper are the matching grant and the provision point mechanism.

A matching grant is a promise made by some authority or significant donor to match private contributions in some fixed proportion. For instance, a philanthropic benefactor might pledge to match public contributions, or the government might offer an income tax deduction for donations to registered charities. Matching grants should in theory boost contributions relative to the VCM, since they effectively reduce the 'price' of a given contribution to a public good. Laboratory experiments have confirmed this hypothesis (Baker *et al.,* 2009; Eckel and Grossman, 2003). However, evidence from field experiments suggests the effect of the match ratio is not large. Rondeau and List (2008) found that the matching donation did not have a positive effect at all, while Meier (2007) found that while a matching grant boosted contributions initially, its subsequent removal actually caused contributions to fall. Using data from a fund-raising campaign in the US, Karlan and List (2007) found that a match offer boosted response rates and the average amount donated, but changing the match ratio had little effect on the amount donated. In other words, to the extent that the matching ratio has any effect at all, the price elasticity of donations appears to decay rapidly as the match offer increases.

A provision point mechanism (PPM) consists of a fund-raising target and a money-back guarantee. The planner announces the fund-raising target to the community, and guarantees to refund all contributions if the target is not met. The PPM is well suited to the provision of lumpy goods, where the target is binding as the minimum amount of money for which the good can plausibly be delivered. It is also simple to explain and implement. Bagnoli and Lipman (1989) showed that, given full information, all perfect equilibria from such a game are Pareto optimal (that is, individual contributions reflect true private valuations).[5] This hypothesis has been tested in the laboratory using an induced value framework, with varying results. Rondeau *et al.* (1999) found that the PPM elicited contributions equal to private valuations. In similar studies by Isaac *et al.* (1989), Bagnoli and McKee (1991) and Poe *et al.* (2002), contributions under the PPM were higher than under the VCM – and provision of the public good more likely – but the mechanism fell short of being fully demand revealing. Rondeau *et al.* (2005) compared the VCM with the PPM in the laboratory and in a small field experiment, and found that the PPM induced generally higher contributions. However, the main effect of the PPM was felt at the top of the distribution (increasing the largest donations). One constraint on the real-world effectiveness of the PPM, relative to the theoretical predictions, might be that Bagnoli and Lipman's (1989) assumption of full information does not hold in practice. However, Marks and Croson (1999) conducted experiments to test the effect of limited information and found that it did not substantially change the impact of the PPM relative to a full-information treatment. There is only limited evidence on the effectiveness of the PPM in real-world applications. Rose *et al.* (2002) found that the PPM increased the rate of participation in a green energy programme substantially above that of a treatment group.

There are various methods for dealing with contributions above the threshold. The nature of this rebate rule matters to the optimality of equilibria. Marks and Croson (1998) tested three such methods in the laboratory: a no-rebate policy, where excess donations are discarded; a proportional rebate, in which the excess funds are divided among the donors in proportion to their contributions; and a utilisation policy, in which excess funds are spent on the public good.

They found that average contributions were significantly higher under the utilisation policy than under the no-rebate and proportional rebate policies. In this study I adopt the utilisation policy.

This is to my knowledge the first field experiment to test the effectiveness of the matching grant and PPM in a developing country. Moreover, these two mechanisms are tested in such a way that I can assess not only their effectiveness relative to a simple voluntary contributions mechanism (VCM), but also relative to each other. Such a comparison has not hitherto been performed in the literature.

3. Introducing the Study Area

The field experiments were conducted between March and December 2009 in conjunction with a year-long household survey in four communities in Akwapim South district, Eastern Region. The survey was part of a three-wave panel, the first two waves having been conducted in 1997-98 (Udry and Goldstein, 1999) and 2004 (Vanderpuye-Orgle, 2008). The original 1997-98 study was concerned with the welfare of farmers in Ghana's export pineapple industry, and the survey area was chosen because of that district's significant involvement in the industry.

The Akwapim South district has historically been a centre of fruit farming – initially cocoa, and more recently pineapple and pawpaw. The district lies immediately to the north of Accra, the country's capital. The growth of the commercial centres of Aburi and Nsawam, which lie on the two main roads heading north from Accra, has changed the pattern of employment in the survey communities (Owen, 2009). Two of the communities (Konkonuru and Darmang) lie close to these towns, and a significant number of the respondents in these communities derive their primary income from non-farm business or waged work. In the other two communities (Oboadaka and Pokrom), which lie in a valley a long way from Aburi and Nsawam, the majority of the respondents are still primarily farmers who travel to the towns weekly to trade. All four communities are quite poor. During 2009, mean per capita consumption (averaged over all five rounds) ranged from GH'54.42 to GH'75.58 per month across the four communities.[6]

All of the communities lack some basic public services. None has piped water, all relying primarily on boreholes for water. Each has at least one primary school and one junior secondary school, but some are in states of disrepair or were never completed. Less than half of households have their own toilet, and none of the communities has sufficient public toilets given its population. Each community has a health clinic and there is a major hospital at Nsawam. Konkonuru and Darmang are accessible by a paved road, while Oboadaka and Pokrom are only reachable by dirt road. All of the communities except Oboadaka have electricity. Public goods are provided by a number of entities: the national government, the district assembly (the local government body), private donors, NGOs and foreign governments. In 2009, the Government of Ghana's Millennium Development Agency (MiDA) commenced an extensive support programme throughout the country, which so far has resulted in the refurbishment of a primary school in one of the survey communities, the training and equipping of farmers, and will soon fund the rehabilitation of a feeder road connecting the two more remote communities to Nsawam. Usually, however, projects are not well coordinated and sometimes left incomplete, resulting in infrastructure which is defective or unusable, and which often decays faster than intended. In one community, the junior secondary school had no doors or windows for one classroom; in another, the school's toilets were not connected to running water and could therefore not be used. In informal discussions community members stated that the poor state of public infrastructure in part reflects a lack of accountability of the providers and a lack of ownership of the projects by the local community. Contractors have an incentive to cut costs in order to boost profits, especially where there is little auditing or follow-up of projects by government to assess quality and durability. If community members were responsible for part of the cost of these projects, they might be more inclined to report defects in the work and take responsibility for the maintenance of the facilities.

4. Sample and Household Survey

The sample consisted of approximately 70 households in each of the four communities. According to our initial listing in January 2009, the four communities had between 180 and 580 households, so that our sample covered between 12 and 40 per cent of households.[7] Around half of these households were part of the initial 1997-98 sample, and the rest were recruited in January 2009 using stratified random sampling.[8] In the original sample, and in the 2009 re-sampling, we selected only from the pool of households headed by a resident married couple.[9] However, we retained households from the 1997-98 sample even if only one of the spouses remained. These 'single-headed households' account for between 7 and 15 of the sample households in each community. Thus, around 150 individuals participated in the experiment in each of the four communities (Table 5.1).

Table 5.1: Sample size by community and respondent type

	Community				
	Darmang	*Pokrom*	*Oboadaka*	*Konkonuru*	*Total*
Husbands	70	67	69	68	274
Wives	77	71	73	68	289
Single males	4	3	1	4	12
Single females	7	5	6	11	29
Total	**158**	**146**	**149**	**151**	**604**

The household survey covered a wide range of subjects, including personal income, farming and non-farm business activities, gifts, transfers and loans, and household consumption expenditures. Each individual was interviewed five times during 2009, once every two months. In addition, we conducted a detailed survey of respondents' in-sample social networks. The social network survey was conducted in the first round. Each respondent was asked in turn about every other respondent in the sample from his or her community. We asked whether they knew the person, by name or personally, how often they saw them, whether they were related, how strong they perceived the friendship to be, whether they had given or received anything of value from the person, and whether they would trust the person to look after a valuable item for them. Summary statistics of the variables used in this study are given in Table 5.2.

Table 5.2: Summary statistics

Variable	*Obs*	*Mean*	*SD*	*Min*	*Max*
Donation (GH′)	2,070	0.70	0.60	0	6
Match ratio	2,070	1.03	0.71	0	2
Household wealth (GH′)	2,070	2,878.22	14,411.10	8.70	^
Monthly per capita expenditure (GH′)	2,070	104.99	87.76	4.01	1,481.35
Household size	2,070	5.22	2.22	1	15
Age (years)	2,070	43.61	13.72	19	85
Sex (male=1)	2,070	0.47	0.50	0	1
Could trust neighbour					
Strongly agree	2,070	0.09	0.28	0	1
Agree	2,070	0.40	0.49	0	1
Neutral	2,070	0.17	0.38	0	1
Disagree	2,070	0.26	0.44	0	1
Strongly disagree	2,070	0.07	0.26	0	1
Social network variables*					
Number known by respondent	2,070	99.72	30.92	4	151
Number who know respondent	2,070	92.78	28.45	15	151
Number trusted by respondent	2,070	27.50	29.89	0	145
Number who trust respondent	2,070	26.55	14.17	3	82
Share trusted by respondent	2,070	0.30	0.31	0	1
Share who trust respondent	2,070	0.28	0.10	0.04	0.55
Status and migration variables					
Holds office	2,070	0.08	0.27	0	1
Akwapim	2,070	0.81	0.39	0	1
Fostered as child	2,070	0.60	0.49	0	1
Lived in village less than 5 years	2,070	0.08	0.27	0	1
Years in village	2,070	26.07	16.08	0	75.42
Share of life spent in village	2,070	0.59	0.31	0	1

Notes: Omitted for privacy reasons. Median wealth was GH′1,099.50. * From census of the in-sample social network. Numbers reported are from the sample of survey respondents in that community.

5. Experimental Design

Two weeks prior to the start of each survey round, we visited each community and conducted one round of the public goods experiment. In all, we conducted five rounds of the experiment. The first round was conducted prior to the second round of the survey, and the fifth followed the final round of the survey.

Before the experiments began, we held an open meeting in each community. We did not give details of the experiment, but explained that participants would be given money for their time in the survey, and would be invited to donate to a public good. Supposing the community could raise around GH′1,000, what would they most like to spend that money on? We gave only a few guidelines: it had to be a self-contained project, affordable with that amount of money. A number of projects were proposed by the community members, which were then categorised as feasible or infeasible depending on their cost.

Those at the meeting then voted on which of the feasible projects to pursue.[10] The final choices were: renovation of primary school toilets in Konkonuru; construction of a maternity ward for an existing health clinic in Oboadaka; a second public toilet block in Pokrom; and renovation of the junior secondary school (JSS) in Darmang. We informed the community members that their choice could be changed later on, provided there was majority community support for the change. The author and an assistant conducted the experiments with support from the survey enumerators. Respondents were called on a given day to report to the local primary school, where they signed in and took a ticket with their individual ID number written on it. One by one, they were invited into a closed classroom to receive their endowment and make a donation if they wished. Care was taken to keep these solicitations private, and the amounts each individual donated were not disclosed to any other community member or participant. Only an interviewer and a record keeper (who took a written note of the donation) were witness to the respondent's decision.[11]

Upon entering the room, the respondent was seated at a desk facing the interviewer and record keeper. The interviewer explained (in Twi, the local language, as most of the respondents did not speak English) that the respondent was to receive a small amount of money (endowment) for their time and co-operation in the previous round's survey.[12] Since most respondents were poor and often short of cash, the endowment was designed to 'even the playing field' of cash-on-hand across respondents, removing potentially contaminating differences in ability to contribute. The endowment varied by round. In round 1, we gave GH'1 to each respondent; in rounds 2 and 3 we gave GH'2, in round 4 we gave GH'4, and in round 5 we gave GH'6. This variation allows me to measure the income elasticity of demand for donations, and test whether the size of the endowment is a binding constraint on larger donations.

The interviewer then explained that we were raising money for a public project, and briefly described the project chosen by that community. The respondent was invited to donate to the project, but was not compelled to. Any donation they made would be kept confidential, and their choice would not affect their ongoing participation in the survey.

The respondent was then invited to draw a token from a bag to determine the matching ratio. There were five tokens in the bag, each a different colour, representing matching ratios of 0, ½, 1, 1½ and 2. We took great care to ensure the draw was blind and random. A table relating the colours to the matching ratios was displayed on a sheet in front of the respondent. The interviewer explained what matching ratio the respondent had drawn, and what that meant. For any matching ratio m, we would add m times the respondent's donation to the total funds raised. If the token representing zero were drawn, no matching grant would be given. We gave the respondent various examples, and quizzed them to check they understood the concept. The respondent was then given their endowment in cash and invited to make a donation if desired. To minimise rounding issues, we gave the first GH'2 of the endowment in 20p coins and the remainder in GH'1 notes.[13] Respondents were able to ask for change, so that any donation was feasible. Once they had made their donation, the match was added. We checked that the respondent was satisfied with their choice, and then the total amount was put in the donation box. Once the respondent had left the room, the match ratio and donation were recorded on a sheet against their name.

In the final two rounds, the procedure was modified slightly to include a provision point mechanism (PPM).[14] After mentioning the project, the interviewer pointed to a sheet in front of the respondent that showed the amount raised and a fund-raising target (including a graphical depiction of the proportion of funds raised). Based on donations from the first three rounds and the realistic minimum cost of the projects, we set targets of GH'750 in three communities and GH'1,000 in Pokrom (which had at that point raised substantially more than the other three). The interviewer explained that the project could not go ahead unless the target was reached, and that if the target was not reached, all donations from the fourth and fifth rounds would be refunded. The funds raised in the first three rounds would be spent on maintenance of existing public buildings. The interviewer explained that the respondent would receive a receipt for their donation, and that they could use this receipt to claim reimbursement if the project did not go ahead. The rest of the experiment proceeded as in the first three rounds, except that at the end a receipt was given to the respondent for the amount donated.

Once all respondents present had been interviewed, we counted the amount raised and cross-checked against the total from the record sheets. The amount was announced to the assemblyman, who in turn informed the community members.[15] We also announced the progressive total amount raised at subsequent meetings with the respondents. At the end of the five rounds, the amounts raised were to be spent on the designated project, provided the target had been reached. Respondents who did not attend the experiment for a given round could claim their endowment in the next round in addition to that round's endowment; therefore, some respondents received larger endowments in later rounds.[16] Funds not claimed at the end of the fifth round were counted as full donations and added (without a matching grant) to the funds raised for the community. Those amounts are excluded from the analysis.

6. Initial Observations

All four communities reached their targets, though Konkonuru did so by only a small margin. Overall, only five per cent of respondents did not donate (Table 5.3). The incidence of non-contribution was much higher in Konkonuru, where 32 per cent of respondents made no contribution in round 1. In the other three communities non-contribution rates ranged from zero to six per cent. In all communities, non-contribution dropped off sharply in rounds 4 and 5 with the increase in endowments and the introduction of the provision point mechanism. Even in Konkonuru, however, the rate of non-contribution was much lower than in similar studies in Western countries, where it is common for more than half of the sample to refuse to donate.[17] In part, this may have been due to the presence of the interviewers. Since Ghanaian social norms dictate that people should not refuse a request for money from a friend in need, they may have felt obliged to give something in response to a request from researchers. For example, in the first round a donation of 20p was the mode in some communities; since the endowment was given in 20p coins, this might have been a 'token donation' by individuals reluctant to give. It could also be due to the fact that the individuals were given an endowment, and could not use the excuse 'I don't have any money'.

Table 5.3: Non-contribution rates (percentage of participants who donated nothing)

	Community				
Round	*Darmang*	*Pokrom*	*Oboadaka*	*Konkonuru*	*Total*
1	5.2	3.2	2.6	32.1	10.7
2	3.4	0	2.4	17.1	5.7
3	7.8	0	6.1	17.5	7.9
4	0	0	0	2.4	0.6
5	0	2.3	0	2.8	1.3
Total	3.2	1.1	2.3	13.5	5.1

These considerations were unavoidable given the experimental design, but should be borne in mind when interpreting the results. However, their presence was constant throughout the year, and should not affect comparisons between individuals or across rounds.

Table 5.4: Mean donations by round and community

	Community				
Round	*Darmang*	*Pokrom*	*Oboadaka*	*Konkonuru*	*Total*
1	29.9	52.8	37.4	34.5	37.6
2	34.7	69.9	36.7	39.7	45.2
3	41.0	65.4	39.8	33.5	44.4
4	76.1	109.7	144.7	66.1	97.8
5	106.4	117.9	145.4	97.2	115.6
Total	58.7	85.1	79.6	56.3	69.5

Table 5.4 presents the mean donations in each round. It is apparent that some communities donated substantially more than others. In part this reflects different characteristics of the respondents (such as differences in wealth), which I will explore in the regression analysis. Even after taking those factors into account, however, there is a residual difference which reflects characteristics of the community and of the project. First, comments by some respondents in the interviews made it clear that the renovation of the school toilet and JSS buildings were markedly less popular for a number of reasons. Some respondents said they were reluctant to donate because their children didn't attend that

school, or because they didn't have school-age children. In Konkonuru (raising money for a school toilet), respondents argued that the teachers locked the toilet even when it was working, and that their children therefore would not benefit from it. Second, there was a distinct difference in the degree of support provided by the community leaders. In Darmang and Oboadaka, the leaders tried significantly harder to garner support and attendance from respondents. However, this appears to have affected attendance more than donations, since Darmang raised the least money despite being the wealthiest of the four communities.

Table 5.5: Summary statistics on matching ratios

	Community				
Round	*Darmang*	*Pokrom*	*Oboadaka*	*Konkonuru*	*All communities*
1	**0.931**	**1.018**	**1.010**	**0.984**	**0.981**
	(0.717)	(0.683)	(0.704)	(0.670)	(0.695)
	[-1.096]	[0.241]	[0.140]	[-0.230]	[-0.567]
	131	83	103	95	412
2	**1.097**	**1.082**	**1.136**	**1.057**	**1.094**
	(0.707)	(0.744)	(0.748)	(0.718)	(0.727)
	[1.464]	[1.120]	[1.874]*	[0.778]	[2.648]***
	113	104	107	97	421
3	**1.009**	**1.005**	**1.083**	**1.099**	**1.050**
	(0.691)	(0.689)	(0.704)	(0.724)	(0.701)
	[0.138]	[0.076]	[1.264]	[1.339]	[1.442]
	110	92	114	96	412
4	**0.961**	**1.057**	**1.062**	**1.123**	**1.049**
	(0.741)	(0.707)	(0.682)	(0.696)	(0.708)
	[-0.566]	[0.794]	[0.930]	[1.813]*	[1.410]
	115	96	105	106	422
5	**1.035**	**1.026**	**0.947**	**1.009**	**1.006**
	(0.721)	(0.728)	(0.703)	(0.669)	(0.705)
	[0.547]	[0.384]	[-0.771]	[0.139]	[0.198]
	130	115	103	115	463
All rounds	**1.005**	**1.039**	**1.049**	**1.054**	**1.035**
	(0.716)	(0.710)	(0.709)	(0.694)	(0.707)
	[0.171]	[1.208]	[1.590]	[1.756]*	[2.312]**
	599	490	532	509	2,130

Notes: Table reports mean match ratio offered in each experimental session. Sample standard deviations are reported in parentheses, and t-statistics (against the null that the mean ratio is 1) in square brackets. The last row of numbers is the sample size. In a test of the hypothesis that the mean ratio is 1, *** denotes significance at the 1 per cent level, ** at the 5 per cent level, and * at the 10 per cent level.

The matching ratio varied randomly across individuals and rounds. Table 5.5 provides a summary of the mean ratios in each village and round, along with standard errors and t-statistics. These are generally around 1 on average, and not significantly larger than 1 at the 10 per cent level in any one experimental session.[18] Looking at a simple bubble graph (Fig.5.1), the matching ratio appears to have had a slightly positive impact on donations, primarily by lifting donations at the top of the distribution.

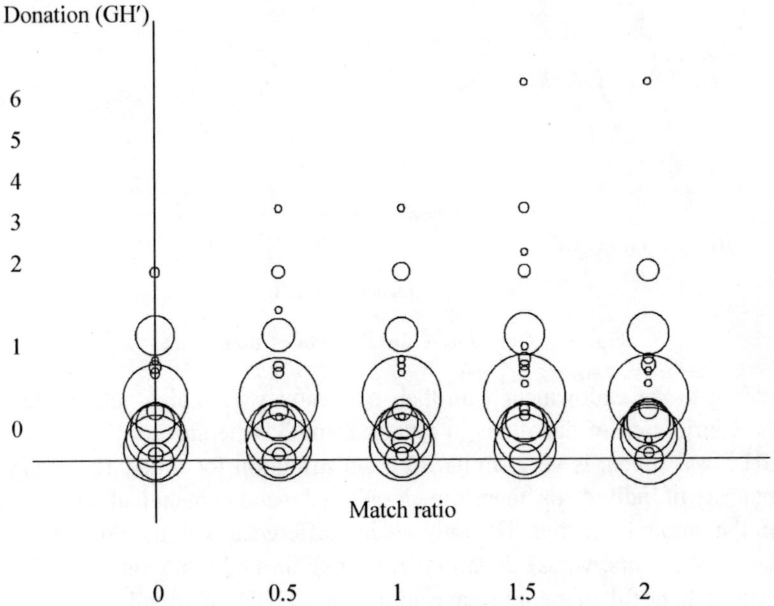

Fig. 5.1: Effect of matching ratio on donations.

Note: Bubble area proportional to frequency.

Fig. 5.2 presents the cumulative distribution function (CDF) of donations for each community. Since donations were almost all in multiples of 10p, the CDFs in Fig. 5.2 are smoothed: uniform random variation of up to 5p was added to each donation in order to separate the lines and make them easier to read. The CDFs show significant clustering of donations at points like 20p, 50p and GH'1, perhaps reflecting people's reluctance to ask for change and donate their true valuation. It might even be a manifestation of 'coherent arbitrariness' due to uncertainty over the true valuation.[19] The 20p mode is apparent in Fig. 5.1, but a number of individuals donated substantially more, a few even

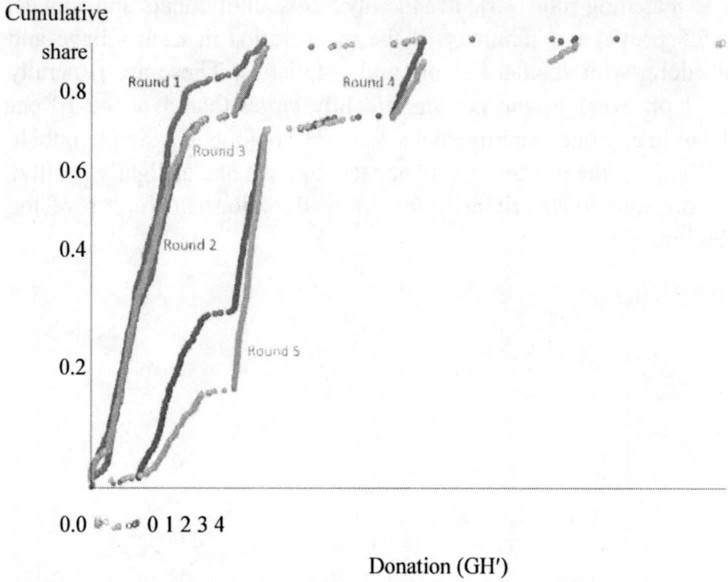

Fig. 5.2: Cumulative distribution of donations.

adding to the endowment with their own money. It is also notable that the distribution of donations in rounds 2 and 3, when an endowment of GH'2 was given, is very similar to the distribution for round 1. For the majority of individuals, therefore, doubling the endowment had no effect on the amount donated. The only visible difference is in the second-top decile of donors, whose donations rose from around 50p to around 80p. Only a handful of people gave more than GH'1 in rounds 2 and 3, suggesting that the GH'1 endowment in round 1 was not a significant constraint on donations.

The effect of the provision point mechanism (PPM) in rounds 4 and 5 is readily apparent. As discussed in Section 2, this mechanism is designed to alleviate the free-rider problem by providing prospective donors with a guarantee that, should the project be underfunded, it will not go ahead and they will get their money back. This assuages concerns that few funds will be raised and the project will be of poor quality, and encourages those who are hesitant to donate. One would therefore expect the PPM to increase contributions, pushing each person's donation closer to their true valuation of the project. The size of contributions indeed rose in the last two rounds, both in absolute terms and in proportion to the endowment (Table 5.4). The increase was substantial and affected the entire distribution.

After including uncollected monies, all four communities passed their targets. We met with each community and, in consultation with experts from the Akwapim South District Assembly, costed each of the projects. The community that had chosen to build a public toilet changed their minds, because the money raised would only build a small toilet which was considered inadequate for their population. Instead, they resolved to spend the money on building a kindergarten. Each community elected a committee to oversee the project work, and also volunteered resources like sand, water, stones and artisanal labour. All four of the projects have now been completed.

7. Regression Analysis

One strength of the experiment's design is the wealth of survey data available on each respondent, which allows me to relate donation decisions to individual characteristics. We collected data on wealth and consumption five times during the year, giving a dynamic picture of the respondents' financial situation over the course of the experiment. In order to measure the effect of characteristics on contributions, I estimate a regression model of the amount donated by each respondent in each round. Because of the likelihood of individual heterogeneity in contributions over the five rounds, I tested an individual-level random effects specification. A Hausman test rejected the random effects model in favour of fixed effects, therefore I focus on the OLS results in the following discussion. This permits inference about key time-invariant characteristics of respondents that are washed out by the fixed effects estimator. I include the random effects and fixed effects results in Table 5.6 for comparison.

The first objective of this analysis is to measure the impact of the matching grant and provision point mechanism (PPM) on donations. The theoretical models of these mechanisms do not provide much guidance on specification. If the matching ratio has an influence on donations by varying the price of contribution, the relationship between the ratio and donations may be nonlinear depending on the functional form of preferences for the public good. Furthermore, we might expect to see threshold effects moving from the no-match treatment (ratio is zero) to a match treatment (where the ratio is non-zero). I present a specification in which the match ratio is included as a set of dummies for the five possible ratios. A linear specification yielded equivalent results; the coefficient estimate is reported in Footnote 23. The PPM was introduced in the last two rounds, therefore its impact can be observed by including a set of round effects. Fig.5.3 suggests the effect of the PPM on

Table 5.6: Main regression results

	OLS		*Fixed Effects*		*Random Effects*	
	Coef.	*Std. Err.*	*Coef.*	*Std. Err.*	*Coef.*	*Std. Err.*
Match ratio (0 omitted)						
	0.018	0.029	0.025	0.032	0.021	0.030
1	0.035	0.030	0.071**	0.032	0.052*	0.030
1.5	0.100***	0.032	0.080**	0.032	0.093***	0.030
2	0.095***	0.031	0.063**	0.031	0.081***	0.029
Extra GH	0.156***	0.020	0.160***	0.012	0.160***	0.009
Log household wealth	0.020*	0.010	-0.024	0.025	0.015	0.013
Age (years)	0.002***	0.001	--	--	0.002**	0.001
Male	0.090***	0.020	--	--	0.083***	0.027
Could trust neighbour ('Strongly disagree' omitted)						
	0.165***	0.056	--	--	0.162**	0.067
Agree	0.080*	0.046	--	--	0.081	0.056
Neutral	0.025	0.047	--	--	0.031	0.061
Disagree	0.043	0.046	--	--	0.045	0.058
Share trusting respondent	0.671***	0.142	--	--	0.730***	0.175
Community (Darmang omitted)						
	0.322***	0.034	--	--	0.332***	0.045
Oboadaka	0.304***	0.034	--	--	0.314***	0.043
Konkonuru	-0.011	0.028	--	--	-0.010	0.038
Round (1 omitted)						
2	0.052**	0.024	0.062**	0.029	0.055*	0.028
3	0.000	0.023	0.014	0.029	0.005	0.029
4	0.558***	0.029	0.557***	0.029	0.556***	0.028
5	0.661***	0.032	0.661***	0.029	0.660***	0.028
Constant	-0.338***	0.099	0.503***	0.178	-0.338***	0.113
N	2,070		2,070		2,070	
Groups	-		515		515	
R2	0.444		0.483		0.515	
Breusch-Pagan $\chi^2(1)$	854.4***		-		-	
Hausman $\chi^2(10)$	-		22.00**		-	

Notes: Dependent variable is donation in GH′. Random and fixed effects are at the individual level. *** indicates significance at the 1 per cent level, ** at the 5 per cent level and * at the 10 per cent level. Robust standard errors reported for OLS regression. The Hausman specification test rejects the random effects model in favour of the fixed effects model at the 5 per cent level.

donations should be substantial. However, the round effects will also pick up other seasonal effects and the variation in the endowment. I control for seasonality in individual income using log household wealth.[20] I estimate the effect of the endowment by looking at the marginal increase in donations among those individuals who were absent in a round and subsequently collected a larger endowment. By subtracting this from the round effect estimate, I get an indirect measure of the impact of the PPM. An alternative approach I then consider is to drop the round effects and make use of the variation in endowment among absentees to measure its effect directly. This isolates the effect of the PPM on contributions in the last two rounds.

The second objective of the regression analysis is to measure the effect of individual characteristics on donations. In addition to log wealth, which is a household-level variable, I add controls for the respondent's age and sex. I also include a measure of trust, since individuals might be concerned about the likelihood of their donations being misappropriated by community leaders (or the survey team) and about the way the public good will be managed once built. To account for this, I use information from a survey module on social attitudes. The module obtained Likert scale responses measuring the respondent's agreement with five statements about trust in neighbours, government and officials. I tested each in the specification; the only one which was significant was 'I feel I could trust my neighbours to look after my house while I am away'. This was measured on a scale of 1 to 5, with 1 representing 'strongly agree' and 5 'strongly disagree'. I include this variable as a set of four dummies called *social* (excluding 'strongly disagree').

The social networks survey collected detailed data on the nature of relationships between the respondent and every other sample member from their community. I test various measures of the size and quality of an individual's social network, including the number of sample members known by the respondent, the number of these the respondent trusts, the number of respondents who report knowing the individual, and the number of these who trust the individual. These variables are represented generically in the specification below by the variable *socnetwork*.

Where å$_{it}$ is a white noise disturbance. The dependent variable, *donation*, is individual *i*'s donation in Ghana cedis in round *t*. The parameters õ^{l} are community fixed effects for the four communities *l*, with Darmang (l = 1) excluded, and ñ^{m} are round fixed effects.[21] The variable *ratio* represents a set of four dummies for the match ratio offered (0.5, 1, 1.5 or 2), excluding zero. The variable *extracash* is the *additional* endowment given to those respondents not collecting money in previous rounds; the remainder is captured by the round fixed effect. The household's wealth in the month just prior to the round is captured by *logwealth*, specified in logs because the variable is approximately lognormal across the population. This measure varies across rounds, capturing seasonal effects and economic shocks to individuals during the year that might affect donations. The respondent's *age* is measured in years, and *sex* takes the value one if the respondent is male, zero otherwise.

The estimates for Equation 1 are presented in Table 5.6. The results are presented with robust standard errors to control for heteroskedasticity. Household wealth has a positive impact on donations, but the effect is small in relative terms. Using the coefficient on wealth, I calculated the wealth elasticity of donations for each individual. Across the entire population, this averaged 0.05. Individual wealth and consumption were not available in the survey data, so I use household wealth as the measure of welfare.[22] Consequently, any differences in the spending power of men relative to women in the same household are captured only by the gender variable. The coefficient on gender is significant and positive, indicating that males donated around 10p more than females on average. It is common in Ghana for the husband to earn a large share of the household's cash income, so this may explain the gender difference in donations. Older individuals also donated more. The greater an individual's reported trust of their neighbours, the higher their contribution. This might reflect the importance of an individual's confidence about the way in which the public good would be built or managed by their community, and potentially also about whether the survey team would act as promised in spending the raised funds.

Effect of the Match Ratio

The coefficients relating to match ratios of 1.5 and 2 are statistically significant at the 5 per cent level, adding an estimated 8-10p to donations relative to the no-match case. This effect compares to a mean donation of 37.6p in round 1 and 69.5p over all five rounds, thus it is quite significant in economic terms. The implied price elasticity of donations is -0.26, therefore inelastic, and not substantially different from the elasticity of -0.38 implied by the results of Karlan and List's (2007) study.[23,24] However, in Karlan and List's study the response rate was very low, so that there was a large difference between the mean overall donation and the mean donation by existing contributors. In contrast, in this experiment there was a small difference between the two due to very high rates of participation. The implied price elasticity for *existing* contributors in Karlan and List's study is effectively zero.[25]

Receiving additional endowment money (from previous rounds) raises donations by around 16p per additional cedi, which is substantially lower than the overall mean donation. It is difficult to infer what donations would have been had the endowment been zero. However, one can use the additional endowment variable to construct an estimate of the income elasticity of donations with respect to the endowment. The mean estimate across all communities and rounds is 0.53, implying that increases in the endowment induce roughly a one-to-two proportional increase in the donation. This is about 10 times larger than the elasticity of donations with respect to wealth, suggesting that the propensity to give out of cash-in-hand is much higher than the propensity to give out of overall wealth.

Provision Point Mechanism

The introduction of the PPM in round 4 had a dramatic positive effect on donations. The round coefficients jumped from between 0.05 and 0 in the second and third rounds respectively (relative to round 1) to 0.56 and 0.66 in rounds 4 and 5. It appears that the PPM was much more effective than the matching ratio in eliciting contributions from community members. The increase in donations in rounds 4 and 5 cannot be explained solely by the increase in the endowment, which doubled from round 1 to 2 with little effect on donations. The estimated coefficient for *extracash* suggests that only part of the increase from round 3 to round 4 (roughly 33 pesewas) could have been due to the additional endowment, leaving a net increase in donations of about 23p attributable to the PPM. This estimate is supported by the CDFs in Fig. 5.3; whereas there was almost no change in the distribution of donations over the first three rounds of the experiment, donations in the last two rounds are stochastically dominant and significantly larger across the distribution. Increasing the endowment by 50 per cent from round 4 to round 5 had only a small positive impact on donations.

As a robustness check, and in order to better isolate the impact of the PPM itself, I re-estimated the model without round effects, including the full endowment (which varied across rounds and within rounds, for those who missed an earlier payment) and a dummy for the PPM rounds. I experimented with first-, second- and third-order polynomials for the endowment, and found a quadratic specification worked best. This modified specification is as follows:

Table 5.7: Estimated effect of the PPM

	Quadratic endowment		Linear endowment	
	Coef.	Std. Err.	Coef.	Std. Err.
Match ratio (0 omitted)				
0.5	0.018	0.029	0.018	0.029
1	0.042	0.030	0.040	0.030
1.5	0.102***	0.033	0.098***	0.033
2	0.098***	0.031	0.096***	0.031
Endowment (GH¢)	0.039	0.026	0.116***	0.014
Endowment squared	0.006**	0.002		–
Log household wealth	0.021*	0.010	0.023**	0.011
Age (years)	0.002**	0.001	0.002**	0.001
Male	0.095***	0.020	0.094***	0.020
Could trust neighbour ('Strongly disagree' omitted)				
Strongly agree	0.161***	0.057	0.160***	0.057
Agree	0.075	0.046	0.073	0.046
Neutral	0.020	0.047	0.019	0.047
Disagree	0.036	0.046	0.037	0.046
Share trusting respondent	0.655***	0.143	0.642***	0.144
Community (Darmang omitted)				
Pokrom	0.317***	0.034	0.311***	0.034
Oboadaka	0.295***	0.034	0.293***	0.034
Konkonuru	-0.011	0.028	-0.014	0.028
PPM (Rounds 4 and 5)	0.328***	0.045	0.216***	0.051
Constant	-0.380***	0.097	-0.507***	0.112
N	2,070		2,070	
R^2	0.438		0.433	

Notes: Dependent variable is donation in GH′. Both equations estimated with OLS. Robust standard errors reported.

*** indicates significance at the 1 per cent level, ** at the 5 per cent level and * at the 10 per cent level.

where *endowment* is the full endowment in Ghana cedis, and *ppm* is a dummy variable taking the value one in rounds 4 and 5 and zero otherwise. The results are presented in Table 5.7. Donations are increasing in the square of the endowment, which suggests the marginal propensity to consume out of the endowment is *increasing*. The introduction of the PPM leads to an estimated 33p increase in contributions, roughly 50 per cent of the mean overall contribution and almost 100 per cent of the mean contribution in rounds 2 and 3. The effect of the PPM is about three times that of the matching grant with a ratio of 2.[26] In the second column of Table 5.7, I report results from Equation 2 where the endowment is specified linearly. In this case, the estimated effect of the PPM is 0.22, which is lower but still more than twice the effect of the match ratio.

Social Network Characteristics

Table 5.8 reports the coefficient estimates for a range of different social network measures, each included individually in an estimation of Equation 1. The measures considered are the number of individuals in the sample whom the respondent knows personally, the number who report knowing the respondent personally, the number of the respondent's contacts she reports being able to trust with a valuable item, and the number of contacts who report being able to trust the respondent. Finally, I try the share of the respondent's contacts she trusts, and the share who trust her. This last variable is by far the most significant, and is therefore the one included in the other regressions in this paper.

It is interesting that *trustworthiness* is the most significant predictor of an individual's contribution. An individual in the top decile in terms of trustworthiness (trusted by 45 per cent of those who know her) would donate around 23p more than an individual in the bottom decile (trusted by only 11 per cent of those who know her). This is roughly one-third of the mean overall donation. The other measures are much less significant, suggesting that it is not an individual's popularity alone that determines her contribution.[27] It is unclear which way the causality might run – whether the result can be explained by more trustworthy people tending to be leaders, and therefore donating more because of their position, or whether those individuals' donations reflect a more generous spirit which has already earned them the trust of others. This is an interesting question for future research, if indeed an experiment could distinguish the channel of influence. What is clear, however, is the crucial role of these trusted individuals in public fund-raising efforts.

Table 5.8: Coefficient estimates for social network variables

Variable	*Coef.*	*Std. Err.*
Number of sample members respondent knows	-0.001	0.000
Number of sample members who know respondent	0.000	0.000
Number of sample members respondent trusts	0.000	0.000
Number of sample members who trust respondent	0.003***	0.001
Share of known sample members respondent trusts	0.049	0.035
Sample members who trust respondent, as share of those who know respondent	0.671***	0.142
Variable	**Coef.**	**Std. Err.**
Number of sample members respondent knows	-0.001	0.000
Number of sample members who know respondent	0.000	0.000
Number of sample members respondent trusts	0.000	0.000
Number of sample members who trust respondent	0.003***	0.001
Share of known sample members respondent trusts	0.049	0.035
Sample members who trust respondent, as share of those who know respondent	0.671***	0.142

Notes: Each row reports the estimated coefficient on the respective social network variable when included individually as the variable socnetwork in an OLS regression of Equation 1.

Dependent variable is donation in GH'. Other regressors in Table 5.6 were included, but are omitted here for simplicity. Robust standard errors reported. *** indicates significance at the 1 per cent level, ** at the 5 per cent level and * at the 10 per cent level.

Is trustworthiness related to higher status in the village? Such individuals might have expected to lead the construction and management of the facilities, or felt responsible for the 'success' of their community's project, and therefore had the greatest interest in seeing it completed. To test these hypotheses, I include a number of measures of status in the regression: dummy variables for holding a village or family office, coming from the local ethnic group, having been fostered as a child, being a new migrant (defined as having lived in the community for five years or less), and the share of the individual's life spent in the community. If it is true that the effect of trustworthiness simply reflects the contributions behaviour of higher-status individuals, one would expect village office-bearers to contribute significantly more. Ethnicity is a significant theme in research on community-driven development, thus we might expect people from the local ethnic group (Akwapim) to have

Table 5.9: Coefficient estimates for status variables

	(1)		(2)		(3)		
	Coef.	**Std.**	**Coef.**	**Std.**	**Coef.**	**Std.**	
	Err.		**Err.**		**Err.**		
Share trusting respondent	0.732***		0.145	0.759***	0.147	0.817***	0.149
Status variables							
Holds village/family office	0.070		0.049	0.071	0.049	0.075	0.049
Member of Akwapim group	-0.079***		0.027	-0.079***	0.027	-0.072***	0.026
Fostered as child	0.002		0.023	-0.002	0.023	-0.007	0.023
New migrant (? 5 years in village)	--		--	0.068*	0.039	--	--
Share of life spent in village	--		--	--	--	-0.089**	0.036
N	2,016	2,016	2,011				
R^2	0.439	0.440	0.440				

Notes: Dependent variable is donation in GH'. Other regressors in Table 6 were included, but are omitted here for conciseness. Robust standard errors reported. *** indicates significance at the 1 per cent level, ** at the 5 per cent level and * at the 10 per cent level.

a greater say (and possibly stake) in public projects and thereby contribute more. Conversely, new migrants to the community are likely to have less. The practice of raising additional funds for local development from community members has a number of advantages. First, these individuals are rarely subject to income tax and therefore shoulder a very small tax burden. Some form of voluntary co-payment seems justified for public projects that offer direct benefits to the local community. The additional funds raised would allow district assemblies to do more with existing funds, and reduce their reliance on central government disbursements and irregular NGO and donor initiatives. Requiring local community members to bear part of the project cost could also increase their sense of ownership of the project and encourage them to take responsibility for its care and maintenance.

Some caveats apply to this analysis. The field experiment was designed to measure individuals' willingness to contribute to a public project. The focus on individual behaviour, and the particular requirements of an experimental setting, means the design of the experiment is somewhat different from the process a district assembly might use to raise funds for a larger public project.

First, donations might have been lower had we not presented respondents with a cash endowment before soliciting contributions. Absent these endowments, more individuals may have refused to contribute because they were short of cash. They may also have been more inclined to contribute because of an 'endowment effect', feeling richer because of their endowment. We tried to offset this by framing the endowment as compensation for their participation in the household survey, and mentioning the payment again during the survey interviews.

Second, the importance of status and social norms in these communities suggests that donations may have been significantly higher had the solicitations been public, subject to the influence of community leaders. Indeed, fund-raising efforts in Ghanaian communities (such as church harvests) frequently raise amounts of money many times higher than those raised in this experiment. One important factor in such efforts is the involvement of outsiders connected to the community, such as family members overseas. If these sources could be harnessed, much more money could likely be raised.

Third, from our interactions with the respondents it was clear that contributions were strongly related to the popularity of the projects. We were limited by our budget and sample size to offering small projects. It is likely that contributions would have been much higher for more desirable and broadly beneficial projects like electrification and road building. However, it is hard to know whether one could raise a similar proportion of the total cost for such a project.

Finally, the results of this study relate to only four communities in one district of Ghana. It is possible that behaviour might be qualitatively different in other parts of the country, l *et al.,* one in other countries. Further research or trials would need to be conducted before broadly implementing such a scheme as policy.

9. Conclusions

This paper presented the results of an experiment designed to measure individuals' willingness to contribute to a local public good. I explored the factors that cause some individuals to give more than others, and tested two incentive mechanisms often used in fund-raising activities. The paper makes a number of novel contributions to the literature. It offers evidence on the actual public goods contributions of individuals in a real-world developing country setting, relating to the financing of an actual public project. This is to my knowledge the first evidence on the effectiveness of the matching grant and PPM in a developing country, and the first comparison of the relative strengths of the two mechanisms in the field. By relating the results of the experiment to a rich dataset on individual characteristics and social networks, the study also sheds light on which individuals in the community are willing to contribute the most to public goods.

In these communities, the rate of contribution was high, but the size of the donations was small relative to the endowment. Older and male respondents donated more, but household wealth had only a small effect on donations. A striking finding was the strong effect of trustworthiness. The more trusted members of the community were more inclined to give, even after controlling for wealth. But somewhat surprisingly, this result was not driven by status alone. Indeed, I found that new migrants to the community donated significantly more, while community leaders did not. Individuals from the dominant ethnic group actually contributed less than others. These results highlight the importance of the social network in determining individuals' willingness to contribute to their communities, reinforcing findings from previous research that social cohesion within communities is conducive to the success of community-led development projects. However, they also bring into question the notion that elites in the community have the most to gain (or capture) from public projects, and the assumption that ethnic homogeneity implies greater participation and success in such endeavours. Perhaps the answer lies somewhere in between: that there is a willingness on the part of minority ethnic groups to contribute to public goods, but generally poorer outcomes in the management of projects resulting from the effect of ethnic fractionalisation on local political co-ordination.

I found that the provision point mechanism (PPM) had a significant impact on the size of donations, while the matching grant had a smaller but also significant effect. That these mechanisms are effective in boosting donations reinforces results from developed country field and laboratory experiments. However, I find that the match ratio has a greater effect in Ghanaian rural communities than has been measured in other places. The broad willingness of individuals to contribute to community projects suggests policy-makers may be able to use such contributions to augment funding for community construction projects. The results from the experiment indicate that the PPM and matching ratio could both be very effective in encouraging donations for such a programme.

Notes

1. For a comprehensive discussion of the history of community-driven development and its outcomes, see Mansuri and Rao (2004).
2. The notion of seeking community views on which projects to pursue is referred to in the literature as *preference targeting*. Evidence on its effectiveness is scarce. In a study of Jamaican Social Funds, Rao and Ibanez (2005) find that better-networked and elite members of the community tended to dominate the choice of project, though in the long run there were high degrees of satisfaction with the projects among all community members.
3. For instance, in her study of piped water schemes in Malawi, Kleemeier (2000) concludes that the infrastructure might have lasted longer had community members been charged user fees to fund maintenance.
4. There are many such mechanisms, the discussion of which is beyond the scope of this paper. List (2007) provides a recent summary of the experimental evidence on the effectiveness of these mechanisms.
5. During 2009, one Ghana cedi (GH′) averaged about 69 US cents. Converting without PPP adjustment, this equates to a mean per capita consumption level of between US $1.24 and US $1.72 per day.
6. Including children, my rough estimates of the populations are 706 in Oboadaka, 1,270 in Konkonuru, 1,768 in Darmang and 2,283 in Pokrom.
7. New sample members were selected randomly from the subset of households in the community headed by a married couple. The sample was stratified by age of the head into three categories: 18-29, 30-64 and 65+, so that the shares of households whose head was in each of these age categories corresponded to the population shares. The stratification was designed to reinstate representativeness given that households with heads under 30 did not exist in 1997-98, and those with heads over 65 had suffered greater natural attrition.
8. Some men in the sample have two or three wives, all of whom were included in the sample.

References

Akramov, K. T. and F. Asante (2009), 'Decentralisation and Local Public Services in Ghana: Do Geography and Ethnic Diversity Matter?' IFPRI Discussion Paper 00872, June 2009.

Ariely, D., G. Loewenstein and D. Prelec (2003), '"Coherent arbitrariness": Stable demand curves without stable preferences.' Quarterly Journal of Economics, Vol. 118, No. 1, pp. 73-105.

Bagnoli, M. and B. L. Lipman (1989), 'Provision of public goods: Fully implementing the core through private contributions.' The Review of Economic Studies, Vol. 56, No. 4, pp. 583-601.

Bagnoli, M. and M. McKee (1991), 'Voluntary contribution games: Efficient private provision of public goods.' Economic Inquiry, Vol. 29, No. 2, pp. 351-366.

Bagnoli, M., S. Ben-David, and M. McKee (1992), 'Voluntary provision of public goods: The multiple unit case.' Journal of Public Economics, Vol. 47, No. 1, pp. 85-106.

Baker, R. J., J. M. Walker, and A. W. Williams (2009), 'Matching contributions and the voluntary provision of a pure public good: Experimental evidence.' Journal of Economic Behaviour and Organisation, Vol. 70, No. 1-2, pp. 122-134.

Clarke, E. (1971), 'Multipart pricing of public goods.' Public Choice, Vol. 11, No. 1, pp. 17-33.

Eckel, C. C. and P. J. Grossman (2003), 'Rebate versus matching: Does how we subsidize charitable contributions matter?' Journal of Public Economics, Vol. 87, No. 3-4, pp. 681-701.

Fehr, E. and S. Gächter (2000), 'Fairness and retaliation: the economics of reciprocity.' Journal of Economic Perspectives, Vol. 14, No. 3, pp. 159-181.

Fischbacher, U., S. Gächter, and E. Fehr (2001), 'Are people conditionally cooperative? Evidence from a public goods experiment.' Economics Letters, Vol. 71, No. 3, pp. 397-404.

Groves, T. and J. Ledyard (1977), 'Optimal allocation of public goods: a solution to the "free rider" problem.' Econometrica, Vol. 45, pp. 783-809.

Isaac, R., D. Schmidtz, and J. Walker (1989), 'The assurance problem in a laboratory market.'

Isham, J. and S. Kähkönen (2002), 'Institutional determinants of the impact of community-based water services: Evidence from Sri Lanka and India.' Economic Development and Cultural Change, Vol. 50, pp. 667-691.

Jimenez, E. and V. Paqueo (1996), 'Do local contributions affect the efficiency of public primary schools?' Economics of Education Review, Vol. 15, No. 4, pp. 377-386.

Karlan, D. and J. A. List (2007), 'Does price matter in charitable giving? Evidence from a large-scale natural field experiment.' American Economic Review, Vol. 97, Issue 5, pp. 1774-1793.

Kleemeier, E. (2000), 'The impact of participation on sustainability: An analysis of the Malawi rural piped scheme program.' World Development, Vol. 28, No. 5, pp. 929-944.

List, J. A. (2007), 'Field experiments: A bridge between lab and naturally-occurring data.' NBER Working Paper 12992, March.

List, J. A. and D. Lucking-Reiley (2002), 'The effects of seed money and refunds on charitable giving: Experimental evidence from a university capital campaign.' Journal of Political Economy, Vol. 110, No. 1, pp. 215-233.

Mansuri, G. and V. Rao (2004), 'Community-based and -driven development: A critical review.' World Bank Research Observer, Vol. 19, Spring, 1-39.

Marks, M. and R. Croson (1998), 'Alternative rebate rules in the provision of a threshold public good: An experimental investigation.' Journal of Public Economics 67, pp. 195-220.

Marks, M. and R. Croson (1999), 'The effect of incomplete information in a threshold public goods experiment.' Public Choice, Vol. 99, No. 1, pp. 103-118.

Meier, S. (2007), 'Do subsidies increase charitable giving in the long run? Matching donations in a field experiment.' Journal of the European Economic Association, Vol. 5, No. 6, pp. 1203-1222.

Messer, K., H. Zarghamee, H. M. Kaiser and W. D. Schulze (2007), 'New hope for the voluntary contributions mechanism: The effects of framing and context.' Journal of Public Economics 91, pp. 1783-1799.

Miguel, E. and M. K. Gugerty (2005), 'Ethnic diversity, social sanctions, and public goods in Kenya.' Journal of Public Economics 89, pp. 2325-2368.

Owen, M. (2009), 'How does proximity to tarred roads impact the pattern of employment and compensation in rural Ghana?' Mimeo, Fenner School of Environment and Society, Australian National University, October.

Palfrey, T. R. and H. Rosenthal (1984), 'Participation and the provision of discrete public goods: A strategic analysis.' Journal of Public Economics, Vol. 24, No. 2, pp. 171-193.

Poe, G., J. Clark, D. Rondeau, and W. Schulze (2002), 'Provision point mechanisms and field validity tests of contingent valuation.' Environmental and Resource Economics, Vol. 23, No. 1, pp. 105-131.

Rao, V. and A. M. Ibanez (2005), 'The social impact of social funds in Jamaica: A participatory econometric analysis of targeting, collective action, and participation in community-driven development.' Journal of Development Studies, Vol. 41, No. 5, pp. 788-838.

Rondeau, D. and J. List (2008), 'Matching and challenge gifts to charity: evidence from laboratory and natural field experiments." Experimental Economics, Vol. 11, No. 3, pp. 253-267.

Rondeau, D., W. D. Schulze and G. L. Poe (1999), 'Voluntary revelation of the demand for public goods using a provision point mechanism.' Journal of Public Economics 72, pp. 455-470.

6

Farmers' Perception on Rainfall and its Impacts on Investment, Output and Food Security in Swaziland

Sipho Felix Mamba

Introduction

Climate change already poses major threats to agricultural production and food security, with particularly negative impacts for developing countries in Africa, Asia and the world's most vulnerable peoples and places. Compelling evidence of such connections has been captured in most recent studies and has been documented by scholars such as Burton *et al.* (2013); Battersby (2012) Smith and Gregory (2013); Battersby (2011); Ziervogel and Frayne (2011). Climate variability, which is the short-term variation in climate, is another critical aspect of climate change that also has a significant impact on crop yield and food insecurity, especially for rain-fed agriculture since it influences rainfall intensity and duration which is key for rain fed agricultural systems. Climate variability also disturbs the farming calendar by making the onset of rainfall highly unpredictable (FAO, 2008; Burke and Lobello, 2010) resulting to low crop productivity (Oseni and Masarirambi, 2011; Vermeulen, Campbell and Ingram, 2012; Wheeler and von Braun, 2013; Manyatsi *et al.,* 2012;

Mamba, Salam and Peter (2015). Scholars argue, however, that while climate is the primary determinant of agricultural productivity in most countries relying on rainfed agriculture, there is need for proper adaptation strategies which may include utilisation of opportunities in favourable years or seasons (wetter years/seasons).

It has also been argued that the widespread food insecurity in Africa, Asia and other parts of the developing world is not because of climate change but rather due to farmers' failure to utilise opportunities in wetter years (Cooper, 2007). Among the factors which contribute to farmers' failure to utilise opportunities in wetter years to boost their crop production and food availability is the way they perceive climate change and variability. Farmers' perception of climate change and climatic variables conditions their initiation of adaptation practices (Misselhorn, 2005; Nelson, 2005; Socio-Economic Team, 2010). Farmers perceive climate change and variability differently and tend to overestimate the negative impacts of climatic variables. Misperception of climatic variables, especially when farmers fail to perceive correctly a good rainfall season and mistook it for low and insufficient rainfall, they may not invest adequately in that farming season. Inadequate investment in a good rainfall year will make farmers miss the opportunity for a good production, and contribute to their food insecurity, which characteristic most countries of the global south (Crush and Frayne, 2010; Tevera *et al.,* 2012; Tawodzera, Zanamwe and Crush, 2012). Thus, it is important that farmers perceive climate change and climatic variables correctly, especially rainfall amount in order to make appropriate decisions and investment.

The problem that has motivated this study was that while climate change and, in particular climate variability is held to be responsible for low agricultural productivity and food insecurity in most developing countries and in Swaziland, we do not know the precise way in which climate variability affects agricultural productivity which in turn impacts on food insecurity. The main objective of the study was to investigate how farmers' perception of climate change and variability, especially rainfall amount, influences investment decisions and the resulting crop yield and food insecurity in Swaziland. Although the study was conducted in Swaziland, findings in this study can be applicable to most developing countries in Africa, Asia and other parts of the world where agriculture still plays a major role in the food security of rural households.

Methodology and Study Area

Study Approach

In this study, FAO (2008) framework on climate change and food security was adopted to assess the influence of farmers' perception on adaptive responses on food systems, food system activities and components of food security. The variables considered under climate change and variability were changes in precipitation and weather variability. The variables considered under precipitation included: increase in frequency, intensity and duration of dry spells and drought as well as changes in timing and amount of rainfall. Under weather variability, the focus was on changes in start and end of growing season and instability in seasonal weather patterns. Food system activities considered were mainly inputs invested in food production: farm size cultivated and planted and quantities of fertiliser applied, types and quality of seeds used. The components of food security assessed were: food availability, access and utilisation. To assess farmers' perceptions of climate change and variability, locally idealised traditional weather cycle was compared with climate change as perceived by farmers of the region using rainfall data to measure the accuracy of perceptions.

Study area

The study was conducted in the Middleveld region of Swaziland which receives adequate rainfall (750-1000 mm) thus support farming of food crops such as maize, which is also the staple food and produces most of the maize consumed in Swaziland. While the area is well drained by many main rivers such as Nkomazi, Mbuluzi, Lusutfu and Ngwavuma, majority of farmers in this region depend exclusively on rainfall for their crops, and any irregularities in rainfall received adversely affect their farming, especially maize yield. Majority of farmers in this region rely on rainfall for maize cultivation. Very few farmers irrigate their crops, and these are sugarcane farmers.

Selection of the communities and households for the study

The Middleveld was purposively selected due to its wide range of agro-ecological conditions that promotes maize cultivation. Spatial sampling was used to sample three constituencies (*Tinkhundla*) from the Middleveld. Three constituencies Ndsingeni, Mthongwaneni and Sandleni were selected. From each constituency, three communities were again spatially sampled and 30 households were purposefully selected from each selected community. The purpose was to ensure an equal number of households with different rainfall perceptions (very plenty, average, low). The total sample households were 270.

Data sources, collection and analysis

The study used primary data supplemented by secondary data and observation. A questionnaire was used to gather information on noticed changes in mean rainfall over a period of 20 years, adaptation strategies employed, size of land owned, cultivated, yield obtained and amount of inputs applied (especially fertiliser) among other essential information. Focus group discussions were conducted with elders in the communities to establish farming ways based on farming experience, changes in rainfall and adaptation strategies used. Analysis involved establishing relationships between farmers' perception of rainfall amount, adaptive responses in terms of inputs used, production outcomes, components of food security and food security status. Comparisons between farmers' perceptions and meteorological data (rainfall) were also carried out to establish accuracy of perception. SPSS was used for facilitate analysis and a chi-square test (sig. level 0.05) was conducted to determine the significance of results obtained. For analysis of household food security access, the household food insecurity access scale (HFIAS) was used.

Results

Perception on rainfall in the 2011/2012 farming season

Rainfall data from the meteorological department for the 2011/2012 farming season was used to calculate the average rainfall amount for the farming season. The results show average rainfall received was 138.5 millimetres with median value of 122.3 millimetres. These results indicate a normal year (average) for the farming season according to Swaziland Meteorological Services. Any amount of rainfall below the median value would indicate below normal (low) rainfall while above normal (plenty) rainfall is indicated by any value above the median value.

The results (Fig. 6.2) indicate that only a few (34 per cent) farmers perceived correctly the amount of rainfall in the beginning of the 2011/2012 farming season while majority (66 per cent) of farmers perceived wrongly the amount of rainfall in the beginning of the 2011/2012 farming season.

The impact of farmers' perception on rainfall on investment decision (inputs used)

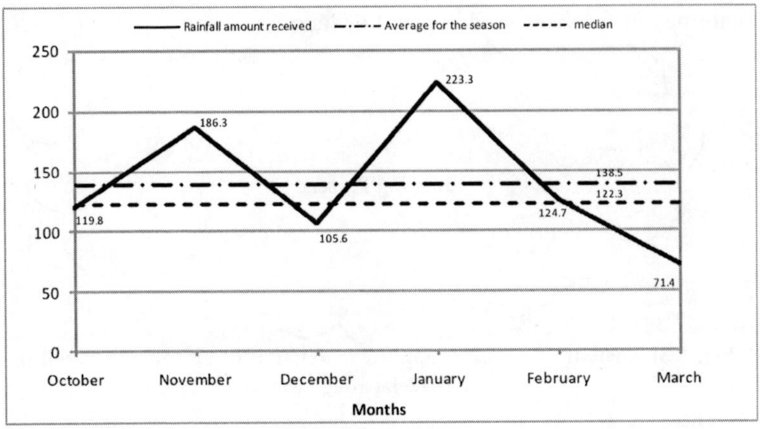

Fig. 6.1: Amount of rainfall received in the Middleveld for the 2011/2012 farming season.

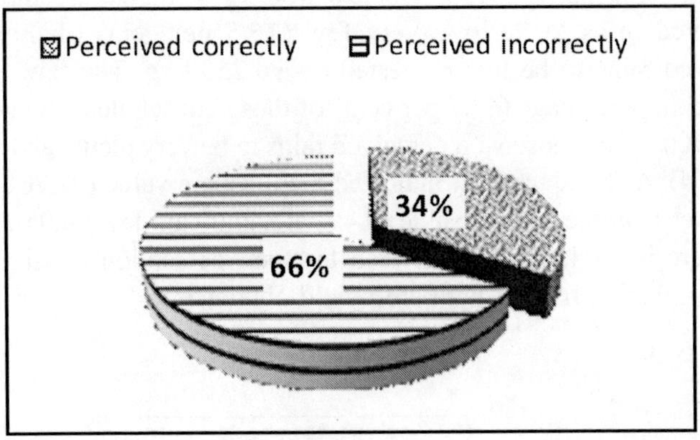

Fig. 6.2: Farmers' perception of rainfall for the 2011/2012 farming season.

Analysis of the amount of fertiliser used per hectare in relation to perceived amount of rainfall indicated that majority (42.1 per cent) of farmers who applied 251-300 kg of fertiliser were those who perceived the amount of rainfall to be very plenty or at least average. Majority of farmers (61.1 per cent) who applied 1-50 kg perceived rainfall to be low. Very few (16.7 per cent) of those who perceived rainfall to be plenty were found to apply 1-50 kg of fertiliser per hectare (Fig. 6.3). The calculated chi-square indicating that there is a relationship between farmers' perception of climate and weather (in this case rainfall) with quantities of fertiliser used per unit of land.

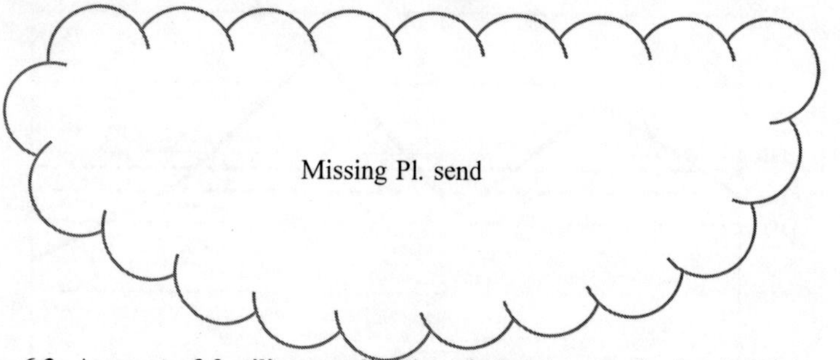

Fig. 6.3: Amount of fertiliser applied in relation to perceived rainfall in 2011/2012 farming season.

Crop yield by rainfall perception

Further analysis was done to establish the amount of maize produced in relation to perceived rainfall. Results indicated that Majority (54 per cent) of households who got below 500 kg of maize are those who perceived rains to be low. Very few (15.5 per cent) of those who perceived rains to be low harvested above 2500 kg. The few, but also significant percentage (42.7 per cent) of those households who get more than 2500 kg are those who perceived rains to be very plenty and average (Fig. 6.4). A chi-square test indicated a chi-square value (27.701) which is greater than the critical value (9.49) at significant level 0.05 meaning that there is a relationship between farmers' perception of climate and weather, that is, rainfall with crop yield obtained.

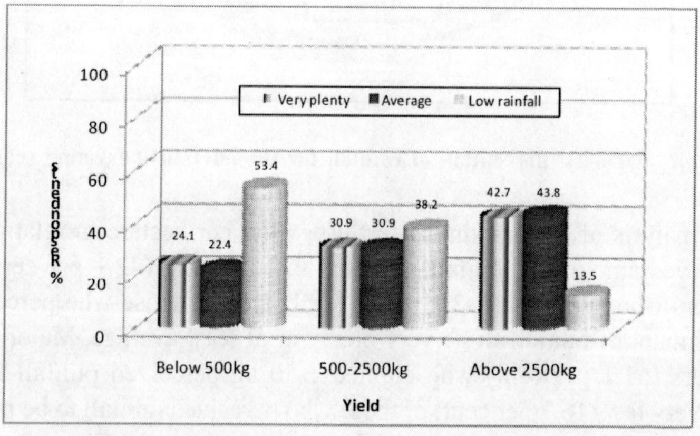

Fig. 6.4: Yield obtained in relation to perception of rainfall

Food security status in relation to perception

Majority (35.6 per cent) of household which are food secure perceived rainfall to be plenty. Majority (27.8 per cent) of the mildly food secure households perceived rainfall to be plenty. It is interesting to note that majority of the moderately food insecure (35.7 per cent) were those who perceived rainfall to be low (Fig. 6.5). Majority of severely food insecure households (25.3 per cent) are those who perceived rainfall to be low. This was tested for significance. The test, however, indicated that the relationship is not significant as the calculated chi-square value (11.706) was less than the critical value (12.59) at significance level 0.05.

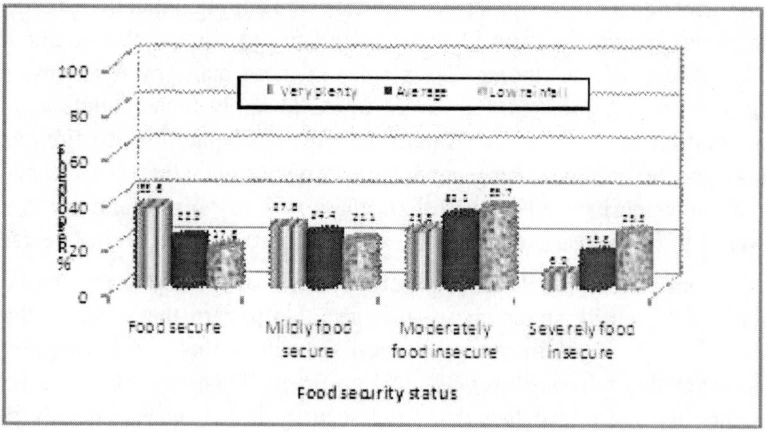

Fig. 6.5: Food security status in relation to perception.

Discussion

Majority of farmers expected low rainfall in the 2010/2011 farming season while the actual rainfall received was very plenty. This indicates that majority wrongly perception the amount of rainfall to be received in the beginning of a farming season (October to March). This supports an argument by Cooper (2007) who noted that farmers tend to over-estimate the negative impact of variable climates and further notes that farmers' perception of climate change does not always tally with national meteorological data. Farmers ability to percive correctly the amount of rainfall expected in the beginning of every farming season is crucial as the FAO (2008) report states that of all the climatic factors, the daily and inter-annual variation in precipitation is most crucial for rainfed agriculture. Farmers in the FGD highlighted that variability in rainfall has caused rains to be highly unpredictable and admitted that it tend to confuse them. This provides an explaination to the findings why farmers fail to correctly predict rainfall within a farming season period (short period) which, unfortunately, is most crucial.

It was also gathered that amount of fertiliser applied varied significantly with perception. Farmers who perceived rainfall to be low invested fewer amount of fertiliser per hectare while those who perceived it to be plenty tend to apply more. Results from a chi-square test indicated that there is a relationship between farmers' perception of climate and weather (in this case rainfall) with quantities of fertiliser used per unit of land). When farmers perceive a good rainfall year, they also tend to invest more inputs (fertiliser) in their production. This was further confirmed in a FGD with farmers (elders) who admitted that this practice is common and it is their adaptation strategies to climate change due to fear of lose. These findings are similar to those made by Ayanwuyi *et al.* (2010) that some farmers were found to apply fewer inputs as an adaptation mechanism or strategy to climate change. These findings confirm the argument by Cooper (2007) who argues that farmers may not apply fertiliser when they think there will be no rain and are "too wary" to incur losses and fail to exploit opportunities in wetter years.

Analysis of the relationship between farmers' perception of rainfall and food security status show an observable pattern that indicate that there is a relationship between food security status and perception, however this relationship was not significant. This, however, was not surprising due to the fact that food security is not measured only by food production but also the power to purchase food yet the perception only covered food production but excluded those who purchased food to ensure food availability. Also, it is worth noting that as farmers' perception influenced input use which in turn affects crop yields, it indirectly influences food security. This is in line with what Cooper (2007) and Socio-Economical Team (2010) observed that farmers' misperception of the impacts of climate change affect crop productivity and eventually contribute to food insecurity.

Conclusion

Based on the findings, the study concludes that farmers perceived correctly the trends climate change and variability. However, some farmers perceived wrongly the amount of rainfall to be expected at the onset of the farming season. Farmers who perceived incorrectly the amount of rainfall in the beginning of the farming season (average or low) make inadequate input investment (in this case fertiliser) and harvest lower yields and are more food insecure. Contrary, farmers who perceived correctly the amount of rainfall (sufficient) tend to make adequate input investment and harvest more yield and are less food insecure. Other farmers were too wary of climate change and missed opportunities in good years and felt bad when other farmers got better yields. The study concluded that farmers' perception of climate change and variability, in particular rainfall, influence investment decision and the resulting crop yield and food insecurity. It is essential that farmers perceive correctly rainfall, especially the onset of the rains so that they can invest adequately.

Recommendation

Recommendations for action

- There is need for adequate communication to farmers on expected rainfall conditions at the onset of the farming season.
- Measures are needed to assist farmers to perceive rainfall conditions correctly.
- Education on climate change and weather variability and skills on how to perceive rainfall correctly should be provided to farmers, especially the young ones.
- Insurance for farmers is needed as a 'fall-back' to help farmers to invest without fear and to reduce their wariness to enable them to utilise opportunities in better years and do so fully.
- There is need for accurate weather forecasting and to communicate this data to farmers more accurately and on time before the onset of every farming season as well as to give them relevant meteorological advice that will help them make informed farming options in each farming season.

Recommendations for further research

- Research needs to be conducted on other factors affecting farmers' perception and mechanisms on how to reach farmers and communicate with them effectively.
- There is also need for research on how to establish insurance for farmers to help them invest without worry or fear.
- Research also needs to be carried out to determine factors that influence input use among maize farmers. Findings in these research avenues will help relieve or even eradicate food insecurity and related stresses by food shortages even beyond household level.

References

Ayanwuyi, E., Kuponiyi, E., Ogunlade, A., and Oyetoro, J. 2010, Farmers' perception of impact of climate change on food crop production on Ogbomosho Agricultural Zone of Oyo State, Nigeria. *Global Journal of Human Social Science*, **3**, *30-55.*

Battersby, Jane. 2011. "Urban Food Insecurity in Cape Town, South Africa: An Alternative Approach to Food Access." *Development Southern Africa* 28 (4): 545–61. doi:10.1080/0376835X.2011.605572.

Battersby, Jane. 2012. *Urban food security and climate change: A system of flows*. EGS Department, University of Cape Town.

Burke, M., and Lobello, D. 2010. Food security and adaptation to climate change. What do we know? Retrieved June 28, 2011, from http://www.ocf.berkeley.edu/~marshall/papers/Chap8 adaptation.pdf.

Burton, Paul, Kristen Lyons, Carol Richards, Marco Amati, Nicholas Rose, Lotus Desfours, Victor Pires, and Rochelle Barclay. 2013. "Urban Food Security, Urban Resilience and Climate Change." National Climate Change Adaptation Research Facility (NCCARF): Gold Coast.

Cooper, Peter. 2007. Climate Change in Africa. ICRISAT. Nairobi.

Crush, Jonathan, and Bruce Frayne. 2010. "Pathways to Insecurity: Food Supply and Access in Southern African Cities". urban food security series no. 3. AFSUN.

FAO. 2008. "Climate change and food security: A framework document". http://www.fao.org/forestry/15538-079b31d45081fe9c3dbc6ff34de4807e4.pdf.

Mamba, Sipho Felix, Abul Salam, and Graciana Peter. 2015. "Farmers' Perception of Climate Change a Case Study in Swaziland" 3 (2): 47–61. doi:10.12691/jfs-3-2-3.

Manyatsi, Absalom M, Michael T Masarirambi, Sepo Hachigonta, Lindiwe M Sibanda, and Timothy S Thomas. 2012. "Southern African Agriculture and Climate Change: A Comprehensive Analysis - Swaziland." Washington D.C. International Food Policy Research Institute (FANRPAN).

Misselhorn, Alison 2005. "What Drives Food Insecurity in Southern Africa? A Meta-Analysis of Household Economy Studies." *Global Environmental Change* 15 (1): 33–43. doi:10.1016/j.gloenvcha.2004.11.003.

Nelson Alson 2009. World food security.

http://www.ifpri.org/publication/climate-change-impact-agriculture-and-costs-adaptation.

Oseni, T O, and M T Masarirambi. 2011. "Effect of Climate Change on Maize (Zea Mays) Production and Food Security in Swaziland." *and Environ. Sci* 11 (3): 385–91.

Socio-Economic Team. 2010. Farm-level climate change perception and adaptation in drought prone areas on Tigray, northern Ethiopia.

Smith, P. and Gregory, P.J. 2013. Conference on 'Future food and health'.

Symposium, I: Sustainability and food security Climate change and sustainable food production. Proceedings of the Nutrition Society, 72, 21–28.

Tawodzera, Zanamwe and Crush. 2012. "The State of Food Insecurity in Harare, Zimbabwe." Urban food security Series. No. 13. Queen's University and AFSUN: Kingston and Cape Town.

Tevera, Daniel, Nomcebo Simelane, Graciana Peter, and Abul Salam. 2012. "The State of Food Insecurity in Manzini, Swaziland." AFSUN Urban Food Security Series.

Vermeulen, Sonja J., Bruce M. Campbell, and John S.I. Ingram. 2012. "Climate Change and Food Systems." *Annual Review of Environment and Resources* 37 (1): 195–222. doi:10.1146/annurev-environ-020411-130608.

Wheeler, T. and von Braun, J. 2013. Climate Change Impacts on Global Food Security. *Natural systems in changing climate. (*341): 508.

Ziervogel, Gina, and Bruce Frayne. 2011. "Climate Change and Food Security in South African Cities." Urban Food Security Series No. 8. Queen's University and AFSUN: Kingston and Cape Town.

7

Achieving Nutritional Food Security Raising Pulses Output and Arresting Price-Rise in India

Gopal Kalkoti

Introduction

The FAO of the United Nations has declared the year 2016 as the international year of pulses which has been very relevant to India in the context of making the country nutritionally food secure when prices of pulses are sky-rocketing and country has to spend Rs 80.67 billion annually on import of 3.44 million tonnes during 2007-08 to 2015-16.

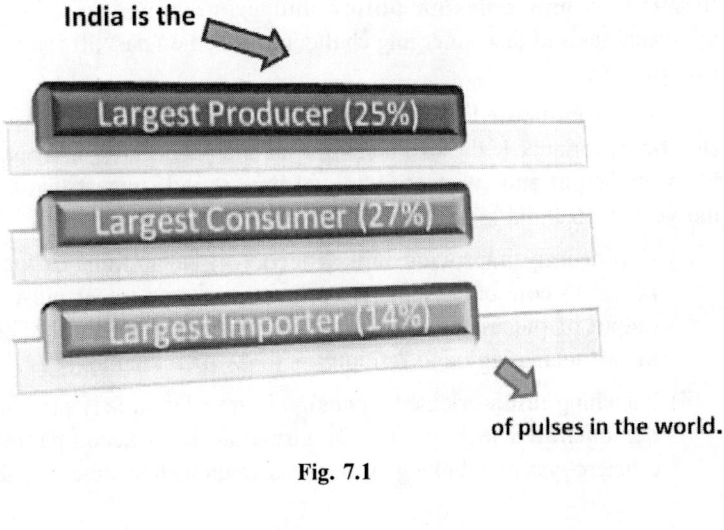

Fig. 7.1

Pulses account for 20 per cent of area under food grains and contribute 7 per cent to 10 per cent of total food output. Rabi pulses contribute more than 60 per cent of total pulses output. Six states (Madhya Pradesh, Maharashtra, Uttar Pradesh, Andhra Pradesh, Karnataka and Rajasthan) contribute about 80 per cent of total pulse production and area.

Despite government's initiatives since 1965 to implement nation-wide programmes to step up pulses productivity, production and profitability, (All India coordinated pulses research Project (1965), intensive pulses development project (1969), central sector national pulses development project (1985), integrated scheme of oilseeds, pulses and maize (2002) and pulses production programme in 6000 villages under the national food security mission (2007)).

India has been importing annually pulses on an average 3.44 million tonnes (MT) amounting to Rs 80.67 billion from 2007-08 to 2015-16. And yet India has been witnessing unprecedented price-rise of pulses which can be controlled by capitalising opportunities when ample scope is available to raise the output and managing the stock and distribution system by formulating and implementing strategic action plan from the year 2016 being the international year of pulses.

International Year of Pulses

When the United Nations' General Assembly has declared 2016 as the international year of pulses, India needs to review and evaluate the strength and weaknesses of all these programmes implemented from 1965 to 2014-15 and redesign policy and programmes to seize new opportunities and face emerging challenges based on past 50 years' field experiences.

Details embodied in this paper, *inter alia,* reveal year to year significant variance in the area under pulses and per hectare yield resulting in lower output and substantial annual import and suggest that during the year 2016 India must initiate strategic actions for

(i) significantly improving India's technical capabilities to forecast nearer to correct season-wise estimates of area under pulses and output of pulses through investing in and better use of state-of-the-art technology and refining methods of estimation;

(ii) launching result-oriented campaign to transfer already proven and demonstrated technologies at farmers' fields accompanied by efficient system of linking institutional credit with on time availability of quality seeds and marketing services that can guarantee expected yield;

(iii) preparing road-map to achieve anticipated output of 35 MT by 2030 and 50 MT by 2050 as envisioned by the Indian Institute of Pulses Research;

(iv) building a need-based buffer stock with accountability for proper management incurring no wastages at all;

(v) keeping close watch on the crop growth in 30 pulse-exporting countries through effective coordination with the FAO and our embassies that can help India negotiate favourable terms for timely import as and when imminent;

(vi) putting in place efficient system to make pulses easily available in the open market throughout the year through rigorous enforcement of essential commodities Act and warranted distribution through public distribution system (PDS) or direct benefit transfer scheme crediting to beneficiary's bank account.

Need to Increase Pulses Consumption and Output

The consumption of pulses needs to be increased as an integral component of country's nutritional food security as they are the major sources of proteins for vegetarians. Pulses contain 22 per cent-24 per cent protein, almost twice the amount of protein available in wheat and thrice that of rice. Pulses supplement the staple cereals in the diets with health-sustaining ingredients viz. proteins, essential amino acids, vitamins and minerals. Pulses are nutritious and are known to reduce impact of several non-communicable diseases such as colon cancer and cardiovascular diseases and avoiding calorie catastrophe by balancing intake of carbohydrates and protein.

Farmers must be incentivised to increase area under pulses including under irrigation since it has unique features viz.

(i) pulses can be grown on a wide range of soil and climatic conditions and in different farming systems, such as crop-rotation, mixed and inter-cropping system. Pulses being legumes help fixing atmospheric nitrogen into soil and release soil-bound phosphorus. They add organic matter into the soil in the form of leaf mould. Some pulses are suitable as green-manure crops. They help check the soil-erosion. All these contribute to maintain soil productivity and fertility level;

(ii) most pulse crops are of short duration which facilitate growing second crop on the same land in a year;

(iii) pulses as industrial crops provide raw material to various industries, such as pulse industry, roasted grain industry, etc.

(iv) they serve as rich source of nutritious fodder for cattle.

More importantly, pulses have low carbon emission and water needs which make them ideally suited in country's farming system. As per recent estimates, one kg production of pulses requires 359 litres of water as against more than 1000 for soybean/groundnut and five times higher than pulses for production of one kg meat. Further, one kg of legumes emits 0.5 kg carbon equivalent as compared to 9.5 kg carbon equivalent for production of one kg meat.

Area under Pulses

India grows varieties of pulses, during monsoon and winter seasons. More popular pulses are chickpea, pigeon-pea, green gram, black gram and lentil. Between 1950-51 and 2013-14, area under pulses increased by 31 per cent from 19.0 million hectare MHA to 25.0 MHA. The CAGR of total area under pulses was 0.08 per cent much lower than 0.21 per cent of total area under food grains, 0.58 per cent for rice, 1.70 per cent for wheat and 1.40 per cent for oilseeds. Most farmers grow pulses in rain-fed/dry land which yield significantly low as compared to pulses under irrigation using high yielding varieties and adequate plant nutrients. Over a period of past six decades, with the expansion of irrigation facilities farmers in the northern India have switched over to cultivation of wheat, rice and maize on a substantially larger area replacing pulses. 1960s and early 1970s witnessed significant fall in pulses cultivation due to substitution by HYV of cereals during the green revolution period in States of Punjab, Haryana and western Uttar Pradesh.

Area under pulses declined by as high as 20 per cent from 10.12 MHA to 8.16 MHA in northern India whereas in Central and Southern India area under pulses increased from 11.34 MHA to 15.01 MHA 32 per cent during last three decades. Chickpea, among all major pulses grown in northern India, witnessed as high as 63 per cent decline under area from 4.98 MHA in 1971 to 1.85 MHA in 2010, mainly due to replacement by wheat. As against this, during this period the chickpea cultivation witnessed a significant swift of about 3.0 MHA from cooler and long season environment of northern India to warmer and short season environment in southern India. The effective coordination between the International Crop Research Institute for Semi-Arid Tropics (ICRISAT) and National Agricultural Research System (NARS) in the evolution and dissemination of short-duration varieties enabled farmers of Central and Southern India to expand area under chickpea and raise its productivity, production and profitability. Following six States in India contributed to 79.48 per cent of total area and 79.35 per cent of total production in India. Yield/hectare in Madhya Pradesh and Uttar Pradesh was appreciably higher than national average.

Table 7.1: Area, Production and Yield of Pulses of Six States Triennium (2014)

State	*Area '000 ha*	*Production '000Tons*	*Yield/hectare Kg)*
Madhya Pradesh	5310 (21.84)	4807 (26.36)	905 (120.66)
Rajasthan	3967 (16.31)	2286 (12.54)	576 (76.80)
Maharashtra	3489 (14.35)	2565 (14.07)	735 (98.00)
Uttar Pradesh	2365 (09.73)	2148 (11.78)	908 (121.07)
Karnataka	2345 (09.64)	1286 (07.05)	549 (73.20)
Andhra Pradesh	1850 (07.61)	1468 (08.05)	794 (105.87)
Others	4990 (20.52)	3674 (20.15)	736 (98.13)
All India	**24316 (100)**	**18234 (100)**	**750**

Figures in parentheses under area and production indicate % share

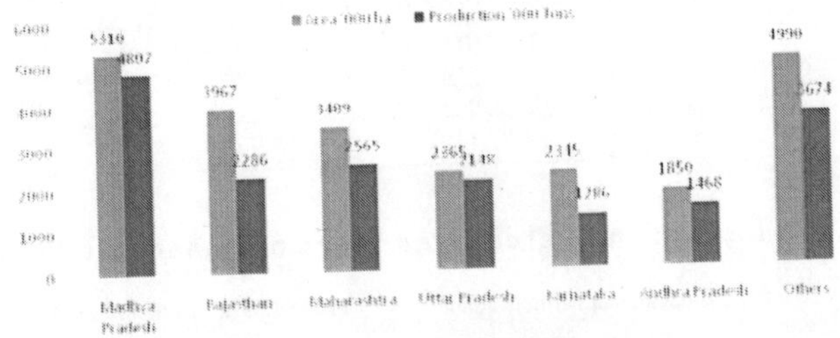

Fig. 7.2. Area and Production of Pulses of Six States (2014)

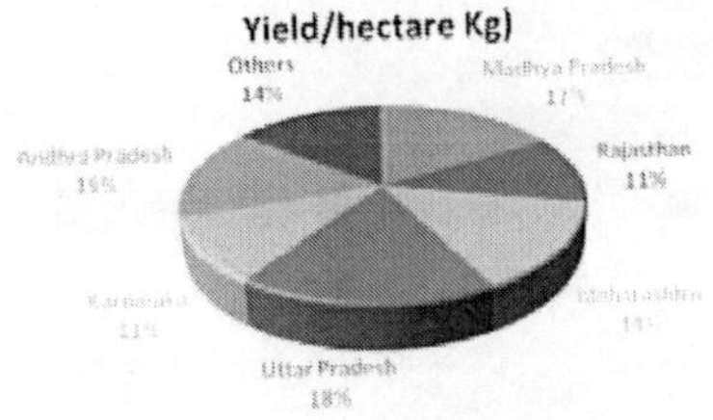

Fig. 7.3

Pulses Production

During 1950-51 to 2013-14 production increased by over 100 per cent from 8.41 million tonnes MT to 19.27 MT. The compound annual growth rate (CAGR) of 0.64 per cent of pulses output was much lower than 2.23 per cent for food grains, 1.90 per cent for rice, 2.75 per cent for wheat and 1.53 per cent for oilseeds. Among 12 pulses crops, chickpea alone had 40.52 per cent share in total pulses production in 2009 which increased to 47.09 per cent in 2014-15. Chickpea along with other three pulses (pigeonpea, black gram and green gram) together had 72.94 per cent and 79.89 per cent share in total pulses production in 2009 and 2014-15 respectively. Between 2009 and 2014-15, black gram recorded 76.47 per cent increase in production followed by chickpea (58.93 per cent) and green gram (42.86 per cent) as against 1.60 per cent by other eight pulses.

Table 7.2: Production and Percentage Share of Important Pulses (2009 and 2014-15)

Pulse-crop	*Production in Million Tons*		*Per cent increase in 2014-15 over 2009*
	2009	*2014-15*	
Chickpea	5.60 (40.52)	8.9 (47.09)	58.93
Pigeonpea	2.48 (17.94)	3.0 (15.87)	20.91
Urad	1.02 (07.38)	1.8 (09.52)	76.47
Moong	0.98 (07.09)	1.4 (07.41)	42.86
Other pulses	3.74 (27.06)	3.8 (20.11)	01.60
Total	13.82 (100)	18.9 (100)	36.76

Production and Percentage Share of Important Pulses

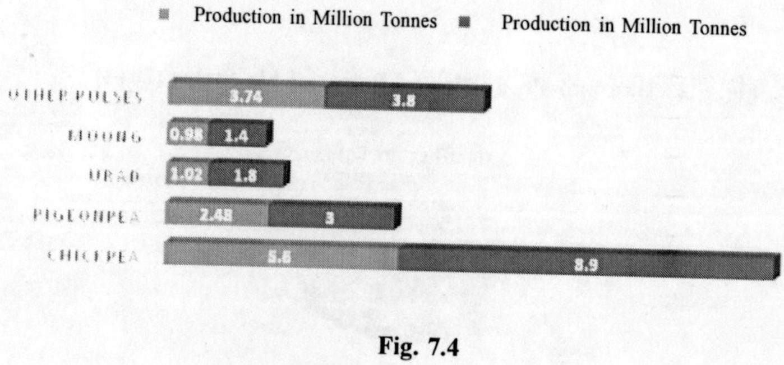

Fig. 7.4

Yield per Hectare

During 1950-51 to 2013-14, the yield per hectare increased by 46 per cent from 441 kg to 764 kg but 0.64 per cent CAGR of yield was much disappointing. The CAGR of pulses yield for five decades 1950-2000) was abysmally low at 0.5 per cent which significantly improved to 2.4 per cent during 2000-01 to 2013-14. Per hectare yield of monsoon pulses ranges between 393 kg and 512 kg whereas the yield of winter pulses varies between 654 and 756 kg. Low yield accompanied by declining area reflected on total output of pulses. Per capita net availability of pulses has been reduced considerably from 51.9 gram/day in 1971 to 41.9 gram/day in 2013 as against requirement of 80 gram/day as recommended by the World Health Organisation.

Import of Pulses

Pulses are often considered poor man's protein but with the urbanisation and rising income of middle class in the country since a decade pressure on protein foods including pulses has increased significantly resulting into price rise when domestic supply is constrained. India, in order to meet the growing domestic demand, imports significant quantity of pulses. Imports ranged from 13.51 per cent to 29.71 per cent of domestic production between 2007-08 and 2015-16. Average annual import was 3.44 MT costing Rs 80.67 billion. Imports are from 30 countries but major ones are Canada, Myanmar, USA, Russia and Australia. India exported 0.30 million tonnes during 2013-14. India has been the important pulse-processor country for some pulse- exporting countries which have inadequate processing facilities. Also, India imports large quantity of pulses viz. desi chickpeas, pigeon-pea, green gram, black gram and kidney bean from Myanmar. Myanmar offers to India wide varieties of pulses with qualities similar to those produced in India and with advantage of low freight rates, and relatively fast delivery. Canada and Australia supply dry peas and kabuli chickpeas to India, each supplying about one-third of India's pulses imports. Other kabuli chickpeas supplying countries are Mexico, Turkey and Iran. Nepal and Syria account for the largest share of India's lentil imports. India cannot afford to import 3.44 million tonnes of pulses annually when the country has the significant scope to improve the productivity, production and profitability as demonstrated by the ICRISAT and NARS.

Table 3: Production and Net Imports of Pulses in Million Tonnes (2007-08 to 2015-16)

Year	*Production*	*Net Imports*	*Year*	*Production*	*Net Imports*
2007-08	14.80	2.00(13.51)	2012-13	18.30	3.80(20.76)
2008-09	14.60	2.90(19.86)	2013-14	19.80	2.70(3.64)
2009-10	14.70	3.60(24.49)	2014-15	18.40	3.90(21.19)
2010-11	18.20	2.60(14.28)	2015-16	17.50	5.20(29.71)
2011-12	17.20	3.30(19.19)	Average	17.05	3.44 (20.19)

Figures in parentheses indicate % of net imports to production

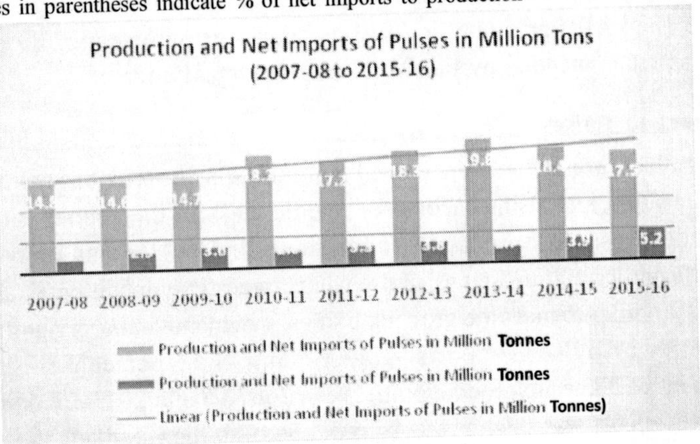

Fig. 7.5

Low Productivity and Production

Factors responsible for low productivity per unit area and resources and output, *inter alia*, include:

(i) around 84 per cent area under pulses is rain-fed with soils relatively of low fertility Between 1966-67 and 2012-13, irrigated area under pulses increased from 9 per cent to 16 per cent as against from 38 per cent to 59 per cent for rice and 48 per cent to 93 per cent for wheat;

(ii) drought and heat stress influence 50 per cent reduction in seed yields particularly in arid and semi-arid regions of the country;

(iii) soils growing pulses have high level of salinity and alkalinity in semi-arid tropics and Indo-Gangetic plains;

(iv) poor drainage leading to water logging during rainy season in the States of Uttar Pradesh, Bihar, West Bengal, Chhattisgarh,

Madhya Pradesh and Jharkhand causes substantial yield losses in pigeon-pea in particular. Farmers use their own saved seeds and practically use no phosphatic fertilisers. Green revolution pushed pulses cultivation in marginal and sub-marginal lands resulting in declining productivity;

(v) pulses being rich in nitrogen and phosphorus content are easy victims of insects, pests and diseases which severely reduce the productivity of chickpea, pigeon-pea and lentil;

(vi) while small and marginal farmers more often prefer growing staple cereals for home consumption, resourceful farmers prefer growing cash crops on larger area rather than pulses;

(vii) inability of small, marginal and tenant farmers to access institutional creditand technical services which discourage them to purchase and use seeds of high-yielding varieties and plant nutrients;

(viii) only three crops (paddy, wheat and sugarcane) have captured 70 per cent subsidies provided for seeds, fertilisers, irrigation and pesticides, leaving insignificant share for pulses growers;

(ix) unattractive and cumbersome claim settlement procedure of crop insurance scheme;

(x) minimum support prices (MSP) for pulses do not benefit pulses growers because of low concern of national agricultural marketing federation (NAFED) and small farmers' agri-business consortium (SFAC) to procure pulses.

In the years to come, the grain yield is likely to be much more affected by extreme temperature under the impact of recent global climate change.

Ineffectiveness of Minimum Support Price

The NAFED and SFAC are responsible to procure pulses under MSP but unfortunately they procured insignificant quantity one per cent to four per cent of output against 28 per cent to 30 per cent of cereals during (2012-13 to 2014-15) despite MSP for pulses in last five years were higher than rice and wheat. Procurement was insignificant amounting to 6.56 lakh tonnes during July 2013- June 2014 reflecting no impact of higher MSP. The expert committee has aptly observed that despite MSP are announced for 23 commodities substantial benefits accrue to wheat and rice growers in selected states leaving pulse-growers often receiving prices much below MSP. Absence of efficient marketing arrangement and production constraints created huge gap between demand and supply resorting to imports.

Demand by 2030 and 2050

According to Indian Institute for Pulse Research, by 2030 and 2050 demand for pulses would be around 32 MT and 50 MT respectively. This would need additional 3.0 to.5.0 MHA area and productivity per hectare to increase to 1361 kg and 1500 kg respectively. In fact, India needs to produce 40 MT of pulses annually in order to meet per capita consumption requirement of 80 grams/day of pulses as recommended by WHO against present consumption of 27.2 grams/day/capita for 1,282 million people. This can be achieved by encouraging farmers to adopt following promising cropping systems which researchers have evolved and successfully demonstrated their economic benefits to farmers. .

Chickpea in Rice-fallows

Agriculture universities in States of Chhattisgarh, Jharkhand, Odisha, West Bengal and eastern Madhya Pradesh have established that short-duration varieties of chickpea and lentil can be successfully grown after rice harvest that can yield 1000 to 2500 kg/ha. Also, farmers preferred *kabuli* varieties (ICCV 2, KAK 2 and JGK) in most areas as they fetch high market prices. More recently, a heat tolerant chickpea variety JG 14 has been found highly adaptable to late-sown conditions in the rice fallow area in above states. India has been one among four countries in the prosperous agricultural Indo-Gangetic plains of South Asia raising rice in about 14.3 million hectares which, however, remain fallow during the winter season. Winter pulses, particularly chickpea, lentil and grass pea can be successfully raised on these rice-fallows which can optimally utilise the available land resources and enhance output of pulses.

Pigeon-pea in Rice-Wheat cropping system

Experiments on research stations and field trials on farmers' fields during 1999-2002 using extra-short duration pigeon-pea varieties, viz. ICPL 88039, in States of Haryana and Western Uttar Pradesh confirmed that pigeon pea can be grown profitably in place of rice during the monsoon season (sown in late-May and harvested in late-October or early November) allowing timely sowing of wheat crop. Pigeon-pea yields were 1500 to 3000 kg/ha with an average of 2000 kg/ha. As pigeon-pea adds nitrogen through biological nitrogen fixation process accompanied by leaf fall (contributing about 40-50 kg N to the system), the succeeding wheat crop needs less nitrogenous fertilisers. The net economic returns under pigeon pea-wheat system were higher as compared to the rice–wheat system. Continuous rice–wheat cropping system being followed for several years in the Indo-Gangetic plain region of India has impacted adversely on soil fertility and increased incidence of pests and diseases posing a serious threat to the sustainability of the rice-wheat cropping system. The inclusion of legumes in rice-wheat cropping system promises to restore soil fertility and reduce other associated problems.

Pigeon-pea at high altitudes

Extra-short duration pigeon pea can be successfully cultivated up to the elevation of 2000 metres above sea level in Uttarakhand. A pilot study along with several on-farm trials across different elevations in Uttarakhand during 2007-08 by agricultural research institute and the department of agriculture, Uttarakhand showed that pigeon pea variety (ICPL 88039) can be grown successfully in low and medium hill regions. It proved to be highly adaptable in regions with high elevations and yielded 1,800 kg/ha of grains. As the long duration of cold and frost can severely damage the foliage and flowers of pigeon pea, its cultivation should be confined only to regions with low and mid-hill regions. Farmers' willingness to cultivate extensively extra-short duration pigeon pea cultivar ICPL 88039 in Uttarakhand can be profitably capitalised.

Application of Micronutrients

Legumes fix atmospheric nitrogen. Arrangement needs to ensure provision of quality Rhizobium inoculum. A recent study by ICRISAT indicated that soils in many states in India are deficient in micro-nutrients such as boron, sulphur, zinc and magnesium. Application of small quantities (0.5 to 2 kg /ha) has resulted in 40 per cent-120 per cent increase in grain yield. Under a mission to boost productivity of rain-fed agriculture through science-led interventions in Karnataka the improved management practices (including application of micronutrients) have increased the yield by 31 per cent-57 per cent in green gram, 26 per cent-38 per cent in pigeon-pea and 27 per cent-39 per cent in chickpea during 2010-11. Similarly, in 2011-12 black gram and green gram grain yields increased by 33 per cent-42 per cent in response to improved management practices as compared to farmers' traditional management practices.

Hence, it is necessary to

(i) replicate these studies in different agro-ecological regions and

(ii) through massive demonstrations make farmers aware of the importance of micro-nutrients and improved management practices and make available micronutrients in remote areas to enhance productivity and production of pulses.

Pulses under Irrigation

Pulses often experience severe moisture stress since they are largely grown in rain-fed conditions. Soil water is limiting the growth and yields of cowpea, pigeon-pea, and chickpea in particular. Field studies suggest that application of small quantity of water as supplemental irrigation to rain-fed pulses during critical stages of growth can substantially improve yield. Studies have shown that by increasing the availability of soil moisture from 150 mm to 300 mm increases yield by 100 per cent to 3520 kg/ha. Studies have shown yields in chickpea and lentil increased linearly with the amount of water applied. Since there is significant scope for providing supplemental irrigation systematic efforts need to be made to educate, incentivise and encourage farmers to adopt drip/sprinkler irrigation system.

Andhra Pradesh State Shows the Way

Farmers in southern India started growing short-duration and wilt resistant chickpea varieties in rain-fed rice-fallow lands. Andhra Pradesh, a State once considered unsuited for chickpea cultivation due to its warm and short-season environment, has now ushered in *chickpea revolution* because of growing early maturing chickpea varieties. During 2000-09, the state increased area five times under chickpea from 102,000 hectares to 602,000 hectares and raised yields 2.4 times per hectare from 583 kg/ha to 1407 kg/ha, synergic effect of which was nine times increase in the output from 95,000 tonnes to 8,84, 000 tonnes. Between 1991 and 2010 average increase in yield of two major pulse crops viz. chickpea and pigeon-pea was as high as 81 per cent to 100 per cent in Andhra Pradesh recording substantially higher increase in yield than national average yield increase.

The attributes to such a phenomenal rise in the output included, *inter alia*

(i) development and on time availability of high-yielding, short-duration, *Fusarium* wilt resistant varieties suited to short-season and warmer environments of southern India;

(ii) motivation and willingness of a large number of farmers to adopt improved varieties and easy access to production technologies;

(iii) successful commercial cultivation by mechanising field operations and efficient management to minimise incidence of pod-borer infestation;

(iv) availability of grain storage facilities to farmers at local level at affordable cost. Andhra Pradesh has now the highest average yield of 1400 kg/ha with more than 80 per cent of the chickpea area under improved short-duration cultivars.

Findings that need focused attention

When already proven and demonstrated technologies as mentioned above are available there is greater need now than before to increase the productivity and production of pulses and arrest abrupt price-rise by focusing attention on following.

Campaign: Launching a massive "Grow More Pulses Campaign" to motivate and incentivise farmers to:

(i) include chickpea in rice-fallows, pigeon-pea in rice-wheat cropping system and pigeon-pea at high altitudes;

(ii) bring more area under pulses, raise pulses under irrigation, use high-yielding varieties of pulses and adopt efficient crop production technologies including application of micronutrients;

(iii) disseminate the technology along with putting in place a farmer-friendly mechanism to make them available on time quality critical inputs including institutional credit and insurance cover at affordable prices among farmers.

Research: Adequate financial and other resources must be committed to research and development efforts exclusively for pulse-crops in proportion to currently provided to cereals and cash crops.

Improved varieties with drought tolerance: Since pulses are raised under rain-fed conditions the development of drought tolerant/resistant varieties of pulses can provide long-term solution against adverse effects of recurrent droughts in one or the other part of the country every year. Economic returns on financial investment in research on evolving/breeding crop varieties drought-proof or drought-tolerance) would be higher compared to spending huge amount of financial and other resources on drought management programmes and strategies every year.

Researches need to be intensified to

(a) match crop maturity period with soil moisture availability as a part of major strategy to avoid drought stress. Hence, emphasis in crop improvement programmes has to be to develop high-yielding, short-duration strains which escape terminal drought. These short duration varieties can facilitate farmers to include them in a given cropping system;

(b) develop varieties with significant amount of diversity in maturity-durations of pulse crops that can facilitate their cultivation in different locations and under different production systems to increase production.

Seed Production and distribution: In order to partially guarantee sustenance livelihood to rising numbers of small and marginal farmers who are often more vulnerable to shocks of crop failure and create an impact of the potential economic benefits of research on evolving drought-tolerant varieties of pulses on rural economy, a well-organised institutional infrastructure in each agro-ecological region would be required for multiplication and distribution of seeds of drought-tolerant varieties to meet farmers' demand on time.

Field surveys show that in recent past a number of improved varieties of pulses have been released for cultivation. However, resource-poor farmers in many locations/states have yet not been motivated to cultivate them. This is because of the fact that a large number of small-holders are not aware of these high-yielding varieties on one hand and on the other most knowledgeable farmers have no easy and reliable access to quality seeds of these varieties. This, therefore, necessitates launching a campaign to create awareness/demand among farmers as also an action-plan to make available quality seeds to farmers at affordable price and on time. For this investment in financial and human resources is a must to create need-based institutional mechanism to create demand of seeds from farmers and cost-efficient seed delivery system and simultaneously augmenting the production of required amount of quality seeds breeder, foundation and certified seeds) under the supervision of the seed regulatory body. Effective coordination is called for among various village PRIs, departments of the State and Union Government.

The seed replacement rate by improved strains in India varies from 14 per cent in chickpea to 35 per cent in soybean, indicating that a majority of the farmers still use their own saved seeds. This is attributed to factors viz. among others

(a) low seed multiplication rate of legumes;

(b) easy access to reuse grains as seeds from previous harvest;

(c) lack of inadequate demand for specific varieties in different agro-ecological regions that suit to consumers' needs;

(d) seed production is mostly confined to potential areas with better infrastructure facilities of seed processing, quality control, storage and skilled workers.

Thus, a strategic action-plan would simultaneously be necessary to motivate farmers to switch over to using these seeds by replacing the use of traditional/home preserved seeds in next three years. Programmes need to be designed and popularised to ensure availability of quality seeds of drought /pest-resistant and high-yielding varieties accompanied by post-harvest technology that can motivate farmers of all sizes of landholdings to allocate fairly reasonable area and resources under pulses.

Acknowledging the importance of quality seeds in crop production as a *sine qua non* the government has established National and State Seed Corporations which have been implementing seed production projects to enhance seed availability of improved varieties to farmers. They need to be strengthened and made efficient to serve the cause of farmers as the informal seed sector is still the dominant player. For example, despite India being the leading global lentil producer, more than 95 per cent of lentil seed in India comes from the informal sector. The situation is similar in respect to other pulses too. Since private companies find pulses-seed business not profitable, accredited seed companies engaged in production, processing and marketing of seeds of other crops can be encouraged to include pulses in their business and create effective demand among pulse-growing farmers. These companies should have easy access to breeder and foundation seed and institutional credit and encouraged to expand their capacities. This should help them put in place appropriate marketing strategies including delivery systems targeting remote areas and small farmers. While research institutes and state agricultural universities have been playing a significant role in evolving high-yielding varieties of pulses and development of seed sector, Public-Private-Partnership mode can facilitate to increase the availability of breeder and foundation seeds to meet the current and emerging needs of seed producer-companies.

In fact, it is time to thoroughly understand and critically assess the current status of formal and informal seed sector, its strength comparative advantages and complementarity and weaknesses in addressing the issue of the delivery of quality seeds to farmers, particularly small and marginal farmers.

Area Expansion: Additional area of 2.5 MHA can be brought under pulses through adopting in cropping system like green/black gram as catch crop in summer season under cereal-based cropping system

(i) inter-cropping with short-duration pulses (mung, urad, cowpea) in sugarcane, millets, cotton etc.

(ii) new cropping system such as pigeon-pea-wheat in northern region, rice-lentil in eastern region and urad-rice in southern peninsula.

Mechanisation: As the currently available varieties of pulses are not suited to mechanical harvesting pulses are harvested manually. In developed countries, such as Australia, Canada and USA, pulses like chickpea, lentils etc. are harvested mechanically which have distinct advantages. In India, with continuously increasing labour cost, farmers find manual harvesting of pulses very expensive and they would like to increasingly opt for mechanical harvesting. The farmers in Andhra Pradesh are anxious to switch over to chickpea cultivars suited to mechanical harvesting and they voice their demand for evolving and supplying such varieties. Therefore, research should focus to reduce cost of cultivation substantially by promoting the use of post-emergence herbicides in controlling weeds by developing herbicide-tolerant cultivars. This is necessary since pulses in general are sensitive to herbicides which compel manual weeding to control weeds. Research, therefore, needs to be pursued to evolve herbicide-tolerant cultivars that offer opportunity of controlling weeds through need-based applications of herbicides. Weed management through application of herbicides can be economical and facilitate zero-tillage or minimum tillage methods.

Marketing : Potential of markets should be harnessed through

(i) value chain approach right from the production at farm level and encompassing post-harvest, processing, packaging, transportation to marketing for small and marginal farmers to reduce losses/ wastages and increase income;

(ii) better price discovery and transparency for which facilities have been created for electronic trading of pulses in few Agricultural Produce Markets in States of Karnataka, Andhra Pradesh and Telangana; and

(iii) recently envisioned National Common Market in India.

References

1. Government of India (2014), Agricultural Statistics at a Glance, Department of Agriculture and Cooperation, New Delhi, India.
2. Government of India (2014), Annual Report, Department of Agriculture and Cooperation, New Delhi, India.
3. Government of India (2015), Commodity Profile: Pulse, Ministry of Agriculture, New Delhi, India.
4. Indian Institute of Pulse Research (2013), Vision 2050, Hyderabad, India.
5. Reddy A. (2016), Spikes In Pulses Prices Kurukshetra, Vol. 64, No. 3, pp. 44-47, New Delhi, India.
6. www.apeda.gov,in/apedawebsite

8

Food Security in India: Issues and Strategies

Parveen Kumar

Asia lies at the centre of the global food security challenge of the twenty first century. The smallholder farmers supplying majority of the continents food confront continued poverty as they struggle to raise output in the face of degrading soils, static productivity, looming water shortages and unpredictable effects of climate change. How countries in the region, particularly China and India feed their citizens in coming decades is vital to the wider security of Asia and rest of the world. Although the rate of population growth in Asia has slowed down, the number of peoples continues to rise and by 2050 the region is still expected to account for around 55 per cent of the world's 9.6 billion peoples (Dutta, B. M., 2014). The history is full of examples when food security has led to riots. This has reawakened fears about the world's future ability to feed itself, as growing populations place greater demands on agricultural systems that have now to operate in increasingly difficult environmental and climatic conditions. Pressures on land, water and energy resources are increasing. Competition over their use is intensifying. The world's population is expected to exceed nine billion by 2050 up from today's seven billion. Feeding nine billion population is estimated to require about 70 per cent more food by 2050 and almost double food production in developing countries according to the Food and Agricultural Organisation of the UN. Under such a scenario, ensuring food security for the masses is going to be the major challenge for the scientific institutions and community all over the globe.

Food security is achieved when all peoples at all times have physical and economic access to sufficient, safe and nutritious food (World Food Summit, 1996). Achieving food security hinges significantly on how inclusive growth is. Economic growth has proved effective in reducing absolute poverty. But unless its benefits are shared equitably, hunger and malnutrition will persist. Rapid growth has come with increase inequality. Evidence shows that food prices increase disproportionately affect the poor and negate efforts aimed at poverty reduction. The poor spends a large portion of their income on food and thus any increase in the prices of food items slows the pace of poverty reduction. Asian Development Bank 2012 reports that each year from 2001 to 2010, an additional 112 million in Asia and the Pacific could have escaped poverty had food prices not increased.

The era of economic reforms in India started in the nineties at the time of Late Prime Minister P.V. Narasimha Rao at the helm and Dr Manmohan Singh being the Finance Minister. It led to the liberalisation, privatisation and globalisation of the economy. The consequent disinvestment, tax and banking reforms saw accelerated GDP growth rate of above five per cent for the period 19911-92 to 2003-04 and above six per cent for the period 2003-04 to 2011-12. Agriculture has been the backbone of Indian economy with a large segment of the population directly or indirectly dependent on agriculture for their livelihood. The country has one of the largest cultivable areas in the world for which we have the largest men power. We have now record food grains production, but yet millions in the country suffer from hunger, poverty and malnutrition. Agriculture it seems is not going the desired way. The farming community itself feels being dejected and deceived. Agriculture sector needs transformation to ensure livelihood for farmers and for food security. This transformation has to be accompanied by enhanced productivity and increased production; judicious use of our resources and efficient utilisation of inputs. Years have witnessed remarkable changes in this sector. Agriculture sector has witnessed structural changes throughout the years and the momentum has now shifted from commodity based approach to diversification, from individual isolated efforts to partnerships while covering all the stakeholders, from chemical intensive agriculture to the climate smart agriculture and much more. The chapter deals with the various issues pertaining to agriculture and food security in India and the strategies to achieve food security for all.

Indian agriculture: Some important aspects

(a) Farmers perception of agriculture

The report of the Swaminathan Commission on Farmers also begins by stating, "This report is designed to serve as a wakeup call on the nation on the deteriorating farm conditions. The very phrase wakeup call implies that agriculture is in serious crisis and if a proper strategy is not evolved to deal with it, the outcome can be disastrous. The findings from a survey conducted by the Centre for the Study of Developing Societies (CSDS) in the late 2013 among 5,480 farmers spread across 18 states reveal that 47 per cent farmers believe that their overall condition was bad; 62 per cent were willing to leave farming if there was an option; 37 per cent would not like their children to be farmers. Today we talk of inclusive development and it cannot be inclusive if we do not include those who are a part and parcel of the agricultural sector and yes of course, I mean the farmers. The rights based model of inclusive development has all the potential to bring larger and larger number of peoples in its ambit. The policy fatigue appears to be constraining the diversification and modernisation of agriculture. Renewed efforts have to be put in this sector for making it more efficient, sustainable and capable of supporting a large percentage of population.

Table 8.1: Perception of farmers regarding agriculture

S. No.	*Parameter*	*Percentage*
1	Overall condition is bad	47
2	Willing to leave farming	62
3	Do not want their children's to be farmers	37

The 70th National Sample Survey Organisation (NSSO) 2014 has estimated that average income of farmers is Rs 6,426 and this is even far less than the monthly salary of a class IV employee in the country. Total allocation of Rs 35,894 crores is a substantial increase from the previous year's budget.

(b) The declining trend

There has been a robust growth in food grain production. While countries like China and Indonesia have experienced more total rapid factor productivity, the technology fatigue in India despite it being an agrarian economy still remains an important area for attention. The agricultural output share is declining faster than the share of employment in agriculture. Agriculture today is the largest employer in developing Asia but not the largest sector by GDP in any Asian country. If we have a critical look on Indian economy, the statistics reveals that 1950; 60 per cent was contributed by agriculture, 13 per cent by industry and 27 per cent by services to the GDP. Similarly the share of labour force in 1950, agriculture accounted for 73 per cent, industry 11 per cent and services 16 per cent of total employment. But a couple of years ago see how the things changed. The share of agriculture came down to 13.7 per cent while those of industry and services went up to 21.5 and 64.8 per cent respectively. Similarly agriculture which was largest employer accounting for 60 per cent of the labour force in 1950 employed 49 per cent followed by service 31 per cent followed by industries at 20 per cent.

Table 8.2: Share of different sectors in the economy over the years (1950-2013)

S. No.	*Sector*	*Contribution (per cent)*	
		1950	*2013*
1	Agriculture	60	13.7
2	Industry	13	21.5
3	Services	27	64.8

Table 3: Share of labour force in different sectors over the years (1950-2012)

S. No.	*Sector*	*Contribution (per cent)*	
		1950	*2012*
1	Agriculture	73	49
2	Industry	11	20
3	Service	16	31

(c) The Defeminisation of Indian agriculture

In one decade there has been a 14 per cent reduction in female agricultural farmers and 24 per cent increase in female agricultural labourers. As far as the data regarding the number of female farmers is concerned figures are not satisfactory. There has been a continuous Defeminisation of Indian agriculture. The decrease in the no. of female farmers and corresponding increase in the female agriculture labourers points out that something wrong with Indian agriculture. Over the years lakh of women have lost the ownership rights over their lands.

Table 8.4: Female farmers and female agricultural labourers over the decade (2001-2011)

S. No.	*Year*	*No. of female farmers (Crores)*	*No. of female agricultural labourers (Crores)*	*Percentage increase/decrease*
1	2001	4.19	4.95	-14
2	2011	3.60	6.16	+24

The average farm size has been declining. The slow growth of opportunities in the non-farm employment sector has led to the proliferation of tiny and economically non-viable holdings (NCF, 2006). The uncertainties in agriculture are increasing. This has also led to distress migration a rise in the number of female headed households in rural areas and general increase in women's work burden and vulnerability (Planning Commission, 2006). The NCF has identified five basic factors which are central to the present crisis. These are unfinished agenda in land reforms, quality and quantity of water, technological fatigue, access adequacy and timeliness of institutional credit and opportunities for assured remunerative marketing (NCF, 2004). The private sector participation in Research and Development has been on the rise. Recent estimates reveal that the business funding (largely private) for agricultural Research and Development constituted about 11 per cent of the total R and D funding (Pal and Jha, 2007).

(d) Peasant Indebtness

With the advent of green revolution in the seventies of the last century dwarf varieties of wheat and rice were introduced which required more water and use of chemical fertilisers and pesticides. Big companies dealing in fertilisers, seeds and plant protection chemicals launched a massive campaign to sell their products resulting in an inordinate use of these inputs in agriculture. Farmers used heavy dose of inputs to get higher yields and when crops failed due to one or the other reason, they found themselves unable to pay for the inputs they had purchased. The situation was further exploited by moneylenders and the '*sahukars*'. The peasant indebtness is also another dimension of the structural change in the agriculture sector of the country. The last NSS report says that in Andhra Pradesh, 93 per cent small and marginal farmers are under debt and in Telangana 89 per cent are under debt. In Tamil Nadu 82.5 per cent are under debt and in Punjab 53 per cent are under debt. The average level of debt in Telangana is Rs 2.40 lakh per house hold. In all, as many 52 per cent farmers households are under debt. About 52 per cent of all the agricultural households in the country were estimated to be indebted. Though the average amount of loan outstanding per farm household has been 47,000. While it is the highest for states like Kerala followed by Andhra Pradesh, it is the lowest for the states like Chhattisgarh and Jharkhand.

Table 8.5: Average amount of loan outstanding per farm household (SECC 2011)

S. No.	*State*	*Loan outstanding*
1	Kerala	2,13,600
2	Andhra Pradesh	1,23,400
3	Punjab	1,19,500
4	Assam	3,400
5	Jharkhand	5,700
6	Chhattisgarh	10,200

Although the state of Kerala has the highest amount of loan outstanding, yet what should be a sigh of relief for the state is that only 2.2 per cent of this loan is from money lenders. In other states the percentage is much higher. In case of Bihar, 51.3 per cent of the loan outstanding is from the money lenders. It is closely followed by Andhra Pradesh (49.5 per cent), Rajasthan (43.9 per cent), Jharkhand (25.9 per cent), Tamil Nadu (25.5 per cent), Madhya Pradesh (24.2 per cent), Punjab (15 per cent) and Maharashtra (5 per cent).

(e) The rising landlessness

The socioeconomic census data (2011) also reveals the sorry state of affairs with regards to the landlessness. It shows that whereas in 2001, 45 per cent schedule tribe farmers were working on their own land, but in 2011 only 35 per cent of them were found working on their own lands. Similarly, regarding schedule caste category we find that in 2001, while 20 per cent farmers were working in their own land, the percentage came down to 15 in 2011. In 2001, 35 per cent of the peoples working in agriculture reported themselves to be landless agricultural labourers and in 2011 this number increased to 44.4 per cent. Thus, we conclude that poor lost land across all categories.

A report of the National Crime Record Bureau (2014) reveals that of the 70 people who commit suicide everyday in agriculture 33 are engaged in agriculture. The report further says that there were 12360 agriculture related deaths in 2014 of which 6,710 were farm labourers and remaining 5,650 were farmers. Again of the 5,650 farmers 4087 were small and marginal farmers. This exposes the vulnerability of the small farmers.

Table 8.6: The declining percentage of Schedule Caste and Schedule Tribe farmers (2001-2011)

Category of farmers (%)	*2001*	*2011*
Schedule Castes	20	15
Schedule Tribes	45	35
Landless agricultural labourers	35	44.4

Over 20 per cent of the farmers who commit suicide 1163 were bankrupt or severely indebted. 965 of these farmers committed suicide after going bankrupt due to crop loan, 952 killed themselves due to crop failure and 250 suicides were attributed to drug abuse and alcoholic character. If we see the age composition of the farmers ending their life, two-third of them were between 30 to 60 years, 59 of them were less than 18 years and 579 were above the age of 60. Five states alone Maharashtra, Telangana, Madhya Pradesh, Chhattisgarh and Andhra Pradesh accounted for 86.6 per cent of the farmers' suicide.

(f) Research drought

Despite tall promises by the successive regimes at the centre to increase the budget to two per cent of GDP, the budgetry support for research in the country has remained static at less than 0.9 per cent. With barely two lakh researchers in a country of over 1.2 billion peoples, India has one of the lowest densities of scientific workforce ranking below Chile, Kenya, USA and UK.

Table 8.7: Researchers per 10,000 labour force

S. No.	*Country*	*Researchers*
1	India	4
2	Kenya	6
3	Chile	7
4	Brazil	14
5	China	18
6	Russia	58
7	UK	79
8	USA	79

What is alarming is the scarcity of papers to publish and unfortunately this leads to negligible patents. In 2013, South Korea filed over 4400 patents per one million of population, while India could manage only 17.

Table 8.8: Patents applications filed per one million populations

S. No.	*Country*	*Researchers*
1	India	17
2	Brazil	34
3	Russia	237
4	China	541
5	Canada	748
6	USA	910
7	Germany	2288
8	Japan	3716
9	South Korea	4451

Even as US spends over US $ 3,43,000 per researcher, India manages to spend US $171,000 which is more than what countries like Pakistan and Spain spend and almost equal to China who is spending US $1,73,000.

Table 8.9: Average spending (in US $) per researcher

S. No.	*Country*	*Researchers*
1	India	1,71,000
2	China	1,73,000
3	UK	1,55,000
4	Canada	1,57,000
5	Brazil	1,81,000
6	South Korea	2,02,000
7	Japan	2,26,000
8	USA	3,42,000

Indian scholarly impact measured by number of times papers from the country are cited in other research work was 30 per cent below the world average in 2013.

Strategies to achieve Food Security

Finance Minister while presenting the union budget 2016-17 has rightly said that we need to think beyond food security and give back to our farmers a sense of income security and to provide socio-economic security to every Indian, especially the poor and the vulnerable.

(a) Increasing productivity

Although we have increased production of food grains in the country many times yet what is alarming is that our productivity is not at par with any of the other countries of the region. For most of the crops our production per hectare has been static just hovering around particular digits. As the land is a limiting resource, it becomes imperative to increase the per hectare production of various crops to increase the production. This can be possible with high yielding varieties, scientific ways of cultivating crops, avoiding loss due to insect, pests and diseases by suitable crop management strategies that make minimum use of the harmful chemicals. Pulses are also an important part of the human diet.

(b) Promoting high value crops

The production of fruits and vegetables is now higher than the food grains. In the past one decade alone, horticultural production has increased by nearly seventy per cent from around 167 million tonnes in 2004-05 to over 283 million tonnes in 2014-15. This is higher than the food grain production of 252.68 million tonnes as per fourth revised estimates for 2014-15. What is remarkable with this achievement is that the small and marginal farmers have taken a lead in this direction and a sizable chunk of land that has been brought under horticulture crops is irrigated. Another interesting fact according to agriculture census 2011-12 is that over 87 per cent of the total vegetables and 90 per cent of the fruits are grown by small and marginal farmers. This is because the cultivation of vegetable is a labour intensive process and the small farmers can manage it with their own family labour. It has been rightly called as the greater diversification of agriculture towards high value commodities such as fruits, vegetables and livestock products (Rao *et al.*, 2004). The year 2012 created a record. For the first time in the country, the total production from horticulture exceeded output from grains. The horticultural production reached 277.4 million tonnes in 2013-14 and to over 283 million tonnes in 2014-15. This figure takes the country to being the second largest producer of horticulture produce after China.

The two consecutive droughts and unfavourable weather in 2014 and 2015 made a dent in the Indian food gain production but horticulture sector escaped these weather shocks and registered record production in 2014-15. A report, 'Horticulture Statistics at a Glance 2015' released by Ministry of Agriculture and Family Welfare, Government of India showed that most horticultural crops are grown with assured irrigation and therefore are more resilient to monsoon deficits. Eight vegetables that make up 74 per cent of the total vegetable production in the country have 73 per cent access to irrigation. In comparison 50 per cent of the area under food grain has access to irrigation. Barring wheat which is an irrigated crop, irrigation access varies from 16 per cent for pulses to 59 per cent for rice. In India, rice and wheat comprise 70 per cent of agriculture produce but less than 25 per cent by value. In other words rice and wheat are low value crops; yet the area under them has not shown any significant decline in the last decade. Government data shows that consumption of wheat and rice has been declining around 1-2 per cent in both rural and urban areas while the demand for fruits and vegetables has been rising by 2-3 per cent annually. Gross returns on an average are double the cost in fruits and vegetables.

Table 8.10: Horticultural Production in India

S. No.	*Item*	*Production (million tonnes)*
1	Fruits	81
2	Vegetables	162
3	Spices	5.7
4	Nuts and Plantation products	17
5	Aromatic horticulture products	1.0
6	Flowers	1.7

(c) Avoiding Food wastage

There is a difference between food loss and food waste. A report of the Food and Agricultural Organisation (2011) distinguished between the two. While Food loss is more common in developing countries and it occurs during the harvest, post-harvest and processing phase. Food loss occurs due to poor infrastructure, poor temperature management, low levels of technology and absence of clod chains and value addition of food products. Food waste on the other hand is more of a problem in developed world like the United States and the United Kingdom where the retailers and consumers throw perfectly edible foods into the trash. About 24 per cent of all calories currently produced for human consumption are lost or wasted. It has been estimated that 30 to 40 per cent of the food produced on earth gets wasted before it can be consumed. The food losses can be avoided by proper understanding of harvest indices of plant foods and how maturity is related to quality and shelf life, proper sorting and grading practices. Adequate temperature and management of relative humidity, appropriate packaging, avoiding unnecessary delay in marketing and adopting suitable post-harvest measures.

(d) Creating Value Chains

From what was once a commodity based approach the focus is now being given to the development of value chains. The most unfortunate aspect of Indian agriculture has been the exclusion of the farmers from the value chain system. The input prices are fixed by the corporate producers and the selling price of the produce is decided by the government. In this process the farmers especially the marginal and the small ones farmers have lost themselves to the market forces. The studies conducted on the producer's share in the consumer's price brings out how under regulated markets in Punjab the share of farmers shrinks as and when the number of intermediate increases. In case of Paddy the producers share is around 53 per cent while in case of wheat it has been 73 per cent. In case of fruits, it falls to 20-25 per cent of the consumer price while in case of vegetables this share ranges from 42 to 50 per cent (Gill, 2016). Actually the system also works in favour of the middlemen. Without bringing the farmers in the value chain their share in the consumer price cannot be increased. The basic objective behind the development of value chains is to cover all the stakeholders including producers, processors who add value to commodities and consumers who always look for better quality with the ultimate aim of providing better returns for producers. Under National Agriculture Innovative Project (NAIP) several good value chains were established and innovative approaches and interventions were made at production stage leading to improved yields. In these value chains 47 Indian Council of Agricultural Research Institutions, 44 state Agricultural Universities, 51 private industries and 19 NGO's participated (Ezekiel, R. 2014). The value chain farmers get enhanced income through better productivity. Also the wastage is reduced considerably. At the same time the processors got better utilisation through use of innovative technologies and quality and exporters and marketers got better utilisation through better price on account of better quality and increased value addition. Another way to bring farmers in the value chain is to promote collective efforts through cooperatives, Self Help groups, Farmer producer organisations. Recently the Government of India has started National Agricultural Market to provide an electronic platform to the farmers for marketing of their produce by integrating local markets with the national markets. For this the concerned state has to amend the Agriculture Produce Marketing (APMC) Act to include provision of electronic trading and to provide a single license to anyone willing to trade in the NAM. Connecting poor farmers with modern market value chains can revitalise Asia Pacific rural economies. A UN FAO report presented recently reveal that the government across the Asia Pacific region should provide an enabling environment to support the integration of agriculture outputs of poor smallholder farmers into more efficient value chains offering them a chance to improve their livelihoods and revitalise rural economies.

(e) Climate smart agriculture

Climate change has become a serious threat to agriculture. The rising temperatures and the uncertainty of climate is severely impacting the yields crops. For that climate smart agriculture is now being practiced and advocated all over the globe. Climate smart agriculture includes simple adaptation practices such as change in sowing dates and crop varieties, bridging yield gaps, development of plant resistant genotypes, providing weather linked insurance and natural resources management through water harvesting mulching, line sowing, use of recommended dose of fertilisers etc.

(f) Contract farming

The rapid urbanisation has also resulted in the rapid emergence and rapid expansion of supermarkets for retailing agricultural goods. Increasing consumer awareness on quality aspects has led to the development of stringent standards that the producers are forced to comply with if they are to gain from these new markets. All these developments have led to the expansion of contract farming arrangements. In order to make contract farming and effective arrangement for strong mechanisms must be in place to monitor contracts and ensure that growers who are often the more vulnerable partners are not exploited (Singh, 2005).

(g) Farmers and Markets

Linking producers with markets improves producer's livelihood. The basic objective of providing linkages to the farmers is to provide them both forward as well as backward linkages. Forward means making an assured supply of inputs and backward means that there produces is being suitable paid. Various private firms have engaged in contract type of farming with farmers in different states and they provide them with the linkages. Various studies have highlighted this fact. In a study in Punjab that examined the operations of fresh food super market (Easy Day) and its interface with farmers revealed that the supermarket farmers realised higher profits compared to non super market (traditional market supplying) farmers mainly because of higher yield and higher price realisation.

(h) Farmer to Consumer (F2C)

The concept of farm direct marketing envisages the farmers to get more shares from consumer rupee by eliminating the middlemen. It also has the advantage that the farmers are in command to set the price. Besides it also meets the satisfaction level of consumers through direct sale of the agriculture commodity by the farmers to the consumers at affordable prices. Since small quantities of farm products can be sold, small producers can participate. Good products and services can get attractive prices and therefore small farmers can be profitable, payment is usually immediate, farmers receive instant feedback from customers on products and services.

Under the F2C umbrella the following marketing strategies can be tried:

1. **Roadside markets:** Farmers mostly remain near their farms and this helps them to considerably reduce the transportation cost that they have to incur if the same would have been brought to market.
2. **Farmers markets:** Daily, weekly or biweekly farmer markets at the village or Panchayat level whereby the farmer's can display their products are also a good option. It also ensures that the consumers get a variety of food products from which to pick and in turn pays the highest price for various food products.
3. **Subscription farming:** A relatively new term the subscription farming involves particular customer base pays for their share of the produce in advance of the growing season. This gives the farmer the necessary capital to invest in the farming besides providing an outlet for the produce of the farmers.
4. **Restaurants/Hotels/ Dhabas:** These can be well suited for niche crops, usually providing year round outlet to the farmers and ensuring an assured supply of food products to the Restaurants/ Hotels/ Dhabas.

(i) Promoting rural development

Various reports have highlighted that rural development improves food security not just through higher incomes but also through increased productivity and thus food availability. Social Safety Nets also play an important role in achieving food security. They provide relief to the disadvantaged groups provided the focus is on the deprived, marginal, the small holder and the excluded one. The economic survey 2016-17 puts the country's growth rate in the year 2016-17 at 7 to 7.5 per cent.

(j) Enhancing the reach of institutional credit

The growing indebtness in agriculture is due to low access to institutional credit. The budget 2016-17 has provided 9.0 lakh crores to farm sector with an interest subvention of Rs 15000 crores. The experience till date suggests that the poor incentives that the bank have in promoting crop insurance is one of the reasons for lesser coverage of insurance schemes. Only four per cent of the premium is paid to bank as service charge, which is very low. The bank employees are overburdened with their official duties and thus they are not much interested in promoting crop insurance. The allocation of Rs 55,000 crores to new Pradhan Mantri Fasal Bima Yojana is a good step which will help more farmers to be under the cover. The new scheme envisages lesser premium by farmers, expansion in coverage of loss, higher claims and increased penetration. It recognises the need to break stagnation in production of pulses and announce incentives in the form of price guarantee for pulses just like Paddy and wheat. Another important issue is the subsidies in Indian agriculture. The subsidies worth over one lakh crore go to the well off. Let me take the case of Urea. The economic survey 2016 revealed that only 35 per cent which make up Rs 17,500 crore of the total urea subsidy of Rs 50,300 crore reached the intended beneficiaries-small and marginal farmers. It therefore suggested a two point reform package which included decontrolling urea imports to increase the number of importers and bringing area under nutrient-based subsidy regime and paying subsidy directly to the farmers. The strategy should be to shift them towards the needful and the deserving. Declaring minimum support prices well before kharif sowing operations, incentivising farmers to produce crops most prone to domestic supply pressures such as pulses should be the essential components of the strategy. Reforming Public Distribution System is also an important aspect that has to be given due importance to provide food security to all.

Allocation of Rs 900 crores as price stabilisation fund in the budget 2016-17 is a welcome step. A national level Agri-market platform called as the National Agricultural Market (NAM) has been launched which can enable the farmers using a mobile phone to sell their produce anywhere in the country where they can get a better price. The last two decades has witnessed the increasing involvement of civil society including research foundations, NGOs and others in agricultural research and extension. Many have been working with poor and helping them to access, adopt and apply new information knowledge and technology. Farmers' mobilisation through self help groups, commodity interest groups and farmer interest groups are also an important mean to fetch good returns to the farmers. Achieving food security will not require a single approach, but a multipronged approach covering all aspects of crop production from sowing to harvesting to storage and finally food distribution. All the concerned stakeholders have to work in tandem to fulfill this objective.

References

Dutta-Monika Barthwal, (2013). In *Food Security in Asia: Challenges, Policies and Implications*. The Adelphi Series.

Ezekiel, R. (2014). Public Private Partnerships in Agricultural Value Chains with Particular Reference to NAIP. Innovation in Indian Agriculture: ways forward. (Abstract).

Hall, A.J., Sivamohan, M.V.K., Clark, N., Taylor, S and Bockett, G.(2001). Why research partnerships really matter: Innovation Theory, Institutional arrangements and implications for Developing new technology for the poor; World Development, 29(5):783-797.

Pray, Carl, E. and Nagarajan, Latha (2014). The transformations of Indian agricultural input industries: Has it increased agricultural R&D? Innovation in Indian Agriculture: ways forward. (Abstract).

Livemint, S. Bera. Deficient rains spare horticulture; record production expected. Hindustan Times January 19, 2015.

Final Area and Production. Estimates for Horticultural crops for 2012-13. Government of India 2014.

Gill, S. S. (2016). First make farmers part of the value chain. The Tribune April, 26.

NCF (2004). Serving farmers and saving farming: First report of the National Commission on Farmers, New Delhi.

NCF (2004). Serving farmers and saving farming: A draft national policy for farmers, Fourth report of the National Commission on Farmers, New Delhi.

Pal, Suresh and Dayanatha Jha (2007). Public Private partnerships in Agriculture R and D: Challenges and Prospects, In Visawa Ballabh (Ed.) Institutional Alternatives and Governance of Agriculture, Academic Foundation, New Delhi.

Planning Commission (2006). Towards faster and more inclusive growth: An approach to the 11th five year plan, Draft approach to the eleventh five year plan, Government of India, New Delhi.

Rao, P. P., Birthal, S. S. Joshi, P.K. and Kar, D. (2004). Agricultural Diversification in India and role of Urbanisation MTID Discussion paper No. 77, International Food Policy Research Institute (IFPRI), Washington DC.

9

Ending 'Mal' nutrition - Food Security and Far Beyond!

Pavan Pandey and Sushrut Sharma

Traditionally a common man thinks that the malnutrition or more appropriately 'under-nutrition' is caused due to inadequate intake of food. However, the pyramid of evidence generated over last many decades proves that malnutrition is multifactorial in origin. It is this multifactorial causation which makes eliminating malnutrition a complicated issue. Everything from the educational status of parents to the place of defecation affects the nutritional status of a child. In conclusion, this chapter explains that to eliminate malnutrition we have to think far beyond 'food' security.

What is Malnutrition

Introduction: The word malnutrition is an amalgamation of two words 'Mal' meaning bad and 'nutrition' meaning food (Last, 2012). In simple terms, it is a condition which arises due to the intake of inappropriate food by an individual. The image which rushes into the mind of a common man on hearing the term "malnutrition" is that of a 'naked small thin child with brown hairs whose ribs outline are clearly visible.'However, speaking in strict scientific terms the word "malnutrition" encompasses all types of nutritional disorders whether it is caused by an insufficient intake of food, i.e., under-nutrition or undernourishment or by overconsumption of food, i.e., obesity or deficiency of specific nutrients such as Iron, Iodine or Vitamin A.

Undernutrition: In this chapter, the term malnutrition will be used in the context of undernutrition only. When the overall caloric value of food eaten by an individual is less than recommended dietary intake, the resulting state of health is known as undernourishment or undernutrition (Young, 2012). Under unfavourable circumstances a person of any gender and all age group can become malnourished but, the effect and implications of being undernourished vary with the age of the individual. Malnutrition in adult deprives the individual with sufficient muscle mass and physical work capacity so as to perform moderate to heavy work such as being employed as labour. By increasing nutritional intake, an adult can regain his/her ability to work. However, this is not the case with children especially those who are under five years of age. Normal biological development of the fetus and a child requires recommended amount of nutrient in right proportion at different stages of development so as to grow into an adult and achieve his/her full potential later in life. Deficiency of all or some nutrient at the various stages of development can result in different disorders. Such nutritional disorder can cause irreversible damage to the child's physical and mental growth.

Overnutrition: It is a type of malnutrition caused by consuming excess calories over an extended period of time (Last, 2012). Overweight and obesity — like hunger, increases susceptibility to disease and disability, reduces worker productivity, and lowers life expectancy.

Specific nutritional disorder: Many times the diet of an individual lacks a specific nutrient ingredient or has an insufficient amount of it. There is an encyclopedia of specific nutritional disorders which can affect humans. However, there are only a handful of specific nutritional disorders which effect significant proportion of world population at the same time, and such disorders are classified as nutritional disorders of public health importance. Deficiency of Iron resulting in anemia is one such problem. Anemia affects mainly women in reproductive age group (19-45 years), adolescent girls and young children. Iron deficiency is the most common and widespread nutritional disorder in the world (WHO, 2015). Iodine deficiency is another example of specific nutritional deficiency. Deficiency of Iodine during pregnancy and in early life can cause mental retardation in children which is permanent (Wu *et al.*, 2006; Zimmermann *et al.*, 2012).

Causes of Malnutrition

The origin of malnutrition is multifactorial and spans biological, social and environmental domains (Haddad *et al.,* 1995; 1999; 2002). Nutritional status of a child or adult is affected mainly by three broad categorical factors, and these are food intake, health system, and required social care (Aldermann *et al.,* 2005; Dewey and Mayers, 2011). Even before the child is born, his/her nutritional status is influenced by many external factors such as dietary intake by the mother during pregnancy, antenatal care received by the mother and hemoglobin level of the mother. After birth, the desired nutritional status of a child can be achieved if he/she is provided nutritionally- diverse and calorie-rich food during the entire period of development. Nutritional status of a child is also tremendously influenced by the health services he/she receive such as postnatal care, immunisation, oral rehydration solution, supplemental Vitamin K, and Vitamin A (Haddad *et al.,* 1999; Aldermann *et al.,* 2005). The nutritional status of a child is also significantly influenced by home and surrounding environment including safe water, sanitation, and good hygiene practices (Caincross, 2004). All these factors are indeed greatly influenced by the educational status of parents, prevailing customs in society, the attitude of health workers and sensitivity of government towards these issues (Box 9.2). A vicious and potentially lethal cycle of deteriorating nutritional status and worsening health status is created because of interaction among above mentioned factors.

Box 9.1

Glossary of terms Stunting: reflects chronic undernutrition. It is defined as a child aged 0 to 59 months whose height for age is below minus two standard deviations (< -2 S.D = moderate and severe stunting) and minus three standard deviations (< - 3 S.D = severe stunting) from the median of the WHO Child Growth Standards.**Wasting:** It reflects acute undernutrition. It is defined as a child aged 0 to 59 months whose weight for height is below minus two standard deviations (<-2 S.D = moderate and severe wasting) and minus three standard deviations (<-3S.D = severe wasting) from the median of the WHO Child Growth Standards. **Underweight:** It is defined as a child aged 0 to 59 months whose weight for age is below minus two standard deviations (< -2 S.D = moderate and severe underweight) and minus three standard deviations (< -3 S.D = severe underweight) from the median of the WHO Child Growth Standards. **Severe acute malnutrition** is defined as a child aged 6 to 59 months whose weight for height is below minus three standard deviations (< - 3 S.D) from the median of the WHO Child Growth Standards, or whose mid-upper-arm circumference less than 115 mm (< 11.5

cm), with or without nutritional edema. **Low birthweight** is defined as a weight of less than 2,500 grams at birth.

Contrary to popular perceptions, undernutrition is not merely a result of food insecurity: many children in food-secure environments and from non-poor families are underweight or stunted because of inappropriate infant feeding and care practices, poor access to health services, or poor sanitation. In most regions of the world where malnourishment among children is rampant, the most crucial factors are inadequate knowledge about the benefits of exclusive breastfeeding and complementary feeding practices and the role of micronutrients in the overall development. Availability of nutritious food, basic healthcare, prevailing customs, and social norms can be influenced by the government policies, politics, economic and social factors prevailing in a state or country. These factors vary from country to country and within the state itself. It is because of variation in these factors the nutritional status of children varies considerably across the world, across Asia and India. The relative importance given to these factors by the respective government of different country varies mainly because of economic reason, political priorities and at some places due to violent conflicts in the region.

Measuring Malnutrition in Children

There are numerous classifications given by several scientist and organisations to classify child's nutritional status. Each of this classificationsis based on anthropometric measurements of child's weight, height, and body parts other anthropometric measurements. Most widely used classification around the globe is the World Health Organisation (WHO) child growth parameters which are accepted internationally, and it is based on data collected at international level from different countries. In 2006, WHO introduced child growth standards for weight and height attained to replace the previously recommended 1977 WHO child growth reference. These new standards were based on breastfed infants and appropriately fed children of different ethnic origins raised in an optimal environment and measured using a standardised technique.WHO Classification of malnutrition builds on the statistical cut-offs for defining wasting (low weight- for- height) and stunting (low height- for- age) like those below minus (–) 2 standard deviation (SD). The new WHO growth standards confirmed earlier observations by different scientists that the effect of ethnic differences on the growth of infants and young children in populations are minimal as compared with the consequences of the environment. These new standards are endorsed by international bodies such as the United Nations Standing Committee on Nutrition, the

International Union of Nutritional Sciences and International Pediatric Association and are adopted by more than 90 countries including India (WHO, 2010).

Consequences of Malnutrition

Consequences of malnutrition can be divided into two broad groups medical/ social and financial/ economical (Richard, 2001; 2002; Hunt, 2005). Medical/social outcomes are can be understood by common man, are clearly visible to everyone and are easy to calculate. Whereas its financial/economic implications are understood only by professionals, not clearly visible, are difficult to calculate and have long-term implications.

Table 9.1: Prevalence of different form of malnutrition among 6-59 month children in India (1992/93-2013/14)

Variable	*NFHS-1*	*NFHS-2*	*NHFS-3*	*RSoC*
Moderately Underweight (Weight for age < -2 SD)	53.4	47.0	42.5	29.4
Severe Underweight (Weight for age < -3 SD)	20.6	18.0	6.4	9.4
Moderate Stunting Malnutrition (Height for age < -2 SD)	52.0	45.5	48.0	38.7
Severe Stunting (Height for age < -3 SD)	28.9	23.0	23.7	17.3
Moderate wasting Weight for height < -2 SD)	17.5	15.5	19.8	15.1
Severe Wasting Weight for height < - 3SD)	3.2	2.8	6.4	4.6

NFHS - National Family Health Survey, RSoC- Rapid Survey of Children/

Table 9.1 details the prevalence of different types of malnutrition in India over last two decades.

(a) Child mortality: About 5.9 million children under the age of five years died in the year 2015. Malnutrition, directly and indirectly, contributed to about 45 per cent of all these child deaths (WHO, 2016). Malnutrition increases the risk of death by making children more vulnerable to a severe form of common diseases. Malnourished children, particularly those with severe acute malnutrition, have a higher risk of death from common childhood illness such as diarrhea, pneumonia, measles, tuberculosis, and malaria (Caulfield *et al.,* 2004). The risk of dying increases even if a child has a mild grade of undernutrition.

Deficiency of vitamin A and Zinc are independently responsible for an estimated 0.6 million and 0.4 million child deaths every year, respectively (WHO, 2016).

(b) Cognitive importance: Development of central nervous system start from the second month of pregnancy, and most of the brain development is completed before child's second birthday (Pitkin, 2007; Pradol and Dewey, 2014). A host of maternal factors including the dietary intake and antenatal care she received have been shown to be significant determinants of intrauterine growth retardation (IUGR). Malnourished children score more poorly on tests of cognitive function, have poorer psychomotor development and fine motor skills, have lower activity levels, interact less frequently with their environments and fail to acquire skills at normal rates (Grantham-McGregor *et al.*, 1997; Grantham-McGregor, Fernald and Sethuraman, 1999). Mental retardation in the form of iodine deficiency is "the most common preventable cause of mental impairment worldwide"(Wu *et al.,* 2006; Zimmermann *et al.,* 2012). Studies in the past have proved that individuals with an iodine deficiency had, on an average, about 10 points lower IQs than comparison groups (Grantham-McGregor, Fernald, and Sethuraman, 1999).

(c) Malnutrition and schooling: Malnourished children have poorer schooling outcomes and may repeat years more often, thus increasing education costs (Hunt, 2005). Children with poor health are likely to have lower human capital (both regarding schooling and health), which negatively affects their productivity and income in the future (Richard *et al.,* 2001; 2002). There are at least two broad means by which nutrition can affect education. First, a malnourished child may have higher rates of morbidity and thus greater rates of absenteeism from school and learn less while in school. Secondly, malnutrition may affect educational outcomes via reduced capacity to learn, a direct consequence of poor nutrition on cognitive development described above.

How much Malnutrition costs to the world?

Every year, malnutrition claims lives of millions of children under age five and makes millions more stunted, which costs the global economy billions of dollars in lost productivity and healthcare cost (Hunt, 2005; Bhutto, 2016; Rollins, 2016). In financial terms, it is estimated that that micronutrient deficiency in the form of anemia, vitamin A deficiency, and Iodine deficiency may cost India nearly US $2.5 billion annually which translates into about 0.4 per cent of India's annual GDP (Gragnolati *et al.,* 2007). Another study, examining only the productivity losses associated with forgone wage employment resulting from child malnutrition, estimates the loss at US $2.3 billion in India (about 0.4 per cent of annual GDP). Malnutrition costs many developing nations an estimated 2-3 per cent of their GDP each year, extends the cycle of poverty and impedes global economic growth. Globally, the direct cost of child malnutrition is estimated at US $20 to US $30 billion per year (Horton and Steckel, 2013).

Why Invest in Malnutrition

A large body of scientific evidence proves that ensuring proper nutrition during the critical 1,000-day window from a woman's pregnancy to her child's second birthday has the potential to save lives (Shrimptom *et al.,* 2001; World Bank, 2010). This approach has potential to help millions of children to achieve their full potential, and deliver greater economic prosperity (Shekar, 2015a; 2015b).Nutritional status in childhood has a long-lasting effect on schooling (Horton and Ross, 2003; Black *et al*., 2007) future health and earning (Johnson and Schoeni, 2007; Smith *et al.,* 2007; Howlader *et al.,* 2012.). Thus, children with poor health are likely to have lower human capital (both regarding schooling and health), which hampers their productivity and earning in the future. Good health and education can lead to a higher future standard of living. Therefore, investment in nutrition is crucial to improving human capital and increase productivity, which in turn enhances economic development (Rollins, 2016). These preventive investments are not limited to the just field of nutrition but include a diverse set of interventions in water, sanitation, hygiene, health education, agriculture, and policies. It is proven that there are many indirect benefits of these investments whose beneficial effects are not just limited to children but extends to the whole population (Hunt, 2005; Penny, 2005).

The strongest and best-documented productivity-nutrition relationships are those related to human capital development in early life. The relation between nutrition and productivity is strongest in the sector of manual labour, to a significant level it has also been found in the manufacturing sector and among white collar workers (Horton and Steckel, 2013). The income–malnutrition relationship is not linear but modest. With economic development, nutritional status of children has steadily improved in most regions of the developing world. However, the pace of economic growth and reduction in malnutrition are uneven. By the past correlation between economic growth and nutrition, it is proven that rate of reduction of malnutrition is not same as the increase in economic growth rate. Countries with different rate economic growth will reduce malnutrition at a various rate, and we as one world cannot let that happen. It is because Good nutritional habit does not come naturally to people: people do not always know what feeding practices are best for their children or themselves. In the age of intense marketing, food manufacturing companies use advertising tactics to change food preferences in their favour to create an unhealthy eating pattern among masses (Caballero, 2005). Because of such misinformation, even when families who make economic progress put additional cash resources in buying unhealthy food for themselves and their children. Thus, economic growth does not always ensure healthy nutritional status for children (Caballero, 2005).

Malnutrition and Sustainable Development Goals

To transform the world, we live in the world leaders met and agreed on a common agenda which came to be known as Sustainable Development Goal. It is a set of 17 goals and has associated 169 targets to monitor its progress.The goal '2' titled "*End hunger, achieve food security and improved nutrition and promote sustainable agriculture*". SDG have given more representation to nutrition as compared to MDGs. Goal 2 has following targets under related to malnutrition under its domain:

(i) By 2030, end hunger and ensure access by all people, in particular, the poor and people in vulnerable situations, including infants, to safe, nutritious and sufficient food all year round;

(ii) By 2030, end all forms of malnutrition, including achieving, by 2025, the internationally agreed targets on stunting and wasting in children under five years of age, and address the nutritional needs of adolescent girls, pregnant and lactating women and older persons.

Road to Eliminate Malnutrition: The 1000 Days Initiatives

Providing every child with the best start in life is not only essential for the child's individual wellbeing but is a necessary investment to protect human capital and achieve world's developmental objectives. As mentioned earlier in this chapter most of the brain development is completed before child's second birthday, i.e., within first 1000 days of life itself (Maalouf-Manasseh *et al.,* 2015). Nutrition has a direct impact on brain development during the first 1,000 days, a period of rapid brain growth and development where sufficient quantities of the main nutrients are needed in differing amounts at critical periods to ensure the brain is developing properly. It is because regions of the brain (e.g., the hippocampus) and brain processes (e.g., synapse formation) require different nutrients at different times and amounts to develop (Pradol and Dewey, 2014). Deficiency of folic acid during pregnancy can cause the neural tube to form improperly and cause birth defects (Pitkin, 2007). It is important to prevent nutritional deficiency during first 100 days of life (Fig. 9.1), as, after a child's second birthday, it becomes increasingly difficult to reverse growth faltering and stunting that has already set in (Victoria *et al.,* 2008). Stunting can begin in utero due to poor maternal nutrition and continues during the first two years of life due in part to inadequate hygiene and infant and young child feeding practices, and reflects a failure to reach one's genetic potential for height.

Adequate nutrition during this period is crucial for brain development and plays a major role in a child's physical, social, emotional, and cognitive development—the four domains of early childhood development (ECD) which each child needs to develop to reach their full potential. Key nutrition risk factors associated with early childhood development during the first 1,000 days include adequate intake of energy, protein, fatty acids, and micronutrients (including iron, folic acid, thiamine and other B vitamins, iodine, vitamin A, zinc, vitamin D, and calcium) which is critical to a child's optimal development and growth (FANTA, 2009).Previously the emphasis was on children under the age of five years, while recent evidence advocates focusing on the 1,000-days of life. These 1000 days include nine month of pregnancy and first two years of child's life. During this time, more than 80.0 per cent of the child's brain develops (Godfrey *et al.,* 2001). During the first year of life infant's length increase by 50.0 per cent and first two years of life his length/height increase by 75.0 per cent of that of birth length (WHO, 2006). This is the highest rate of growth in the lifetime of humans. Evidence from a study which analysed data from 54 low- and middle-income countries point out that growth faltering on average begins during pregnancy and continues to about 24 months of age (Shrimpton *et al.,* 2001). Pre-term birth, intra-uterine growth retardation (IUGR) and low birth weight children prove that growth faltering can occur even before birth.

Traditionally the fight against malnutrition is concerned with providing nutrition, health and other forms of care to a malnourished child. All these are necessary as the malnourished child is at an increased risk of getting diseases and are at higher risk of dying from such diseases. However, this approach has one big flaw; it cannot reverse the loss of

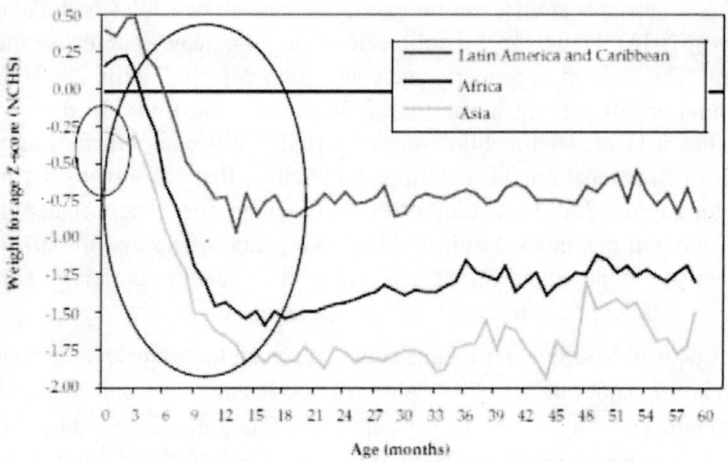

Fig. 9.1: The window of opportunity for addressing undernutrition.

The window of opportunity for improving nutrition is small—from before pregnancy through the first two years of life. The damage to physical growth, brain development, and human capital formation that occurs during this period is extensive and largely irreversible. Therefore, interventions must focus on this window of opportunity.

Source: Shrimpton and others (2001).

time, money and health that has already taken place (Mendez and Adair, 1999). For example, this approach does not reverse the neural tube defect that has already occurred or cures the mental retardation that has already occurred due to deficiency of Iodine. 1000 days initiative differs from the above approach in a way that it advocates the prevention of malnutrition. It believes that every child should attain their full potential, and it is the duty of the parents, society and the government as a whole to provide the recommended care during the critical period of first 1000 days of life (Kar *et al.,* 2008). Although one may argue that a child can become malnourished after two years of age. Following two sentences provide the rational counter-argument in this regard. First as mentioned numerous times earlier in this chapter most of the development of child's brain takes place before 100 days of life. So if a child escapes malnourishment during this period, then chances of suffering irreversible change during coming years are less. Secondly, if a woman, a family, and community are empowered to undertake the desired care of their mothers and children during the first 1000 days of life, then they would simultaneously acquire sufficient knowledge in the due process about how to take proper care of their children and mother in the coming years of life.

Components of 100 Days Initiatives

This approach does not advocate any particular or new intervention. What it does is to ensure that each mother-child pair gets the recommended evidence-based care at the most crucial stage of their life.

(i) Care before pregnancy: The neural tube formation starts within the first month of gestation.Folic acid is involved in the formation of the neural tube (Pena *et al.,* 2012). If a woman is deficient in folic acid, then there are chances that she will give birth to a child with neural tube defects. So to prevent neural tube defect it is essential to provide every woman with prophylactics folic acid before conceiving a pregnancy.

(ii) Antenatal care: During pregnancy, babies are entirely dependent on their mothers for all the nutrients supply. In simple words during pregnancy "baby eats what mother eats". The speed of brain's development can be estimated from the fact that when the baby is born their brain will contain 100 billion neurons (Pradol and Dewey, 2014). To ensure that every pregnant woman, eats the recommended diet several nutritional interventions have been assessed. These includes simple dietary advice to pregnant women, provision of balanced energy protein supplements, and high protein or isocaloric protein supplementation. A Cochrane review concluded that balanced energy protein supplementation reduced the incidence of small for gestational age (SGA) by 32 per cent and risk of stillbirths by 45 per cent (Krammer *et al.,* 2003). WHO recommends daily iron supplementation during pregnancy as part of the standard of care in populations at risk of iron deficiency (WHO, 2012). Table 9.2 details the variations in maternal health indicator in India over last two decades. Other than this all pregnant women should be given the recommended healthcare e.g. tetanus injection, screening for sexually transmitted infection etc.

Table 9.2: Maternal Health Indicator over two decade in India (1992/93- 2013/14)

Variable	*NFHS-1*	*NFHS-2*	*NHFS-3*	*RSoC*
Mothers who had at least 3 antenatal care visits for their last birth (%)	43.9	44.2	50.7	63.4
Mothers who consumed IFA for 90 days or more when they were pregnant with their last child (%)	NA	NA	22.3	23.6
Women whose Body Mass Index is below normal (%)	NA	36.2	33.0	NA
Women who are overweight or obese (%)	NA	10.6	14.8	NA
Ever-married women age 15-49 who are anaemic (%)	NA	49.7	56.2	NA
Pregnant women age 15-49 who are anaemic (%)	NA	NA	57.9	NA

NFHS- National Family Health Survey, NA-Not available (not measured), RSoC- Rapid Survey of Children

(iii) **Maternal calcium supplementation:** Gestational hypertensive disorders are the second leading cause of maternal morbidity and mortality and are associated with increased risk of preterm birth and fetal growth restriction (Srinivas *et al.,* 2009). Calcium supplementation during pregnancy in women has been shown to reduce maternal hypertensive disorders and preterm birth. Hofmeyr *et al.,* (2010) showed that calcium supplementation during pregnancy reduced the incidence of gestational hypertension by 35 per cent, preeclampsia by 55 per cent, and preterm births by 24 per cent.

(iv) **Maternal iodine supplementation or fortification:** In all regions affected by iodine deficiency, use of iodised salt is the most cost-effective way to prevent deficiency.

(v) **Early initiation of breastfeeding and avoidance of pre-lacteal feeding:** Breastfeeding within one hour of life protects the child from infections and reduces the risk of neonatal death by up to 22 per cent (Edmond, 2006). Early initiation of breastfeeding is also beneficial to the mother. Skin-to-skin contact with the mother through breastfeeding keeps the child warm and reduces the child's risk of dying of cold ('hypothermia') and fosters mother-infant bonding (Moore *et al.,* 2012). A major hurdle in ensuring

100.0 per cent initiation of breastfeeding within one hour of birth is the prevailing customs, beliefs and social norms in a different society which advocates the introduction of various types of pre-lacteal feed to newborn. A noble effort in this regard is baby friendly hospital initiative which ensures that the hospital staff supports, encourages and teaches the parents about correct breastfeeding practices (BFHI, 2006). Table 9.3 details the progress in breastfeeding and child feeding practices made in India over last two decades. WHO, UNICEF, and other prominent health agencies support the practice of exclusive breastfeeding by mothers, i.e., to give newborn only breast milk up to six months of age, no other liquid or solid not even water should be given during the six months of age (WHO, 1997). After six months of age, breastfeeding must be continued along with complementary feeding up to two years of age (WHO, 2002). Exclusively breastfed infants – are at a lower risk of diseases like diarrhea and infections involving the nose, throat and lungs, leading causes of death among infants. To ensure that exclusive breastfeeding is practiced by all mothers, it is necessary that the mother be with the newborn all the time, and it is thus essential to remove barriers in the work environment and supportive strategies such as maternity leave provision be ensured. To achieve this, we need to develop practical guidelines and tools for the implementation and monitoring of laws related to maternity entitlements.

(vi) Complementary Feeding: Complementary feeding for infants referred to the timely introduction of safe and nutritionally rich foods in addition to breastfeeding at about six months of age and provided until 24 months of age (WHO, 2002). Optimal complementary feeding involves factors such as the quantity and quality of food, frequency and timing of feeding, food hygiene, and feeding during/after illnesses. Rates of malnutrition among children usually peak during the time of complementary feeding. Growth faltering is most evident between 6-12 months, when foods of low nutrient density begin to replace breastmilk and rates of diarrheal illness due to food contamination are at their highest (Arimond *et al.,* 2004; Dewey *et al.,* 2008; 2013). Foods from different food groups such as grains, eggs, poultry, fish, meat, dairy products, fruits, and vegetables provide children with a variety of nutrients that helps

Table 9.3: Trends for Breastfeeding practices in India (1992/93- 2013/14)

Variable	*NFHS-1*	*NFHS-2*	*NHFS-3*	*RSoC*
Initiating breastfeeding with 1 hour of birth	9.5	15.8	23.4	44.6
Median duration (months) of breastfeeding among last born child	1.4	1.9	2.0	NA
Children exclusively breastfed	51.0###	55.2###	46.3***	64.9***
Children age 6-9 months receiving both solid or semi-solid food and breastmilk	31.4	33.5	55.8	50.5

###- data for exclusive breastfeeding among 0-3 months age infant

***- data for exclusive breastfeeding among 0-6 months age infant

NFHS- National Family Health Survey

them grow strong and develop completely (Arimond *et al.,* 2004). If all children in the developing world received adequate complementary feeding, stunting rates at 12 months could be cut by 20 per cent (Bhutto *et al.,* 2013).

(vii) **Vitamin A supplementation:** Children who are deficient in vitamin A have lower resistance to infections, and severe deficiency causes irreversible corneal damage, leading to partial or total blindness. Vitamin A capsules given to children twice a year can prevent blindness and lower a child's risk of death from common childhood diseases – at a cost of only 2 cents per capsule (Darlow *et al.,* 2007).

(viii) **Prevention of Anemia in children: Iron supplementation and deworming:** Children who do not have enough iron in their body are at a higher risk of developing anemia, which has devastating consequences for the child's brain development and school performance (WHO, 2012). Regular intake of iron supplements and deworming protect children against anemia and poor development.

(ix) **Feeding nutritious foods during and after illness to ensure child's appropriate recovery:** Sick children need a higher amount of food and fluids, but they have a decreased appetite; feeding them nutritious foods in small quantities and giving fluids frequently, including breast milk, helps them recover faster (Brown, 2003). Diarrhea is one of the most common causes of death among children under five. For the treatment of diarrhea, oral rehydration salts (ORS) to replace lost fluids and zinc supplements to reduce

Table 9.4: Child Health Indicator over one and half decade in India (1992/93- 2013/14)

Variable	*NFHS-1*	*NFHS-2*	*NHFS-3*	*RSoC*
Children 12-23 months fully immunized (%)	35.5	42.0	43.5	65.3
Children with diarrhea in the last 2 weeks who received ORS (%)	17.8	26.9	26.2	54.5
Children with diarrhea in the last 2 weeks taken to a health facility (%)	61.9	65.3	61.5	NA
Children with acute respiratory infection or fever in the last 2 weeks taken to a health facility (%)	NA	NA	70.5	76.9
Children age 6-35 months who are anaemic (%)	NA	74.2	78.9	NA

NFHS- National Family Health Survey, NA-Not available, RSoC- Rapid Survey of Children

the duration and severity of diarrhea and the risk of it happening again within short time (de Onis *et al.*, 2012). Table 9.4 details the some of the key child caring practices by caregivers in India.

(x) **Complete Immunisation:** Ensure every child is immunised against common diseases.

Eliminating 'Mal'nutrition; Moving from Food Security to Nutrition Security

The function of food is to provide necessary ingredient to the body so that body can carry out vital functions. No matter what kind of food a child eat, where a child eats, how expensive the food is, in the stomach, it would always be broken down into the fundamental units of nutrient viz. carbohydrate, fat, proteins, vitamins, and minerals. Each of these basic nutrients has well defined and specific role in the body's metabolism (Shekar *et al.,* 2008).

The agricultural transformation that occurred in several developing countries, including South-Asia nations, has largely ignored the nutritional transformation. Achieving nutritional transformation requires making whole agriculture and food systems sensitive towards the nutritional requirement of citizens (Masset *et al.,* 2011). Moreover, this transformation should happen in all sectors of agriculture viz. cereals, vegetable, food, milk, fish, and poultry (Herforth, Jones, and Pinstrup-Andersen, 2012). Food security must always be seen as a tool to fulfill the nutritional requirement of every individual of the different age group of the entire world(Kulwa *et al.,* 2006). Although most of the world's citizens including South Asian have access to food to meet their energy needs, their food is deficient in many essential micronutrients such as proteins, iron, vitamin A, and iodine (World Bank, 2012).

Box 9.2

What should we wish for Food security or Nutrition security?

To achieve the goal of malnutrition free world it is essential to understand the difference between food security and nutrition security, these are two different terms having entirely different outcome are very often used interchangeably. Food security, is related to access to food both in physical and economic dimensions. It means ensuring food of sufficient quality and quantity to everyone in a socially and culturally acceptable manner. It is related to agriculture and food policies. Nutrition security is multidimensional and it is dependent not only on food intake but also depends on healthy environment, and good caring practices. For example, a family may have proper access to the components of a healthy diet, but due to lack of knowledge about feeding practices, she may not be able to or may not utilises the available food in a nutritionally sound manner, thereby becoming nutritionally insecure. Nutrition security is achieved for a family when food security is complemented with a clean water, sanitary environment, adequate health services, and knowledgeable care to ensure a healthy life for all household members. In the same manner a country may be food secure, yet have children, women, girls who are nutritionally insecure. Thus, food security is an essential but not the sole requirements for nutrition security. Adopted from: Repositioning Nutrition as Central to Development *A Strategy for Large-Scale Action-World Bank (2006).*

Food security is defined as a condition related to the supply of food, and individuals' access to it. The final report of the 1996 World Food Summit states that food security exists "when all people, at all times, have physical and economic access to sufficient, safe and nutritious food to meet their dietary needs and food preferences for an active and healthy life" (FAO, 1996). As per Food and Agriculture Organisation, there are four dimensions or pillars of food security, and they are food 'availability', food 'access', and food 'utilisation' and food 'stability' (FAO, 2009; 2013). In this section we will discuss the scope of eliminating malnutrition in the concept of above mentioned four pillars of food security and will lay emphasis on why it is necessary to move from the food security to providing nutrition security.

What is food security? Two things determine the food and nutrition security framework: a physical and a temporal determinant (Perez-Escamilla *et al.,* 2008). The physical determinant compromises of first three dimensions of food security viz. availability, accessibility, and utilisation (Smith *et al.,* 2005). *Availability* refers to the supply of food in the market after cultivation in farms reflecting prevailing conditions of production and trade. So the first step in providing nutrition security is to ensure that nutritious food is available in all the market at all the time. *Access* is at the household level, reflecting the purchasing power of all households. Access is ensured when all households and all individuals within the household have sufficient resources to obtain appropriate foods for a nutritious diet.Therefore, second step in ensuring nutrition security is to ensure that the every household has access to nutritious food. To ensure nutrition security, each family should have financial means to buy food, in other words; the nutritious food should not be costly so as to hinder the family's access to a nutritious diet. Also, the family should have access to the nutritious food in their locality, in other words, they do not have to travel a long distance to get nutritious food. So just ensuring availability of food at the market is not essential but ensuring families access to it both in spatial and financial terms is equally important. Food access has an intrahousehold dimension; it is not always necessary that the available food be equally distributed within house members. Numerous factors including gender inequality hinder equity in food distribution within a given family. It must be ensured that pregnant woman, lactating mother and young children should get the food that is most appropriate in sufficient amount. The *utilisation* pillar reflects the fact that even when a household has access to food, it does not necessarily achieve nutritional security. Food utilisation is multidimensional. It refers, how the family consumes the available food. It involves the food storage, food preparation, knowing the right combination of food, knowledge about what to eat and what not to eat. Nutritional demands of a pregnant woman, lactating mother and growing child differs markedly from a normal full grown adult (Smith *et al.,* 2005). Growing children require a higher amount of protein per kilogram of body weight in comparison to adults. Not only quantity, but growing children also require good quality of proteins which must have all the essential amino acids in the right amount. Whereas as the diet of a pregnant woman should be rich in energy, protein as well as in Iron and Calcium (Ramakrishna *et al.,* 2012). Thus, caregivers should be well informed about these facts so that they can choose the right kind of food from the available options in order to ensure nutritional requirements of all household members are met. Food *stability* refers to the temporal determinant of food and nutrition security framework, and it affects all three physical elements. It refers to the fact that all the arrangement for ensuring the first three dimensions of food security must be in place around the time so as to ensure continuity in nutrition security. In short to eliminate malnutrition, each household members should have nutritious food is available to him/her at a nearby place, at a price the house can afford and it can utilise this food keeping in mind the nutritional demand of body (Kaiser *et al.,* 2002). Nutrition-sensitive agricultural interventions are recommended to address the shortcomings in the current model of agricultural transformations so as to completely solve the issue of nutrition security and malnutrition in many developing countries (Gross *et al.,*1998). A strategic intervention for translating the foods produced at the farm level into increased nutrition in rural households is the need of the hour to ensure the desired nutritional outcome (Pinstrup-Andersen *et al.,* 2011).

Food Fortification

Food fortification is a popular, safe and cost-effective in the prevention of micronutrient deficiencies and has been widely adopted by many countries at the national and sub-national levels (WHO/FAO, 2006). Foods can be fortified at three levels: mass, targeted, and household. Mass or universal fortification possible through legislation has the potential to produce nutritious food products that are widely consumed by the general population (e.g., salt iodisation). Mass fortification is also a highly cost-effective nutrition intervention (WHO, 2010). Targeted fortification (e.g., fortified complementary foods for children aged 6-24 months) is necessary for subgroups of nutritionally vulnerable populations (Riely *et al.,* 1995). A meta-analysis of 60 trials showed that iron fortification of foods resulted in 41 per cent reduction in the risks of anemia and a 52 per cent reduction in iron deficiency (Gera, 2012). Common salt is fortified with Iodine to curb its deficiency in population (WHO/FAO, 2006).

Bio-fortification

Bio-fortification is a nutrition-sensitive agricultural intervention which focuses on breeding of crops that have high nutritive value. Biofortified food as a source of micronutrient is better suited for the provision of daily doses to prevent the development deficiencies in individuals throughout the lifecycle, outside the 1000 days critical period. Bio-fortification cannot achieve the high concentrations of micronutrients needed to treat severe deficiencies or to fulfil the high requirements (e.g., of iron) of pregnant and lactating women and infants (Saltzman *et al.,* 2013). Bio-fortification is considered as one component of a larger strategy which must include nutritional supplementation, dietary diversification, and traditional fortification programme (Hotz, 2012a; 2012b).

Water, Sanitation and Hygiene

History of water, sanitation, and hygiene goes back to the birth of 'public health' as a distinct area of public policy and as a professional discipline. WASH practices are divided into four categories; two of these are related to 'water' viz.: water 'quantity' and water 'quality'. The first involves interventions that improve the amount of drinking water available to each of every household, and the second describes interventions that improve the physical, chemical and most importantly biological (microbial) quality of drinking water, both at the level of the source and at the point of consumption (Bain *et al.,* 2014). Sanitation refers to technique and behaviours that relate to safe containment of human excreta, preventing human contact, and hygiene is commonly used to mean washing body especially hands with soap at critical times (e.g. after defecation and before eating).

These public health interventions together form a 'sanitation barrier' that prevents exposure of humans to disease-causing organisms via five transmission object, and they are fingers, flies, fomite, food and feces (Wagner and Lanoix, 1958). Everyone relates WASH interventions with his or her role in curbing malnutrition and promoting the health of the population, but its benefit has far-reaching impacts. For example improvements in water supply reduces the distance travelled to the water source leading to significant saving of time and energy for households, and it can transform the lives of the women and children whose responsibility is in large part to collect water. This fact was long ago recognised by a senior World Bank economist who argued that this benefit alone provide sufficient economic justification for the investment costs of water supply without any consideration of the health benefits that may accompany (Churchill *et al.,* 1987).

How can safe water sanitation, and hygiene prevent stunting?

Biological mechanisms: There is a pile of evidence to explain the biological mechanism by which WASH factors can cause malnutrition. These are divided into two broad categories.

(1) Via repeated bouts of diarrhea in a child (Richard *et al.,* 2013). The frequency of the diarrheal disease, as a syndrome, irrespective of its causes, is strongly correlated with growth faltering (Checkley *et al.,* 2008). A recent pooled analysis of data from nine countries with longitudinal morbidity and anthropometry provides evidence that repeated bouts of diarrhea cumulatively increase the risk of stunting in children (Checkley *et al.,* 2008).(2) Soil-transmitted chronic helminth infections can be prevented with adequate sanitation (Strunz *et al.,* 2014) and are strongly associated with childhood undernutrition (Prüss-Üstün and Corvalán, 2006). Hookworm infections during pregnancy can lead to malabsorption of nutrients and maternal anemia, which in the long run is associated with stunting at birth (Black *et al.,* 2013).

Social and economic mechanisms: When the source of water is not located nearby, as is the case in numerous villages, it results in energy cost for carrying water for long distances. When professional vendors perform the water-carrying, as is more often in the case in urban areas, it proves far more expensive to the consuming household. In this way, expenditure related to water makes a significant proportion for a poor household. In this way, water supply affects nutritional status not only via the complex metabolic links described above but also by the most direct social route.

Social and Behaviour Change

Before concluding this chapter, one essential component needs to be discussed. Despite the availability of all evidences, the fight against malnutrition can only be won, when all the woman, mothers, fathers, and caregivers of every child start adopting and practicing these evidence in a regular manner (Bhandari *et al.,* 2004). We have discussed that undernutrition is not merely a result of food insecurity, many children in food-secure environments and from better-off families are malnourished because of inappropriate infant and child care practices, poor access to health services, or poor sanitation. We have discussed that often the most important cause of undernutrition is inadequate knowledge among caregivers about the benefits of exclusive breastfeeding, complementary feeding practices and other child care techniques. Community members must be given proper health education in a manner which ensures social and behaviour change. Social and Behaviour Change Communication (SBCC) can guarantee the elimination of malnutrition as well as the promotion and maintenance of good nutrition practices not only for the children but also applicable to the whole population (Ghosh, 2002).

In the case of malnutrition, the SBCC campaign targets strong determinants of child nutrition such as antenatal care for pregnant women, breastfeeding and young child feeding practices, care during illness, psychosocial care of the child, food preparation, and hygienic practices (Santos, 2001; Marriots, 2012). The way caregivers carry out these practices depends not only on the resources available to them but also on the knowledge and attitude of caregivers. Improving child's nutritional status can be accomplished by addressing inappropriate feeding and caregiving practices through Behaviour Change Communication (BCC) programs. It involves efforts far beyond simply educating individuals or delivering information about healthy practices. It involves working with communities to understand their perceptions about the problem of malnutrition and hurdles they face in dealing with malnutrition and ultimately identifying the potential solutions for addressing nutritional problems. For example, to improve breastfeeding practices, all women especially pregnant and lactating women either individually or in a group can be taught right attachment method for breastfeeding through a demonstrationof models and pictures. In some cases, this approach alone might not be helpful e.g. destitute families, unemployed family members. However, in most cases, this behaviour change interventions can address the problems of malnutrition in a particular community. Evidence generated from Bangladesh Integrated Nutrition Project proves that even in the presence of food insecurity, mothers were able to provide the recommended complementary foods from their resources, as they were highly motivated by the nutritional education (Roy, 2005).

Social Safety Nets and Aid

Under some circumstance, all the above measure will fail. Such circumstances include famine, floods, wars, conflict in the region, unemployed families, extreme poverty, sudden loss of income, and death of earning member of the household. In these conditions, it is the responsibility of government and international agencies to provide resources to such families and children who are at risk of being malnourished.

Conclusion

Traditionally the world has focused on curbing undernutrition among children, but a new challenge is brewing in many different parts of the world. With the increase in food production, a decrease in fertility rates, and changing feeding habits the world is witnessing an increase in the proportion of children who are either overweight or obese. I want to conclude this chapter by stating that together, we can eliminate malnutrition from the face of this earth, if each one of us whether it's an adolescent girl, a newly married couple, pregnant women, lactating mother, community health workers, farmers, doctors, policy makers and most of all the government fulfills their respective duties. Eliminating malnutrition is not a one-time effort but a never ending journey. As long as there will be children on this earth, there are chances that they can become malnourished. So the only permanent solution is to be vigilant forever!!!

References

1. Alderman, Harold, Hoogeveen, J.G.M. andMariacristina Rossi. 2005. "Reducing Child Malnutrition in Tanzania: Combined Effects of Income Growth and Program Interventions." Washington, DC: World Bank Policy Research Working Paper 3567.
2. Arimond, M, Ruel, M.T. Dietary diversity is associated with child nutritional status: evidence from 11 demographic and health surveys. *J Nutr*2004; 134: 2579–85.
3. Arnold, B.F., Null, C., Luby, S.P., Unicomb, L., Stewart, C.P., Dewey, K.G. *et al.,* (2013). Cluster-randomised controlled trials of individual and combined water, sanitation, hygiene and nutritional interventions in rural Bangladesh and Kenya: the WASH Benefits study design and rationale. BMJ open 3, e003476.
4. Bain, R., Cronk, R., Hossain, R., Bonjour, S., OndaK.,Wright, J. *et al.,* (2014). Global assessment of exposure to faecal contamination through drinking water based on a systematic review. *Tropical Medicine and International Health* 19, 917–927.
5. BFHI, 2006. Baby Friendly Hospital Initiative
6. Bhandari, N, Mazumder, S, Bahl, R, Martines, J, Black, R E, and Bhan, M. K. (2004). "An Educational Intervention to Promote Appropriate Complementary Feeding Practices and Physical Growth in Infants and Young Children in Rural Haryana, India." *The Journal of Nutrition* 134 (9) (September): 2342–2348.

7. Bhutta, Z.A., Ahmed, T., Black, R.E., Cousens, S., Dewey, K., Giugliani, E. *et al.,* (2009). What works? Interventions for maternal and child undernutrition and survival. *The Lancet* 371 (9610), 417–440.

8. Bhutta, Z.A., Das, J.K., Rizvi, A., Gaffey, M.F., Walker, N., Horton, S. *et al.,* for the Maternal and Christian P., Lee S.E., Donahue A.M., Adair L.S., Arifeen, S. E., Ashorn, P. *et al.,* (2013). Risk of childhood undernutrition related to small-for-gestational age and preterm birth in low- and middle-income countries. *International Journal of Epidemiology* 42, 1340–1355.

9. Bhutta, Z. (2016). Early nutrition and adult outcomes: pieces of the puzzle. The Lancet 382: 486-487.

10. Biran, A., Jenkins, M.W., Dabrase, P. and Bhagwat, I. (2011). Patterns and Determinants of Communal Latrine Usage in Urban Poverty Pockets in Bhopal, India. Tropical Medicine and International Health 16 (7), 854–862.

11. Black, Robert E., Lindsay, H. Allen, Zulfiqar, A. Bhutta, Laura E. Caulfield, Mercedes de Onis, Majid Ezzati, Colin Mathers, and Juan, Rivera (2008). "Maternal and child undernutrition: global and regional exposures and health consequences." *The Lancet* Series on Maternal and Child Undernutrition. *The Lancet* 371: 243-60 (January 19).

12. Black, R.E., Victora, C.G., Walker, S.P., Bhutta, Z.A., Christian, P., De Onis M. *et al.,* (2013). Maternal and child undernutrition and overweight in low-income and middle-income countries. *The Lancet* 382, 427–451.

13. Briend, A. (1990). Isdiarrhoea a major cause of malnutrition among the under-fives in developing countries? a review of available evidence. *European Journal of Clinical Nutrition* 44, 611–628.

14. Brown, K.H. (2003). Diarrhea and malnutrition. *The Journal of Nutrition* 133, 328S–332S.

15. Caballero, B. (2005). "A nutrition paradox—underweight and obesity in developing countries." *N Engl J Med* 352(15): 1514–1516.

16. Cairncross, S. (2004). Editorial: water supply and sanitation: some misconceptions. *Tropical Medicine and International Health* 8, 193-195.

17. Casey, G., Montresor, A, Cavalli-Sforza, L, Thu H, Phu, L, Tinh, T *et al.,* Elimination of iron deficiency anemia and soil transmitted helminth infection: evidence from a fifty-four month iron-folic acid and deworming program. *PLoSNegl Trop Dis.* 2013; 7(4): e2146. doi:10.1371/journal. pntd. 0002146.

18. Caulfield, Laura, E., Mercedes de Onis, Monika Blössner, and Robert, E. Black (2004). "Undernutrition as an Underlying Cause of Child Deaths

Associated with Diarrhea, Pneumonia, Malaria, and Measles." *American Journal of Clinical Nutrition* 80: 193–98.

19. Checkley, W., Buckley, G., Gilman, R.H., Assis, A.M., Guerrant, R.L., Morris, S.S. *et al.,* (2008). Multi-country analysis of the effects of diarrhoea on childhood stunting. *International Journal of Epidemiology* 37, 816–830.

20. Christiansen, L. and Tollens, E. (1995). Food security: From concept to action—A status questionis. K. U. Lueven and B.A.D.C. research project in the framework of policy preparing research in the field of cooperation in development, Nr 2, Brussels, Belgium.

21. Churchill, A., Ferranti, D.D., Roche, R., Tager, C., Walters, AA, Yazer, A. (1987). Rural water supply and sanitation; time for a change. In: World Bank Discussion Paper No. 18. World Bank: Washington DC.

22. Darlow, BA, Graham, PJ. (2007). Vitamin A supplementation to prevent mortality and short and long-term morbidity in very low birthweight infants. *Cochrane Database Syst Rev* 2007; 4: CD000501.

23. Dewey, K.G. (2003). Nutrient composition of fortified complementary foods: should age-specific micronutrient content and ration sizes be recommended? *Journal of Nutrition* 133, 2950S–2952S.

24. Dewey, K.G. (2013). The challenge of meeting nutrient needs of infants and young children during the period of complementary feeding: an evolutionary perspective. *Journal of Nutrition* 143, 2050–2054.

25. Dewey, K.G. and Adu-Afarwuah S. (2008). Systematic review of the efficacy and effectiveness of complementary feeding interventions in developing countries. *Maternal and Child Nutrition* 4, 24–85.

26. Edmond, KM, Zandoh, C, Quigley, MA, Amenga-Etego, S, Owusu-Agyei S, Kirkwood, BR. Delayed breastfeeding initiation increases risk of neonatal mortality. *Pediatrics* 2006, 117: e380–6.

27. FAO (2009). *Declaration of the World Food Summit on Food Security* (PDF). Rome: Food and Agriculture Organisation of the United Nations.

28. FAO, WFP, IFAD. "The State of Food Insecurity in the World 2013. The multiple dimensions of food security." FAO. Retrieved 26 November 2013.

29. FANTA-2. *Preventing Malnutrition in Children Under 2 Approach (PM2A): A Food-Assisted Approach. Version 1: October 2009.* Washington, D.C.: Food and Nutrition Technical Assistance II Project (FANTA-2), Academy for Educational Development (AED), 2009.

30. Gardner, J.; Grantham-McGregor, S.M.; Himes, J.; and Chang, S. 1999. "Behaviour and Development of Stunted and Nonstunted Jamaican Children." *Journal of Child Psychology and Psychiatry*. Vol. 40(5), pp. 819–827.

31. Gera, T, Sachdev, HS, Boy, E. Effect of iron-fortified foods on hematologic and biological outcomes: systematic review of randomised controlled trials. *Am J ClinNutr* 2012; 96: 309–24.

32. Ghosh, Shanti, Kilaru, A, and Ganapathy, S. (2002). "Nutrition Education and Infant Growth in Rural Indian Infants: Narrowing the Gender Gap?" Journal of the Indian Medical Association 100 (8) (August): 483–484, 486–488, 490.Giles J, Satriawan E (2012). Protecting child nutritional status in the aftermath of a financial crisis: evidence from Indonesia. Policy Research

33. Godfrey, K.M., and Barker, D.J., (2001). Fetal programming and adult health. *Public Health Nutr.* 4(2b), 611–624.

34. Gragnolati. M., Shekar.M., Dasgupta. M., Bredenkamp. C., and Lee. Y. K., (2006). *The Challenge of Persistent Child Undernutrition in India and the Role of the ICDS Program.* Washington, DC: World Bank.

35. Grantham-McGregor, Sally, Lia Fernald, and K. Sethurahman. 1999a. "Effects of Health and Nutrition on Cognitive and Behavioural Development in Children in the First Three Years of Life." *Food and Nutrition Bulletin* 20(1): 53–99.

36. Grantham-McGregor, Sally, Lia Fernald, and K. Sethurahman. (1999b). "Effects of Health and Nutrition on Cognitive and Behavioural Development in Children in the First Three Years of Life." *Food and Nutrition Bulletin* 20(1): 53–99.

37. Grantham-McGregor, S. (2007). "Developmental Potential in the First 5 Years for Children in Developing Countries." *Lancet.* Vol. 369(9555), pp. 60–70.

38. Gross, R., Schultink, W., and Kielmann, A.A. (1998). Community nutrition: definition and approaches. Encyclopedia of human nutrition. Ed. by M. Sadler, S. Strain and B. Caballero. Academic Press, London, UK..

39. Herforth, A, Jones, A, Pinstrup-Andersen, P. Prioritising nutrition in agriculture and rural development: guiding principles for operational investments. Washington, DC: World Bank, 2012.

40. Hofmeyr, GJ, Lawrie, TA, Atallah, AN, Duley, L. Calcium supplementation during pregnancy for preventing hypertensive disorders and related problems. *Cochrane Database Syst Rev* 2010; 8: CD001059.

41. Hoddinott, J., Maluccio, J., Behrman, J.R., Martorell, R., Melgar, P., Quisumbing, A.R. *et al.,* (2011). The consequences of early childhood growth failure over the life course. In: Discussion.

42. Hoddinott, J., Alderman, H., Behrman, J.R., Haddad, L. and Horton, S. (2013). The economic rationale for investing in stunting reduction. *Maternal and Child Nutrition* 9 (Suppl. 2), 69–82.

43. Hofmeyr, GJ, Lawrie, TA, Atallah, AN, Duley, L. Calcium supplementation during pregnancy for preventing hypertensive disorders and related problems. *Cochrane Database Syst Rev* 2010; 8: CD001059.

44. Horton, S, and Ross J. (2003). The economics of iron deficiency. Food Policy. 2003;28: 51–75. doi:10.1016/S0306-9192(02)00070-2.

45. Horton, S. and Steckel, R. (2013). Global economic losses attributable to malnutrition 1900–2000 and projections to 2050. In: The Economics of Human Challenges (ed. B. Lomborg). Cambridge University Press: Cambridge, U.K.

46. Hotez, P.J., Brooker, S., Bethony, J.M., Bottazzi, M.E., Loukas, A. and Xiao, S. (2004). Hookworm infection. New England Journal of Medicine 351, 799–807.

47. Howlader, S.R., Sethuraman, K., Begum, F. Paul D. Sommerfelt, A.E. Kovach, T. (2012). Investing in nutrition now: a smart start for our children, our future. Estimates of benefits and costs of a comprehensive programme for nutrition in Bangladesh, 2011–2021. PROFILES and Nutrition Costing Technical Report. Washington, DC: Food and Nutrition Technical Assistance III Project (FANTA), FHI 360.

48. Hunt, J.M. (2005). "The Potential Impact of Reducing Global Malnutrition on Poverty Reduction and Economic Development." Asia Pac J ClinNutr 14(S): 10–38.

49. Imdad, A. and Bhutta, Z.A. (2012). Routine iron/folate supplementation during pregnancy: effect on maternal anaemia and birth outcomes. Paediatric and Perinatal Epidemiology 26, 168–177. doi: 10.1111/j.1365-3016.2012.01312.x.

50. Kaiser, L.L., H. Melgar-Qui˜nonez, C. Lamp, (2002). Food security and nutritional outcomes of Latino Preschoolers. *J. Am. Diet. Assoc.* 102: 924–929

51. Kar, B.R., Rao, S.L. and Chandramouli, B.A. (2008). Cognitive development in children with chronic protein energymalnutrition. Behavioural and Brain Functions 4, 31.

52. Kramer M.S. and Kakuma A. (2003). Energy and protein intake in pregnancy. Cochrane Database of Systematic Reviews. Issue 4. Art. No.: CD000032. doi: 10.1002/ 14651858.CD000032

53. Kulwa, K. B., Kinabo, J. L. and Modest, B. (2006). Constraints on good child-care practices and nutritional status in urban Dar-es-Salaam, Tanzania. *Food Nutr Bull,* 27, 236-44.

54. Last, M J (2012). Dictionary of Epidemiology p. 139.

55. Maalouf-Manasseh, Z; Oot, L; Sethuraman, K. (2015). *Giving Children the Best Start in Life: Integrating Nutrition and Early Childhood Development within the First 1,000 Days*. Washington, DC: FHI 360/ FANTA.

56. Marriott, BP, White, A, Hadden, L, Davies, JC, Wallingford, JC. World Health Organisation (WHO) infant and young child feeding indicators: associations with growth measures in 14 low-income countries. *Matern Child Nutr*2012; 8: 354–70.

57. Masset, E, Haddad, L, Cornelius, A, Isaza-Castro, J. A systematic review of agricultural interventions that aim to improve nutritional status of children. London: EPPI-Centre, Social Science Research Unit, Institute of Education, University of London, 2011.

58. Mendez, M.A. and Adair, L.S. (1999). Severity and timing of stunting in the first two years of life affect performance on cognitive tests in late childhood. Journal of Nutrition 129, 1555–1562.

59. Moore, ER, Anderson, GC, Bergman, N, Dowswell, T. Early skin-to-skin contact for mothers and their healthy newborn infants. *Cochrane Database Syst Rev* 2012; 5: CD003519.

60. deOnis, M., Dewey, K., (2013). The World Health Organisation's Global Target for Reducing Childhood Stunting by 2025: Rationale and Proposed Actions, *Maternal and Child Nutrition* (2013), 9 (Suppl. 2), pp. 6–26.

61. Pena-Rosas, JP, De-Regil, LM, Dowswell, T, Viteri, FE. Daily oral iron supplementation during pregnancy. *Cochrane Database Syst Rev* 2012; 12: CD004736..

62. Penny, ME, Creed-Kanashiro, HM, Robert, RC, Narro, MR, Caulfield, LE, Black, RE. (2005). Effectiveness of an educational intervention delivered through the health services to improve nutrition in young children: a cluster-randomised controlled trial. The Lancet. 2005;365(9474):1863–1872

63. Perez-Escamilla, Rafael; Segall-Correa, Ana Maria (2008). "Food insecurity measurement and indicators". *Revista de Nutrição*21: 15–26. doi:10.1590/s1415- 52732008000500003. Retrieved 31 July 2013.

64. Pinstrup-Andersen, P. The food system and its interaction with human health nutrition. Leveraging agriculture for improved nutrition in health. 2020 Conference: Leveraging Agriculture for Improving Nutrition and Health. Brief 13. Washington, DC: International Food Policy Research Institute, 2011.

65. Pitkin, R.M. (2007). "Folate and Neural Tube Defects." *American Journal of Clinical Nutrition*. Vol. 85 (supplement), pp. 285S–288S.

66. Prado, E.L. and Dewey, K.G. (2014). "Nutrition and Brain Development in Early Life." *Nutrition Reviews*. Vol. 72(4), pp. 267–284.

67. Prüss-Ustün, A., Bartram, J., Clasen, T., Colford, J.M., Cumming O., Curtis V. *et al.,* (2014). Burden of disease from inadequate water, sanitation and hygiene in low- and middleincome settings: a retrospective analysis of data from 145 countries. Tropical Medicine and International Health 19, 894–905.

68. Ramakrishnan, U., Grant, F.K., Goldenberg, T., Bui, V., Imdad, A. and Bhutta, Z.A. (2012). Effect of multiple micronutrient supplementation on pregnancy and infant outcomes: a systematic review. *Paediatric and Perinatal Epidemiology* 26, 153–167.

69. Richard, S.A., Black, R.E., Gilman, R.H., Guerrant, R.L., Kang, G., Lanata C.F. *et al.,* (2013). Diarrhea in early childhood: short-term association with weight and long-term association with length. *American Journal of Epidemiology* 178, 1129–1138.

70. Richards, M, Rebecca, H, Diana, K, and Michael, E.J. W. (2001). "Birth Weight and Cognitive Function in the British 1946 Birth Cohort: Longitudinal Population Based Study." *British Medical Journal* 322: 199–203.

71. Richards, M, Rebecca, H, Diana, K, and Michael, E.J.W (2002). "Birthweight, Postnatal Growth, and Cognitive Function in a National UK Birth Cohort." *International Journal of Epidemiology* 31: 342–48.

72. Riely, F., Mock, N., Cogill, B., Bailey, L., and Kenefick, E. (1995). Food security indicators and framework for use in the monitoring and evaluation of food aid programs. Food security and nutrition monitoring project. IMPACT, Arlington, USA.

73. Rollins, N *et al.,* (2016). Why invest, and what will it take to improve breastfeeding practices? *The Lancet* 387: 491-504.

74. Roy, SK, Fuchs, GJ, Mahmud, Z, Ara, G, Islam, S, Shafique, S, Akter, SS, Chakraborty, B. Intensive nutrition education with or without supplementary feeding improves the nutritional status of moderately-malnourished children in Bangladesh. *Journal of Health, Population and Nutrition*. 2005;23(4):320–330. 32.

75. Saltzman, A, Birol, E, Bouis, H, *et al.,* Biofortification: progress toward a more nourishing future. *Global Food Secur* 2013; 2: 9–17.

76. Santos, I, Victora, CG, Martines, J, Goncalves, H, Gigante, DP, Valle, NJ, Pelto, G. (2008). Nutrition counseling increases weight gain among Brazilian children. *Journal of Nutrition*. 2001;131(11):2866–2873.

77. Shekar, M. Delivery sciences in nutrition. *Lancet* 2008; 371: 1751.

78. Shekar, M *et al.,* (2015a). Scaling Up Nutrition in the DRC: What Will It Cost? Health, Nutrition, and Population (HNP) Discussion Paper. Washington, DC: The World Bank Group.

79. Shekar, M *et al.,* (2015b). Scaling Up Nutrition for a More Resilient Mali: Nutrition Diagnostics and Costed Plan for Scaling Up. Health, Nutrition, and Population (HNP) Discussion Paper. Washington, DC: The World Bank Group.

80. Shrimpton, R., Victora, C.G., De Onis M., Lima, R.C., Blössner, M. and Clugston, G. (2001). Worldwide timing of growth faltering: implications for nutritional interventions. *Pediatrics* 107, e75–e75.

81. Smith, Lisa C., Harold Alderman, and Dede Aduayom (2005). "Food Insecurity in Sub-Saharan Africa: New Estimates from Household Expenditure Surveys." Draft. Washington, DC: International Food Policy Research Institute.

82. Srinivas, SK, Edlow, AG, Neff, PM, Sammel, MD, Andrela, CM, Elovitz, MA. (2009). Rethinking IUGR in preeclampsia: dependent or independent of maternal hypertension? *J Perinatol* 2009; 29: 680–84.

83. Strunz, E.C., Addiss, D.G., Stocks, M.E., Ogden, S., Utzinger, J. and Freeman, M.C. (2014). Water, sanitation, hygiene, and soil-transmitted helminth infection: a systematic review and meta-analysis. PLoS Medicine 11, e1001620.

84. Udani, P.M. (1992). Protein energy malnutrition (PEM), brain and various facets of child development. *Indian Journal of Pediatrics* 59 (2), 165–186.

85. UNICEF (1990). Strategy for improved nutrition of women and children in developing countries. In: A UNICEF Policy Review. UNICEF: New York.

86. UNICEF (2010). Progress for Children: Achieving the MDGs With Equity NewYork: UNICEF.

87. Victora, CG, Adair, L, Fall, C, *et al.,* for the Maternal and Child Undernutrition Study Group. Maternal and child undernutrition: consequences for adult health and human capital. *Lancet* 2008; 371: 340–57.

88. Wagner, E.G. and Lanoix, J.N. (1958). Excreta Disposal for Rural Areas and Small Communities,WHOMonograph series No 39. WHO: Geneva.

89. WHO (2008). Safer Water, Better Health: Costs, Benefits and Sustainability of Interventions to Protect and Promote Health. WHO: Geneva.

90. WHO and UNICEF (2003). Global Strategy for Infant and Young Child Feeding. Geneva: World Health Organisation.

91. WHO (2012). Guideline: daily iron and folic acid supplementation in pregnant women. Geneva: World Health Organisation, 2012.

92. WHO, FAO. Guidelines on food fortification with micronutrients. Geneva: World Health Organisation; Food and Agricultural Organisation, 2006.

93. WHO/FAO/UNU. (2007). *Protein and amino acid requirements in human nutrition: Report of a joint WHO/FAO/UNU expert consultation.* WHO Technical Report Series No. 935. Geneva: WHO. http://whqlibdoc.who.int/trs/WHO_TRS_935_eng.pdf.

94. World Bank (2006). Repositioning Nutrition as Central to Development: A Strategy for Large-scale Action. World Bank:Washington, DC.

95. World Bank (2010). Scaling up nutrition. In: What Will It Cost? World Bank: Washington, DC.

96. World Health Organisation. WHO guidelines on nutrition (http://www.who. int/publications/guidelines/nutrition/en/, accessed 21 May 2016).

97. Wu, T, Liu, GJ, Li, P, Clair, C (2006). Iodised salt for preventing iodine deficiency disorders. *Cochrane Database Syst Rev* 2006; 3: CD003204.

98. Young, E.M. (2012). *Food and development*. Abingdon, Oxon: Routledge. pp. 36–38. ISBN 9781135999414.

99. Zimmermann, MB. The effects of iodine deficiency in pregnancy and infancy. *Paediatr Perinat Epidemiol*2012; 26 (suppl 1): 108–17.

10

Calorie Availability to Realise Food Security : Some Evidences in the District of Burdwan

Maniklal Adhikary and Khokon Sarkar

One of the biggest problems facing the world with its progressive severity over time is food insecurity. Defined and interpreted in various ways, the term 'Food Security/Insecurity' has been introduced in the dictionary of social sciences. But, the fundamental idea states that weather a person is able to purchase sufficient food that provides him/her required calorie to prove him/her medically fit to live an active and healthy life. So, the attainment of threshold calorie level is necessary to treat oneself as a food secure person. Regarding the requirement of minimum calorie for a person there are many controversies between FAO and WHO's. In this paper, we have intensively calculated according to our prescribed manner (Recommended Dietary Allowances, 2010) the calorie available at the family level for those food items which were reported to be consumed by the households. The requirement of the total calorie of the family has been calculated by Harris-Benedict method. The difference between calorie requirement and calorie available shows the calorie deprivation or food insecurity situation at the family level. We have obtained partial elasticity of calorie available per day at the household level with respect to family income, family size, sex of the household head, years of basic education of the household head, religion and caste by applying the Lin-Log model. And it is has been empirically found that except religion all other explanatory variables have significant effects on the household calorie availability in our model.

Introduction

The first and the foremost essential criteria for a person is to ensure his daily requirement of minimum calorie. But the attainment of minimum calorie does not necessarily mean that the person/family is in the secured level in respect of food. Of course, there are other several factors which are equally important as minimum calorie for achieving food security. For example protein, micronutrients, vitamins, safe drinking water, hygienic sanitation system, clean environment, proper medical facilities and the ability to meet the future needs of the food against the odds etc. are also important in the achievement of food security. Inability of access to any one of the stated facilities may lead oneself to food insecurity in the present as well as in the future. Therefore, it is very difficult to define and identify oneself as secured in terms of food. Since the term 'food security' has been introduced in the literature of the social sciences, thousands of definitions have been made by the various authors depending on their level of understanding of the problem. Among all these definitions, in our view, the definition provided by FAO (2002) is the best one in defining food security. FAO (2002) has stated that 'Food security is a situation that exists when all people, at all times, have physical, social and economic access to sufficient, safe and nutritious food that meets their dietary needs and food preferences for an active and healthy life.'

There are so many indicators of food security/insecurity widely used by different authors in different studies, e.g. minimum calorie cut of point, minimum monthly per capita expenditure and anthropometric parameters etc. Among all these indicators, calorie deprivation is the direct measure of the magnitude of food insecurity of the individual or households. Though the method is controversial and is not very easy to calculate, especially, at individual level. It is not easy to observe and measure the actual amount of food intake by each and every member of the households for a week/month/year throughout the day.

In our study, we have tried to find out the gap prevailing in the family between the required calorie and the acquired calorie that is the extent of one family's capability of meeting their dietary needs in terms of calorie requirement. We define calorie deprivation as the difference between the actual physically required calorie and actual daily acquired calorie at the household level. The negative value of calorie deprivation for the family can be termed as the food insecurity situation in the form of calorie at the family level. To serve our purpose, we have collected the information on the monthly purchase of essential food items (cereals, pulses, sugar, mustered oil, vegetables and flesh food items) and converted them into their calorie value. And also we have collected the biometric information of each and every member of the households to obtain their medically requirement of daily calorie. Thus, we have defined the daily calorie deprivation/surplus as the simple differences between daily requirements to that of daily availability of calorie at the household level. Finally, we have tried to identify the factors which may have very significant effects on the calorie deprivation of the family.

Measuring calorie availability in our daily purchased food is not an easy task and more importantly there is not any single method which is free from criticism. Since, each raw food items brought from the market are passes through many process (of cooking) to make it edible. No one can satisfactorily measure how much calorie value from the said food items, when cooked, has been utilised. To measure the calorie value of food items, we have followed the nutritive value table of various food items (edible per 100 g) proposed by 'Food Science (B. Srilakshmi, 2008)'.

Another important task is to measure the daily requirement of calorie for each and every member of the family. Here, we know that the calorie requirement varies from parson to person according to their biometric nature (age, sex and height) as well as their daily activities and geographical circumstances of the area. In this regard, we have tried to obtain the requirement of daily calorie of a person as it is prescribed medically. Following Harris- Benedict (1918), we have obtained the minimum requirement of calorie for sustaining his/her livelihood according to their biometric information.

This paper has been arranged as follows. In section-2, we have reviewed some selected literatures related to our study. We have depicted our objectives of carrying out this study in section-3. In section-4, we have provided information about our data collection and methodology that we have used. The discussion regarding our result is presented in section-5. Finally, in section-6, we have concluded our study with some useful recommendations.

Literature review

Rushed Faridi and Syed Naimul Wadood (2010) *et al.,* analysed the factors of food security for the agricultural households following the footsteps of Feleke, Kilmer, and Gladwin (2005). To this end, they have collected data on Bangladeshi households from the income expenditure survey of 2005. And they have empirically estimated their model of determining the various components of food insecurity with the help of logistic model. They have found that other than consumption level, there are so many factors of food insecurity which are found to be significant. Different household characteristics as the quality of house, level of ownership, tenancy status, electricity connection and education have been found to be significant determinants of food security. It has been noted in the study that the wage earner groups are the worst affected in response to the increase in prices of food items.

In a response paper (FAO March, 2013) it has been broadly noticed that economic development in the country alone is not sufficient to get rid of hunger and malnutrition. The report has mentioned many examples from the various countries' experiences that the process of development may lead to inequalities, which may trigger the hunger and malnutrition. It criticises the estimation method of the minimum calorie threshold because of the fact that the minimum calorie requirement differs due to the geographical location of the country. In estimating hunger and malnutrition, food price fluctuation was not taken into consideration. In order to reduce hunger and malnutrition, the social protection measures through chief credit facilities, land reform programmes (as these are evident from China, Ghana, Thailand, Vietnam, Indonesia, Brazil and Bangladesh) may be successfully implemented.

Luther Tweeten (1997) in his panel discussion, pointed out that food accessibility is a larger problem than food availability. In his view, the definition of food security would be "Utilisation by all people at all times of sufficient food or sufficient nutrition for an active, healthy life". He has suggested ten food security principles to execute well to fill food gaps as fully as possible. These are summarised as follows:

1. Food inaccessibility is a greater source of food insecurity than food availability.
2. Food inaccessibility stems primarily from poverty.
3. The most efficient way to alleviate poverty is by economic growth.
4. Transitory food insecurity is also the effect of impoverishment.

5. General poverty is basically the consequence of public policy failure that brings slow economic development.
6. Right economic policy can guarantee economic growth.
7. Another essential component for food security besides economic development is a safety mesh.
8. An imperfect political system, ignorance, greed and apathy are the main reasons to reduce poverty and to increase food security.
9. It is better to address food crisis before they come out.
10. Severe food insecurity is often best addressed in the short run by food aid, in the intermediate run by a broad-based sustainable economic development and in the long run by lower birth rates and reduced population growth.

P. S. Amaza, J. C. Umesh, J. Helson and A. D. Adejabi (Aug, 2006), in their study of Borno State of Nigeria have tried to find out and analyse the measures of food protection. They have collected data from 1200 households through multistage sampling and analysed cost-of-calories (COC) through logit model. The result shows that over 58 per cent of the sample households are food insecure. In this study, the determinants of food insecurity are household size, gender, educational level, farm size and types of family-farm enterprise. The household size, educational level, farm size, ratio of quality produced to the ratio of quantity consumed, household's access to extension agents, household head's membership of cooperative societies and values of family assets are found to be negatively correlated with food insecurity. The gender of the head of house, type of family enterprises, extent of agricultural output commercialisation, expenditure on education are found to be positively correlated with food insecurity.

Sharon I Kirkpatrick and Valerie Tarasuk (2011) have analysed the influence of housing circumstance on household food security. They have collected data from the Toronto, Canada from 2005 to 2007, using a quota sampling to achieve a balanced sample of households in subsidised and market rental accommodations. They have applied clustering in the sampling design to approximate sampling error. Linear regression was applied to evaluate associations between income, housing cost and food consumption and housing type, and they have also applied logistic regression. After examining the data they have found that there is an association between housing tenure and household food insecurity. The balance of income allocated to housing was also inversely related with food expenditures. It was also noted that a positive association exists between being in a dwelling in need of major repair and food insecurity among market families.

Siddharth Agarwal, Vani Sethi, Palak Gupta, Meenakshi Jha, Ayush Agnihotri, Mark Nord (2009), have pointed out the levels and determinants of households food insecurity (HFI) in an urban slum of Delhi, India. They have collected data from Delhi by interviewing of 410 adult females. They have studied on the socio-demographic characteristics of the respondents by using multiple logistic regressions. To assess the reliability and internal validity of their study they have tested Cronbach's alpha and Rasch model. After examining the data they have concluded that fifty one per cent of households were food insecure.

Christine M. Oslon, Barbara. S. Rauschenbach, Edward A. Frongillo, Jr. Anne Kendall (1996) have identified the elements that contribute to household food insecurity in upstate New York. They have collected data from the rural upstate of New York in 1990. To select the best predictors of food insecurity, they have applied stepwise logistic regression. It has been noted that being a single parent, lack of savings, larger household size, having unexpected expenses, adding US $50 or more in food stamps to purchase sufficient food and having low food consumption are significant determinants of food insecurity.

Amartya Sen (1987) has outlined some of the primary issues that are intended to be carried out in research for eliminating famines and the removal of endemic hunger across the globe. He expressed his doubt on many methodologies about estimating the number of the hungry and the undernourished by comparing calorie intake figures with "requirement" norms. According to him, in the case of food insecurity, the actual issue is not the over-all availabilities of food, but its acquisition by individuals and households. So, to understand hunger, one should analyze the people's entitlements, i.e., what commodity bundles they can create for their own. A man can fall down into starvation if some changes take place in his endowment, e.g., alienation of land, or passing of labour power due to ill health, fall in wages, rise in food prices, loss of employment etc.

Daman Prakash (February, 2003) has tried to make the relationship between rural women and agricultural cooperatives in combating food insecurity. Rural women are actively involved in the operation of food production, processing and selling but they often lack the legal status, which forbids them to sustain access to credit, education and engineering. Cooperative institutions can help speed up the process of development and participation of women in the organisational and job actions. Women cooperatives, e.g. cooperative banks, consumer stores, fruits and vegetable vendors, have done extremely well and provided a whole range of services to their members. In most of the South-Asian countries women's membership in cooperatives is generally low as compared to those of the other countries. In states like India, Nepal, Bangladesh, Sri Lanka and Pakistan, women comprise just 7.5 per cent as compared with men (92.5 per cent). The troubles faced by the rural women's behind their lower participation in agricultural cooperatives are high illiteracy rates and poor living conditions, lack of leadership, absence of rights to property inheritance, unequal healthcare services, lack of marketing facilities and opportunities and socio-cultural obstacles etc.

Peter Svedberg (2001) has criticised that the measurement of the prevalence of undernourished (POU) of FAO is a biased estimator. In the POU method the parameters used are same for all states and regions. Generally, it is overestimated number of undernourished. The minimum calorie requirement varies from nation to nation and region to region, as it primarily depends on the individual Physical Activity Level (PAL) whereas anthropometric method is free from such prejudices.

Objectives

The broad objectives that inspire us to carry out this study are as follows

(i) To obtain the actual minimum calorie requirement of the family necessary for sustaining the livelihood of the family.

(ii) To obtain the total calorie that a family is capable of meeting in their daily calorie consumption.

(iii) To identify the gap of each family between required calorie and acquired calorie.

(iv) To identify the main factors those are responsible for calorie deprivation in the family.

Methodology and Database

Our first task of this study is to obtain the calorie deprivation at the household level or the observed difference between required calorie and the acquired calorie at the household level. For obtaining the required calorie at the household level per day, our necessary task is to calculate the requirement of calorie per day of each person. We have followed the method proposed by Harris-Benedict (1918). And calculate the medically requirement of minimum calorie of a person to sustain his/her livelihood according to his/her weight, height and age. Therefore, the Individual requirement of calorie per day is obtained by using the equation sated below

For men, h = 66.4730 + 13.7516 w + 5.0033 s - 6.7550 a

For women, h = 655.0955 + 9.5634 w + 1.8496 s - 4.6756 a

Where h = total heat production per 24 hours, w = weight in kilograms, s = stature in centimeters, and a = age in years.

Once the requirement of each and every individual being obtained we sum up them for all the members of the family that will give us the daily calorie requirement of the family.

In order to obtain the acquired calorie of the family we first converted all monthly purchased food amounts (kg) into calorie value following the nutrition value table (per 100 g) of 'Food Science (B. Srilakshmi, 2008)'. The converted calorie of all food items (cereals, pulses, oil, sugar, fish, flesh food and vegetables) together is the monthly available calorie for the family. From this we can easily obtain the daily calorie available for the family by dividing monthly calorie available with 30 days.

Then we obtain the observed calorie deprivation as

Calorie Deprivation (CD) = Daily calorie Requirement of the family – Daily Available Calorie of the family

To identify the determinants of our sample calorie deprivation we proceed as follows:

Let y = Observed Calorie Deprivation (CD).

x_1 = Income of the family (fi)

x_2 = Total members of the family (fs)

x_3 = Years of education of the head of the family (yoe)

x_4 = Sex of the head of the family (shh)

Where

shh =1 if head of the household is male

= 0 otherwise.

x_5 = Religion of the family

Where

religion = 1 if family belongs to Hindu

= 0 otherwise.

x_6 = Caste of the family

Where

caste = 1 if family is general caste

= 0 otherwise.

A model that accomplishes this purpose can be written as

$$y_i = \beta_1 + \beta_2 \ln x_1 + \beta_3 \ln x_2 + \beta_4 x_3 + \beta_5 x_4 + \beta_6 x_5 + \beta_7 x_6 + u_i$$

Where the coefficient β_2 and β_3 = change in *y*/change in *x* = change in *y*/relative change in *x*

We have,

$$\beta_2 = \frac{dy}{dx_1 / x_1}$$

$$\beta_3 = \frac{dy}{dx_2 / x_2}$$

This states that the absolute change in $y(= \Delta y)$ is equal to slope times the relative change in x_2 or x_3. If the latter is multiplied by 100, then (2) gives the absolute change in y for a percentage change in or Thus, if $(\Delta x_1 / x_1)$ or $(\Delta x_2 / x_2)$ changes by 0.01 unit (or, 1 per cent), the absolute change in y is 0.01 (β_2) and 0.01 (β_3) respectivly.

And β_4 represents simply $\frac{dy}{dx_3}$

But, x_4, x_5 and x_6 are Dummy = 1 or

= 0

Here our testing hypotheses are that

$$H_0 : \beta_i = 0 \text{; where } i = 1, 2, ...6$$

Against the alternative hypothesis

$$H_1 : \beta_i \neq 0$$

For the empirical estimation we have collected data from the district of Burdwan, West Bengal. For our purpose we have selected purpusively two Blocks from the district of Burdwan. Again from each block again we have selected two villages and two municipalities purposively. Then from each village and municipalities we have randomly selected 7 or 8 panchayts or wards respectivly. Finally, from each panchayat and Wards, 10 households are randomly selected and interviewed total 316 houeseholds respectively. We have collected data on demographic, socio-economic status and indivisual biometric information.

5. Discussion

Table 10.1 below shows the summary statistics of our 316 sample households. The average calorie deprivation is 742 Kcal, which is positive, indicating that the most of the families have a surplus calorie as per the minimum requirement. And this is also substantiated by the diagram-1. Here, we can see that most of the families lie above the zero line. But, there are some families which are lying below the zero line. And even some of the families have calorie deprivation of more than 4000 unit. As in table 10.1 we can see that the minimum of the calorie deprivation is -4906. The average monthly income of the families is Rs5280, but ranging from Rs 2500 - Rs 11000. So there is a wide inequality in income distribution of the families in the district of Burdwan. And the number of family members also varies from 2 to 10 with an average of 4.5 members. Average years of education of the head of the families are very low of approximately 1 with a range from 0 year to 15 years.

Table 10.1: Summary Statistics

Variable	*Obs*	*Mean*	*Std. Dev*	*Min*	*Max*
cd	316	742.4508	2356.329	-4906.54	7869.446
shh	316	0.89557	0.306303	0	1
yoe	316	2.800633	4.005726	0	15
fs	316	4.5	1.298351	2	10
fi	316	5279.747	1810.806	2500	11000

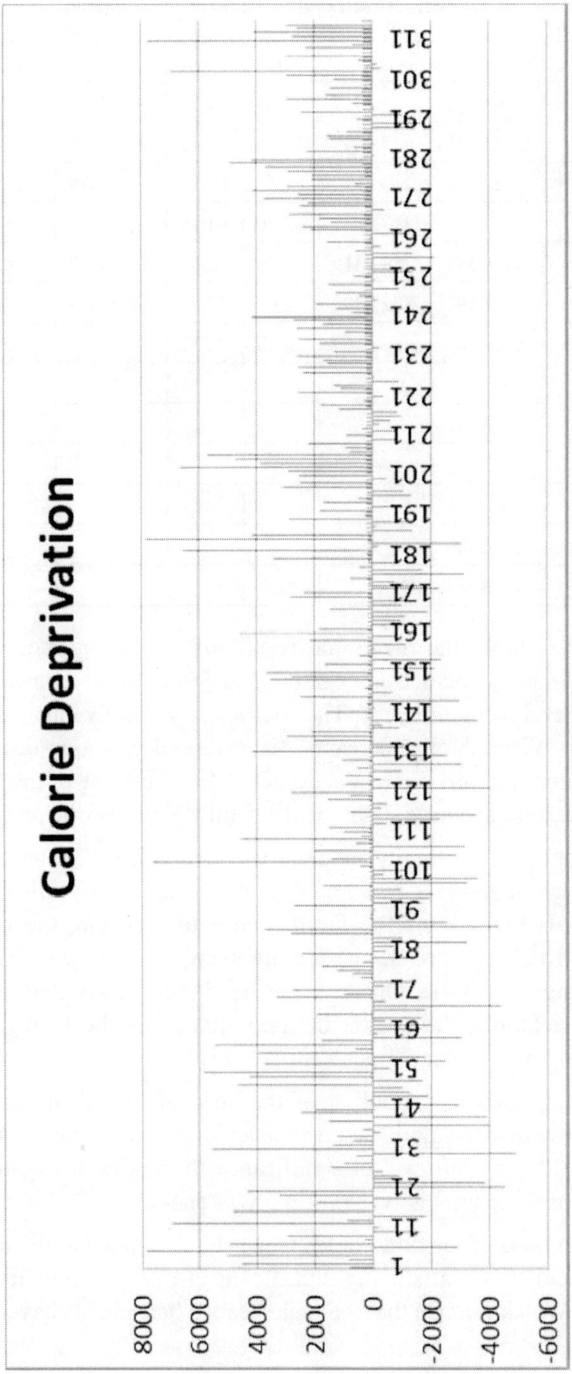
Calorie Deprivation
8000
6000
4000
2000
0
-2000
-4000
-6000
1
11
21
31
41
51
61
71
81
91
101
111
121
131
141
151
161
171
181
191
201
211
221
231
241
251
261
271
281
291
301
311

Diagram 10.1

Table 10.2: Regression results (Calorie Deprivation)

	Coef.	*Std.*	*t*	*P>|t|*	*[95% Conf. Interval]*	
log_fi	-931.14	346.3727	-2.69	0.008	-1612.69	-249.592
log_fs	5442.346	413.7093	13.16	0	4628.303	6256.39
yoe	42.3758	26.87375	1.58	0.116	-10.5029	95.2545
shh	-855.986	347.3821	-2.46	0.014	-1539.52	-172.452
religion	-496.652	257.7419	-1.93	0.055	-1003.8	10.49913
caste	-222.884	332.2405	-0.67	0.503	-876.624	430.8555
cons	1759.503	2809.369	0.63	0.532	-3768.41	7287.417
obs	316					
F(6,309)	33.31					
Prob>F	0					
R-squared	0.3927					
Adj R-squared	0.3809					
MSE	1854					

Table 10.2 shows the regression results of our lin-log model. The coefficient of family income is negative and found to be significant at one per cent level of significance. The coefficient of family income states that if income of the family increases, the calorie deprivation decreases by 9.31 per cent. And obviously it is expected that if income of the family increases, the food security status of the family will also increases.

The number of the family member (fs) is possitively related with calorie deprivation and it is also found to be statistically significant. We can say that as the size of the family tends to increase, the calorie deprivation will also go up. Because, more member of the family means greater demand for calorie. On the other hand we can say that smaller the size of the family, the greater the opportunity for the family to be food secure by more than 50 per cent.

Number of years of schooling of the head of the family (yoe) is also positively related to calorie deprivation and it is found to be significant at more than 10 per cent level of significance. It implies that education have some possitive effects on nutrition awardness.

Sex of the head of the households is negatively related to the calorie deprivation and it is statistically significant at one per cent level of significance. Which implise that the male headed households have lower deprivation of calorie in terms of the requirement of the calorie at the household level. In other words, we can say that the male heads are more aware/capable than the women heads in aquiring sufficient amount of food to provide the necessary amount of calorie for their families.

Religion is negetatively related with calorie deprivation and also significant at five per cent level. Which indicate that Hindu families are in a better possition than the non-Hindu families in terms of calorie deprivation.

And caste of the families are also negatively related with calorie deprivation, but it is statistically insignificant. Since, most of the families of our sample populations are belongs to the general categories, so, the comparatively smaller amount of non-general caste's are may, unable to make any significant impact in our estimation.

6. Conclusion

Calorie deprivation is not the actual measure of food security but it is the most essential indicator of food security. In the district of Burdwan of West Bengal, our sample population indicating that most of the families are able to purchase sufficient calorie for their livelihood, though not all. From our empirical analysis we can see that the family income is negatively related to calorie deprivation. So to elevate the families with lower calories to their required calorie level, we need to provide them sufficient employment opportunity with healthy wages.

Another truth is that smaller the size of the family, smaller is the requirement of the calorie. As a result smaller will be the deprivation of calorie. In rural areas the size of the families is quite large. Because of illiteracy they are unable to make any proper family planning. In consequence, the family tends to increase year after year. Providing basic education regarding family planning may help them in making family planning so that they can keep their calorie requirement at the low level.

Acknowledgement

We must thankfully acknowledge and express our appreciation to University Grants Commission for recognising and accepting our Minor Research Project proposal and extending necessary fund to carry out this study.

References

1. Rushad Faridi and Syed Naimul Wadood (Sept, 2010). "An Econometric Assessment of Household Food Security in Bangladesh"; The Bangladesh Development Studied. Vol. XXXIII.

2. FAO (March, 2013). "The State of Food Insecurity in the World 2012: Economic Growth is Necessary but not Sufficient to Accelerate Reducing Hunger and Malnutrition".
3. Luther Tweeten (May, 1997). "Issues in Performance Measurement of Food Security: An Overview"; Panel discussion Paper No.1, Proceedings of the USAID Workshop on Performance Measurement for Food Security, USAID Development Information Services Clearinghouse. 1611. W. Kent, St. Suite-200, Arlington, VA 22209-2111.
4. P.S.Amaza, J.C.Umesh, J. Helson and A.D.Adejabi (Aug, 2006). "Determinants and Measurement of Food Insecurity in Nigeria: Some Empirical Policy Guide"; International Association of Agricultural Economists Conference, Gold Coast, Australia.
5. Sharon I Kirkpatrick and Valerie Tarasuk (March, 2010). "Assessing the Relevance of Neighbourhood Characteristics to the Household Food Security of Low Income Toronto Families" ; Public Health Nutrition (1139-1148), Toronto, Canada.
6. Sidddharth Agarwal, Vani Sethi, Palak Gupta, Meenakshi Jha, Ayush Agnihotri, Mark Nord (Aug, 2009). "Experiential household Food Insecurity in an Urban Underserved Slum of North India"; Springer Science+Business Media B.V and International Science for Plant Pathology 2009.
7. Christine M. Oslon, Barbara. S. Rauschenbach, Edward A. Frongillo, Jr. Anne Kendall (1996). "Factors Contributing to Household Food Security in a Rural Upstate New York Country"; Institute for Research on Poverty Discussion Paper No. 1107-96. www.ssc.wise.edu/irp.
8. Amartya Sen (November, 1987). "Hunger And Entitlements"; World Institute For Development Economics Research United Nations University, Auranen, Forssa, Finland.
9. Daman Prakash (February 2003). "Rural Women, Food Security and Agricultural Cooperatives"; Rural Development and Management Centre 'The Saryu', J-102 Kalkaji, New Delhi 110019. India.
10. Peter Svedberg (2001). "Under nutrition Overestimated", Seminar paper no.693 October 2001. Institute for International Economic Studies, S-10691 Stockholm, Sweden.
11. Peter Svedberg (1998). "41 MILLION UNDERNAURISHED? ON THE TYRANNY OF DERIVING A NUMBER", seminar paper no.656, October 1998. Institute for International Economics Studies, S-10691 Stockholm, Sweden.
12. J. Arthur Harris and Francis G. Benedict (1918). "A BIOMETRIC STUDY OF HUMAN BASAL METABOLISM", Nutrition Laboratory And Station For Experimental Evolution, Carnegie Institution of Washington.

11

Food Security: Concept, Determinants and Initiatives in India

Milan Banik

India is the second largest producer of food grains in the world, feeding 17 per cent of the world's population on only three per cent of the world's arable land, yet 194.6 million under nourished people call India their home. About 18 per cent of the India's total population are undernourished. Nearly 40-45 per cent of children under the age of three years are underweight and stunted. Almost 58 per cent of pregnant women aged between 15-49 years and 75 per cent of children below five years of age suffer from anaemia. This is despite the fact that the country's food grains production has touched all time high record of 257 million tonnes in 2011-12 and the production curve is on an upward trend. In fact, lack of proper and adequate food caused for their hunger, malnutrition and under nutrition. Several food-related schemes and measures were taken by the central government and the state governments to reduce hunger and ensure food security. Yet, India's efforts in achieving food security for all remain unimpressive. India now ranks 55th position out of 76 countries before Bangladesh and Pakistan (rank 57), but still trails behind her neighbouring Nepal (rank 44) and Sri Lanka (rank 39). India's hunger status is still classified as "serious". Accordingly, this paper attempts to take an overview of the food security in terms of its concept, global scenario of food insecurity, determinants of food security in India, hunger and its underlying components for major states for better understanding of the grievous situation with reference to India.

Introduction

Adequate nutrition is essential for growth, good health and physical and cognitive development, and requires a diverse diet including staple food, vegetables, fruits, animal-source foods and fortified foods. Nutrition is affected not only by food availability and access, but also by disease, sanitation including access to safe drinking water and availability of preventive health services (FAO, 2010).

The world body convened the World Food Conference in 1974 which was the biggest effort ever to discuss global food issues threadbare. The conference set the goal of eradication of hunger, food insecurity and malnutrition within a decade. In 1996, 185 nations met at the Rome headquarters of the Food and Agricultural Organisation (FAO) to discuss the ways to end hunger. At the met, it was committed to reduce the number of undernourished to half by 2015. This pledge was reiterated in the Millennium Summit in 2000 and the World Food Summit in 2002 (Pandey and Kedia, 2007). Thereafter, FAO has been constantly monitoring the global food situation and suggesting corrective actions for fighting hunger and ensuring food security for all.

India is the second largest producer of wheat and rice in the world, growing 12 and 22 per cent of the world's total wheat and rice crop respectively, yet over 300 million people in the country go without two square meals a day. According to the Global Hunger Index (GHI) 2012, India is ranked 65th position in the list of 79 countries. With over 200 million people unsure about accessing their daily bread, 50 per cent of our children undernourished and stunted, and about 68 out of 1000 dying before the age of one year, food security is undoubtedly a major concern and top priority for the government to-day.

Concept of Food Security

Sustainable food security involves strengthening the livelihood security of all members within a family by ensuring both physical and economic access to balanced diet including the needed micronutrients, safe drinking water, and environment, sanitation, basic healthcare and primary education (Razi, 2009).

The concept of food security has further been refined and enlarged by the National Commission on Farmers (2006), which states that every individual has- physical, economic, social and environmental access to a balanced diet that includes the necessary macro and micro nutrients, safe drinking water, sanitation, environment, hygiene, primary healthcare and education as to lead a healthy and productive life (NCF, 2004, cited by Modgal, 2014). In a study in Murshidabad District of West Bengal, Sultana and Ahmed (2015) conclude that with the increase of per capita room availability, education, pucca houses, earning family members, sanitation facility, livestock availability, monthly income, food security increase. In a study, Iram and Butt (2004) state that food security is a broad concept which includes issues related to nature, quality, food access and security of the food supply. Food security also includes access to food, its exchange and utilisation (Sen, 1981).

FAO (2010) has defined the concept of food security as enlisted below:

Food security exists when all people, at all times, have physical, social and economic access to sufficient, safe and nutritious food that meets their dietary needs and food preferences for an active and healthy life. Household food security is the application of this concept to the family level, with individual within households as the focus of concern.

Food insecurity, according to FAO (2010), exists when people do not have adequate physical, social or economic access to food as defined above. It is the underprivileged individuals and families who are often prevented from satisfying their basic need of food and become food insecure. Food insecurity is the most common manifestation of protracted crises and about 22 countries are currently considered to be in protracted crises.

There are two aspects of the food situation in India – 'food grains security' and 'food security'. A distinction is made between food security and food grains security below:

The food basket of the people in India has become considerably diversified during the last couple of decades. A much greater share is now occupied by non-food grain items such as edible oils, sugar, milk, meat, eggs, vegetables and fruits. These non-food items now account for 60 per cent of the consumer expenditure on food. Therefore, while physical and economic access to food grains implies 'food grains security', the 'food security' would require the same for non-food grain items of food basket (Dhingra, 2014).

Food security has three essential components which are as follows:

(i) Food Availability

It concerns with the availability of sufficient quantities of food of appropriate qualities, supplied through domestic production or imports.

(ii) Food Accessibility

It refers to the factors like household incomes and individual wages, food prices, consumer credit etc. In short, it implies the purchasing power of the households.

(iii) Food Utilisation

The utilisation of food through adequate diet, water, sanitation and healthcare bring forth the importance of non-food inputs in food security.

Global Scenario of Food Insecurity

The Global Hunger Index Report (GHI), 2015 shows that levels of hunger in the developing world have declined by more than one-quarter since 2000. Despite the progress made, the level of hunger in the world remains unacceptably high, with 795 million people still going hungry, more than one in four children affected by stunting, and 9 per cent of children affected by wasting. The data revealed that levels of hunger remain serious or alarming in 52 of the 117 countries, which was in 16 of the 76 countries and more than an estimated 2 billion people globally affected by hidden hunger in 2014. Effects of hidden hunger include child and maternal death, physical disabilities, weakened immune system, and un-promised intellects. It also holds countries back in a cycle of poor nutrition, poor health, cost productivity, persistent poverty, and reduced economic growth (IFPRI, 2014). Among the world regions, South Asia and Africa South of the Sahara continue to experience the highest levels of hunger.

The report also explores the relationship between armed conflict and hunger. More than 40 countries affected by internal conflict since 2000 and had already suffered one or more civil wars over the previous three decades. Countries that suffer protracted or repeated violent conflict may experience much higher levels of under nutrition, reduced access to education, and much higher infant mortality that staple countries of similar economic standing. The report also shows that the level of hunger in developing countries as a group has fallen by 27 per cent, yet the state of hunger in the world remains serious and nearly half of all child deaths under age five are due to malnutrition, which claims the lives of about 3.1 million children per year (IFPRI, 2015).

The situation of global food insecurity is very much reflective from the following table. The results of the GHI report 2015 shows the continued overall severity of the hunger situation in the world, while revealing the variation in hunger across the selected nations in the world.

Table 1: Global Hunger Index and its Underlying Components (2014-15) (in per cent)

Country	*Proportion of under-nourished (%)*	*Prevalence of wasting under-5 years (%)*	*Prevalence of stunting under-5 years (%)*	*Under-five Mortality rate (%)*
Bangladesh	16.4	14.3	36.1	4.1
Bhutan	-	5.9	33.6	3.6
China	9.3	2.3	9.4	1.3
Ethiopia	32.0	8.7	40.4	6.4
India	15.2	15.0	38.8	5.3
Indonesia	7.6	13.5	36.4	2.9
Malaysia	2.0	10.7	11.2	0.9
Myanmar	14.2	7.9	35.1	5.1
Nepal	7.8	11.3	37.4	4.0
Pakistan	22.0	10.5	45.0	8.6
Philippines	13.5	7.9	30.3	3.0
Sri Lanka	22.0	21.4	14.7	1.0
Thailand	7.4	6.7	16.3	1.3
Zimbabwe	33.4	3.3	27.6	8.9

Source: Global Hunger Index Report 2015, (IFPRI), Washington, DC.

Notes: 1. Child wasting refers to the proportion of children under the age of five who suffer from wasting i.e., low weight for their height, reflecting acute under-nutrition.
2. Child stunting refers to the proportion of children under the age of five who suffer from stunting i.e., low weight for their age, reflecting chronic under-nutrition.

It is evident from the Table 11.1 that almost in all the countries have a serious hunger problem. In India, 15.2 per cent people are suffering from under-nourishment, 15.0 per cent of wasting under five years age, 38.8 per cent are stunting under five years age and the under five mortality rate is 5.3 per cent which is more than even Bangladesh (4.1 per cent), Sri Lanka (1.0 per cent) and Nepal (4.0 per cent).

Determinants of Food Security in India

Production and income are two most important determinants of access to food (Sen, 1981) and are classified as 'entitlements' of an individual or household, which included endowment (i.e., physical, natural, human, social, financial, etc.) and exchange. Studies reveal that food self-sufficient countries at the national level can have food insecurity at national and household level due to unequal distribution of food within the country and unequal accessibility by the households owing to poor purchasing power. Researchers have used a large number of determinants to evaluate the food security of the households. Here, availability of food grains and access to safe drinking water are used to determine the food security in India.

Availability of Food Grains

It concerns with the availability of sufficient quantities of food of appropriate qualities, supplied through domestic production or imports (Dhingra, 2014). Food security also involves adequate physical availability of food, a determinant of food security, to the entire population in a country. While India's population was steadily rising, the production of food grains – cereals and pulses had rosed equally (Table 11.2). The net availability of cereals per capita per day had gone up from 422.7 grams in 2000 to 468.9 grams in 2013. The per capita per day net availability of pulses had increased from 31.8 per cent in 2000 to 41.9 per cent in 2013. Obviously, while moving towards food grain security, India has succeeded to increase the production of food grains with the growing needs of the population. But, India ranks 66 in the list of 88 countries in the Global Hunger Index (GHI) 2008 which is at present 55th position among 76 countries, just before Bangladesh and Pakistan (rank 57), but still trails behind neighbouring countries Nepal (rank 44) and Sri Lanka (rank 39) in the GHI 2014.

Table 11.2: Population and Per Capita per Day Net Availability of Food Grains in India

(in grams)

Year	*Population (in million)*	*Cereals*	*Pulses*	*Total*
2000	1014.8	422.7	31.8	454.4
2001	1033.2	386.2	30.0	416.2
2002	1050.6	458.7	35.4	494.1
2003	1068.2	408.5	29.1	437.6
2004	1085.6	426.9	35.8	462.7
2005	1102.8	390.9	31.5	422.4
2006	1119.8	412.8	32.5	445.3
2007	1136.6	407.4	35.5	442.8
2008	1153.1	394.2	41.8	436.0
2009	1169.4	407.0	37.0	444.0
2010	1185.8	401.7	35.4	437.1
2011	1201.9	410.6	43.0	453.6
2012	1213.4	408.6	41.7	450.3
2013(p)	1228.8	468.9	41.9	510.8

Source: Economic Survey, 2014-2015, Government of India, p. A28.
Note : P- Provisional.

Studies reveal that the causes of hunger in India currently are the wide prevalence of poverty and the inability of a large section of the population to buy food or to establish entitlement over an adequate amount of food. The pattern in the availability of food grains indicates that the six decades of economic planning has not been successful in ensuring sustainable food grains availability either through its production and pricing policy or through its initiatives launched towards fair distribution of food grains to the vulnerable poor in the country.

Access to Safe Drinking Water

Water is known as life line. Safe drinking water, another determinant of food security, decreases the probability of water borne diseases and increases the food security of the people. India has 4 per cent of water resources of the world, while it supports 16 per cent of the world's population and 15 per cent of livestock. In India, 50 per cent of villages do not have safe drinking water. Annually, 37.7 million people are affected by water borne disease, 1.5 million children are estimated to die of diarrhoea and 62 million people are at the risk of suffering from fluorosis due to excessive fluoride in the ground water (Gautam, 2009:4). It is heartening to note that while only 78 per cent of households had access to safe drinking water in 2001 which went up to 86 per cent in 2011. Much of the progress has been in the rural areas with the number of households having access to drinking water went up from a mere 73.2 per cent in 2001 to 82.7 per cent in 2011(Table 11.3). That merely 26.8 per cent households in rural areas do not have adequate drinking water in 2001 which was 17.3 per cent in 2011.

Although the production of food grains and access to safe drinking water were made available, they did not reach the target people in adequate measure due to mismanagement of the various components of the food distribution system. And, now, India is home to more than 230 million undernourished people – highest for any country in the world and more than 27 per cent of under nourished population globally live in India (FAO, 2008).

This situation would be more serious if appropriate policy initiatives are not taken in time to increase the food production along with the distribution of essential food items at affordable prices to the consumers.

About 43 per cent of children below five years of age in the country are underweight. About 30 per cent of babies in India are born underweight. Malnutrition accounted for nearly 50 per cent of child deaths in India. About 70 per cent of children below five years of age are suffering from anaemia and more than 80 per cent do not get vitamin supplements (Hazra, 2009). All these deficiencies are very much reflective from the following table.

Table 3: Access to Safe Drinking Water for Major States in India

(in per cent)

States / Union Territories	*2001*			*2011*		
	Rural	*Urban*	*Total*	*Rural*	*Urban*	*Total*
Andhra Pradesh	76.9	90.2	80.1	88.6	94.5	90.5
Assam	56.8	70.4	58.8	68.3	78.2	69.9
Bihar	86.1	91.2	86.2	93.9	94.7	94.0
Gujarat	76.9	95.4	84.1	84.9	97.0	90.3
Haryana	81.1	97.3	86.1	92.0	96.7	93.8
Himachal Pradesh	87.5	97.0	88.6	93.2	97.8	93.7
Jammu & Kashmir	84.9	95.7	65.2	70.1	96.1	76.8
Karnataka	80.5	92.1	84.6	84.4	92.3	87.5
Kerala	16.9	42.8	23.4	28.3	39.4	33.5
Madhya Pradesh	61.5	88.6	68.4	73.1	92.1	78.0
Maharashtra	68.4	95.4	79.8	73.2	95.7	83.4
Odisha	62.9	72.3	64.2	74.4	79.8	75.3
Punjab	96.9	98.9	97.6	96.7	98.9	97.6
Rajasthan	60.4	93.5	68.2	72.8	94.3	78.1
Tamil Nadu	85.3	85.9	85.6	92.2	92.9	92.5
Uttar Pradesh	85.5	97.2	87.8	94.3	97.9	95.1
West Bengal	87.0	92.3	88.5	91.4	93.9	92.2
India	**73.2**	**90.0**	**77.9**	**82.7**	**91.4**	**85.5**

Source: Economic Survey 2014-2015, Government of India, p. A133.

The Table 11.4 reveals that not a single state in India is either low or moderate in terms of its index score, most of the states have a "serious" hunger problem and only one state, namely, Madhya Pradesh has an "extremely alarming" hunger problem as it covers 59.8 per cent underweight children below five years of age and its mortality rate under five years of age is 9.4 per cent. Other states like Gujarat, Chhattisgarh, Bihar, Jharkhand, etc., are also suffering from acute hunger problem as they bear the burden of 44.7 per cent, 47.6 per cent, 56.7 per cent and 57.1 per cent of underweight children respectively. The mortality rate of children below five years of age in these states is 6.1 per cent, 9.0 per cent, 8.5 per cent and 9.3 per cent respectively. Alarming on the Hunger Index are the states of UP, Rajasthan, Haryana, Bihar, Jharkhand, Weat Bengal, Odisha, Chhattisgarh, Tamil Nadu, Maharashtra, Karnataka, and Gujarat. The serious states on the Hunger Index are Punjab, Kerala, Haryana and Assam. Studies reveal that India has made a slow progress in ensuring food security and it could feed its growing population. But, it is indicated that India has the highest numbers of hungry children in the world and it has been placed in 65th position out of 79 countries in the GHI 2012.

Nearly half of the total population in the country still suffer from chronic hunger and under-nutrition. Without reducing hunger, it will not be possible to attack gender related problems like child and maternal mortality, diseases, illiteracy, even AIDS etc.

Table 11.4: Hunger Index and its Underlying Components for Major States in India

States	*Prevalence of Under-nourishment (%)*	*Proportion of underweight children Below five years (%)*	*Under-five mortality rate (Deaths per 100)*	*India State Hunger Index Rank*
Punjab	11.1	24.6	5.2	1
Kerala	28.6	22.7	1.6	2
Andhra Pradesh	19.6	32.7	6.3	3
Assam	14.6	36.4	8.5	4
Haryana	15.1	39.7	5.2	5
Tamil Nadu	29.1	30.0	3.5	6
Rajasthan	14.0	40.4	8.5	7
West Bengal	18.5	38.5	5.9	8
Uttar Pradesh	14.5	42.3	9.6	9
Maharashtra	27.0	36.7	4.7	10
Karnataka	28.1	37.6	5.5	11
Odisha	21.4	40.9	9.1	12
Gujarat	23.3	44.7	6.1	13
Chhattisgarh	23.3	47.6	9.0	14
Bihar	17.3	56.1	8.5	15
Jharkhand	19.6	57.1	9.3	16
Madhya Pradesh	23.4	59.8	9.4	17
India	**20.0**	**42.5**	**7.4**	-

Source: India State Hunger Index Report 2008.

Government of India's Initiatives for Food Security

The access to food for all people is of utmost importance ever since the beginning of humanity. Access to enough food is their fundamental human right. The Government of India, in partnership of the state governments has been initiating several programmes for increasing access to food in the country with an emphasis on poorer sections of the society, a few of them are enumerated below:

(i) Rationing System

In India, rationing system was introduced at the time of World War II by the British government through which the government provided rice, wheat and other food items to the ration card holders. The basic aim was to provide essential commodities such as rice, wheat, sugar, edible oils, soft coke and kerosene at subsidised prices to the vulnerable sections of the society. After the War in 1943, the rationing system was abolished by the British government. After independence in 1947, the Government of India re-introduced the rationing system in 1950 to distribute food items at low prices. It was called the National Food Security System (NFSS). In order to strengthen the Public Distribution System (PDS), the Government of India established the Food Corporation of India (FCI) in 1964 to ensure food security in India. The PDS was emerged as government's participation in food commodities trade out of Fair Price Shops (FPS) in 1950s and 1960s as a double benefit program, i.e., to facilitate price support to farmers and food subsidy to consumers.

(ii) Integrated Child Development Services Scheme (ICDS)

ICDS started in 1975 was intended to cater to the poorer sections of the Indian society by providing supplementary nutrition with primary healthcare and pre-school education to children. The target groups of the scheme include children in the age group of up to six years, pregnant and nursing women from the poorer sections of the population in rural areas. It offers an integrated package of services that includes supplementary nutrition, pre-school education, immunisation, health check-up, referral services and nutrition and health education. It also envisages effective convergence of inter-sector services in the Anganwadi Centres.

(iii) National Drinking Water Mission (NDWM)

It was launched in 1986 which was re-named as 'Rajiv Gandhi National Drinking Water Mission' (RGNDWM) in 1991 with the following objectives:

(a) Providing safe drinking water to all villagers;

(b) Assisting local communities to maintain source of safe drinking water in good conditions;

(c) Giving special attention for water supply to scheduled castes (SC) and scheduled tribes (ST).

(iv) Mid-Day Meal Scheme (MMS)

The Ministry of Human Resource Development, Government of India, launched this scheme on 15 August, 1995 to benefit students in the primary schools located in the area of 'Employment Assurance

Scheme' (EAS), earlier known as 'Revamped Public Distribution Scheme (RPDS), launched in 1992. Students in classes I to V in the government primary schools as well those run by the local bodies are covered in this scheme. The programme was re-named as 'Targeted Public Distribution System' in 1997.

(v) Antyodaya Anna Yojana (AAY)

It was launched on 25 December, 2000 for the down-trodden in the society. Under the scheme, 25 kg. of food grains were made available to each eligible family at highly subsidised rates of Rs 2.00 per kg. of Wheat and Rs 3.00 per kg. of Rice. The quantity since then has been enhanced to 35 kg. on 1 April, 2002.

(vi) The Integrated Cereal Development Programme (ICDP)

This programme was in operation since 4 October, 2000. It covers rice, wheat, and coarse cereals which cease to function in the identified districts once the NFSM—rice and wheat start functioning there.

(vii) National Food for Work Program (NFWP)

This scheme is operating since 13 October, 2004 and implemented in 150 most backward districts in India. The scheme ensures food security through creation of need based economic, social and community assets in the above districts.

(viii) National Commission on Farmers (NCFS)

It was re-constituted through its new resolution dated 3 November, 2004 with partial modification of earlier resolution dated 10 February, 2004 under the chairmanship of Dr M.S. Swaminathan. The main purpose of NCF was to suggest and workout a medium term strategy for food and nutrition security for the country in order to achieve the universal food security over time.

(ix) Mahatma Gandhi National Rural Employment Guarantee Act (MGNREGA)

This scheme was launched on 2 February, 2006 to empower all rural adults with right to work and earn minimum wages of at least Rs 125 per day in all states of India which will create 12 million jobs per year for five years starting 2009.

(x) National Food Security Mission (NFSM)

It was launched on 29 May, 2007, which comprised of the food items like rice, wheat, and pulses to make the country self-sufficient in food grains and to strengthen India's food security by increasing the production and productivity of this three crops in the country.

(xi) National Food Security Act (NFSA)

Recently, the Government of India has notified the National Food Security Act, 2013 with the objective to provide for food and nutritional security in human life cycle by ensuring access to adequate quantity of quality food at affordable prices to live a life with dignity. The act covers up to 75 per cent of the rural population and up to 50 per cent of the urban population for providing subsidised food grains under TPDS from 2000. It lays a special focus on the nutritional support to women and the children covering 11 states.

Apart from above, the Government of India has been implementing several other programmes like National Rural Livelihood Mission (NRLM), Development of Women and Children in Rural Areas (DWCRA), National Rural Health Mission (NRHM), Integrated Disease Surveillance Programme (IDSP), Total Literacy Campaign (TLC), etc. which are important for ensuring food and nutritional security for the vulnerable sections of the society in India.

Conclusion

Sustainable agriculture, affordable pricing policy and inclusive growth initiative are the three most important aspects of ensuring "Food for All" in a predominantly rural and agricultural country like India. Food insecurity exists when people are undernourished as a result of the physical unavailability of food, their lack of social or economic access to adequate food and/or inadequate food utilisation.

India has witnessed green revolution and is readying for the second round of green revolution with newer farm technologies and innovations in farming systems. Agricultural progress i.e., crop and animal husbandry, fisheries, forestry, and agro-forestry, and agro-processing etc. will be the most effective social safety net against poverty and hunger. There is an urgent need for enhancing investment in agriculture and rural infrastructure development along with allied sectors through second round of green revolution scientifically and to analyse its relationship to resources, markets, services, policies and institutions in their local cultural context.

Apart from above, there is also a need for encouraging the production of major cash crops like cotton, jute, groundnuts, tea, coffee, coconut, cashew, rubber etc. which will enhance the income of the farming community and help to ensure food security. Recently, it has been urged to reduce the number of hunger, undernourished and malnutrition in the developing countries. For India with around 30 crores chronically hungry population, it is indeed a great challenge to plan strategies to gradually reduce underweight children from the present 30 per cent to nil in the next ten years. But this can be achieved if the focus on the rural sector remains unhindered. The strategy should also try to the revival of the agricultural sector and in turn of rural sector wherein nearly 70 per cent of the total population engaged directly or indirectly for their livelihood.

The solution to the problem of food security in the world lies in increasing production and productivity in the low-income, food-deficit countries. The growth rate in India has down from nine per cent GDP in 2007-08 to 5 per cent annual GDP in 2012-13. India's exports have also been affected adversely as well the capital flow from abroad is impacted due to protectionist policies of the developed countries. Hence, the immediate need of the hour is to invest more resources into research for increasing food production and productivity along with procurement of food grains from farmers at remunerative prices, building up and maintenance of buffer stocks, storage and distribution of food grains at affordable prices, management of natural resources, environment, market and price stability of food grains which are important for ensuring food and nutritional security in India.

References

Dhingra, I. C. (2014). "The Indian Economy-Environment and Policy", Sultan Chand and Sons, New Delhi, 2014.

Economic Survey-2014-15, Government of India, Ministry of Finance (Economic Affairs), New Delhi, 2015.

FAO (Food and Agricultural Organisation of the United Nations) 2010. "The State of Food Insecurity in the World- Addressing Food Insecurity in Protracted Crises", Rome, online available at www.fao.org/013/i1683e/pdf, accessed on 10/03/16.

___, (2008). "The State of Food Insecurity in the world".

Gautam, H. R. (2009). "Food security the next Big Challenge", Kurukshetra, A Journal on Rural Development, Publication Division, Ministry of Information and Broadcasting, Govt. of India, New Delhi, 2009, Vol.11(57): 16 - 18.

Hazra, A. (2009). "Food for All – Still A Distant Dream", Kurukshetra, A Journal on Rural Development, Publication Division, Ministry of Information and Broadcasting, Govt. of India, New Delhi, 2009, Vol-11(57). 12-15.

Iram, U. and Butt, M. S. (2004). "Determinants of Household Food Security. An Empirical Analysis for Pakistan", International Journal of Social Economics, Vol.31 (8):753-766.

IFPRI (International Food Policy Research Institute) 2014. "Global Hunger Index – The Challenge of Hidden Hunger", online available at www.ifpri.org/ghi/2014 , accessed on 12/03/16.

___, (International Food Policy Research Institute) 2015. "Global Hunger Index 2015", online available at www.ifpri.org/ghi/2015, accessed on 28/03/2016.

Modgal, S. C. (2014). "Food Security of India – An Overview", National Book Trust, New Delhi, 2014.

Padey, M. and Kedia, O. (2007). "United Nations in the Service of the Common Man", Publication Division, Ministry of Information and broadcasting, Govt. of India, New Delhi, 2007 (Reprint).

Razi, S. (2009). "Food Security the Next Big Challenge", Kurukshetra, A Journal on Rural Development, Publication Division, Ministry of Information and Broadcasting, Govt. of India, new Delhi, Vol.11 (57). 3-7.

Sultana, B. N. and Ahmed, S. N. (2015). "Determinants of Rural Household Food Security in Murshidabad District of West Bengal", Man and Development, Vol. xxxvii (4):63-77

Sen, A. (1981). "Poverty and Famines: An Essay on Entitlement and Deprivation", Clarendon Press, Oxford, 1981.

12

Quantitative Assessment: Beneficiary Nutritional Status and Performance of ICDS Supplementary Nutrition Programme in Bihar

Andrew Fraker, Neil Buddy Shah and Ronald Abraham

Introduction

Child malnutrition is a critical problem in Bihar, where the prevalence of underweight children is far worse than the Indian average and higher than any country in the world.[1] Recognising this, the Bihar State government (along with the Central government) commits over Rs 1,100 crore per year (US $200 million) to the Integrated Child Development Services (ICDS) Supplementary Nutrition Programme (SNP). However, the government is aware that programme funds are regularly pilfered, and it is common for anganwadi centre staff to fail to provide meals and dry rations to the intended beneficiaries.

This assessment quantifies the shortcomings of ICDS'SNP by providing in-depth analysis of ground-level realities through independent, primary data collection. Evidence from this assessment will provide a foundation for ICDS to work on.

The main findings from this quantitative assessment are:

1. Fifty-three per cent of the SNP budget was "missing" due to lea 71 per cent of the budget for food served at AWCs was missing 38 per cent of the budget for take home rations was missing.

   The main sources of fund leakage were:

   - Anganwadi centres were open 76.5 per cent of the time they should have been.
   - Meals were only served 77 per cent of the time when centres were open, and 59 per cent of the time overall.
   - When meals were provided, only 386 calories (77 per cent of stipulated amount) and 11.7 grams of protein (78 per cent of stipulated amount) were served per child per day.
   - On days when the centres served meals, child attendance was only 56 per cent of the number of children for which the centres get funds.
   - Eithy-four per cent of beneficiaries received take home rations (THR), and those that got THR only received 61 per cent of the stipulated amount, on average.

2. Nutrition levels were very low

   - Forty-three per cent of children are underweight-for-age, 58 per cent have low height-for-age, and 20 per cent have low weight-for-height, a prevalence beyond "critical" as per the World Health Organisation.
   - thirty-nine per cent of nursing mothers are underweight

The remainder of this report is organised as follows:

1. Background
2. Anganwadi centre performance
3. Beneficiary nutrition levels and nutrition at home
4. Conclusion

1. Background

Child malnutrition in Bihar

In India, 43 per cent of children under age five are underweight for their age.[2] Bihar has the third highest prevalence of underweight children (56.1 per cent) among Indian states, after only Jharkhand (57.1 per cent) and Madhya Pradesh (59.8 per cent).[3] The prevalence of underweight children in Bihar is higher than any country in the world.[4]

ICDS and the Supplementary Nutrition Programme

The Integrated Child Development Services (ICDS) scheme was launched in India in 1975 to address issues critical for child development. The scheme addresses three inter-sectoral aspects of child development –nutrition, early childhood education, and health –and is one of the largest community-based child development programmes in the world. To specifically address child malnutrition, ICDS launched the Supplementary Nutrition Programme (SNP), which provides nutritional food to vulnerable populations such as children up to 6 years of age, pregnant women and nursing mothers.

The SNP has two components

- Hot cooked meal and morning snack served daily at anganwadi centres to children ages three to six, and adolescent girls, for 25 days per month
- Monthly take home rations (THR) for children ages six months to three years, pregnant and nursing mothers, and adolescent girls

The government currently spends over Rs 1,100 crore (US $200 million) per annum on the SNP.[5] However, leakage of funds from public service delivery programmes like the SNP is endemic in India and Bihar.

Purpose of this quantitative assessment

ICDS in Bihar wanted to quantify the current level of performance and asked insight to conduct this assessment as part of a larger initiative to refine the Supplementary Nutrition Programme (SNP). The main purposes of this assessment are to quantify:

- Missing expenditure from the SNP.
- Quality and quantity of nutrition actually received by beneficiaries.
- Nutritional levels of beneficiaries.

This assessment will serve as a quantitative description of the status quo, which will serve as the foundation that the ICDS leadership intends to use to support its work in improving the delivery of nutrition to children and the overall performance of the SNP.

Sample and methods

The survey was conducted between November 6 and December 15, 2012. Three districts (Gaya, Muzzafarpur and Madhubani) were selected in a manner to maximize representativeness of the sample to the state of Bihar. At least one district from the Magahi and Maithili cultural-language regions were chosen, and the districts were selected to be as close to the Bihar state averages on key indicators from the 2011 census.

Table 12.1: Comparing study districts and Bihar on key characteristics

Characteristic	*Bihar average*	*Study districts*
Female literacy	53.0%	53.7%
Population density (pop. per km^2)	1,222	1,102
Gender ratio (girls per 1,000 boys, ages 0-6)	933	936
Children ages 0-6 as % of population	17.9%	17.3%

Source: Census of India, 2011

Within the three districts, 20 blocks were selected and within each block an average of 10 panchayats were randomly selected. In each panchayat, one anganwadi centre was randomly selected for surveying.

To gather the data, surveyors[6] made unannounced visits to anganwadi centres between 11:45 am – 1:00 pm – the hours during which ICDS has specified that anganwadi staff must prepare meals.[7] The surveyors undertook the following eight activities at the anganwadi centre:

- Direct observation of meal preparation or the lack thereof.
- Weighing of amount of food prepared.
- Sample collection of food for nutritional analysis at a laboratory.
- Staff and beneficiary attendance.
- Examination of child attendance, THR, and monitoring registers.
- Random selection of one SNP beneficiary from the children attending on the day of the survey for home visit, anthropometric measurements, and nutrition survey.
- Random selection of one THR child beneficiary from the THR register for home visit, anthropometric measurements, and nutrition survey.
- Random selection of one THR mother beneficiary from the THR register for home visit, anthropometric measurements, and nutrition survey.

The final sample includes:

- 200 anganwadi centres.
- 200 children ages six months to three years (one per centre).
- 200 pregnant or nursing mothers (one per centre).
- 153 children ages three to six (one for each centre open on the day of visit).
- 172 shopkeepers (minimum of six per block).

3. Anganwadi Centre Performance

Missing expenditure

ICDS leadership is keenly aware that leakage exists in the SNP system, but does not know the precise level or the main sources. This assessment carefully quantifies missing expenditure according to each of the possible margins on which funds could go missing.[8] As stated previously, SNP has two components:

- Hot cooked meal and morning snack served daily at anganwadi centres to children ages three to six, and adolescent girls, for 25 days per month.
- Monthly take home rations (THR) for children ages six months to three years, pregnant and nursing mothers, and adolescent girls.

Missing expenditure from the daily lunch component

If the anganwadi centre is open on all 25 days per month, and the anganwadi centre staff serve the government prescribed quality and quantity of food to the number of children that are officially recorded in their registers as attending, then average anganwadi expenditure per month would be Rs 5,497, while the monthly allotment is Rs 4,592. This difference is due to the higher prices of foodstuffs in the local markets, as compared to the price list used by ICDS.

However, from the allotment of Rs 4,592 only 1,326 Rs are spent per month, due to the fol-lowing five factors: (1) closed anganwadi centres, (2) anganwadi centres that were open, but did not serve meals, (3) children that are not present for the meal, if a meal is served, (4) insuf-ficient amount of ingredients, and (5) the cost of the ingredients. Graph 12.1 below illustrates the measured levels of each of these factors, and each is explained below.

1. **Closed anganwadi centres**: 24 per cent of anganwadi centres were found closed on the day of the surveyor visit, reducing expenditure by 24 percentage points.[9]

2. **Meals not served when centre is open**: Of the open anganwadi centres, meals were not served 23 per cent of the time. This pushes expenditure down a further 18 percentage points.[10] Thus, it follows that meals were only served on 59 per cent of days when they should be.
3. **Children not present for meals:** On average only 22 children out of the 40 that should attend (and for whom the anganwadi worker is receiving funds) are present for meals. This pushes expenditure down a further 26 percentage points, from 59 per cent to 33 per cent.
4. **Ingredient underutilisation**: Only 73 per cent of the stipulated ingredients (mostly rice and dal) are used, further pushing the total expenditure down nine percentage points from 33 per cent to 24 per cent.
5. **Ingredient cost**: Ingredients needed to prepare the meals on average cost 20 per cent more on average than the amount allocated by ICDS. This increased total expenditure 5 percentage points, from 24 per cent to 29 per cent

Taken together, **an estimated 71 per cent of funds the anganwadi worker receives for this com-ponent of SNP are not spent on the beneficiaries.** This means Rs 3,267 are effectively pil-fered per anganwadi centre per month through the hot cooked meal and morning snack component of SNP.

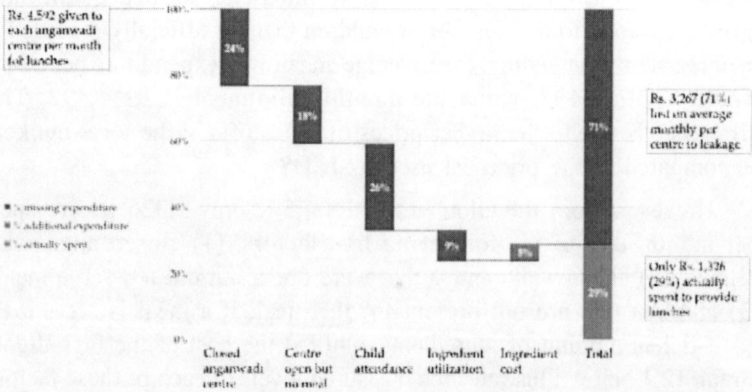

Graph 12.1: Missing lunch expenditure: contribution of each factor.

Missing expenditure from the take home rations (THR) component

The THR component is intended to provide bags of rice and dal to young children, and pregnant and nursing mothers once per month. Missing expenditure in THR is due to three factors: (1) the percentage of intended beneficiaries that do not receive any THR, (2) benefi-ciaries not receiving the intended quantity of THR, and (3) the price of rice and dal. Graph 12.2 below summarizes missing expenditure for rice, and Graph 12.3 for dal.

For rice:

1. **Not receiving any rice**: 83 per cent of beneficiaries reported receiving THR of rice, which translate to a leakage of 17 percentage points
2. **Receiving insufficient quantities of rice**: Beneficiaries reported receiving only 68 per cent of the government prescribed quantity of rice, increasing leakage by 27 percentage points.
3. **Cost of rice**: Rice cost 14 per cent more than what ICDS provides for, decreasing leakage by 8 percentage points.

In total for THR rice, 36 per cent of funds received by the anganwadi worker

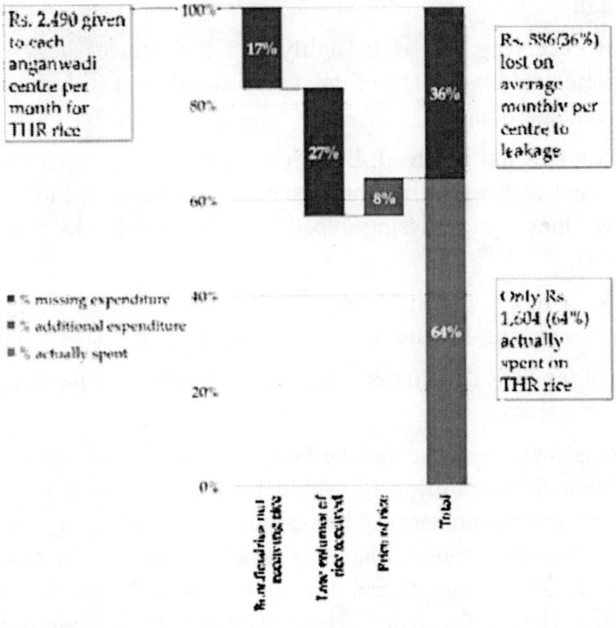

Graph 12.2: Missing THR rice expenditure: contribution of each factor.

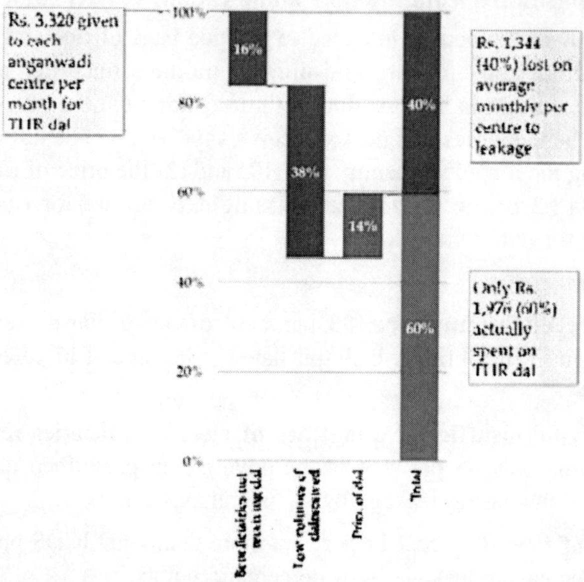

Graph 12.3: Missing THR dal expenditure: contribution of each factor.

For dal:

1. **Not receiving any dal**: Eighty-four per cent of beneficiaries reported receiving THR of dal, which translates to a leakage of 16 percentage points
2. **Volume of dal received**: Beneficiaries reported receiving only 54 per cent of the government prescribed volume of dal they should have, increasing missing expenditure/leakage by 38 percentage points.
3. **Cost of dal**: Dal cost 31 per cent more than what ICDS provided for, decreasing missing expenditure by 14 percentage points.

In total for THR dal, 40 per cent of funds received by the anganwadi worker are leakage.

There is some evidence that the missing THR expenditure is slightly underestimated. In addition to asking beneficiaries how much they received, on the November take home ration distribution day surveyors visited 34 anganwadi centres randomly selected from the 200 anganwadi centres in the survey sample and directly measured the quantity of take home ra-tions being distributed. These average quantities are lower for rice and dal than what bene-ficiaries reported. See Graph 12.4 below. For the purposes of this analysis the beneficiary reported values are used.

Overall for THR, 38 per cent of funds received were not spent on beneficiaries. This means Rs 2,230 are pilfered on average per anganwadi centre per month through the THR component.

Overall missing expenditure

Table 12.2: SNP missing expenditure per programme component per anganwadi centre per month (in Rs)

SNP Component	*Budget*	*Amount spent*	*Missing expenditure*	*% of component funds missing*	*Share of total SNP funds missing*
Lunch	4,592	1,326	3,267	71%	59%
THR	5,810	3,580	2,230	38%	41%
Total	**10,403**	**4,906**	**5,497**	**53%**	**100%**

More than half –53 per cent of funds received by the anganwadi workers – are not spent to provide food to the children and mothers. If the observed anganwadi centres are typical of others throughout Bihar, this amounts to an estimated loss of over Rs 581 crores (US $ 106 million) per year for the state and central exchequer. Some of the key anganwadi centre performance factors are analysed below.

Nutritional quality of the meals: calories and protein

For the daily lunch and snack component of SNP, food samples were taken from the cooked meals at the anganwadi centre, preserved with formaldehyde solution and ice, and sent to Mitra S. K. Private Limited[11] in Kolkata to measure caloric and protein content. On the 59 per cent of days when children were actually served a meal, children were provided with 386 calories per meal each, and 11.7 grams of protein, on average.[12] This is 77 per cent and 78 per cent of the government-required amounts of 500 calories and 15 grams of protein per meal, respectively.

Staff attendance

Each anganwadi centre is staffed by a Sevika, who runs the centre, and a Sahayika, who assists the Sevika, and is responsible for cooking the meal. However, only in a minority (40.0 per cent) of cases were both found present at the anganwadi centre at the time the surveyor arrives. Graph 12.6 also shows that in 18.5 per cent of cases only the Sahayika was there, in 16.0 per cent only the Sevika was there, and in

25.5 per cent neither were present, usually resulting in the anganwadi centre being closed. Overall Sevikas were present 56.0 per cent of the time, and Sahayikas 58.5 per cent.[13]

Staff presence is closely correlated with meal provision. In the cases where both staff members were present, meals were served 86.3 per cent of the time. When the Sevika was absent, the meal provision rate fell to 78.4 per cent, and if the Sahayika was absent, meal provision was only 56.3 per cent. If neither were there meals were only served 3.0 per cent of the time.[14]

Child attendance

Anganwadi centres are provided funds to feed 40 children. In cases where the anganwadi centre was open, on average only 17.1 children were present when the surveyor arrived. Attendance increased slightly to 20.3 children[15] by the time the meals are usually served. Of the children in attendance, 58 per cent were girls.

Child attendance is closely associated with meals being served. An average of 22.4 children attend when a meal is served, but when the anganwadi centre is open but not serving a meal, average attendance is only 12.8. According to the official attendance registers for the past three working days, Sevikas reported an average attendance of 37.1 children, which is evidence of over reporting.

If anganwadi centres functioned as they should: open 25 days per month with 40 children attending, surveyors would have observed 8,000 children. In fact, they only saw 3,041 children, or 38 per cent of the number they should have seen.

Child activities

Not only do anganwadi centres do a poor job of providing meals for children, they offer few learning opportunities. Graph 12.10 shows that in only 28.5 per cent of cases were children participating in an organised activity, and 8.5 per cent of the time they were playing. 39.5 per cent of the time the children were simply sitting idle, while 23.5 per cent of the time no children were present, usually because the anganwadi centre was closed on that day.

4. Beneficiary nutrition levels and nutrition at home

Nutrition levels

Children under age five

Overall, 43 per cent of children under age five in the sample are underweight for their age,[16] as shown in Graph 12.11. This is lower than what the 2005 National Family Health Survey-3 survey indi-cates, but is almost identical to the data from a 2011 survey conducted by the Naandi foundation.[17] Fifty-eight per cent of children suffer from stunting (low height-for-age) which is due to chronic malnourishment. Almost 20 per cent of children suffer from wasting (low weight-for-height), which is often related to acute malnutrition.[18] These high levels are cause for concern: the World Health Organisation deems a prevalence of low weight-for-height over 10 per cent as "serious"and over 15 per cent as "critical".

Mothers

The pregnant and nursing mothers also suffer from high levels of malnutrition. 16.4 per cent of pregnant mothers are below the underweight threshold for non-pregnant mothers (body mass index below 18.5 kg / m^2), despite the necessary weight gain due to pregnancy. Low maternal body mass index is associated with increased risk of intrauterine growth restriction,[19] which increases the risk of illness, disability and death.[20] In addition, nearly 2 in 5 (38.6 per cent) of nursing mothers are underweight.

Association between nutrition levels and anganwadi centre performance

Table 3: Association between nutrition levels and anganwadi centre performance

	AWC open	*Sevika present*	*Sahayika present*	*Both present*	*Meal served*
Weight-for-age (3-6)	-	0.46	0.01	0.27	0.16
Height-for-age (3-6)	-	0.19	0.29	0.35	0.42
Weight-for-height (3-6)	-	0.51	-0.25	0.08	-0.17
Weight-for-age (6m-3y)	-0.13	-0.02	0.04	0.06	0.07
Height-for-age (6m-3y)	-0.32	-0.09	0.05	0.14	-0.02
Weight-for-height (6m-3y)	0.07	0.05	-0.02	-0.06	0.13
Body mass index (mothers)	0.73*	0.59*	0.46	0.44	0.16

* indicates statistically significant with $p<0.10$. Values shown are z-scores.

The following table shows how anganwadi centre performance variables are correlated with beneficiary nutrition. However, most are not statistically significant, and no causal relationships can be claimed. It is possible that better performing anganwadi centres increase beneficiary outcomes, however it is also possible that areas with better nutrition levels are more developed in general, and also have better functioning anganwadi centres. The coefficients in the table are the average difference between z-scores[21] for beneficiaries belonging to an anganwadi centre found to be of a certain status (indicated by the column heading, such as Sevika being present or absent) on the survey day. Observations at the anganwadi centre are positively correlated with nutritional outcomes of children eligible for meals (ages 3–6) in 9 out of 12 cases.

Home nutrition

Meals at home

Children who attend the anganwadi centres eat meals and snacks 3.3 times a day at home. They usually eat once in the morning before attending the anganwadi centre, then two or three times after returning home. Households do not seem to respond to whether or not the AWC served a meal: children have 3.3 meals on days when the AWC served a meal and 3.1 on days when they did not.[22,23]

Children and mothers usually have dal once per day, and that is their main source of pro-tein. Graph 12.13 below shows that 71 per cent of children and 72 per cent of mothers had eaten dal on the day before the survey, and 39 per cent and 41 per cent had eaten other protein sources. Only 23 per cent of children and 17 per cent of mothers had not eaten any protein sources on the previous day of the survey.

Conclusion

There are no easy solutions guaranteed to reduce leakage and increase the provision of nu-tritious food to Bihar's millions of malnourish assessment was a first step that provides evidence of what the sources of leakage and areas of concern are overall. This report provides the foundation for the design of interventions by ICDS to improve the Supplementary Nutrition Programme. Ideally, each intervention should be piloted, refined, and rigorously evaluated for impact before scaling across the state. The Government of Bihar and ICDS' to improve eagerness the performance of to in no SNP provides hope that the status quo can improve, ultimately benefiting millions.

Notes

1. Menon, P., Deolalikar, A. and Bhaskar, A., 2009. India State Hunger Index: Comparisons of Hunger Across States. IFPRI.
2. The most recent data is seven years old, from NFHS-III, 2005.
3. Menon, P., Deolalikar, A. and Bhaskar, A., 2009. India State Hunger Index: Comparisons of Hunger Across States. IFPRI.
4. World Bank, 2012. World Development Indicators. Accessed online at: http://data.worldbank.org/data-catalog/world-development-indicators.
5. http://www.icdsbih.gov.in/
6. The surveyors were hired, trained, and managed by a third-party evaluation organisation, IDinsight, and have no relationship with the government or ICDS. This was done to ensure integrity of data collected from the random visits.
7. During the winter, anganwadi centres are open from 10AM to 2PM.
8. Anecdotally, supervisory staff such as CDPOs sometimes extract rents from the Sevikas. This assessment was unable to capture what portion of the missing expenditure is goes in that channel. This report is also unable to quantify how much missing expenditure was due to not providing daily snacks to children (5.2 per cent of the SNP budget), which anecdotally was not done frequently.
9. We confirmed with villagers and ICDS that these centres were not permanently closed, but rather closed on that particular day.
10. 17 percentage points is calculated as following: 76 per cent of centres are open * 23 per cent that do not serve meals = 17 per cent.
11. Mitra SK's laboratories are recognised by the National Accreditation.
12. We did not find systematic evidence of surveyor effects on the amount of food being prepared or the type of ingredients used. Comparing cases where surveyors arrive at the food preparation stage vs. after the meal had already been cooked, the amount of protein per child was very similar, after accounting for 1 extreme outlier. Likewise the number of calories per child was somewhat higher on an average for the preparation stage observations, but this was not statistically significant.
13. Sevika attendance was lower (42.1 per cent) during the quarterly polio immunisation campaign and higher (61.5 per cent) for the majority of the survey that occurred after polio week. Sahayika attendance remained the same, and meals were served less frequently, though this was not statistically significant at $p=0.10$.
14. In these cases one of the staff members had been there to prepare the meal, and would return when she learned a surveyor was there.
15. This figure includes centres that did not serve meals, which had lower attendance on an average.

16. Technically, underweight is defined as "percentage-for-below minusof twochildren u standard deviations of the NCHS/ WHO reference median," stunted is the height-for-age below minus two standard deviations of the National Center for Health Statistics (NCHS)/WHO reference median," and the percentage wasted of children is under five years who have a weight for height below minus two standard deviations of the NCHS/WHO reference median. *Source*: http://www.who.int/healthinfo/statistics/indchildrenstunted/
17. HUNGaMA (2011), *Fighting Hunger and Malnutrition, The HUNGAMA Survey Report 2011*. In their survey in 112 districts in 9 states, 2 were in common with our survey. Our measures of the prevalence of underweight and stunted children were near identical in each of these districts.
18. See this source for further explanation and interpretation of the nutrition metrics: http://www.who.int/nutgrowthdb/about/introduction/en/index2.html
19. Fishman SM, Caulfield L, de On is under weight M, et. al In: Ezzatial. M, Childhood Lopez AD, Rodgers A, and Mur-maternal ray CLJ, eds. Comparative quantification of health risks: global a risk factors. Geneva: World Health Organisation, 2004: 39-161.
20. Black, RE, Allen, LH, Bhutta, ZA, *et al.*, for the Maternal and Child Undernutrition Study Group. Maternal and child undernu-trition: global and regional exposures and health consequences. Lancet 2008; 371: 243-60.
21. A z-score is the standard deviation above or below the NCHS/WHO reference median for a given age and gender.
22. The difference is not statistically significant.
23. We are unable to comment on whether the quantity of food received at home lessens in response to food received at the anganwadi centre.

13

Children's Development Baby Steps in Odisha

Reetika Khera

"The Integrated Child Development Services scheme and maternity entitlements can play a crucial role in improving children's food and nutrition security. Both interventions are part of the National Food Security Act, though maternity entitlements have yet to be activated. Odisha has experimented with several creative policies, including initiating a maternity entitlements scheme in 2011 before the NFSA was enacted, introduction of eggs and decentralised procurement of take-home rations in the ICDS. This article, based on a field study of the two children's schemes in four districts in December 2014, reports how they perform and identifies areas for further action."

The survey was organised by the Office of the State Adviser to the Commissioners in the Right to Food Case in the Supreme Court (Odisha). The Office of the State Adviser is supported by Dan Church Aid. I thank Rajkishor Mishra (state adviser) and Naman Garg for help with the survey, Jean Drèze and Arti Ahuja for helpful comments.

At the Tasarda (Mayurbhanj) anganwadi, as the auxiliary nurse and midwife (ANM) pulled out the blood pressure (BP) instrument to check a pregnant woman, the children at the anganwadi began playing "nurse":

with their little sts, they pumped an imaginary BP instrument, and a short while later, squealed with laughter as they let off the pressure with a "pphssss" sound. The ANM had come for her scheduled "Mamata Divas" where pregnant and lactating mothers receive antenatal care (ANC). The endearing moment at the Tasarda anganwadi was significant because it suggested that ANC activities, such as checking BP, were regular enough for the children to have learned how to imitate them. The Integrated Child Development Services (ICDS) scheme is the largest universal government programme that reaches children under the age of six years. The ICDS includes supplementary nutrition, pre-school education (pse), growth monitoring, immunisation, health check-ups and referral for children. In addition, there are some interventions for adolescent girls, pregnant and lactating mothers also. Given that a child's future well-being (in terms of health, nutrition and education) is determined substantially in this period, the ICDS is a very important programme. Along with maternity entitlements, mid-day meals and the public distribution system (PDS), ICDS is also one of the four pillars of the National Food Security Act (NFSA), 2013. For a programme that is so important, there have been few reliable studies of the implementation of ICDS. An important study was the Focus on Children Under Six (FOCUS) report, prepared by the Citizen's Initiative for the Rights of Children Under Six (CIRCUS). The FOCUS report studied ICDS in six states (Chhattisgarh, Himachal Pradesh, Maharashtra, Rajasthan, Uttar Pradesh and Tamil Nadu) in 2004 and found that the ICDS was "dormant" in Chhattisgarh, Rajasthan and Uttar Pradesh, and active in the other three states. Recently, several studies have noted the activation of the services that are supposed to be provided through the ICDS scheme. Between July and December 2009, an independent evaluation of the ICDS was undertaken by the Planning Commission (Government of India, 2011a, 2011b). They found that less than half of eligible children were covered by the ICDS, cited in Government of India 2011a and Odisha Advisor's Office 2010). The Public Evaluation of Entitlement Programmes (PEEP) Survey 2013 interviewed mothers of three–six-year-old children. In Odisha, the PEEP Survey covered two districts (Sundergarh and Koraput) and found that 96 per cent of mothers reported receiving Supplementary Nutrition Programme (SNP) regularly, 76 per cent reported regular immunisation. The proportion of mothers who report regular growth monitoring (84 per cent) and PSE (76 per cent) was also high. Among the 10 states in which the PEEP Survey 2013 was undertaken, Odisha was ranked third for implementation of the ICDS (Drèze and Khera, 2013). However, the sample size in the PEEP Survey was quite small and did not include interviews with AWWs or visits to the anganwadi centre (AWC). To overcome these limitations, we conducted the Odisha ICDS Survey 2014 from 11 to 20 December 2014 using a subset of the FOCUS survey instruments. However, in addition to studying the ICDS scheme, we interviewed beneciaries of maternity entitlements under the Mamata scheme of the Government of Odisha, introduced in 2011. Odisha is among the few states that has a universal scheme for maternity entitlements. Four districts, one each from coastal (Ganjam), northern (Mayurbhanj), western (Bargarh) and southern (Koraput) Odisha were selected. Within each district, two blocks were selected; in each block, three sample and three replacement gram panchayats (GP) were randomly selected. In each GP, two AWCs were selected through random sampling.[1] From the register at the AWC, the teams took a random sample of three mothers from the three–six-year-old enrollment list and three from the seven months to three years list. In addition to this, the team randomly sampled ve women who had received all four instalments of Mamata maternity e ntitlements. The full sample has 147 mothers of preschool children (three–six-year age group), 146 mothers of under-three-year-old children and 233 Mamata beneciaries from 49 AWCs. Table 13.1 presents a snapshot of the improvement in the ICDS in Odisha, using data from the National Family Health Survey 2005–06 and the Odisha ICDS Survey 2014. On each of the services—SNP, PSE, immunisation, growth monitoring and health check-ups—there is a big jump. For example, from about half in 2005–06 to nearly universal for SNP; from less than one- third to 85 per cent for PSE and so on.

1. Anganwadi Workers and Their Work Environment

AWWs are the front-line workers as far as the ICDS scheme is concerned. They play a key role in ensuring that the six ICDS are provided at the AWC. Good education and training, decent employment conditions for them are crucial to make ICDS work. On average, AWWs were 36 years of age and had studied up to Class 11. Adivasi and Dalit AWWs made up 20 per cent each of the sample; Other Backward Class (OBC) members were 40 per cent. Most AWWs were getting their full salary, and they reported getting it once in every two–three months (over

70 per cent had salary due to them). Apart from the delays, there were no major salary-related complaints. A majority (85 per cent) of AWWs said that their salaries had improved in the past five years. The are paid between Rs 3,500 and 4,000 per month. (The state government "tops up" AWW salaries: the central government contributes Rs 3,000 and the state government has been paying an additional Rs 500 for AWWs who have not completed Class 10 and Rs 1,000 who have studied beyond Class 10.) However, AWWs at mini-AWCs—with exactly the same responsibilities as AWWs at regular AWCs—are paid only Rs 1,500–2,000 per month and do not even have a helper to assist them. Though few AWWs report harassment (for example, 10 per cent said they had to pay a bribe to get work done), one complaint they often had was an increase in the number of duties. This may be a result of the Right to Education Act which does not allow school teachers to be assigned non-teaching duties. ICDS-related paperwork had increased: on an average, they maintain 28 registers, and spend nine hours a week to maintain these registers. AWWs are able to manage the increased workload because the team of ICDS frontline workers is functional in Odisha: the AWW works closely with the anganwadi helper (AWH), ANM and the accredited social health activist (ASHA). There was a clear division of tasks among them (more on this below). This means that the AWWs are in a position to full their basic duties (even though, say, registers were patchily maintained) without being impossibly burdened as noted in earlier studies of the ICDS. The coming together of this team was one significant finding of the Odisha ICDS Survey. Their work was also appreciated by the community: mothers were generally positive about AWWs. About one-tenth of the mothers felt that the AWWs' motivation levels were "very" or "rather" low.

2. Services at the Anganwadi

Survey teams were instructed to reach the anganwadi during opening hours. We found that a regular routine is in place: most AWCs were open when the teams arrived and in about 70 per cent of AWCs, the AWW were also present at the time of arrival. Three-quarters of mothers of preschool children (three–six years) said that their child attended yesterday; a higher proportion (80 per cent) reported that the child attends regularly. However, the teams found there can be considerable variation in opening time and opening hours. On an average, mothers reported that the anganwadi opens for three hours daily.

Table 13.1: Improvement at the Anganwadi: NFHS 3 (2005–06) vs Odisha ICDS Survey (2014)

	NFHS 3 (2005–06)[1]		*Odisha ICDS Survey (2014)*	
Percentage of 0–71 Month Children	0–71	36-71	7–36	6–71
Who Received from AWC	Months	Months	Months	Months
Any service[2]	66	99	98	
Supplementary food	53	98	97	
Any immunisation	42	76	54	
Health check-up	43	58	53	
Percentage of children who received				
Preschool education	–	28	-	85
Percentage of children who were weighed	–	56[3]	58	76

1. Table 46, p. 73, International Institute of Population Sciences (2008).
2. Includes supplementary nutrition, growth monitoring, immunisation, health check-ups and pre-school education. For the Odisha ICDS Survey 2014, these services were received within the past six months.
3. 0–59 months old children.

ICDS provides six services through the anganwadi. Tables 13.2 and 13.3 report on the state of these services at the AWC, and are discussed below in some detail.

Table 13.2: Anganwadi Centre

	Number of enrolled children (average)
Under three years	31
Toddlers (three–six years)	23
Toddlers present on average on the last working day (as per AWW)	18
Toddlers present at the time of the arrival of the investigators	11
Average credit into AWC account in the past six months	Rs 12,843
Proportion (%) of AWCs reporting delays in receiving funds	
Always/frequently	31
Sometimes	49
Rarely/Never	20
AWWs (%) who reported that they had to put in own funds	71
Proportion (%) of AWWs reporting	
ANM visited in the last month	96

contd...

Fixed schedule for ANM visit	83
Visit is helpful	88
Proportion (%) of AWWs reporting ASHA appointed	92
Work with ASHA (where appointed)	96
Met ASHA at least once a month in the past three months	94
Physical infrastructure of anganwadi Own building	46
Toilet	15
Separate space for cooking	31
Separate space for playing	29
Safe drinking water	49
Storage space	27
Electricity	14

Table 13.3: Access to ICDS Services among Under-Three Children and Preschool Children

	Under- Three-Year-Old Children	*Preschool Children (Three–Six Years)*
Caste group of respondent (%)		
SC	17	18
ST	38	39
OBC	37	34
Other	9	10
Proportion (%) of mothers who live in the same hamlet as the AWC	75	76
Say they/their child find it difficult to reach the AWC	23	13
Number of eggs received in the past seven days	1.5 (2.0)[1]	2.4
Proportion of mothers who say that the AWC is "very" or "quite" important for their child's well-being Regularity of other ICDS services	91	91
Supplementary nutrition, within past week	65	92 (85[2])
Preschool education	Not applicable[3]	90

contd...

	Under-Three-Year-Old Children	*Preschool Children (Three–Six Years)*
Immunisation within past three months	62	54
Growth monitoring within past month	83	76
Health check-up within past month	59	–
Deworming within past six months	62	60
Proportion (%) of mothers, who perceive an improvement over past five years in Infrastructure	35	37
Parents' interest	78	82
AWWs' training	66	65
Inspection and monitoring	65	68
Total number of respondents	148	147

1. Average without Bargarh (see text for explanation).
2. Reference period is "Yesterday or today" among those who attended yesterday.
3. 25 under-three year-old were going to the AWC.

Supplementary Nutrition Programme: At all AWCs, a hot meal is cooked by the AWH and/or AWW for preschool children. Wherever appointed, the AWH has the main responsibility for preparing the hot-cooked meal. In addition to this, the AWH plays an important role in bringing the three–six-year-old "preschool" children to the AWC from their homes. As far as SNP is concerned, the main tasks of the AWW include helping the AWH, purchasing eggs, dal and other ingredients, distributing take-home rations (THR) and maintaining records. Hot cooked food is provided as per the weekly menu and includes eggs thrice a week (Wednesdays, Fridays and Saturdays). On average, mothers reported that their child had received 2.4 eggs in the past week at the anganwadi. There is also a provision for serving a morning snack at the AWC—only two-thirds of the mothers of preschool children said that their child gets the morning snack regularly. In almost all cases, vegetables and dals are bought locally by the AWW and AWH, whereas the grain (rice) is supplied by the Child Development Project Ofcer's (CDPO) ofce. In April 2011, the Government of Odisha put in place a system for decentralised procurement of vegetables and dals, whereby money is transferred into the joint account of the AWW and a GP member for the provision of hot cooked meals.[2] Since the account is jointly held with a panchayat member, panchayatiraj institutions and members are also involved in the running of the ICDS. This has been combined with putting in place village *jaanch* (monitoring) committees and mother's committees. The system appeared to work reasonably well, though the accounting practices need to be tightened (see discussion on corruption below). For children under three years of age, there is a provision THR. The THR includes two packets of *chhatua* (roasted mix of wheat, dal, groundnut and sugar) each month and two eggs a week. Women's self-help groups supply chhatua. Mothers reported getting, on average, 1.6 packets of chhatua in the past 30 days, and 1.5 out of their entitlement of two eggs in the past one week.[3] Mothers of younger and older children were happy with the SNP: 87 per cent reported that it was regular and 90 per cent said that they were very satisfied or somewhat satised with the quality of the food provided. An important reason for the regularity is that mothers were aware of their child's entitlements. For instance, only four per cent mothers (of preschool children) did not know that their child was entitled to eggs at the AWC. Among mothers of younger children in Bargarh where eggs were not being distributed, nearly two-thirds were not aware of the provision of eggs.

Preschool Education: AWWs have the sole responsibility for undertaking PSE activities (such as teaching child songs). These PSE activities have become relatively regular: more than 90 per cent of mothers of preschool children (that is, three–six-years-old) said that some PSE activity had taken place within the last week, though some mothers complained that not enough was done. The expectation among mothers that the AWC should not be only about dal–rice and eggs was encouraging to see.[4]

At each AWC, the teams requested children to sing a song—at more than three-quarters of AWC, children were able to sing a rhyme. (Some AWWs said that there were 12 songs, one for each month, in Arunima, a book provided to them by the state government.) However, toys and other PSE material was sorely lacking—for example, less than one-third of AWCs had toys and about half had pictoral charts. Often, it was not clear if these were being used.

Growth Monitoring, Immunisation and Maternal Health: For other services, such as growth monitoring, immunisation and antenatal health check-ups, the main responsibility lies with the ANM and the ASHA. The AWW and AWH support and assist them in these activities. ASHAs were appointed in 90 per cent of the AWCs. Over 80 per cent of AWWs said that the date for the visit of the ANM was fixed. The schedule was adhered to at nearly all AWCs: only two AWCs reported that the ANM had skipped one month's visit. Mothers confirmed that these activities are taking place: 94 per cent of mothers of children under three years and 83 per cent of mothers of preschool children said that they had a Mamata card, and between 54 per cent and 78 per cent (of under-three children and preschool children) of these cards were fully maintained according to the investigators. Another one-fifth of the cards were partially maintained. Between 62 per cent and 76 per cent mothers said that their child had been weighed in the past month. About 60 per cent of mothers said they had received deworming medicine in the past six months. Health referral services continue to be weak or non-existent. Quite likely, this is because the public health services have not been activated in the same way as the ICDS. Further confirmation of these activities comes from the fact that while the survey teams were in the field, they met ANMs at the AWC conducting these activities, including antenatal check-ups for pregnant women, and when mothers were able to tell the survey teams what their child's weight was when they were asked (not systematically). In fact, activation of these services was one of the most impressive achievements in the ICDS in Odisha. It was quite heartening to see this team of four women: AWW, AWH, ANM and the ASHAs working together at many centres. Overall, mothers were highly appreciative of the services provided there. Over 90 per cent said that the AWC was very important for their child's well-being. When asked why they felt that way, apart from the provision of eggs (even otherwise clueless fathers knew about eggs), mothers mentioned preschool acti vities, that her child formed the habit of going to the AWC, that her child enjoyed being with other children, etc. Because of regular weighing of her child at the AWC, a young mother in Ganjam was able to consult a doctor as her younger child's weight had caught up with the older child's weight.

3. Mamata: A Scheme for Maternity Entitlements: The Government of Odisha is among a handful of states in India to launch universal maternity entitlements for the first two pregnancies. Odisha's Mamata scheme provides Rs 5,000 as maternity entitlements, that is, a cash transfer. There are some conditions, for example, registration with the AWW and getting a Mamata card, one antenatal check-up, iron/folic acid tablets, one tetanus vaccination and one counselling session for the first instalment, registration of child's birth and immunisation for the next instalment and so on.[5] As mentioned earlier, at the sample AWC, we selected five mothers who were supposed to have got all four instalments by random sampling, from the Mamata Tracking Register maintained at the anganwadi. Table 13.4 presents the main findings.

Table 13.4: Maternity Entitlements in Odisha

Average number of Mamata beneficiaries per AWC	22
Proportion (%) of mothers of children in seven months to three years age group who were on the Mamata list	67
Among mothers who ought to have received all four instalments, proportion (%) who reported	
All four instalments are due	9
Some instalments are due	14
Only last instalment is due	4
All four instalments have been received	72
Average amount received (among those who had got all four instalments)	Rs 4,722
Problems reported by respondents (%)	
Opening a bank account	13
Meeting conditionalities	12
Delays	20
Corruption	9
Uses of cash transfer, as reported by respondents (%)	
Health	74
Food	64
Saved	36
Celebration	9

Coverage: The Mamata scheme is supposed to be a universal scheme. According to the registers at the anganwadi, out of 1,544 enrolled children in the seven months to three years age group, 1,035 mothers had got Mamata benefits, that is, two-thirds of mothers who had a child in the past three years were on the list of the Mamata scheme. The scheme appears to have taken root in the state. We spoke to 233 mothers, that is, about one-fifth of the 1,035 beneficiaries. Nearly one-third were illiterate, and on average, they had five years of schooling. Boys marginally outnumbered girls (120 vs 111) among bene ciary children. About one- third each were Adivasis or belonged to "other backward castes"; 20 per cent were Dalits and the rest were from the general caste or other groups. We did not come across any serious complaints of social discrimination.

Large number of mothers reported having used the money for food-related expenses for herself or the child (64 per cent) and health-related expenses (74 per cent). About one-third said that they had saved the money.

Schedule of Payments: As per the official schedule, the rst instalment is due in the sixth month of the pregnancy, the second (Rs 1,500) when the child is three months old; the next two instalments, Rs 1,000 each, are due when the child is six months and nine months old respectively. Awareness about the payment schedule was low. In many cases, the amount had not been credited as per the offcial schedule. One-fifth of the respondents reported delays.

Awareness and Corruption: Only 11 (that is, 5 per cent) beneficiaries were unaware of being on the beneficiary list. Among those who were aware of being on the list, 14 (7 per cent) had not got any money. Even though all payments are made through bank accounts, out of 233 respondents, about 10 per cent had corruption-related complaints. Seven per cent of the respondents reported having to pay someone to get the money. Similarly seven per cent of respondents had not received any money, even though according to the AWW's records she had received all the instal ments. The teams found several cases of erroneous transfers—for example, some instalments were credited twice, clubbing of several instalments and so on. In some cases, recovery of the excess amount had also been initiated. Among those who had received all instalments, on average, they got six per cent less than the full amount. Few respondents reported problems related to opening bank accounts (13 per cent), meeting conditionalities, for example, registering with the ANM, antenatal check-ups, etc, associated with each instalment (12 per cent).

Discussion: The level of functionality achieved in the ICDS in Odisha is remarkable because as recently as 2009, when anganwadis opened, the main activity was providing supplementary nutrition (Government of India 2011a). A study in 2009 in seven districts found that the "Take Home Ration under Supplementary Nutrition Programme is found to be the only activity that is going on everywhere. Sometimes the team felt that ICDS centre has been turned into distribution centre of the THR. On the other hand there is massive irregularities and corruption found in SNP (both THR and Spot Feeding) almost everywhere" (sic) (Advisor's Office 2010). Today, there appears to be a regular routine, which extends beyond providing hot cooked food to some pse activities as well as growth monitoring and immunisation. This has been achieved, partially at least, because of the coming together of a team of four workers (AWW, AWH, ANM and ASHA), with the AWW playing a key role. What remains a puzzle is how they were convinced to perform their duties regularly, when in neighbouring states (for example, Jharkhand) even today the AWW can be difficult to trace. Anecdotal evidence suggests that AWCs opened more or less regularly even earlier. In recent years, several factors have helped to build on that initial momentum: one, the work is to be done locally, which makes it possible for the AWW to do it regularly; two, initially, the workload was quite negligible—with few children enrolled and lack of monitoring or public pressure, it may have appeared to be an easy job. Three, as monitoring and public pressure increased the workload, salaries and work conditions also improved (for example, the appointment of helpers, working with the ANM). Finally, and unfortunately, the scope for keeping the "leftover" from the AWC account (amounting to about 20 per cent of the monthly salary) is likely an important part of the story of the activation of the ICDS in Odisha. The gains in the implementation of ICDS are largely on a ccount of creative policymaking in the eld of child nutrition in Odisha. Simple measures such as providing uniforms for the ANM, AWW, AWH and ASHA as well as anganwadi children helps create an environment of seriousness associated with, say, schooling or at health centres. Another example is decentralised procurement for items required for Supplementary Nutrition Programme (SNP). Instead of routing funds through the CDPO's of ce, the money goes straight into a joint account operated by the AWW and a GP member. This has freed AWWs from the tyranny of CDPOs, a common complaint elsewhere. Along with decentralised devolution of funds, the state has also introduced a model of decentralised procurement for THR. The most common form of THR is powdered mixes such as chhatua. Though such mixes can be reasonably nutritious, one problem has been keeping out commercial interests which will come primarily for the pro t. The decentral ised procurement model in Odisha where the standardised mix is prepared by self-help groups shows one way of surmounting that concern. The most interesting initiative as far as nutrition is concerned, of course, has been the introduction of eggs as THR. It is more nutritious than chhatua and given that its shelf life is longer than most other foods with comparable nutritive value, it can be given as THR. Political and administrative will is partly responsible for the observed improvement. Two examples that demonstrate this can easily be given. First, enhanced budgets for the ICDS: for example, the per child allocation has increased from Rs 2/child/day in 2008 to Rs 4 in 2009, and is currently at Rs 6 and the salary top-up given by the state government. Second, the government of cial in charge of the programme (Secretary, Women and Child Development) enjoyed a long stint in the same department (from 2010 to 2014). This allowed her to build a fuller understanding of the challenges and to put in place adequate systems (for example, decentralised procurement, computerisation, staff training for computer use) to deal with those challenges. Obviously, things are far from perfect. Two areas of serious concern in the functioning of the ICDS emerged clearly in our survey: poor physical infrastructure and corruption. The most basic physical infrastructure is still sorely lacking: less than half of the sample anganwadis were running in their own building.[6] One-fifth were operating from the AWW or AWH's house and another 30 per cent were running in a village "club" or a school room (Table 13.2). The lack of a dedicated physical space impeded the functioning of the centre in many ways– preschool activity (for example, the use of pictorial charts) could not always be conducted, the lack of storage space for AWC equipment (such as weighing scales, registers, etc), also caused inconvenience. Sometimes this meant that these activities were not conducted in the manner that they should be. For instance, among children who were at an anganwadi which had its own building, 94 per cent were able to sing a song. This proportion was much lower (61 per cent) among children whose anganwadi did not have its own building. Only 30 per cent AWCs had a functional kitchen. When there was no kitchen, the AWH cooked in the open or at their homes.[7] We did not investigate misappropriation of funds in a direct manner but it seems that tighter accounting practices would help. While SNP was the most regular service provided at the AWC, there remains scope for siphoning off money. The per child per day norm is Rs 6 for hot cooked meals, which is credited into the account of the AWW, jointly held with a ward member. AWWs are required to submit accounts for hot cooked food and the morning snack to the CDPO on a monthly basis. It is not clear whether these are verified in any way. As per the records, on an average, 23 children in the three–six-year age group were enrolled at the AWC. According to the AWW, 18 were present on the previous working day. (The attendance register also recorded the same number). This suggests that, on average, each day the SNP allocation for at least ve children remains unused. This comes to Rs 750 per month, a ssuming that SNP is allocated for 25 working days, that is, just over one-fifth of the funds for hot cooked meals remain unused.[8] We did not check if the balance remains in the account or if it is used, how. In the absence of regular monitoring, it is likely that some of it ends up being misappropriated. There were some complaints that cash for children's uniforms had not been distributed; even in the distribution of chhatua there appears to be some scope for cheating (for example, by distributing fewer packets than what people are entitled to). The sort of creative policy ideas mentioned earlier need to be devised for reducing corruption (for example, publicly displaying the bank account statement). With the constitution of village jaanch committees, mothers' committees as well as involvement of panchayat members, the means for community monitoring may get strengthened. Public pressure has quite likely played an important role in some of the improvement (for example, pressure through the media in 2011 led to the implementation of decentralised procurement for the SNP, and has made a difference). Ultimately, the findings point to the possibility of improvement in children's programmes in a relatively short span of time, with political and administrative will and public pressure.

Notes

1. Replacement AWCs were visited when the sample AWC was closed and unlikely to open on the day of the team's visit (for example, the worker at one mini-AWC was away for her own wedding). This happened in ve anganwadis out of 49 sample AWCs. Two anganwadis in Hinjilicatu Block (Ganjam) had to be replaced because the AWWs were attending a sector meeting at the CDPO's of ce. The AWCs were open, but there were no children at the time of the arrival of the team. In the replacement GP, the AWH were present with some children. In the light of the ongoing training in the block, the block was replaced, and the team worked in Digapahandi Block.
2. The move towards decentralised procurement was in response to a scam involving supply of poor quality of dal through a centralised mechanism. See Orissa Diary (2011a) and Orissa Diary (2011b).
3. The average number of eggs in the past week is two (leaving out Bargarh where THR eggs were not being distributed due to an objection from the AWWs union). Less than one-tenth (8 per cent) of the respondents said that they had received no chhatua packet in the past one month. Out of 24 mothers who reported that their child had been classified as malnourished, only 10 reported getting extra "red" chhatua packets.
4. Though, admittedly, most mothers associated anganwadis with food. About two-thirds of the mothers were able to associate with AWC with preschool education activities.
5. Details of the conditions can be found online at http://wcdodisha.gov.in/node/46.

6. According to the Government of India (2011a) study, 54 per cent of AWCs had their own centres. Where centres existed, they were in reasonable condition, though many were in need of minor repairs (for example, damaged ooring). Only half had drinking water facilities and three-quarters had a functional baby weighing scale. Toilets were hardly being used in the few AWCs where they existed. Survey data from 2009 suggests that things have become worse. If the older data is reliable and comparable, the decline in the indicators of physical infrastructure could be on account of the substantial increase in the number of AWCs in 2010–11.
7. However, the lack of a kitchen did not affect the number of eggs children got adversely.
8. In fact, we found that attendance on the day of the visit was lower. At the time of the team's arrival at the AWC, there were on average 11 children at the AWC. This number often increased, as the team arrived while children were still trickling in. If we assume that 15 children eat every day, then the money for eight children is left over, that is, Rs 1,200 per month. Further, on average, AWWs reported getting Rs 12,843 over the past six month to run the AWC (including money for uniforms), which also suggests that the leftover may be higher.

References

Advisor's Office (2010): "Study on Compliance of Supreme Court's Orders on Universalisation with Quality," unpublished report.

Citizen's Initiative for Rights of Children Under Six (2006): "Focus on Children Under Six," New Delhi: Right to Food Campaign.

Drèze, Jean and Reetika Khera with the PEEP Team (2013): "A Peep into Another India," Outlook, 24 March, available online http://www.outlookindia.com/article/Water-For-The-Lee- ward-India/289801, last accessed on 6 January 2013.

Government of India (2011a): Evaluation Study on Integrated Child Development Services (ICDS), Vol. 1, PEO Report No. 218, Programme Evaluation Organisation, Planning Commission, New Delhi: Government of India, available online at http://planningcommission.nic.in/reports/peoreport/peoevalu/peo_icds_v1.pdf

— (2011b): Evaluation Study on Integrated Child Development Services (ICDS), Volume 2, PEO Report No. 218, Programme Evaluation Organisation, Planning Commission, New Delhi: Government of India, available online at http:// planningcommission.nic.in/reports/peore- port/peoevalu/peo_icds_v2.pdf

Orissa Diary (2011a): "Orissa Vigilance Submits Preliminary Report on Dal Scam," 5 February, available online at http://www.orissadiary. com/CurrentNews.asp?id=24412, last acces sed on 6 January 2011.

— (2011b): "Congress, BJP Seek Orissa CM's Resignation over Dal Scam," 6 February, available online at http://www.orissadiary.com/CurrentNews.asp?id=24422, last accessed on 6 January 2011.

14

The Goal and Realities of Food Security - The Way Forward

K. Baby

The UN Millennium Development Goals are one of the initiatives aimed at achieving food security in the world. The first Millennium Development Goal states that the UN "is to eradicate extreme hunger and poverty" by 2015. Olivier De Schutter, the UN Special Rapporteur on the Right to Food, advocates for a multidimensional approach to food security challenges. This approach emphasises the physical availability of food; the social, economic and physical access people have to food; and the nutrition, safety and cultural appropriateness or adequacy of food. India is home to 25 per cent of the world's hungry population. An estimated 43 per cent of children under the age of five years are malnourished (WFP, 2012). India remains an important global agricultural player; despite the fact that agriculture's share in the country's economy is declining. It has the world's largest area under cultivation for wheat, rice, and cotton, and is the world's largest producer of milk, pulses, and spices (World Bank, 2012). Nearly three-quarters of India's households are dependent on rural incomes. Agricultural productivity in the country's semi-arid tropical region is impeded by water shortages and recurrent drought, while environmental degradation and vulnerability to weather-related disasters pose challenges to the country as a whole.

Introduction

The Economic Survey 2015-16 emphasises that the main aim of food management policy is to provide food security to the population. Providing food security entails making food available at affordable prices at all times, without interruptions. In order to provide food security, in the current agriculture scenario, India has to focus on supplies which are timely and uninterrupted and affordable for the poor. Though India's GDP growth has been impressive and the agricultural production has also increased over the past few decades, hunger and starvation still persist among the poorer section of the population. There has been moderation of inflation including food inflation during the last two years, but more needs to be achieved by freeing up markets, augmenting supply of food and leveraging the use of IT.

Need for Food Security

According to the data of the 66th round of the National Sample Survey (2009-10), the average dietary energy intake per person per day was 2147 Kcal for rural India and 2123 Kcal for urban India. As per the Report of Nutritional Intake in India, 2011-12 (NSSO, 68th round), among the bottom 5 per cent of rural population ranked by Monthly Per Capita Expenditure (MPCE), 57 per cent of households had calorie intake below 2160 Kcal/consumer unit/day. The average protein intake per capita per day rises steadily with MPCE level in rural India from 43 gm for the bottom five per cent of population ranked by MPCE to 91 gm for the top five per cent, and in urban India from 44 gm for the bottom 5 per cent to about 87 gm for the top five per cent. Economic Survey 2015-16 states that India has the second highest number of undernourished people at 194.6 million person (FAO, State of Food Insecurity in the World, 2015) which warrants immediate attention. Moreover, with 27 per cent of the population below the poverty line, the rise in prices of food impacts the poor adversely, with a greater proportion of their household incomes being spent on food. Therefore, along with provision of food subsidy, stability in agricultural commodity prices is essential for making poorer sections food secure. There is a strong correlation between stability in agricultural production and food security. Volatility in agricultural production impacts food supplies and can result in spikes in food prices, which adversely affect the lowest income of the population.

With a large number of people who remain undernourished and the issues of volatility in agricultural prices, India has one of the largest scheme of food schemes in the World to ensure food security. There is entitlement feeding programmes like the Integrated Child Development Scheme (ICDS) (All Children under six, pregnant and lactating mothers) and MDMS (Mid Day Meal Schemes), food subsidy programmes like the Targeted Public Distribution System, Annapurna (10 Kgs of free food grain for destitute poor) and the Employment Programmes like Mahatama Gandhi National Rural Employment Guarantee Scheme (100 days of employment at minimum wages) to ensure food security.

Food Security in India

While India has seen impressive economic growth in recent years, the country still struggles with widespread poverty and hunger. India's poor population amounts to more than 300 million people, with almost 30 per cent of India's rural population living in poverty. The good news is, poverty has been on the decline in recent years. According to official Government of India estimates, poverty declined from 37.2 per cent in 2004-05 to 29.8 per cent in 2009-10. Rural poverty declined by 8 percentage points from 41.8 per cent to 33.8 per cent and urban poverty by 4.8 percentage points from 25.7 per cent to 20.9 per cent over the same period (World Bank, 2012). Poor populations also face a lack of access to productive assets, financial resources, education, health care, and basic social services. The government has recently begun to focus on microenterprise development as a way to address these challenges, as well as initiatives to bring basic services to the rural poor. With the country's population and economy continuing to grow, huge demands will be placed on critical infrastructure in the coming years. It is estimated that US$1 trillion will be needed to meet India's infrastructure needs in the next five years (World Bank, 2012).

Food security is a condition related to the supply of food, and individuals' access to it. The term "food security" was defined with an emphasis on supply. Food security, is the "availability at all times of adequate food supplies of basic foodstuffs to sustain a steady expansion of food consumption and to offset fluctuations in production and prices".. The final report of the 1996 World Food Summit states that food security "exists when all people, at all times, have physical and economic access to sufficient, safe and nutritious food to meet their dietary needs and food preferences for an active and healthy life". Household food security exists when all members, at all times, have access to enough food for an active, healthy life. Individuals who are food secure do not live in hunger or fear of starvation. Food insecurity, on the other hand, is a situation of "limited or uncertain availability of nutritionally adequate and safe foods or limited or uncertain ability to acquire acceptable foods in socially acceptable ways", according to the United States Department of Agriculture (USDA). Food security incorporates a measure of resilience to future disruption or unavailability of critical food supply due to various risk factors including droughts, shipping disruptions, fuel shortages, economic instability, and wars. In the years 2011-2013, an estimated 842 million people were suffering from chronic hunger. The Food and Agriculture Organisation of the United Nations, or FAO, identified the four pillars of food security as *availability, access, utilisation, and stability*. Food Security is the ability to assure, on a long-term basis, that the system provides the total population access to a timely, reliable and nutritionally adequate supply of food.

Food security can be visualised in four stages:

(i) Making an adequate quantity of cereals available to all to ensure survival.

(ii) Adequate availability of cereals and pulses.

(iii) Food security to include cereals, pulses, milk and milk products.

(iv) Food security to include cereals, pulses, milk and milk products, vegetables and fruits, (fish, egg and meat in case of non-vegetarians).

India has now reached a stage where the country is no longer exposed to real famines. All the same there still exist pockets within the country where people have to face acute starvation year after year.

Challenges to achieving food security

- Global water crisis
- Land degradation
- Climate change
- Agricultural diseases
- Dictatorship and kleptocracy
- Availability of Food Grains.

Food Prices Stability

India may increase the size of a fund used to stabilise food prices by as much as 80 per cent after an unexpected acceleration in inflation to a 17-month high. The price stabilisation fund will probably be increased to Rs 9 bn (US $131mn) from Rs 5bn. The fund, handled by the food ministry, is spent on buying commodities such as onions and pulses for sale in the local market to boost supplies during shortages. The gGovernment is taking steps to control prices of essential food commodities after first back-to-back shortfall in monsoon rainfall in three decades trimmed production of rice, oilseeds, sugar cane and cotton. The fund, which was set up in March last year, will be used to advance interest-free loans to state governments and agencies to meet their working capital and other expenses on procurement and distribution of staples. State governments or their agencies will procure commodities directly from farmers or their organisations and sold to the consumers at reasonable prices. India's retail inflation unexpectedly accelerated to the fastest pace since August 2015, adding pressure on the government to contain spending when it presents its annual budget on February 29. The consumer food price index rose 6.85 per cent in January from a year earlier after a 6.4 per cent gain in December; the increase was led by a 43 per cent surge in pulses.

Agricultural Condition

Several agricultural conditions complicate this dilemma. Farming is an energy intensive business. Crops must be transported efficiently to market, and petroleum-based fertilisers and pesticides are widely used. Energy price spikes hurt farmers around the world and in the future are likely to hit with even greater ferocity than the spike in 2007 and 2008. Water scarcity will intensify because of population growth, urbanisation, and land use pressures. According to a report by the Royal Institute of International Affairs, a half billion people currently live in countries with chronic water shortages, a figure that is expected to rise to 4 billion by 2050. Finally, climate change is challenging farmers on every continent to deal with altered weather patterns, novel agricultural pests, and new water conditions. These challenges will be felt most intensely by smallholders in some of the poorest regions of the world.

Need for Self-Sufficiency

India suffered two very severe droughts in 1965 and 1966. Food Aid to India was restricted to a monthly basis by USA under the PL-480 programme. Prime Minister Jawaharlal Nehru had foreseen such a situation and declared, "It is only when we attain self-sufficiency in food that we can progress and develop ourselves. Otherwise there is the constant pressure of circumstances, there is trouble and misery and sometimes shame and humiliation." The Green Revolution made a significant change in the scene. India achieved self-sufficiency in food grains by the year 1976 through the implementation of the seed-water-fertiliser policy adopted by the Government of India. Food grain production increased four-fold during 1950-51and 2001-2002 from 51 million tonnes to 212 million tones. The country is no longer exposed to real famines. Total lack of purchasing power however continues to haunt people in some parts of the country. They starve even when the country's granaries are overflowing.

Role of Government in Food Security

The role of the government in providing food security involves:

- Promoting domestic production to meet the demands of the growing population.
- Providing minimum support prices for procurement and storage of food grains.
- Operating a Public Distribution System, and
- Maintaining buffer stocks to counteract any pushing up of prices of food grains during periods of shortages.

Well before the harvest time, the government declares a minimum floor price at which the government would buy cereals to maintain its own buffer stocks. Minimum support prices ensure that the growers do not suffer if the traders form syndicates and force low prices on the farmers for their produce.

Impact of Public Distribution System (PDS)

"Excessive stocks of food grains on the one hand, and prevalence of widespread hunger and malnutrition on the other, call for an expansion of the PDS operations"

The main purpose of the Public Distribution System was to act as a price support programme for the consumer in 1960s. Those were the years of food shortage. The basic items covered were rice, wheat, sugar, edible oil, and kerosene to be sold at subsidised prices. The coverage was extended to rural areas by some states during the 1980s. Effort was made to cover the tribal blocks with a population around 57 million persons in 1985. There had been a growing feeling that the non-poor were the beneficiaries of the PDS in large numbers especially in respect of sugar and Kerosene oil. Under the new system, the non-poor sections have been kept out. The Public Distribution System was very well conceived. However, it has remained very ill manned. PDS has remained an expensive and largely untargeted programme. The very poor are unable to take the benefit of the PDS for a variety of reasons. They do not have a regular income. They are unable to lift a month or a fortnight's quota at one time for want of enough money. In most cases the PDS shops are closed by the time the labourer is back home.

PDS and Wage Employment Programmes

Wage employment programmes are a much better option for helping the poor sections of the society. Employment Guarantee schemes and the Jawahar Rozgar Yojna create improvements in agricultural labourers wages and even create some assets. The non-poor are excluded from such programmes since those who can afford to buy food from open market would not come to work under these schemes. It is not that there would be no leakages under wage employment schemes. Cases of fake muster rolls are not unknown. But these can be checked by better surveillance. Co-operative Marketing Societies need to be encouraged to sell food grains to consumers directly. This will eliminate the middlemen and also eliminate profiteering and black marketing. Bigger societies could have their own storage and warehousing facilities. This will go a long way in reduction storage losses. The Food Corporation of India should buy food grains from co-operative marketing societies. Cooperative marketing has made good progress in Maharashtra, Andhra Pradesh, Tamil Nadu, Uttar Pradesh and Bihar. The sugarcane marketing societies in Bihar and Uttar Pradesh protect the interests of the members. Punjab, Maharashtra, Gujarat and Uttar Pradesh account for 75 per cent of the total value of the agricultural produce marketed by cooperatives.

Long-term Food Security Measures

Public Distribution System can at best be a Blood Transfusion exercise. It does not act as a permanent poverty alleviation measure. While it does provide some immediate relief, it fails to provide enduring food security to the poor. It would be more appropriate to focus on strategies that reduce poverty and stabilise prices of food grains. At one time we had 300 million people at various degrees of starvation while there were 64 million tonnes of food grains rotting in the godowns of the Food Corporation of India. The rural poor did not have the purchasing power to buy food grains even at the PDS prices. Food grains were being transferred to private mills and traders through collusion on the part of corrupt civil supplies officers. Only the very inferior grains were supplied to the ration card holders. The minimum buffer stock now required in India has been fixed at around 16-17 million tonnes of food grains.

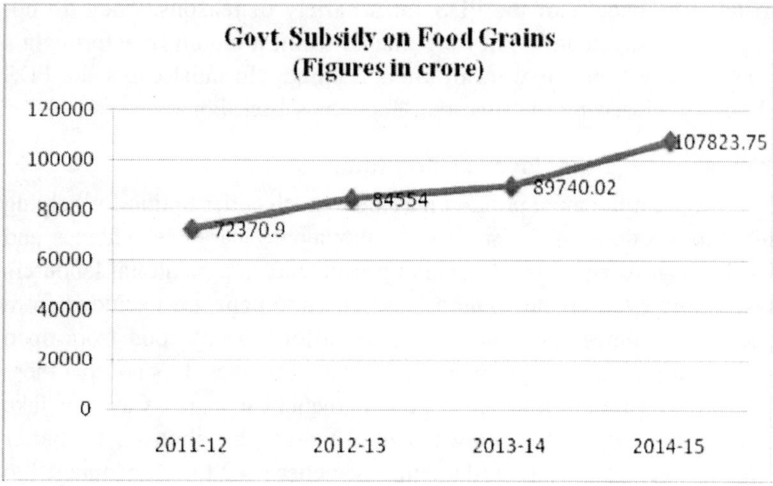

Source: Dept. of Public Distribution, GoI, Annual Report 2014-15.

National Food Security Act (NFSA), 2013

As passed by the Parliament, government has notified the National Food Security Act, 2013 on 10th September, 2013 with the objective to provide for food and nutritional security in human life cycle approach, by ensuring access to adequate quantity of quality food at affordable prices to people to live a life with dignity. The Act provides for coverage of up to 75 per cent of the rural population and up to 50 per cent of the urban population for receiving subsidised food grains under Targeted Public Distribution System (TPDS), thus covering about two-thirds of the population. The eligible persons will be entitled to receive 5 Kgs of food grains per person per month at subsidised prices of Rs 3/2/1 per Kg for rice/wheat/coarse grains. The existing Antyodaya Anna Yojana (AAY) households, which constitute the poorest of the poor, will continue to receive 35 Kgs of food grains per household per month. The Act also has a special focus on the nutritional support to women and children. Besides meal to pregnant women and lactating mothers during pregnancy and six months after the child birth, such women will also be entitled to receive maternity benefit of not less than Rs 6,000. Children up to 14 years of age will be entitled to nutritious meals as per the prescribed nutritional standards. In case of non-supply of entitled food grains or meals, the beneficiaries will receive food security allowance. The Act also contains provisions for setting up of grievance redressal mechanism at the District and State levels. Separate provisions have also been made in the Act for ensuring transparency and accountability.

All India Allocation and Off take under TPDS
January 2016 (Quantity in Lakh MT)

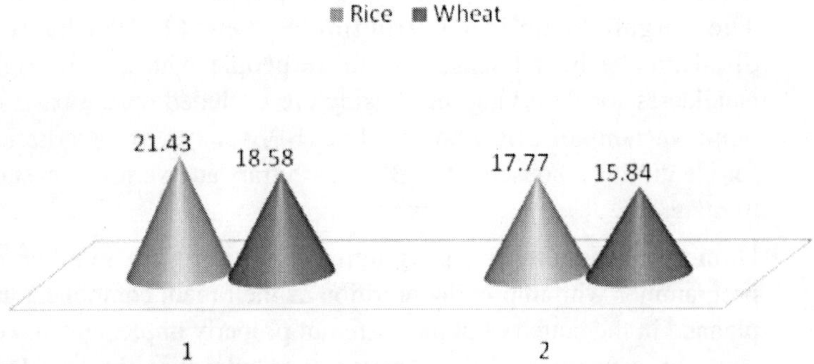

Source: IISFM 2016.

Challenge of Food Security in India

There is a perception that China has, by and large, solved its 'food problem', whereas India has not. This rings true in a very specific sense. The crux of India's food problem today pertains not so much on increasing food availability or production but with the distribution of food.

- This is not to suggest that the challenges associated with ensuring food availability in sustainable ways is not a policy concern, but rather, in terms of the immediacy of challenges, ensuring food access would appear to score over concerns over food availability in rural and tribal areas. This is mainly due to lack of improvement in agricultural productivity owing to inadequate resources and markets needed to obtain agricultural stability.
- The key issue which catalyses the problem of food insecurity in urban areas and needs to be addressed is the large proportion of informal workforce resulting in unplanned growth of slums which lack in the basic health and hygiene facilities.
- The children are food insecure because of factors attributed to overpopulation, poverty, lack of education and gender inequality. Poverty is a major cause as it limits the amount of food available to children. Overpopulation is linked to competition for food and can lead to malnutrition amongst children, especially in rural areas where access to food is limited.
- Lack of adequate knowledge amongst mothers regarding nutrition, breast-feeding and parenting is another area of concern.

- Faulty food distribution system: Inadequate distribution of food through public distribution mechanisms (PDS i.e. Public Distribution System) is also a reason for growing food insecurity in the country. The Targeted Public Distribution System (TPDS) has the disadvantage in the sense that those people who are the right candidates for deserving the subsidy are excluded on the basis of non-ownership of below poverty line (BPL) status, as the criterion for identifying a household as BPL is arbitrary and varies from state to state.
- Unmonitored nutrition programmes: Although a number of programmes with improving nutrition as their main component are planned in the country but these are not properly implemented. For instance, a number of states have yet to introduce the Mid Day Meal Scheme (MDMS). In states such as Bihar and Odisha where the poverty ratio is very high, poor implementation of nutritional programmes that have proven effectiveness has a significant impact on food security.
- Lack of inter-sectoral coordination: Lack of coherent food and nutrition policies along with the absence of inter-sectoral coordination between various ministries of government such as Ministry of Women and Child Health, Ministry of Health and Family Welfare, Ministry of Agriculture, Ministry of Finance etc have added to the problem.

Challenges and Way Ahead

There is a compelling need to operationalise the concept of nutrition security which implies physical, economic and social access to balanced diet, clean drinking water, safe environment, and health care. Ensuring food security alone will aid in reducing hunger but will not eliminate malnutrition or impact nutrition status largely if other components such as safe drinking water and healthcare are also not envisaged.

Implementing Measures to Improve Agricultural Productivity and Food Storage

The government policy needs to adopt an integrated policy framework to facilitate the increased use of irrigation and newer farming techniques. The measures should focus mainly on rationale distribution of cultivable land, improving the size of the farms and providing security to the tenant cultivators apart from providing the farmers with improved technology for cultivation and improved inputs like irrigation facilities, availability of better quality seeds, fertilisers and credits at lower interest rates.

Ensuring Food Availability and Accessibility to Below Poverty Line (BPL) Families

It is essential to ensure availability of food grains to the common people at an affordable price. This can be done by more accurate targeting of the BPL population so that they get food at substantially low price. There is a problem associated with the BPL listing. There is a debate about the exact number of people falling under this category. The estimates of the government are around 30 per cent of the population. The Planning Commission (under the Government of India) has now recommended a 37 per cent cut off based on the Tendulkar Committee report.

Improving Purchasing Power through Employment Generating Schemes

The government should come up with more holistic schemes like Mahatma Gandhi National Rural Employment Guarantee Act (MGNREGA) Poverty alleviation programmes like the Integrated Rural Development Programme (IRDP) and employment generation schemes like Jawahar Rozgar Yojana, Nehru Rozgar Yojana etc need to be re-oriented and up scaled to make a positive impact on the purchasing power of the lower socio-economic segment of the population. Also, it is equally important to enhance the quantity and quality of wage-paid employment

Crop Diversification, Establishing Food Grain Banks and Promoting Family Farming

Another area which needs to be explored is 'crop diversification'. Higher profitability and the stability in production highlight the importance of crop diversification, e.g. legumes alternative with rice and wheat. Growing of non-cereal crops such as oilseeds, fruits and vegetables etc need to be encouraged. The creation of decentralised food grain banks in each village or block of the district, from which people may get subsidised food grains against food coupons, will be a good option. This concept will improve the delivery of food grains and eliminate corruption.

Community Awareness through IEC Activities and Social Marketing

Need based IEC and training materials should be developed for effective dissemination of nutrition messages. Local community education on key family health and nutrition practices using participatory and planned communication methodologies will be helpful. Incorporating health and nutrition education into formal school curriculum for girls and adult literacy programmes could greatly improve women's health and nutrition. Social marketing of iodised salt, iron and folic acid and vitamin A supplements, nutritious food mixes and other low cost vitamin/mineral preparations will prove to be beneficial.

Monitoring and Timely Evaluation of Nutritional Programmes

A complete community-based approach needs to be adopted. Focus on even simple interventions like promoting exclusive breastfeeding, proper complementary feeding and growth monitoring and promotion (GMP) can be expected to give outstanding results. Efforts should be made by the concerned health departments and authorities to initiate and supervise the functioning of the nutrition related schemes in an efficient way.

Community Participation and Inter Sectoral Coordination

Revamping of existing direct nutrition programmes to enable management by women's Self Help Groups (SHGs) and /or local bodies along with orientation and training of community health workers, Panchayati Raj Institution (PRI) members, other opinion leaders, care givers and other stakeholders can be another area, if addressed, can give positive results. Delivering very basic, well-targeted package of nutrition services through a multi-sectorial approach will improve the nutrition level of people.

Conclusion

First Millennium Development Goal states the target of "Halving hunger by 2015". Sadly, the recent statistics for India present a very gloomy picture. India currently has the largest number of undernourished people in the world and this is in spite of the fact that it has made substantial progress in health determinants over the past decades and ranks second worldwide in farm output. The causes of existing food insecurity can be better viewed under three concepts namely the: 'traditional concept' which includes factors such as unavailability of food and poor purchasing capacity; 'socio-demographic concept' which includes illiteracy, unemployment, overcrowding, poor environmental conditions and gender bias; 'politico-developmental concept' comprising of factors such as lack of inter-sectoral coordination and political will, poorly monitored nutritional programmes and inadequate public food distribution system. Priority has to be assigned to agriculture and rural development along with promoting women empowerment, ensuring sustainable employment and improving environmental conditions.

References

Annual Report (2015). Department of Food and Public Distribution Ministry of Consumer Affairs, Food and Public Distribution, Annual Report,2014-15/

Athreya, VB, Bhavani, RV, Anuradha, G, Gopinath, R, Velan, AS. Report on the state of food insecurity in rural India. 2008 Dec; 14. M S Swaminathan Research Foundation.

Basu, K *(*2011*)*. Food Management in India. Working Paper, Ministry of Finance. Government of India, New Delhi.

Chattopadhyay, N. (2008). Climate change and food security in India. International symposium on climate change and food security in South Asia; August 25–30, 2008, Dhaka, Bangladesh.

Economic Survey 2014-15, Govt. of India Publication.

Government of India (2010). Report of the Expert Committee on National Food Security Bill, Planning Commission. Government of India, New Delhi.

Identifying and addressing food insecurity among the urban poor. Summary of the FSN forum discussion No. 35. 27 April – 15 June, 2009. Sujata Balasubramanian (2015). 'Is the PDS Already a Cash Transfer? Rethinking India's Food Subsidy Policies' HKUST IEMS Working Paper No. 2015-16- March 2015 Shweta Saini and Ashok Gulati (2015). 'The National Food Security Act (NFSA) 2013- Challenges, Buffer Stocking and the Way Forward' Indian Council For Research On International Economic Relations-Working Paper-297 2015 March.The state of food insecurity in the world. Eradicating world hunger-taking stock ten years after the World Food Summit. FAO corporate documentary repository 2006. p. 14, Related websites.

15

Seeds, Soil and Survival: Towards a Saner Agricultural Future

Ashish Kothari

> "In just two years, we gave up all pesticides as we saw the results of vermicompost and *amritpani* ... now we are well on way to stopping chemical fertilisers too" Villagers of Kedia village, Bihar.
>
> "This year I planted 45 varieties of crops, and got enough produce to last the family the whole year, plus had some left over to sell in the market and earn Rs 2 lakhs. My expenditure for the year? Rs 18000. Would have been better were it not for drought conditions this year!" Nadimidoddi Vinodamma, dalit woman farmer of Nagwar village, Telangana.
>
> "On my 3 acres I have this year grown 72 crop varieties, enough to feed family of 10, plus income from sale of ragi, sesame, pigeon pea ... in a year with 30 per cent less than normal rainfall" Loknath Navri, Talia Kondhadivasi farmer of Kerandiguda village, Niyamgiri, Odisha.

These three narratives are representative of a slow but steady transformation that is taking place in India's agriculture, providing flickers of hope in an otherwise bleak scenario of farming distress symbolised most tragically by the spate of farmer suicides across the country. Over the last few decades an industrial model of agriculture has certainly increased yields of crops, milk, and other produce, but at ecological, economic and social costs so high that even scientists within the government establishments are recognising its unsustainability. It's a bit like being on steroids for a while, and collapsing then the steroids are withdrawn or no longer effective, because meanwhile the body itself has been shorn of its inherent strengths. Externally generated or artificial inputs of fertiliser, pesticide, lab-grown seeds, and surface irrigation have been the steroids, but in many places not only are they no longer working, but have damaged the soil, eroded seed and livestock diversity, erased centuries of in-depth knowledge, pushed marginal and small farmers out of business because they can no longer afford even subsidised chemicals and seeds, reduced the independence and self-reliance of rural communities, and distorted state and national economies because of the thousands of crores of subsidy having to be paid by governments. Increasingly also agricultural policy, R&D, and resources like seeds are being controlled by private corporations. It is an oft-repeated story that I do not want, or need, to go into here.

Does the latest budget, labeled by many as a pro-farmer, pro-village exercise that will help revive agriculture and rural livelihoods, signal a shift in government policy towards agriculture? The fact that the central government has finally recognised, even if on paper, the need to boost the rural economy seems to be a sign of hope. That the budget even contains, for the first time ever, provision for organic farming, is also encouraging, and I will come back to this later. But the overall neglect of farming continues to be shocking; Neeraj Jain of Lokayat puts it in perspective when he says: "the fact that most eloquently brings out the absolute unconcern of India's policy-makers with regard to the severe crisis gripping the agricultural sector is the total government spending on agriculture as a proportion of its total expenditure / the country's GDP. It works out to an abysmal 0.3 per cent of the GDP, and just 2.25 per cent of the total budget outlay—for a sector on which even today nearly 70 per cent of the people are dependent for their livelihoods. Compare this to the tax concessions given to India's rich, some of whom are amongst the most wealthy people in the world—they amount to 4.1 per cent of the country's GDP, and are equivalent to nearly one-third of the union budget!"

Enough said on the crisis of agriculture; in this piece I'd like to concentrate on initiatives that are trying to get us out of this mess (noting, importantly, that I do not deal with pastoralism here, a usually neglected topic that needs separate treatment). Briefly describing three examples,

I will also try to look at policy implications, directions that the country needs to take if agriculture is to be revived and food security achieved.

Seeds of resistance and transformation

The three quotes above represent stories of resistance and transformation, resistance to the continuing push for Green Revolution kind of farming, and transformation towards more sustainable, equitable forms.

Kedia village, which I visited in February this year, is in the Jamui district of Bihar. The economy of its 94 households is predominantly agriculture-based. Till 2013 its agriculture was typical of so many across India, with an increasing homogenisation of crops, heavy dependence on chemical pesticides and fertilisers, poor market returns for their produce, and consequently the inability to generate a decent livelihood from farming. It was in 2013 that Kedia's residents, being on the route of a 'Living Soils' padayatra that Greenpeace (GP) India had taken out, offered their village as a testing ground for what this organisation proposed. They started with sample plots where GP India and enterprising farmers experimented with the use of biofertilisers and biopesticides, including vermicompost. The results were remarkable enough for an increasing number of households to turn to organic methods; GP India helped them in obtaining government funds allocated for activities like vermicomposting (itself a big struggle as bureaucratic hurdles had to be overcome!), the village's considerable cattle wealth (all of a local *desi* breed) was harnessed, and over just two years the residents were convinced that they could completely stop pesticides, and reduce chemical fertilisers by about 70 per cent.

I asked if yields have declined? "Yes, a bit", said Kedia's farmers, "but we are confident they will go back to the yields we were getting earlier as the fertility of the soil returns, and even higher over time. Besides, our inputs costs have gone down significantly, and so we are better off." Increasingly they are also going back to or trying new mixed and inter-cropping techniques, enhancing overall food yields and maintaining the soil fertility.

Nadimidoddi Vinodamma, ably helped by her husband Vinayappa, is part of a woman's *sangha* set up by the Deccan Development Society. I met her and her husband in their field, where, surrounded by a bewildering array of jowar, bajra, ragi, red gram, green gram, til, sama, korra, and other crops, she spoke about how she is merely using knowledge handed down over generations, trusting the land and traditional seeds. This year there has been about 40 per cent less rainfall than usual, she said, so they may need to go to the market to buy vegetables; otherwise the produce is enough to feed the family. The surplus jowar is sold and fetches a handsome amount.

As we walk through Vinodamma and Vinayappa's farm, they point to five varieties of jowar (sorghum), telling us how one grows quite fast and with very little water (and is therefore called 'poor person's jowar'), another is good for diabetics, a third one has high productivity, and so on. We notice some trampled jowar and bajra; Vinayappa tells us that wild pigs sometimes get into the field, but even after the pigs and birds and other creatures have done their damage or taken their share, there is enough for the family! As in the case of Kedia village, Vinodamma and other members of DDS Sanghas use natural products for dealing with pests or adding fertility to the soil, such as vermicompost, cowdung powder, dried neem powder, jaggery water (attracting ants that will feed on pests!).

In Odisha, at the foothills of the Niyamgiri hills (globally famous for the iconic struggle of the Dongria Kondh adivasis against a multinational mining company Vendanta), I visited Loknath Navri, a Talia Kondh adivasi farmer of Kerandiguda village. His crop diversity was even higher than that of Vinodamma, and in the three acres he farms, he produces enough to feed a family of 10. Members of the NGO Living Farms, which has been documenting and helping farmers like Loknathji, told me that the area is full of farmers continuing to thrive on agriculture based on traditional knowledge, diversity, and organic inputs, in some cases with recent innovations or new seeds but still with relative independence from the market and the government. As in the case of the dalit women farmers of Telangana, here too much of the farming is dryland, rainfed, not with heavy surface irrigation.

Factors of success

What makes these three examples tick, why are these different from the very many places in India where farmers, especially dryland farmers, are in severe distress? There are many factors, and I only present a few here (not in any order of importance); a full picture of the complexity of factors would need more in-depth study and much more space than I have here.

One crucial reason for the success of the farmers of Kedia, Zaheerabad, and Niyamgiri is that they are part of or helped by larger collectives. For instance, Vinodamma's Sangham is one of several such

Sanghams in 45 villages affiliated to the DDS, with about 3000 women members. Through seed exchange, fund collection and management, knowledge sharing, collective labour, and other joint activities, the Sanghams have overcome the barriers and limitations that each individual marginal farmer faces, especially as a woman. As the umbrella organisation, DDS has helped in many ways: getting credit and linking women to banks, conducting participatory natural resource documentation and planning exercises, overcoming resistance from men and upper castes, trying to get women ownership over or rights to lands they are cultivating, dealing with hostile or indifferent government officials and bringing in helpful ones, providing information on the dangers of chemicals and hybrids and genetically modified seeds, helping build capacity to understand policies and laws, marketing of organic produce through a cooperative called Sangham Organics, and in many other ways facilitating the empowerment of women to take back control over their lives.

Another important factor in success has been the facilitation and support of civil society organisations. In Kedia, Greenpeace India's help was instrumental not only in reviving the village's belief in organic fertilisation techniques while introducing technical innovations, but also in advocacy with local government agencies responsible for agriculture and rural development. In Niyamgiri the group Living Farms has helped network many of the farmers, and the activist researcher Debal Deb has shown innovations in combining diversity with productivity through some painstaking scientific work in his small fields (he lives in a hut in the same village as Loknath Navri, carrying out what is possibly the most rigorous research on rice diversity undertaken in India).

None of the above would have worked, of course, were it not for the farmers' own knowledge and skill base, and the availability of essential inputs like seeds, biomass (*gobar*, leaf manure, cow urine, neem or other trees, etc). One reason Kedia's farmers asked GP India to work with them, and GP India too agreed, was the presence of a large number of cattle and therefore of *gobar.* Unfortunately this is a significant constraint now in many parts of India, where even if farmers want to move away from chemical fertilisers, the options are limited. This is where a policy shift of the incredibly high subsidy on fertilisers (Rs 70,000 crores) towards organic inputs, could play a massive role in promoting organic farming.

Policy shifts

Other than the need for reorienting government subsidies towards organic, there are a number of other policy changes that are needed if these three examples (and many others like them) are to be multiplied across the country. These include providing better market access and prices (the government's minimum support prices for most crops have remained shamefully low, and farmers in Kedia complain about this being the biggest hurdle). This can be done in many ways. One of DDS's most important innovations is the parallel Public Distribution System (PDS) in which the organic jowar produced by the farmers is offered at reasonable rates to residents in the villages, helping create a local cyclical economy that benefits both producers and consumers. This example has been used to advocate fundamental changes in the official PDS system across India, including its decentralisation (in terms of democratic control) and localisation (in terms of diverse foods relevant to local ecologies and cultures). Perhaps as a result of this and advocacy from other groups, the Food Security Act 2013 states that "the Central Government, the State Governments and local authorities shall, for the purpose of advancing food and nutritional security, strive to progressively realise the objectives specified in Schedule III", and Schedule III includes "(a) incentivising decentralised procurement including procurement of coarse grains; and (b) geographical diversification of procurement operations." Without any mandatory, time-bound provision, however, it is not clear if this part of the Act will get implemented in the near future, or at all.

There are some other hopeful signs of policy shifts; well before the central government recognised the need to support organic farming, over a dozen states had already instituted policies or programmes for this. Sikkim's move to become 100 per cent organic is by now well-known, though the continuing dependence on exports to fuel this shift is worrying given the fickleness of export markets and the fact that the ecological costs of transporting food long distances is simply being externalised. Kerala, Andhra Pradesh, and a number of other states are actively promoting organic cultivation; to this they need to add a focus on biologically diverse farming, particularly traditional crops like millets, old rice varieties, indigenous vegetables and fruits. When I visited Vinodamma and other farmers near Zaheerabad, I participated in a programme titled 'Organic Medak', organised by DDS, where the District Collector D. Ronald Rose and Superintendent of Police B. Sumathi assured help in transforming the district into a hub for organic farming with millets as a fulcrum. In Jamui, Bihar, the Block Agricultural Officer Haroon Rashid was all praise for the organic initiative in Kedia, and said the Bihar government is substantially increasing its support to vermicomposting and other such inputs (he also gave the hopeful news that fertiliser consumption on the district had decreased by 30 per cent!). According to the 2016 budget speech of the Finance Minister, there is now a provision for "10 lakh compost pits for production of organic manure", and a Rs 412 crore "scheme called 'Organic Value Chain Development in North East Region', (with) emphasis on value addition so that organic produce grown in these parts find domestic and export markets." If implemented in earnest the latter could support states in north-east India that have avowed commitments to promote organic.

Yet another major policy shift has to be to provide farmers a central place in agricultural R&D. They are after all the ones who, over millenia, have generated India's incredible diversity of crops and livestock, created and sustained sophisticated knowledge systems regarding soil and weather and other components of agriculture, and linked all these to complex cultures. Yet in the last few decades of the Green Revolution, they have been relegated to 'recipients' of what 'experts' in laboratories produce. What we need now is to place the farmer back in the centre of research and innovation, with the formally trained scientists facilitating them. In fact the Krishi Vigyan Kendra (Agricultural Science Centre) at Pastapur is run by the DDS women with the help from government-appointed scientists, one of the few in India where the curriculum is set by farmers. The collaboration between Kondh farmers and workers of Living Farms and scientists like Debal Deb is another example of different knowledge systems combining to achieve sustainable farming.

Facilitating linkages between farmers and consumers is another important arena for policy support. To make the local organic food more popular, DDS has set up Café Ethnic and a Sangham Organics shop in the town of Zaheerabad, where millet-based products and dishes predominate. The group Timbaktu Collective has set up Dharani, a farmers' company that enables more collective processing of organic agricultural produce, its branding, its enhanced pricing for the market, outreach to consumers, and equitable sharing of revenues; similar producer companies or cooperatives are coming up in many agricultural communities.

Certification is also a crucial part of policy support. Private or govenrnment certification of organic produce is costly, way beyond the ability of small farmers. But several groups like Timbaktu and DDS have pioneered a peer-review based certification system (the Participatory Guarantee Scheme) in which farmers are involved, recognised by the government. Providing farmers across India an orientation on how PGS can be used, is important.

All this will not work, of course, unless we also stop the corporate grab of India's agriculture, the increasing stranglehold that companies (domestic and multinational) have not only on farmers but also on decision-making in government circles, the entry of genetically modified crops with all their attendant problems. But people much better equipped than I have written extensively, and networks like Alliance for Sustainable and Holistic Agriculture (ASHA), Anti-GM Coalition, and Millets Network of India (MINI) have been lobbying hard against these forces, so I'll leave it as a mention, not in any way to undermine its tremendous importance.

Over and above all this, is something all of us reading this article must reflect on: how much do we respect the farmer? Every time I am with extraordinarily 'ordinary' farmers like Vinodamma and Loknathji, I am reminded of the fact that I may be starving, or be eating substandard artificial food dished out by corporations, were it not for people like them. Recognition of the absolutely crucial role played by the small farmer, and especially of women, is long overdue; across the world they remain the major producers of our food. And yet for us in the middle or richer classes, they are a forgotten category, and even the periodic reports of farmer suicide are treated by us like any other news. Are we prepared to move out of our comfort zones, build relations with farmers and provide facilitation to their voices and needs, bring them into our institutions as teachers and co-learners and colleagues, and honour them as our *annadatas*?

16

Food Security, FTA and Trade Protectionism in Asian Countries

Aruna Kumar Nishanka

Food security is the broad area of the food for the forthcoming generation. Asia's famous economic rise as the "global factory" over several decades was facilitated by outward-oriented development strategies and a multilateral approach based initially on the General Agreement on Tariffs and Trade (GATT) and then its successor, the World Trade Organisation (WTO). Free trade agreements (FTAs), as trade-policy instruments in Asia, were largely absent in the region's trade policy architecture during Asia's economic rise. Four main factors underlie the recent spread of FTA initiatives in Asia: (1) deepening market-driven economic integration in Asia, (2) European and North American economic integration, (3) the 1997–98 Asian financial crisis, and (4) slow progress in the WTO Doha negotiations. Food security is mixed blessing because it is providing substitute domestic industrial and agricultural production and made a country more efficient for the production of particular product in international production for trade disruption and co-ordination failure.

Introduction

Hunger and poverty reduction is the main focus for this millennium Development Goal having the principle and motto for food security. The principle and the policy focus regarding this subject is evolutes to

Food security in different continent. Hunger in the general population is measured by dietary energy supply and its deficiencies. Some experts recommend a minimum of 2,200 calories for adults undertaking light activity; others suggest variations of this.[1] This income effect is reinforced by the fact that people with higher incomes demand a larger proportion of protein in their diets, which in turn leads to a demand for grains as animal feed (United Nations Environmental Programme 2009). Food supply cycle may be taken into account for this reason that the supply factor is responsible i.e. in 2006 there were some drought and natural calamities (Drought, flood) in constant with major food shortage, due to export and trade ban in foreign food trading market in Asia, is the main focus in this paper. The world is reflecting the changes in its food production to the previous year's i.e. the world is decreasing 1 per cent in the production of wheat as compare to other years on whole world the rice production was 727.2 million tonne of wheat, which is decreased to 720 million ton in 2015. So the import dependency ratio is increasing.

Literature review

There is no universally accepted dentition of hunger or its measurement, although food is different to different person, but the energy, the kilo-calorie is unique to this scientific anthropocentric world. Over the years, the discussion has transferred from availability to the nutritional presence of food i.e. the focus for the nutritional fact in the world.At the World Food Summit of 1996, the Food and Agriculture Organisation(FAO) (1996) posited that hunger can be eliminated and food security would exist "when all people, at all times, have physical and economic access to sufficient, safe and nutritious food to meet their dietary needs and food preferences for an active and healthy life" (Para 1 of Plan of Action). The region is unlikely to achieve the MDG hunger targets. The target on reduction of underweight children will not be reached, given current trends (ESCAP, ADB, and UNDP 2012).

The poor do not necessarily spend more on food consumption (or on food with high-calorie content, such as foodgrain when their incomes increase. In a study of 13 countries, Banerjee and Duo (2006) found that the extreme poor (i.e., those existing on less than US $1 per day) do not put all their income into food. Rural poor households spend 56 per cent to 78 per cent of their cost of living on food, and the urban poor spend 56 per cent to 74 per cent. So the regional impact is the main cause for this nutritional consumption and food take up. Here a great question arise that, why the urban and rural people have the great difference on their calorific food consumption.? The main answer is the rural urban divide national policies and the absence of any international plan and policies for this spawning problem for the Asia like emerging continent and the growing emerging market in the world. The main focus for this area is local national budgetary allocation and lack of balance in the maintenance in the investment plan of the different Government. For the Foreign Direct Investment and Institutional Investment as well as searching the cheap market for local business with operation and management (O&M) in the country. First time in history of the statistics shows that the urban dwellers are so more than the rural dweller in the world. The expected statistics shows that it will touch to two billion within the year 2050. The consumption pattern of rural is so quality than the urban, but the migration of the rural people to urban is growing a large rate than regional balance fund allocation in Asian country. If urbanisation isn't solving all our problems, it is perhaps time to go back to villages and start looking for more sustainable solutions (Ehtesham, Shahid).

In the world economic forum inform the world that 793 million human being means one among the nine is getting hungry with food in Asia. Thin markets and export restrictions were widely referred to as key contributing factors to the food price spikes of 2007-2008 (Headey and Fan, 2008).

Global or regional sufficiency v/s domestic self-sufficiency

Domestic shortage is the main focus for the international and inter regional motto for huger free world. Taken into consideration of main case of India, which is banning the export ban of rice , wheat and sugar, is also the main cause for this artificial trade gap, which multiplying the internal headache for the food supply in Asian countries .Some countries regional resource is not good for producing a cheap product, but some country have the quality like this. The cheaply produced food also required for food requirement for import as per their national requirements. This production can be possible through regional cooperation with avoidance of trade restriction in the market with double assistance of both (investment and expertise) to the technical deficient countries for gaining the production capacity in the sensitive and targeted area. It would also require the necessary trade, port, and shipping infrastructure to enable the handling of grains in large quantities. Conclusion here knock us that domestic infrastructure is also taken into account for sufficiency in procurement of food grain. Domestic availability of food grains also can be furthered through regional cooperation efforts promoting regional food security by building regional food reserves. The South Asian Association for Regional Cooperation (SAARC) Food Bank, established in 2007, is an example. In 1988, the Food Bank established a food security reserve comprising nearly 250,000 tonnes of food grains. A similar arrangement has been in existence since 1983 in the Association of Southeast Asian Nations – the ASEAN Emergency Rice Reserve – with a stock of 50,000 tonnes. This was later augmented to 67,000 tonnes when Brunei Darussalam and Viet Nam joined the association. Regional entity is must for regional production capacity with avoidance regional international business negligence and diplomatic dispute in the smooth trading in Asia like emerging. (ESCAP, ADB, and UNDP, 2010). The free Trade agreement in Asian Countries is increasing from time to time but the for m internal restriction for the food to different country also increasing from time to time . The relationship between these two,indicating the food security in different countries. The gap or the mathematical relationship in different country showing the food security consciousness to the word in and in he particular world. Asian FTAs are often viewed as discriminatory and a drain on scarce trade negotiation capacity in developing countries (Bhagwati, 2008).

The world consumption pattern of import is taking the lion share of a thing i.e. the international and total trade and the global value chain is the import of process food and the agriculture food. The increasing food price in different continent can be solved through the import only and , is the last option for the various local Government now, because few local Government have known that globalisation is realised by every person in the world.

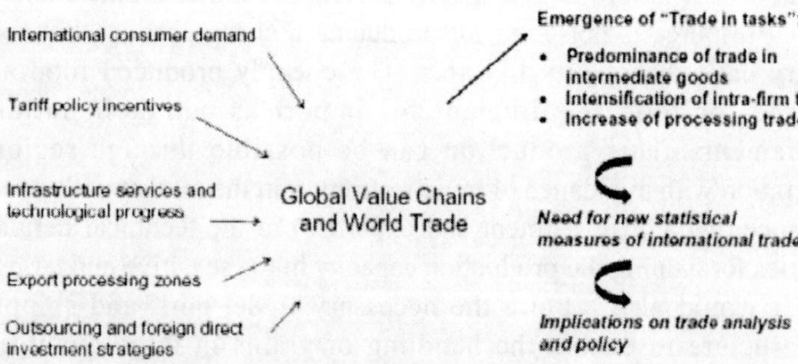

Fig. 16.1: Global Value Chains and World Trade – Ins and Outs

Source: World Trade Organisation.

According to Food and Agriculture Organisation (FAO), the International food price is increasing from time to time and sure to this the price of the food is increasing. As compare to the price index of the different years we see under the graph the market is increasing from time to time. In the sense the market is influence by international price and the trade relation. The main cause of the price inflation in different economy may be due to local or regional both monetary and fiscal problem or may be the international factor like absence of dynamic governance system in the country as proportion to the spawning population. So in this sense we recommend and conclude the inflationary situation in the market.

Another main cause for food insecurity and the inflationary situation is democratic imbalance and system paralysis in different the country. Though majority of World as well as Asian Countries are taking democratic system as wayward, some time we realise that the market is influence by some political factor and the political bad decision. We may say its demerit of political democratic system of the world. The graph showing that the index is increasing at very large on the year 2008 and 2011. These years are the crisis years of the major market of USA and UK with the beginning of the Euro Crisis is the market. Due to political and economic policy paralysis, it was showing the lack of sucking of international product in the market. Some may think that how it is possible that trade restriction is responsible for increasing food restriction. On the one side the trading or exporting countries have the specialisation over that product. On other hand the glut situation in the market is creating under minimum supporting Price Situation on the trading countries. Second the market may have some slow influence over the international market is providing the good at low price to the importing countries with economic crisis and food crisis in the economy. It has the multifarious effect on the market. The restricted market has been creating such bad situation in the economy.

As compare to the real food price index in different country is totally antidote each other. As shown in the graph we see that the real food price is increasing continuously from year, 2008. But the price of the staple food is decreasing as compare to previous years before 2002. Then the price index of major cereal, Free trade is intrinsically an incentive for the development of GVCs, but low tariffs on intermediate goods. Exchanged within supply chains, are even more conducive to their expansion. Highlights that tariffs on semi-processed goods were lower in Asia in 2011 compared to either raw materials or processed products.

Actual tariff escalation can only be observed for a few economies, such as pulse, wheat and rice is increasing but at very less proportion to the previous years. Some logical political factor is responsible for this. First thing is that to maintain balance the on the minimum supporting price in internal food market is a political phenomenon. Secondly, the restriction for export of these items is also keeping huge amount of stock to keep the price lower as compare previous stock. Third, international growing dumping is creating a risk for different developing growing food absorbed country. Fourth is the absence of dynamic anti-dumping measures were not taken suddenly for this regard is also the main factor for this. Fifth the growing demand for food item like diary, semi-processed food, meat and others price were increase at a vast rate as proportion to other main food items .

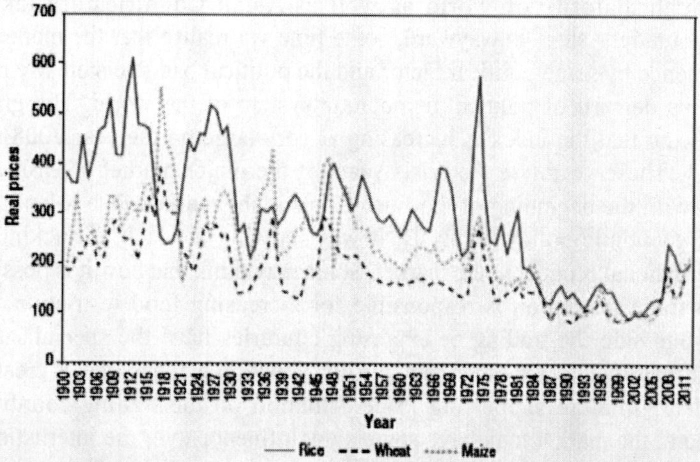

Notes: Prices of all three cereals are indexed to 2002–2004. Cereal prices are deflated using the Manufactures Unit Value (MUV) index.

Sources: For data up to 2010, estimates by Grilli, E., and M. Yang. 1988. Primary Commodity Prices, Manufactured Goods Prices, and the Terms of Trade of Developing Countries: What the Long Run Shows. *The World Bank Economic Review*. 2 (1). pp. 1–47; as updated by Pfaffenzeller, S., P. Newbold, and A. Rayner. 2007. A Short Note on Updating the Grilli and Yang Commodity Price Index. *The World Bank Economic Review*. 21 (1). pp. 151–163. ADB calculations for 2011 and 2012 based on the methodology of Grilli and Yang (1988) with data on commodity prices from the World Bank Commodity Price Data (Pink Sheets) and MUV from the World Bank Development Prospects Group, http://go.worldbank.org/4ROCCIEQ50 (accessed 15 May 2013).

Fig. 16.2: Real Prices of Majhor Cereals, 1900-2011 (2002-2004 =100).

Indonesia and Malaysia, however progressive application of low tariffs can be partially offset by non-tariff measures (NTMs) such as licensing, quantity controls, phyto-sanitary measures, and antidumping, to which governments resort to limit imports. Some procedures established within the multilateral trading system, such as rules of origin or trade remedies measures (such as anti-dumping), may impact a country's own producers and exporters. (youking; youking; youking).

Protectionism in Asian Nation towards Food Security

Asia has been acquainted itself with some traditional protectionism in Asian trade market and the tariff with trade , trade governance, and local import barrier is the main warrior of this form of this un-conjugal form of international focus for food security in Asia. Increases in protection on import-competing goods. Tariffs on food trade are highest for goods from middle and high-income countries, averaging 22 per cent (Boumellassa, Laborde, and Mitaritonna, 2009).

The world's total protection in Asia is the more than the half in Asia, is a indication of trade disturbances in the Asian countries. The intra-regional trade negotiation, FTA limitation of is nothing but creating a bad impact on the global dependency world in the global market economy. Asia is implementing 28.5 per cent of the total protectionism implemented in the world market. World trade is decreasing very negatively due to protection and the domestic price inflation and the import tariff and restriction for international trade consisting both export and import. Trade specially the international trade is requiring huge restrictive measures and policy as compare to the history, as it is increasing the trade restriction after the year 2011.

Second thing to protect, the international prices shock and insulation of the market, local as well national Government and authorities are taking huge amount of strict tariff as well as increasing the price level , may be by restriction, duties and the challenges with Government supported MSP (Minimum Support Price) for the market ad international food market. The remedy for this problem is to support the price intervention with international standard by opening all the market.

The indicator of total no. of measures taken by the world and different Asian Pacific countries showing that the no on liberalising measure is so less as compare to the total of protection measure, which means total world is very in favour of protection and restriction for import and the restriction of the product in the food product market. As per the table we see that in developing Asian Pacific country the imposition of measure is 71 per cent and most of the tariff and trade defence still in force is 93.4, where as high Asian Pacific countries force is 76.3 per cent and total world order is 88.2 per cent. It shows that developing countries have taken more measures to the trade and tariff in the market.

Table 16.1: Indicator of the resort to protectionism from November 2008- Oct,2013.

Groups of countries	*measures imposed from November 2008 - Sept. 2013*					*Measure still in force on 6 October, 2013*	
	Total no of liberalising measure	*Total no of protecti onist measur e*	*Total no of protectionist tariff and trade defence measure*	*Percentage of imposed measures that are protectionist*	*% of protectionist measure that are tariff and trade and defence*	*% of all protectionist measure still in force*	*% of Tariffs and trade defence measures still in force*
Developing Asian pacific	241	591	304	71.0	51.4	90.4	93.4
High Asian Pacific.	129	462	131	78.2	28.4	88.1	76.3
World	787	2441	888	75.6	36.3	85.7	88.2s

Tariff Escalation of Some selected country.

Tariff escalation means the restriction for discouraging exporting to different countries for internal restriction both political and market. The data shows that the Korea is having the good market restriction for raw material, but not the processed and semi- processed good in the international trade market. India and the next is the Thailand . So it is indicating that globalisation is not a meaningful principle for their international business, but it is a word itself. Global market like global behaviour should not be based on local restriction in the market.

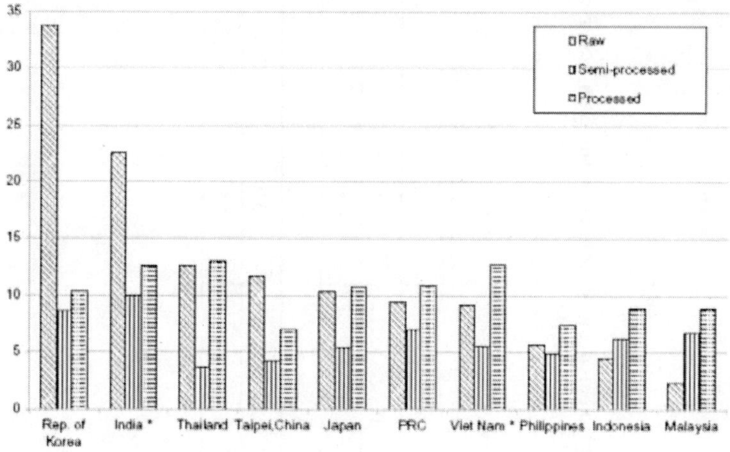

Notes: "Raw" products include agricultural and food products. *Data for 2010. PRC = People's Republic of China.

Source: World Trade Organization, integrated database.

Fig. 16.3: Tariff escalation in selected Asian economies, 2011 (per cent)

Market is now forcing them to different international market, are in escalation mode to enter in to the different market. In the sense the figure given above is showing that Republic of Korea is putting highest amount of escalation in the international market. The figure here indicating that the counteract of the countries for competition of aggression n the market is taking the raw material market in Korea market, where as india market is the second one as compare to the Korea market then, one of the most important thing in this matter is that the raw material market is less escalating position than the processed and the least is the semi processed product, as compared to the processed. it indicate that some countries are now restricting their export and import market for semi-processed

Fig. 16.2: Annual totals of protection measures implemented by economies in the Asia and Pacific region and the rest of the world

Year	*High Income Asian Pacific nation*	*% of the total world*	*Developing Asian Pacific Nation*	*% of the Total world*	*Rest of the world*	*% of the Total world*	*Total in the world*
2008	30	7.35	90	22.06	288	70.58	408
2009	104	21.22	104	21.22	282	57.55	490
2010	85	16.80	134	26.48	287	56.71	506
2011	69	15.27	118	26.10	265	58.63	452
2012	110	22	127	25.4	263	52.6	500
2013	119	27.87	116	27.16	192	44.96	427

**Source: ADB, Data Bank, 2013

food to processed food. Every trade participating countries ,required to sell only final processed food so that it would be a good asset to its balance of Payment and International Investment position, in the economy.

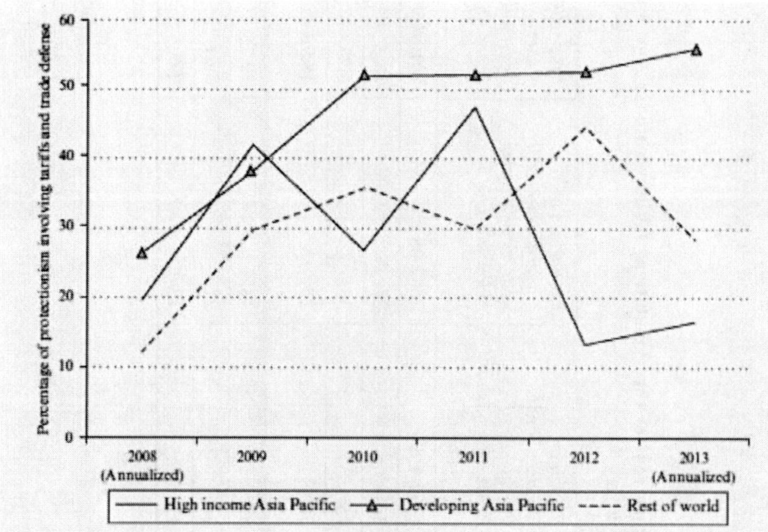

Fig. 15.4

** From global Trade Alert Data October, 2008.

The graph is showing that developing Nation has been taking the most restriction as compare to different Asian Pacific nation and some extent the high income countries are taking so less restriction for the gobal market. But on the rest of the world has been continuing with so less amount of restriction on trade and tariff in international market.

Prevalence of under nourishment child under Age 5 in different Asian Countries

As per data available in the website of WHO and world bank as well as UNICEF the underweight with under-nourishment child in different country is some extent reducing. But the data is indicating that some improvement have seen on the East Asia, which was 60 on 1990, now in 2010-15 it is reduced to 6.25 per cent. Central Asia is also performing so nicely, which was reducing from 51 per cent to 5.61 in 2010-15. As like Pacific nations are also performing so well as compare to other nation i.e. 41 per cent in 1990 to 2.6 per cent in the year 2010-15. In this case we see South Asian nation's performance is as low as compare to other

Table 16.3: Prevalence of undernourishment and under weight (per cent of the Population) Children under Age 5 in different Asian Country

Region or sub-region	*Headcount ratio % ($1.25-per-day purchasing power parity*		*Prevalence of undernourishment underweight (% of population) children under age 5*		*Region or Headcount ratio Prevalence of Proportion of sub-region (%) ($1.25*	*Proportion of Undernourishment underweight under below the age 5*	*Proportion of Undernourishment underweight under below the age 5*
	1990	2004-10	1991-94	2001-06	1992-1999	2002-08	2010-15
Asia and Pacific	54	22	21	16	34	27	18
East Asia	60	13	18	10	15	07	6.25
South East Asia	44	16	24	14	30	20	18.98
South Asia	51	34	22	22	52	43	32.25
Central Asia	51	17	24	22	34	27	5.61
Pacific	41	24	21	16	11	12	2.6

**Sources*: World Bank, UNICEF & WHO Data Bank, 2016.

nation. It is reducing to only 32.25 in 2010-15 from 51 per cent in the year 1990. It is reflecting the bad sustainability in that group of nations. Like South Asia, South East Asian country's performance is not comparatively so good. It is reducing to 18.98 per cent in 2010-15 from 44 per cent in the year 1990. On the previous table we see that the more protection of export and import is on the Asian Developing Countries i.e. 93.4 per cent, which is blocking the free trade and relation between the different trading nations of the world , which have the direct and positive correlation between them. But in the pacific nation is reducing to 2.6 per cent and the restriction in the 2013 is 73.6 per cent, which is reducing from time to time. The Government taking so much endogenous trade measures to restrict the market, but due to that the important product are freely traded among the nations. That's why the particularly South Asian countries and the developing Pacific nations are suffering so much on this issue.

Conclusion

The analytical conclusion entrusted and focus on the facts and figures, , encompassing multifarious effect of the market and give solution for the society and the market regulate according to the en-focused logic in the international market. International market is nothing the dynamism . it is nothing but the dynamic behaviour of the market and different continent and the different nationalities in the world. We see the more restriction and tariff escalation in the market, the more the under nourishment in the international social market. In the sense we say that the market the processing industry and semi-processing industries in different countries are not exporting or importing goods. But those countries which are not exporting processing goods, but those countries are trading processing goods not the raw material. As conclusion processing goods in the market is available aplenty in the market. it means final processing food is one type of good food security, but on the other way it is a full coverage of final business in the market.

Another most important conclusion here is that in this context, we could say here that the more restrict and tariff escalation of the country , the more multifarious forward linkage of the food security of the Asian countries. As we see our market not open we predicted as in the globalisation way, but w are very openly close one nation in the world. Having such type of thing in the world market we are predicting a long-term, co-operative good market in the international social and good market.

Notes

1. For example, Ahmed *et al.,* (2007) dened three categories of the hungry based on the number of calories consumed per day: the subjacent

hungry, consuming 1,800 to 2,200 calories per day; the medial hungry, consuming 1,600 to 1,800 calories per day; and the ultra-hungry, consuming fewer than 1,600 kilo calories per day. The poor are also classified according to intensity of poverty being experienced: the subjacent poor live on US $0.75 to US $1 per day; the medial poor live on US $0.50 to US $0.75 per day; and the ultra-poor live on less than US $0.50 per day. The authors found a strong association only between ultra-poverty and hunger.

References

Barro and Jong-Wha Lee, Robert J. 2011. Costs and Benefits of Economic Integration in Asia. *Costs and Benefits of Economic Integration in Asia.* s.l. : Asian Development Bank and Oxford University, Manil, Philippines, 2011.

Clapp, Jennifer. 2014. *Trade Liberalisation and Food Security.* Quaker United Nation's Office, 2014.

Development, Department of International. Jan, 2013. Can Trade Improve Food Security. *Trade and investment analytical paper.* Topic 9-19-8, Jan, 2013, 1.

2007. Economic Partnership Agreements: A Threat to Food Sovereignty. 2007, Policy Briefing Paper 1.

Editors, Board of. 2014. Economic Corridor Development for Inclusive Asian Regional Integration. 2014, Vol. 1, p. 116.

2014. *Ending Asian Deprivation.* New York : Routledge, 2014.

Unit, The economist Intelligence. 2014. Feeding Asia-Pacific: Australia's role in regional food security. *The Economist.* 2014.

V, Chongsuvivatwong. 2011. *Health and Health Care Systems in Southeast Asia: Diversity and Transitions.* s.l. : The Lancet. 377 (9763). pp. 429–437, 2011.

2014. Evolving trade policy architecture and FTAs in Asia. (book auth.) Masahiro Kawai and Ganeshan (Editors, 2014) (2007) (Unit, 2014) (V, 2011) (2014) John S. Wilsona, John S, Otsuki, Tsunehiro. 2001. *Global Trade and Food Safety:Winners and Losers in a Fragmented System.* Washington, USA : World Bank , 2001.

Swaminathan, MS. 2015. *Combating Hunger and Achieving Food Security.* New Delhi : Cambridge University Press, 2015.

Yashira, Tadahiro. March,2004. *East Asian Regionalism and Japan.* Japan : APEC Study Centre, March, 2004.

FAO. (2012). FAOSTATS, Food and Agriculture Organisation of the United Nations. (Online) available: HYPERLINK "http://faostat.fao.org" http://faostat.fao.org.

UN Conference on Trade and Development, Trade and Development Report, 2008, iv-v, http:// www.unctad.org/en/docs/tdr2008fas_en.pdf (accessed October 15, 2008)

UN Conference on Trade and Development, "Tackling the global food crisis," UNCTAD Policy Briefs, No. 2, June 2008. (Swaminathan, 2015) (2014).

17

Various Approaches for Sustainable Food and Nutritional Security

B.P. Mahapatra and B. Patra

Introduction

Economic growth is an objective of every country in the world. However, the deleterious impact of such growth on environment has alerted the global community to think about an alternative strategy of development which is now popularly called sustainable development. But the term sustainable development is perceived as paradoxical as "development" implies change, while "sustainability" implies permanence. However, this contradiction is actually consistent with economic thinking; namely, it implies the selection of policies that maximise objectives subject to constraints and the aim of these policies are the maximisation of well being, which is the concern of the global community. The efforts of the global community are reflected in different declarations and goals. For example, in 1987 Brundtland Commission defined sustainable development "as development that meets the needs of the present without compromising the ability of future generations to meet their own needs." Recently in September 2015, UN General Assembly adopted a set of Sustainable Development Goals (SDGs). These goals are the successor to the Millennium Development Goals which ran from 2000 to 2015 as the world's framework for development. Hence achieving sustainable development is a challenge to global community the developing and developed countries alike.

In many ways, well being of the human being can be ensured by food security. Food security is achieved at the individual, household, national, regional, and global level when all people, at all times, have physical and economic access to safe and nutritious food sufficient to meet their dietary needs and food preferences for an active and healthy life. (World Food Summit, 1996). On the other hand, food insecurity is defined as a situation that exists when people lack secure access to sufficient amounts of safe and nutritious food for normal growth and development and an active and healthy life. From the WFS, 1996 definition, sustainable food and nutritional security ensures the availability, access and the utilisation of nutritionally reach but culturally acceptable food for all times and so that all people can lead a healthy and active life.

At the time of Independence, India faced two major nutritional problems. One was the threat of famine and the resultant acute starvation due to low agricultural production and the lack of an appropriate food distribution system. The other was chronic energy deficiency due to (i) low dietary intake because of poverty and low purchasing power; (ii) high prevalence of infection because of poor access to safe-drinking water, sanitation and healthcare and (iii) poor utilisation of available facilities due to low literacy and lack of awareness. (Tenth Five Year Plan, Government of India).The country adopted multi-sectoral, multipronged strategy to combat these problems and to improve the nutritional status of the population.

This article is an attempt to find various approaches adopted for ensuring food and nutritional security from international perspective. After that, an attempt has been made to explain various approaches to food security adopted in India.The article concludes after giving some idea on the challenges and possible solutions.

Main approaches to food security

The approaches and paradigm shift to food security may be attributed to among others, World Oil and Food Crisis in 1972-74; Universal Declaration of Human Rights (1948), African Famine of 1984-85, publication of Amartya Sen's "Poverty and Famines: An essay on entitlement and deprivation in 1981", "Hunger and Public Action" written by Jean Dreze and Amartya Sen in 1989 and Cairo declaration and international conference on nutrition in 1992. Let us discuss various approaches to food security first briefly. These approaches will help us to understand the implications as well as unit of measurement of food policies.

Food Availability Approach/Malthusian approach : An oldest approach reflected in the declaration of world food conference 1974, focuses on the (dis)equilibrium between population and food. The policy implication of this approach is two-fold. One, on demand side, the population should be controlled and on supply side, the (per capita) food production-through agriculture should be increased. In this approach the unit of analysis can range from the world, to a country, a region, down to a community, a household, or a single individual. From the economic point of view, the approach can focus on a single sector, on a cluster of sectors (e.g. the "food system" or "chain") or can be economy-wide. Considering these characteristics, the units of analysis generally used in the food availability approach are the country (and its food balance sheet) or the world, and the agricultural sector (its production and productivity).

Income Approach to Food Security: The approach is very similar to assessment of the poverty. While poverty is conceived as a lack of enough income necessary to buy a bundle of goods to guarantee the survival (or minimum standard of living) of a person, food insecurity is implicitly assumed as a sub-category of poverty (often referred to as "food poverty"), i.e. lack of enough income necessary to buy at the given conditions the amount of food required. In particular, the different foods are converted into calories (characteristics of the food): if people's calorie availability is lower than a threshold identified by international nutritionists, they are considered food insecure. Household surveys on income and expenditure are used normally to understand the food security under this approach. Income of the individual is considered as unit of analysis.

Basic needs approach: In the second half of 1970s, the International Labour Organisation (ILO) has proposed the basic needs approach which aims to ensure the satisfaction of the basic needs of all the people. Among the basic needs of life like food, shelter and clothing, food is the most basic need of all. Food first approach in food security literature is an outcome of basic needs approach which calls for a micro level analysis of food security. There are different ways to assess food security coherently with this framework. They are: Food frequency assessment, direct observation of food consumption and diversification of the diet.

Entitlement approach

The publication of Amartya Sen's "Poverty and Famines: An essay on entitlement and deprivation in 1981" enabled the thinkers to shift from availability to access to food security. "The entitlement approach concentrates on each person's entitlements to commodity bundles including food, and views starvation as resulting from a failure to be entitled to any bundle with enough food". Entitlements depend on two elements: (1) personal endowments, which are the resources a person legally owns such as house, livestock, land, and non-tangible goods (2) the set of commodities the person can have access to through trade and production, i.e. the "exchange entitlement mapping". The entitlement approach reduces the role of aggregate food supply and give relevance to the socio-economic conditions of people. "Starvation is a matter of some people not having enough food to eat and not a matter of there being not enough food to eat" as quoted by Amartya Sen in 1981.

Sustainable livelihoods approach

The Sustainable Livelihoods (SL) framework is mainly concerned with pentagon of assets- natural capital, physical capital, human capital, financial capital, social capital. This approach has two analytical features- a long-term perspective and the attention to the context (political, economic, physical, social, cultural, etc.). Although the latter is often confined to the agricultural activities and the rural areas, and seldom it considers macroeconomic or economy-wide issues. The combination of these two analytical features brings three inter-related concepts like vulnerability (which means not lack or want but exposure and defenselessness. It has two sides: "the external side of exposure to shocks, stress and risk; and the internal side of defenselessness, meaning a lack of means to cope without damaging loss", Sustainability ("a livelihood is sustainable when it can cope with and recover from stresses and shocks and maintain or enhance its capabilities and assets both now and in the future" and Coping strategies (that "represent a set of activities that are undertaken, in a particular sequence, by a household in response to exogenous shocks that lead to declining food availability").

Human Development and Capability approach to food security

The capability approach to food security is dominantly influenced by the book *Hunger and Public Action* written by Jean Dreze and Amartya Sen in 1989. This approach switched the focus from "command over food" to "nutritional capabilities". In food security literature, this approach goes beyond the "access" dimension of food security - that is the main concern of the basic needs, entitlement and SL approaches- and includes also the "utilisation" dimension. This is one of the most important innovations of the capability approach to food security.

Human development is the process of enlarging people's choices. These choices are infinitive and can change over the time but some of them are changeless and common to every human being: adequate nutrition, access to safe water, better health services and access to knowledge. Human Development Index (HDI) is an index used to measure and compare development between countries since 1990 and it is calculated as the mean of three components: GDP per capita, life expectancy at birth (LE) and educational level (EL) - measured as adult literacy rate and combined gross enrollment ratio for primary, secondary and tertiary school. However, this indicator has not included food and nutritional security. Therefore, a fourth indicator in the form of Food and Nutrition Security (ISAN by its Spanish Acronym) can be added with three indicators to assess the well being of the countries.

Plan and Prgrammes of Government for food and nutritional Security in India

India does not have a food policy. Approaches to Food Security in India has been associated agricultural development strategy. To analyse the approaches of Government of India, the period after independence can be divided into four phases, viz., 1947 to mid-1960s, the mid-1960s to the early 1980s, the 1980s and from the early 1990s to the present day.

The main concern of the food policy until the mid-1960s was to ensure that the gap between demand and supply of food did not result in an excessive rise in consumer prices of food. During the early 1960s, the intensive agriculture district programme (IADP) and intensive agriculture area programme (IAAP) were launched in selected districts having the potential to increase food production. A programme of land reforms was also initiated during such period. However, this strategy did not address the food shortage problem until the middle of the decade.

By the mid-1960s, India started a new agricultural strategy in order to overcome the over-dependence of country on import for wheat and drought. In order to maximise the production, this atrtegy was based on a foundation of three elements viz., (i) the provision of an improved high-yielding technological package for the farmers; (ii) the delivery of modern farm inputs and services, including credit; and (iii) the assurance of remunerative pricing and marketing environment to the farmers, was. To achieve these objectives, several policy instruments were used. Some of the main instruments reflecting the policy orientation (Acharya, 2002b) among others are:

(i) The creation, strengthening and expansion of the national agricultural research system (NARS) to develop and perfect new production and post-harvest technologies.

(ii) The establishment, strengthening and expansion of agricultural education and training system for agriculture extension workers and the transfer of new technology to the farmers.

(iii) Arrangements for the production, imports and distribution of high-yielding farm inputs like improved seeds, fertilisers, plant protection chemicals and other services, including credit, to the farmers.

During the early 1980s, in order to balance between demand and supply of foodgrains, the objective of agricultural development was modified from 'maximising the production of foodgrains', to 'evolving a production pattern consistent with the emerging demand pattern'. For this, three support approaches were extended to non-foodgrain crops, i.e., technology, inputs and marketing. The result was an increase of production of non-cereal food items such as edible oilseeds, fruits, vegetables, spices and livestock products. Besides, attention was given to household and individual food security. To provide food assistance, create employment opportunities, and provide supplementary nutrition programmes, several schemes were launched. The approach of the government for improving household food security implicitly was the entitlement approach, which recognised that people, especially in the rural areas, derive their livelihoods from production-, exchange-, labour-, and transfer-based entitlements (Acharya, 2002). Marginal and small farmers earn their livelihood and meet their food requirements mainly through self-production on their farms. For these households whose marketable surplus is negligible, provision of production inputs such as seeds, fertilisers, and irrigation water at reasonable prices was considered as the means of assuring food security.

After facing serious financial crisis in 1991, India initiated a structural adjustment programme which included liberalisation of industry and trade along with agriculture. However, the approach to agricultural reform was cautious and gradual. G S Bhalla and Gurmail Singh (2009) while making a state level analysis of levels and growth of agricultural output during 1962-63 to 2003-06, they have found that during the post-green revolution period beginning in the mid-1960s, the new technology was instrumental in raising the yield and output levels of wheat and was confined to irrigated states in the north-western region of India. This resulted in raising crop yields and promoting growth of agricultural output in most of the north-western states and agricultural worker productivity. The new technology matured during the period 1980-83 to 1990-93 when it spread widely to more areas and encompassed more crops. The result was a notable increase in the levels and growth rates of yields and output as well as in agricultural worker productivity in most states and regions of India during 1980-83 to 1990-93. However, significant increase in crop diversification away from coarse cereals towards more valuable oilseeds crops in the rainfed states of central India was visible in 1980-83 and 1990-93.

At the national level, food availability has often been viewed mistakenly as a food self-sufficiency problem. As a result, government food security strategies have frequently emphasised increased domestic food production, through the distribution of Green Revolution technologies, as the key means for addressing malnutrition. In India, two major programmes like National Food Security Mission and Rashtriya Krishi Vikash Yojana (RKVY) have been launched to ensure the availability of food. To ensure access to food India has started a Public Distribution System (PDS).To tackle the malnutrition, India has employed three kinds of interventions: food supplementation for vulnerable groups, particularly women and children; nutritional education and health interventions to address the physical symptoms of malnutrition, micronutrient deficiencies and child and maternal health. The Integrated Child Development Scheme (ICDS), the Supplementary Nutrition Programme (SNP) and the Mid-day School Meal Scheme (MDMS) are the major nutrition-oriented programmes that are being implemented in India.

Recently, the National Food Security Bill (NFSB) was passed by both the Houses of Parliament, and was given a nod by the President on September 12, 2013, and has now become an Act. The legislation is a landmark, and perhaps the largest food security programme in the world. The Act proposes to cover 75 per cent of the rural population, and 50 per cent of the urban population. This Act is based on the life-cycle approach to food security.

Challenges before the Indian Government

Sabhu Ghatak (2014) mentioned that green revolution has significantly contributed for achieving self-sufficiency in food production. Food grain production has increased by five-folds from 50.8 million in 1950-51 to 257.4 million tonnes in 2011-12 (*Economic Survey,* 2012-13) yet the country is struggling hard to fighting the scourge of hunger and malnutrition despite running the programmes like PDS, MDM, ICDS.

According to FAO report 2010, over 225 million Indians remain chronically under-nourished i.e. India is home to one-third of the world's undernourished children. According to the third National Family Health Survey (NFHS-3, 2005-06), one-third of Indian children are born with low birth weight, 45 per cent of children below three years of age are stunted, 23 per cent are wasted, and 40 per cent are underweight. Under nutrition among adults is substantial too: Around one-third of all Indian women have body mass index (BMI) below 18.5. India currently accounts for more than 17 per cent of the global population and 456 million poor, or 41.6 per cent living on less than US $1.25 a day.

Agricultural growth in India was high from the Fifth Plan period to the Ninth Plan period - highest being in the Sixth Plan period, at around 5.7 per cent. If we consider longer periods, growth of agriculture decelerated from 3.5 per cent between 1981-82 and 1996-97 to around 2 per cent between 1997-98 and 2004-05, although there have been signs of improvement in recent years. (GoI, 2008).

Rural Food Insecurity Atlas revealed that the Punjab-Haryana region which is today India's bread basket could lose its production potential within a few decades if the current patterns of groundwater extraction and pollution, soil salinisation and monoculture of rice and wheat persist.

Supply of these non-cereal commodities is lagging in comparison to the demand, resulting in increased food inflation in recent years. Analysing the Household Consumption Expenditure Survey, NSSO 66th round 2009-10, the Working Group on Food grains for the Twelfth Five Year Plan (2011) observed that people get higher incomes they are likely to switch away from cereals, and go towards more of fruits and vegetables, milk and milk products, edible oils, and eggs, meat and fish etc. This may put a little pressure on the feed demand in due course.

Roshan Kishore (2014) has mentioned about a new report by the National Academy of Agricultural Sciences (NAAS) which reveals that despite nutritional value of millets, otherwise known as coarse cereals(barring some varieties), there has been a drastic reduction in the area under its cultivation from 36.34 million hectares in 1955-56 to 18.6 million hectares in 2011-12 thanks to the wrong agricultural and price policies of the government.

Possible solutions for sustainable food and nutritional security

Agriculture-based strategies have been proposed or used to address malnutrition by researchers, governments and international organisations for over two decades (Levin *et al.,* 2003). For example, Gopalan (2013) suggested that food based approach can solve the double burden of malnutrition- like under nutrition and obesity of India. Global evidence suggests that many developing countries are exploiting the links between agriculture-health and nutrition, but India seems to lag behind (Headey, 2011). This may be attributed to incomplete convergence of different sectors in policy formulation, lack of attention to institutional modifications to facilitate convergence, and lack of monitoring mechanisms to assess convergence of programmes on an ongoing basis.

Ved and Menon (2012) have suggested two types of nutrition interventions- nutrition specific and nutrion sensitive to address the challenges of malnutrition. The nutrition specific actions are behavioural interventions to improve feeding, care, and hygiene practices; and interventions to deliver micronutrients, to improve maternal nutrition, and to prevent and treat illnesses and severe malnutrition. The nutrition sensitive actions are actions to address issues like household poverty, food security, social equity, women's empowerment, and other underlying factors. To ensure the proper implementation of all key actions for nutrition, they call for convergence between the fields of nutrition, health, agriculture, livelihoods, and women's empowerment. There should be convergence in planning formulation and planning policy, convergence in implementation and convergence in monitoring and evaluation.

Mahendra Dev (2012) also supported for the convergence in order to protect the poor from the harmful effects of inflation especially protein inflation. He has suggested to redesign agricultural policies to improve the supply of protein-rich foods and to further diversify the diet in India. Government of India has lunched major agricultural programmes like Rashtriya Krishi Vikas Yojana (RKVY), National Horticulture Mission (NHM), and National Food Security Mission (NFSM) to improve nutrition security, especially in districts with a substantial overlap between poverty and under nutrition. He suggested a minimum of 15 per cent of all RKVY and NHM funds should be channeled to plans that integrate nutrition-security concerns into their planning, implementation and monitoring.

While making an empirical enquiry about the recent evidence on nutrition from 1983 to 2006, Deaton and Dreze (2008) has urged the need for better nutrition monitoring arrangements in India. There are serious gaps in India's nutrition statistics, and even the most basic nutrition trends are far from clear. For example, National Nutrition Monitoring Bureau (NNMB) surveys are not particularly informative, given their small sample sizes, limited geographical coverage, obscure methodology, and uncertain quality. The National Family Health Survey (NFHS) surveys, for their part, are conducted at wide intervals (six to seven years), and the reports focus mainly on state-level indicators. Effective action in this field requires regular and reliable large-scale surveys that would make it possible to monitor the nutrition situation at the district level at intervals of, say, two to three years at most. Revamping the District Level Health Surveys (DLHS), and conducting NFHS surveys at more regular intervals, are two possible steps in this direction. Another useful option would be to "link" these surveys with NSSO surveys from time to time, making it possible to combine detailed nutrition data with household expenditure data.

Conclusion

Climate change is a threat to food and nutritional security as the availability of food is mostly determined by agriculture, which is largely dependent on rain. While irregular monsoon and drought- a major fall out of climate change is affecting the agriculture and hence food availability, lowering of water table-another effect of climate change, is also affecting the major components of nutrition security i.e. drinking water and sanitation. Therefore, any policy for ensuring food and nutritional security should consider the influence of climate change. However, before formulating any policy, a thorough understanding of the concept of food security is essential. It is in this context, this article has been prepared. Agriculture sector faces a lot of challenges. Agricultural growth decelerated from 3.5 per cent during 1981-1997 to 2 per cent during 1997-2005. Furthermore, the scope for increase in net sown area is limited. Land degradation has increased in the form of soil depletion, fertility issues, erosion, and water logging. Agriculture is an important element in a number of other interlocking systems. It has strong ties to water, land, and energy, which are, like agriculture itself, under increasing pressure. At the same time, double burden of malnutrition in India poses a serious threat to economy and society. Food security is also linked to other notions of security like economic security (related to employment, incomes, and gender), socio-political security (related to inequality, governance, and conflicts), and environmental security (related to natural resources). It is high time for agriculture, nutrition, and health to join forces in pursuit of the common goal of improving human well-being .Then only the SDG goal to eradicate hunger by 2030 can only be fulfilled.

Notes

1. David Zilberman, The Economics of Sustainable development, *Amer. J. Agr. Econ.* 96(2): 385–396; doi: 10.1093/ajae/aat075 Published online September 24, 2013.

2. WP, 2012-009: February 2012: A Human Development and Capability Approach to Food Security: Conceptual Framework and Informational Basis By Francesco Burchi and Pasquale De Muro.

3. Even though the core idea of this approach could be traced back to the Venetian thinker Giovanni Botero (1588), it was Thomas Malthus (1789) that popularised it, and, in fact, it also known as the Malthusian approach.

4. SL Framework is very popular among development organisations

5. Like (e.g., CARE, Oxfam), in governmental agencies (e.g. DFID) and UN agencies (e.g., FAO, IFAD, WFP, UNDP).

6. Afonso Gallegos, A., Trueba I (2008) : Taking Into Account Food And Nutrition Security in the Measurement and Assessment of Human Development. Universidad Politécnica De Madrid.

7. Economic Liberalisation and Indian Agriculture: A State-wise Analysis, December 26, 2009, EPW, Vol xliv no. 52.

8. Sambhu Ghatak: Clear and Present Challenges before 21st Century Bharat in Access to Food, Essays, E-Book April 2014, Irish Knowledge Foundation, Mumbai.

9. Food Insecurity Atlas of Rural India FIARI (MSSRF-UNWFP, 2001).

10. (2011): Report of Working Group on Food Grains for Twelfth Five Year Plan. Crops Division Department of Agriculture and Cooperation, Ministry of Agriculture, Krishi Bhawan, New Delhi.

11. Roshan Kishore: Policy Issues Concerning Food Security in Taking Note of the Small Producers in Access to Food, Essays, E- Book, April 2014, published by Irish Knowledge Foundation, Mumbai.

12. C. Gopalan (2013): The changing nutrition scenario: *Indian J Med Res* 138, September 2013, pp. 392-397.

13. Rajani Ved and Purnima Menon: Analysing Intersectoral Convergence to improve child nutrition in India- Development and Application of a Framework to Examine Policies in Agriculture, Health and Nutrition: IFPRI Discussion paper 01208, September 2012.

14. S. Mahendra Dev (2012): Agriculture-nutrition linkages and policies in India: IFPRI Discussion paper 01184, May 2012.

15. Angus Deaton and Jean Drèze (2008), Nutrition in India : Facts and Interpretations, Working Paper No. 170, Centre for Development Economics, Department of Economics, Delhi School of Economics.

18

Technologies for Enhancement of Agriculture Production and Sustainability of Rural Livelihoods

Rekha Dhanai and R.S. Negi

A majority of the Himalayan rural population is dependent on agro-based activities for their livelihood, but over 70 to 75 per cent of them are threatened by the problems of unemployment and food insecurity. Although India has made significant progress to achieve self-sufficiency in food production, the growth of the agriculture sector has been stagnant in this hilly region. This is a serious threat, which should be addressed through a paradigm shift by focusing on the development of rain-fed areas and degraded lands, whose potentials have not been fully exploited so far. The present need of the area is to promote productive self-employment to enable the rural poor to earn sustainable livelihood, while enhancing food production. There is essentially a need to develop production in rain-fed areas with integration of livestock, horticulture and agro-forestry. As the main target of the study are women and poor household of the region, greater emphasis on building the capacities should also be aimed. This paper is based on field experience from five villages of Rudraprayag district, Garhwal Himalaya.

Introduction

India is one of the fastest growing economies in the world. But at the same time, the challenge before the country is how to ensure future growth in a sustainable and inclusive mode. It has various challenges in different nature in terms of employment, agriculture and rural development. Challenges have also been imposed by exclusive and inequitable access due to multiple deprivations of class, caste and gender. New technological approaches and solutions, and looking beyond the conventional mode of performing various tasks are required to solve these problems. New technologies could play a crucial role to ensure inclusion of vulnerable groups besides making the development environmentally sustainable.

The vast majority of farmers in developing countries are smallholders, with an estimated 85 per cent of them farming less than two hectares (World Bank, 2007). These farmers mostly dependent on agro-based activities for their livelihood, but over 30 to 35 per cent of them are threatened by the problems of unemployment and food insecurity. Hence, World Development Report (2008) emphasised that the potential of agriculture to contribute to growth and poverty reduction depends on the productivity of smallholder farmers. And raising that productivity will require a much higher level of adoption of new agricultural practices and technologies than presently observed in the smallholder farming population (De Janvry and Sadoulet, 2002; World Bank, 2007).

The methods described in this paper have been developed from a basic understanding of the way that different assets and activities contribute to peoples' livelihoods. This understanding builds upon the livelihood approach to consider the functions of assets (such as land and livestock) and activities (such as agriculture and livestock husbandry) within people's livelihood strategies.

Study area

The area of the present study is district Rudraprayag, Garhwal Himalaya. The study area is situated in the north-western part of the Garhwal Himalaya. The district covering an area of 2439 km^2 lies between latitude 30°19' and 30°49' North and longitude 78°49' and 79°21' East. The surveyed villages situated in the Agustmuni block of the district. According to the census 2011, Agustmuni block has 351 villages and a population of 1,06,881 with 24,505 households. The region contains diverse vegetation types due to different altitudinal gradient, ranging from tropical deciduous to temperate and subalpine forest. Forest and water is the most important natural resources of the district.

Data and Methodology

The study has been conducted in the Agustmuni block of Rudraprayag district, Garhwal Himalaya, Uttarakhand and is based on the primary and secondary data. To select the sample households, an amalgam of purposive and random sampling procedure was followed. To begin with, five villages, namely Sumerpur, Ratura, Kandara, Kansil and Akhori were purposively selected to represent different micro-climatic niches and cropping patterns. A sample of 105 households was selected randomly from these villages through proportional allocation method. The data on different aspects of agricultural development, livestock rearing and natural resource management specially water and land, were collected through personal interview and semi-structured questionnaire method during March 2013 to February 2014. The data were analysed using simple statistical tools like averages and percentages.

Result and Discussion

Sustainable Development and Rural Livelihood

India has already established its leadership in information technology and heavy engineering. The current challenge is how to sustain the growth and ensure economic prosperity, particularly in rural areas. Rural development in India requires priority because more than 65 per cent of the population is still living in villages and over 85 per cent of the rural people are dependent on agriculture for their livelihood (Hegde, 2011). Most of the farmers in the study area are small and marginal holders and large part of their earnings are utilised to ensure food security. The growing population and over-exploitation of natural resources affect the quality of rural life. Hence, it is necessary to develop a suitable strategy to improve the economy of the rural households through agricultural development and sustainable use of natural resources.

To achieve the rural prosperity in this vulnerable Himalayan region, it is necessary that the development strategy should focus on improved agricultural production while generating productive self-employment for the farmers. Agriculture and allied activities is the main source of rural employment, but being deprived of irrigation facilities, a majority of the small and marginal farmers are heavily under-employed for 6-8 months in a year in this region while the MGNREGA provide alternative for short time in some rural areas. Even under well established irrigated conditions of the area, the growth of the agriculture sector itself has been almost stagnant from the last 10-15 years. Therefore, the policy-makers and agriculture experts have been urging to accelerate growth in the agriculture sector. However, the task is more challenging as the potentials for enhancing crop yields have already been exhausted in the fertile agricultural belts covered under assured irrigation.

Scope for Enhancing Agricultural Production

While rich farmers in the area will continue to make efforts to increase agricultural production through adoption of new technologies and innovative inputs developed in the private sector, farmers in the rain-fed areas and backward regions will depend on the public sector research and development institutions to help them to improve agricultural productivity, with low investment in agricultural inputs. Hence, it is necessary to identify the target areas where there is good scope for improving agricultural production and its diversification. Approaches to this challenge include reducing the use of external inputs, increase the organic farming practices and integrating a wide range of low cost management technologies that build on services using natural resources.

Table 1: New technology adoption by the farmers of surveyed villages

Innovation/technology adopted	*Frequency of adoption**	*Percentage*
Organic farming (farmers used only manure or organic fertiliser)	69	65.7
Improved livestock breed	44	41.9
Water harvesting tank (all the structures supported by government)	04	03.8
Agroforestry (in last few years farmers starting plantation on agriculture fields bunds)	71	67.6
Bio/Vermicomposting (all supported by government)	17	16.2

*multiple response recorded

The low external input and sustainable agriculture (LEISA) approaches involve limiting the use of external inputs such as inorganic fertilisers and pesticides and relying more on local and naturally available resources and a combination of traditional and improved methods to manage soil fertility, water, pests and other agronomic needs (Pender, 2008). The particular methods used in the area include a wide range of technologies, such as water harvesting; agroforestry for soil and water conservation, the application of manure and organic fertiliser

(Bio/Vermicompost), the incorporation of crop residues, the transfer of biomass and mulching, the use of leguminous cover crops, shrubs, or trees in improved fallows or intercropping systems.

Organic farming

The distinct geographical features of this Himalayan region, makes it a unique region to grow variety of fruits and other horticulture and cereal crops. The traditional farming practices of the region encourage use of manure or organic compost for agriculture as a way of life. Organic farming development in the region could have wide ranging ramifications in rural employment, ecological sustainability and remunerative agriculture. Organic agriculture is a specific type of low external input agriculture that adheres to certain principles in the production and transformation of agricultural commodities. Organic agriculture have the ability to improve the livelihoods of poor farmers in less-favoured areas. Either it is certified or non-certified. Certified organic agriculture must meet certain standards in the production, processing and handling which developed in accordance with basic standards established by the International Federation of Organic Agriculture Movements (Kilcher *et al.,* 2004). Organic agriculture is based on minimising the use of external inputs and avoiding the use of synthetic fertilisers and pesticides (FAO and WHO, 2001). Based on certification, price premiums of 10 to 50 per cent are common for developing country exports of organic products (Scialabba and Hattam, 2002; IFAD, 2005). Producers of organic products may also benefit from a more assured market than they may find for non-organic products. Organic farming has grown rapidly in the past few decades, and organic

Table 18.2: Major crop grown under organic farming in the study area during Kharif and Rabi season

Major crops cultivated	*Kharif Season*	*Rabi Season*
Cereals	Figermillet	Wheat
	Barnyard millet	Barley
	Maize	
	Amaranthus	
Pulses	Black Gram	Gram
	Horse Gram	Pea
	Pigeon Pea	Lentil
Oil Seeds	Soybean	Mustard
	Sesame	

products are one of the most rapidly growing segments of the retail food industry. There are two types of organic farming in the region; one is part of the sustainable agriculture promoted by NGOs, and the second is promoted through government departments.

Organic farming is traditional method of farming in this hilly region of Uttarakhand but last few years villagers start using inorganic fertilisers in their fields mainly for the paddy and potato crops. But recently government of Uttarakhand banned the inorganic fertiliser in the district for promoting organic farming. The government officials (Horticulture and Agriculture Departments) aware the people about the benefits of organic farming and also provide them training and support for construction of compost pit. Thus, it is suggested that ample opportunities exist for the farmers to increase their income through production of organic crops. Now most of the small and marginal farmers grow organic and only few large farmers (about three per cent) procure inorganic fertiliser (Urea and DAP) from outside as fertiliser depot is closed in the district.

Fig. 18.1: Organic paddy farming in village Sumerpur and vegetable cultivation in village Ratura.

Water Resource Management: Water is a crucial input required to enhance agricultural production as well as for drinking purposes. As most of the small farmers living in hilly regions are deprived of irrigation facilities, promotion of water resource development schemes and sustainable use of all the available water resources should be ensured to improve the crop yields. In the absence of adequate water conservation measures, water scarcity is likely to be a serious bottleneck in the future.

Water crisis can be a serious problem with the anticipated global warming and climate change. With increasing exploitation of natural resources and environmental pollution, the atmospheric temperature is expected to rise. If it happens, most of the rivers originating from the

Himalayas may dry up and cause severe shortage of water for irrigation, suppressing agricultural production by 40-50 per cent (Hegde, 2011). Rainfall is expected to be erratic and the water requirement for crops is likely to increase due to a significant increase in evaporation and transpiration losses. Therefore, greater awareness needs to be created to make efficient use of water resources and to prevent global warming through environmental protection. In the study area different type of water harvesting structure were observed such as polylined tank, ferro cement tank, simple tank etc., but these structures were present in very small number only 4 tanks were observed in all the five villages. And all the structure supported by government under MGNREGA and other schemes. Low adoption may be due to lack of awareness among the people about water harvesting and sustainable use of water resources and high construction cost as farmers are poor. There is a scope for introducing new technologies in the following areas for efficient management of water resources in the region:

1. Efficient harvesting and storage of rain water.
2. Reducing loss of water by evaporation in reservoirs and tanks.
3. Development of alternate and renewable sources of energy for rural uses.
4. Technologies for low water consumption by crops and trees.

Fig. 18.2: Water Harvesting Structure in the Study Area

Livestock Husbandry: Livestock development is an important opportunity to provide gainful self-employment and food security for the rural poor households. The small and marginal farmers in the region, who do not have sufficient land for agriculture, are dependent on livestock for supplementary income. Small farmers consider livestock as an important asset for earning their livelihood, especially in this region where the huge demand of livestock and livestock products such as milk and milk products, meat, wool, manure, transport (Goods and human in remote area) etc., for various purposes. Therefore, livestock is well distributed among the weaker sections of the community compared to land. Promotion of dairy husbandry along with agri-horti-pasture, can generate remunerative employment for small farmers throughout the year. Probably, dairy husbandry is the only programme where poor families are able to build new assets every year in the form of crossbred cows, each worth over Rs 25,000. There is also a need to strengthen veterinary healthcare through an extensive network of vets and para-vets to ensure good health, which has a direct impact on the cost of milk production and the quality of milk. In the study area almost all the household rearing livestock special cow and buffaloes ranging from two to six but the production is very low with the traditional animals. Farmers now improve the breed through artificial insemination and about 42 per cent of farmers rearing cross breed cow and buffaloes. Villagers of the surveyed villages complaint that the number of livestock were decreasing significantly during last five to ten years. This may be due to lack of fodder resources, low production and over exploitation of fodder species from the nearby forest.

Following are the areas requiring new technologies to increase the productivity of the livestock industry in the area:

1. Genetic improvement for enhancing production and quality of livestock which in turns increase the income.
2. New technologies for increasing hygiene and sanitation in the cattle shed which decreases the intensity of disease.
3. Low cost animal healthcare using nuclear and light therapies in remote rural areas which provide resistance to livestock loss by disease.
4. Low cost cooling and processing of milk, meat and other food products which not only provides better income options to poor farmers but also reduce product loss.
5. Value addition for milk, meat and other products for better income.

Agro-forestry on Degraded Lands: The development focus should be on generation of employment for small and marginal farmers, who are dependent on agricultural production on un-irrigated areas. Presently, these lands are not being used intensively for high value crops. In fact, farmers often incur losses by farming on such lands, due to natural calamities. These lands can be profitably used for establishment of drought tolerant fruit crops and agri-horti-pastures. Tree crops have the ability to withstand the vagaries of nature while protecting the soil from erosion and runoff of rain water. Promotion of tree-based farming in such lands will also enrich soil fertility and increase the water table while absorbing atmospheric carbon dioxide all round the year.

Fig. 18.3: Livestock rearing and biocomposting of animal waste in the study area.

Besides this farmers can easily earn a net income of Rs 45,000 - Rs 60,000 per ha from crops like mango, cashew, custard apple, *amla* and tamarind once the orchards start bearing fruits (Hegde, 2011). Apart from foodgrains and vegetables, there are many under-utilised plant species having food, medicinal and nutraceutical uses which can be planted as inter-crops to fetch premium price even in local markets. Income from inter-crops can start from the first year itself to sustain livelihood of the participant families. Promotion of horticulture in these lands can further open up opportunities for post-harvest processing and marketing which not only reduce the wastage but also generate the additional employment in rural areas.

For enhancing agricultural production on the degraded and unproductive wastelands, it is necessary to introduce new technologies which can help in proper diagnosis of various problems and develop suitable solutions to address them. Following are some of the technologies useful while developing degraded lands and improving agricultural production in the region.

Water Conservation and Utilisation

1. Ground water storage, rain water harvesting and conservation through rain water harvesting tank, roof top harvesting, trenches etc.
2. Water requirement of crops to determine irrigation schedule and sustainable utilisation of water for irrigation by using drip and sprinkler irrigation.

3. Measuring salt and mineral contents in water and soils and use proper technologies for improving the quality of land and irrigation water.

Crop Protection

1. Improving crop yields and quality through genetic modification.
2. Use of bio-compost, bio-fungicide, bio-pesticides, disinfectants.
3. Eco-friendly techniques for sterilisation, control of pests and diseases.
4. Drying and storage of seeds and food grains by using low cost techniques.
5. Foodgrain storage using techniques like low humidity, oxygen free chambers.
6. Techniques for long shelf life of fruits, vegetables and other food products.

Post-harvest Management

Effective post-harvest management of the produce should be possible by using following techniques:

1. Preservation of food by using safe techniques (chemical free).
2. Dehydration of fruits and vegetables through low cost techniques.
3. Protection of natural colours and flavours in processed food.

Capacity Building of Rural Households: To ensure agricultural prosperity, it is necessary to build the capabilities of the poor households, particularly the women. Status of rural women has a direct influence on the agricultural production in the Himalayan region, as about 65-70 per cent of the labour in crop production is contributed by women due to migration of male in urban and semi-urban areas in search of employment. Due to male dominant society it is thinking that women cannot be able to contribute to agricultural improvement and also due to their low literacy and often lack confidence, thus it is necessary to build their capacity through training and awareness programmes and provide various essential services related to agriculture development at their doorsteps by well-trained extension workers. While there are solutions to address the anticipated technical problems, it is essential to re-build the infrastructure to establish backward and forward linkages while launching various programmes. Presently, the organisations which deal with agricultural extension, input supply, credit and marketing at the village level are extremely weak so it is necessary to strengthen them.

Most of the poor families are not able to take advantage of various development schemes. Thus, we need to create awareness among the poor about various opportunities and motivate them to take active part in socio-economic development. There are many unsolved problems affecting the quality of life of the people living in rural areas. There is a need to tackle all these problems and find solutions for betterment of rural poor.

Conclusion

As poverty or unemployment is a serious problem in the region, we need to enhance agricultural production through promotion of organic farming as people gain more benefit from selling of organic produce, development of agri-horti-pastures on wastelands or degraded lands and livestock development, particularly dairy husbandry with a special focus on generation of productive self-employment for the rural poor. These activities should enhance agricultural production by involving a large number of small farmers with integration of women empowerment, literacy and development of community organisations, for ensuring its success. The remote areas are deprived of basic amenities so they should be the target areas of current development programmes. This type of programmes can empower the rural poor to come out of poverty and enable the country to achieve the development goals, for a sustainable future. There is a need to develop low cost economically viable technologies as our target population is poor. Such technologies can empower the poor to take active part in the process of strengthening the regional economy.

References

De Janvry, A., and Sadoulet E., 2002. World poverty and the role of agricultural technology: Direct and indirect effects. Journal of Development Studies 38(4), 1–26.

FAO (Food and Agriculture Organisation of the United Nations) and WHO (World Health Organisation). 2001. "Guidelines for the Production, Processing, Labelling and Marketing of Organically Produced Foods". CAC/GL 32-1999-Rev.1-2001. FAO and WHO Codex Alimentarius Commission, Rome. ftp://ftp.fao.org/codex/standard/booklets/Organics/gl01_32e.pdf.

Hegde, N.G., 2011. New technologies to enhance agricultural production and sustainable rural livelihood. www.baif.org.in.

IFAD 2005. Organic Agriculture and Poverty Reduction in Asia: China and India Focus; Thematic Evaluation. Report No.1664. International Fund for Agricultural Development, Rome.

Kilcher, L., Huber, B., and Schmid, O., 2004. "Standards and Regulations." In: H. Willer and M. Yussefi (eds.), The World of Organic Agriculture: Statistics and Emerging Trends. 6th revised edition. Bonn: International Federation of Organic Agriculture Movements. www.ifoam.org.

Pender J., 2008. Agricultural technology choices for poor farmers in less-favoured Areas of South and East Asia. The fifth discussion papers produced by the Asia and the Pacific Division, IFAD.

Scialabba, N., and Hattam, C., 2002. "General Concepts and Issues in Organic Agriculture". In: N. Scialabba and C. Hattam (eds.), Organic Agriculture, Environment and Food Security. Environment and Natural Resources Series 4. Rome: Food and Agriculture Organisation of the United Nations.

World Bank 2007. World Development Report 2008. Agriculture for Development. Washington, DC.

19

Aadhaar Enabled Public Distribution System (AEPDS) in Jharkhand

Dipti Paridhi Kindo

The Food Security Act (FSA) came into force on July 5, 2013 but Jharkhand failed to meet two deadline and months of delay before the launch of the Act and it got delayed in the State due to various reasons. Earlier, the State Government had announced to implement it from July 1 with eight districts to start with but following the Centre's objection it was decided to roll out before October 1 throughout Jharkhand. On 25th Sep. 2015, the Jharkhand Government has implemented the Food Security Act that targets at providing subsidised food grains to around 80 per cent of the state's population after preparing data and collecting records of beneficiaries based on the socio-economic survey of 2011.

This article will examine the Aadhaar Enabled Public Distribution System (AEPDS) in Jharkhand; newly carved state with 29,955,161 Aadhaar numbers generated as on March 2016. The scheme is covering 51,70,159 total number of families and more specifically 2,33,40,832 people have been identified for getting rice at Re 1 per kg per head with 23,516 dealers involved in the distribution. As many as 37,37,609 people in the list are from Antyodaya. In particular, article will also posits the challenges during implementation process of AEPDS and the opportunity through which it is addressing the food security issues of Jharkhand.

Further, the article will also emphasize on the advantages over the traditional method of Public Distribution System by AEPDS.

Introduction

Food security is achieved when "all people at all times have physical and economic access to sufficient, safe, and nutritious food" *(World Food Summit, 1996)*.

Food Security is a multifaceted issue and economic growth, international trade, consumption models, different sites and locations and ecological change is increasing its multifariousness and it's becoming more complex. Public policies in context to these multifarious challenges should address in the most synchronised manner addressing the requirement of each section of the community.

About the Department of Food, Public Distribution and Consumer Affairs in Jharkhand

The principal Policy objective of the Department of Food, Public Distribution and Consumer Affairs is to ensure food security through well-timed and efficient procurement and distribution of the food grains for the whole state. This engages procurement of various food grains especially rice and wheat, building up and maintenance of food stocks, their storage space, movement and deliverance to the distributing agencies and monitoring of production, stock and rate of food grains. The priority is on incentivising farmers through fair value of their produce by way of Minimum Support Price mechanism, distribution of food grains to Below Poverty Line (BPL) families and covering poor households and PVTG (Primitive Vulnerable Tribal Groups).

Mission Statement

- Management of Public Distribution System (PDS) operations in the State through efficient storage and distribution of food grains.
- Undertake procurement of food grains, at Minimum Support Price (MSP).
- Ensuring availability of food grain, Kerosene oil through appropriate policy instruments including maintenance of buffer stocks of foodgrain.
- Making food grain accessible at reasonable prices, especially to the weaker and vulnerable section of the society.

- Safeguarding consumer welfare through efficient functioning of Consumer forum and Consumer Protection Councils
- Distribution of other items such as clothing, sugar, salt etc. as per direction of the State Government

Public Distribution System (PDS)

The PDS distributes a number of necessary commodities to households across India. These commodities primarily consist of food grains, kerosene, sugar and salt. Prior to 1997, the programme was in principle accessible by more or less all the households and was intended to stabilize food prices and provide food security. Since 1997, there has been an emphasis on involving the underprivileged households only in the programme. The PDS commodities are distributed through a network of Fair Price Shops (FPSs). Eligible households take delivery of ration cards that entitle them to predefined quantities and prices of PDS grains. Households below the poverty line (BPL) receive the most favoured prices.

Aadhaar Enabled Public Distribution System (AEPDS)

In Jharkhand, the key objectives and envisaged output from the procedure of end to end computerisation are multiple ranging from overall improvement in process efficiencies starting from food grain allocation cycle to the distribution of food grains to the accurate beneficiaries. Presently, greater part of the processes depends heavily on manual work and coordination. As on March, 2016, 29,955,161 Aadhaar numbers have been generated. The scheme is covering 51,70,159 total number of families and more specifically 2,33,40,832 people have been identified for getting rice at Re 1 per kg per head with 23,516 dealers involved in the distribution. As many as 37, 37,609 people in the list are from Antyodaya.

In AEPDS, a micro-ATM is used to record all the transactions. Aadhaar Authentication is used as a means to ensure that the commodities are distributed to the correct family members who are authorised. The real-time updating of inventory takes place at the back-end. The device which is used is light weight last mile device as it is not having a large amount of data because the data lies at the back-end. The supply chain module uses the balance stock as the basis for replenishing the stock in the next month. The portability of the entitlements is built in the system.

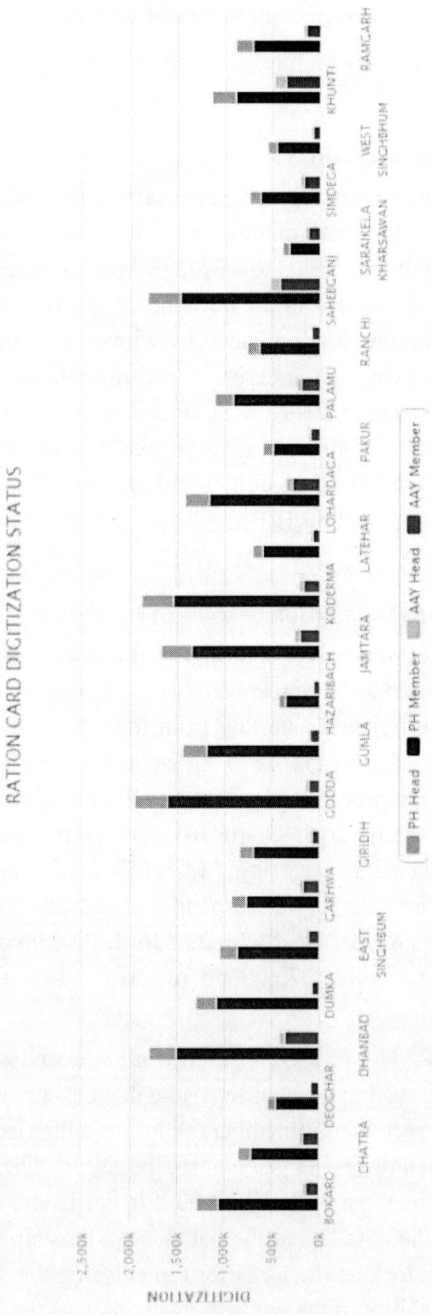

Fig. 19.1 Source: http://nicjharkhand.nic.in/pds.html dated 18/05/2016

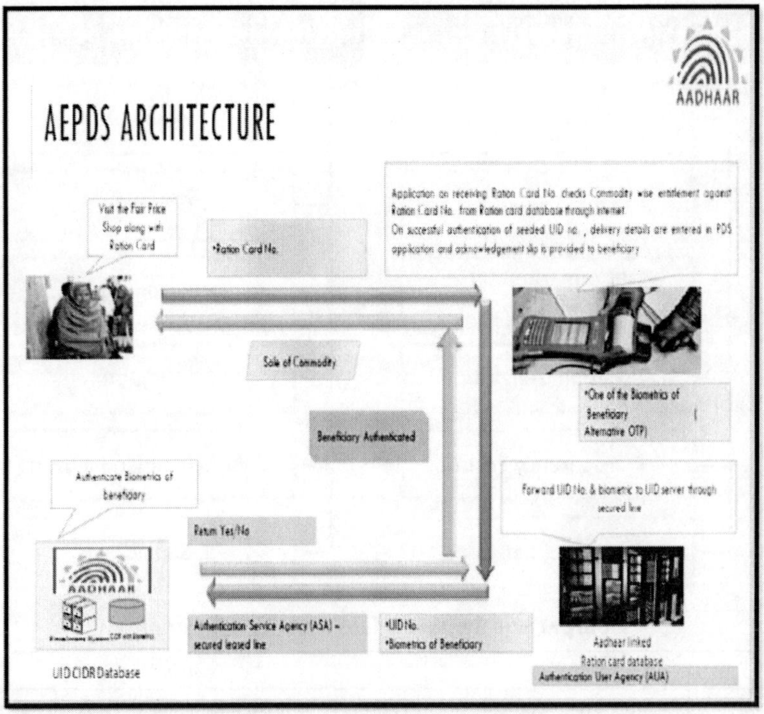

Fig. 19.2: AEPDS Architecture

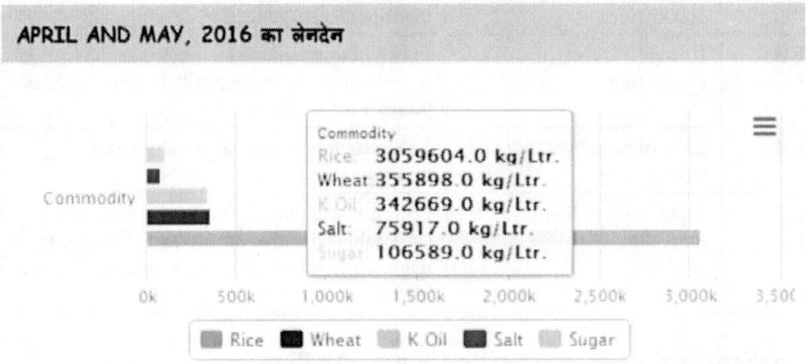

Fig 19.3: Distribution of Commodity in the month of April and May, 2016.

Source: http://nicjharkhand.nic.in/pds.html dated 18/05/2016

In first stage of computerisation, Jharkhand Government has identified following milestones–

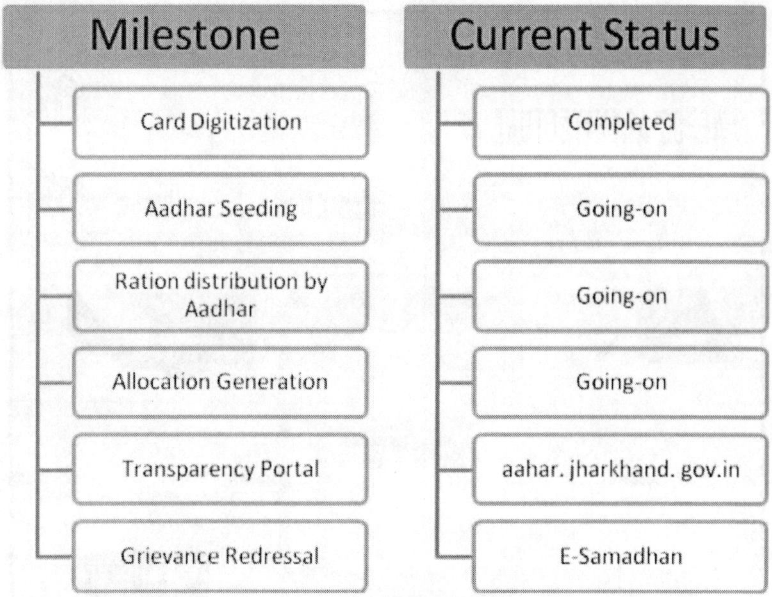

Comparison between Old and New System

S.No.	*Old System*	*New System*
1	Manual Transaction	Transactions through handheld devices using Aadhaar authentication over internet.
2	Compilation of reports is complicated	Comprehensive MIS with data representation through charts/graphs.
3	Chance of falsified transaction	Falsified transactions eliminated as beneficiaries are authenticated using Aadhaar biometric authentication.
4	Lack of accountability and transparency	The system is accountable, robust and transparent.
5	Probability of black marketing	Prevents black marketing by ensuring ration card holders receive the amount allocated to them which automatically gets reflected in the MIS.

Challenges during implementation of AEPDS

(i) The mobile number has to be accurate in the case the person is not enrolled in Aadhaar.

(ii) The vehicle carrying the PDS material can't be tracked so, GPS ttracking of vehicle can be done.

(iii) The people's representative/PRI members are unaware so, a SMS based alert can be done for them.

(iv) Black Marketing has been reduced in terms of distribution but the distribution of less food grains as per the allocation is also a challenge.

Conclusion

However, in Jharkhand, the Department besides, launching the scheme AEPDS for all, is also working hard to make it leakage proof. The AEPDS has increased transparency which has not only increased transparency and accountability but promoted the paperless and electronic transactions. Due to aadhaar authentication falsified transactions to ghost beneficiaries has been reduced. Low cost and low maintenance devices with comprehensive MIS System in AEPDS has given new dimensions to the food security in Jharkhand but most significant issue is not just ensuring ample quantities only, but also to accomplish the malnutrition which is a major issue in context to Jharkhand should also be addressed.

20

Feeding the Hungry Assessing the Imperative of FSA

Samit Kar

Introduction

India is home to the highest number of hungry people in the world at 19.4 crore surpassing China according to the *United Nations Annual Hunger Report, 2015*. At the global level, the corresponding figures dropped to 79.5 crore in 2014-15 from 100 crore in 1990-92 with East Asia led by China accounting for most of the reductions. *The Report of the UNICEF, 2014* states that India heads the table in the number of mal-nourished children in the world accounting to more than 50 per cent of the world's total number. Moreover, the gradual withdrawl of farm subsidies at the behest of the WTO in the post-liberalised regime had led to steep increase in the cost of cultivtion rendering many villagers in India, mostly dependent on agriculture as principal livelihood had led to an alarming rise of suicide cases and deaths due to starvation, mal-nutrition and other hunger-related diseases. Thus, the practice of agriculture across the world, including India has become critically non-remunerative and scholars and experts had mentioned that the introduction of the post-liberalised regime had rendered the peasants the most deprived social category in the world.

According to the *Annual Report of the Ministry of Agriculture*, GoI published in 2014 the sharp fall in the participation of rural youth in the practice of agriculture as the principal livelihood has plummeted as low as only seven per cent of the net rural youth workforce in India. This has led to the emergence of a very grim social scenario in rural India making the spread of despair among the villagers clearly discernible. In the backdrop of these depressing social realities, the enactment of the Food Security Act (FSA) by the Government of India in 2013 is indeed commendable and demands a preliminary assessment about the need and relevance of the speedy implementation of the Act considering the sluggish role of many States to go ahead with rapid strides amidst various allibis. The introduction of mechanisation of farming practice at a very rampant way with the government providing huge subsidies, severely curtailing the scope of manpower involvement to derive a bare minimum income from the farm sector in a significantly populous countryside in India may lead to the growing pauperisation of the common people making the veracity of FSA more significant. Thus, an assessment of the Act in the wake of this critical scenario is, no doubt, immensely necessary.

Food Scarcity

Few years ago, a former President of the United States George W Bush irked the Indians, in particular and the people across the world, in general by saying, a notable cause of global food crisis is the increasing intake of food by the global population. He was, in fact referring to the rising income of the Indians and many people living in the Developing Countries (DCs) leading to the requirement of higher volume of food supply across the world. Bush's argument may sound surprising as he was trying to accuse the Indians for the cause of shortage of food supply as he was referring to 'too much food intake' of our countrymen. Whereas sufficient per capita consumption of food is a basic necessity of a nation, the cash-rich western countries considered our achievement as a possible threat of food scarcity tantamount to rising cost of food in their nation. The concern for food security became a serious challenge to many nations due to a number of reasons, the rising volume of food intake due to a relatively increasing per capita income of more number of individuals across the world being a major social factor. This stark social phenomenon had apparently decreased the severe problem of starvation or semi-starvation, the growth in the number of mal-nutrition children, amongst others. Moreover, due to rapid increase of population and the significant spread of urbanisation i.e. the conversion of villages to towns or cities, there had been a gradual decrease in the availability of necessary agricultural lands to cultivate the required volume of food to feed the world population now numbering over 700 crore. Therefore, the achievements regarding the rise of income of world population was found to be largely negated by the decreasing landspace needed for the practice of agriculture to meet the yawning volume of food supply to cater to the needs of all people living around the world.

Concern for Food Security

Food is the most essential source of human survival. There is a universal consensus that the appearance of food fit for human consumption in the Earth led to the appearance of human species. Without food, mankind can hardly survive for more than 48 hours. The nature and type of food and dietary habits underwent a sea-change along with the passage of time. Even today, in many civilised parts of the modern world, people still prefer to have the type of food, which was consumed no less than 5000 years ago. But due to a spectacular rise of population around the world and the growing income differentials between the individuals living in the Northern and Southern Hemisphere of the world, a serious challenge in the form of dreaded threat to human survival emerged in the form of global food crisis. In order to meet this lethal challenge, in 1996, the *World Summit on Food Security* was held in Rome at the behest of The Food and Agriculture Organisation (FAO) of the United Nations. The Conference produced two key Documents, the Rome Declaration on World Declaration or World Food Security and the World Food Summit Plan of Action. The Rome Declaration calls for the members of the United Nations to work to halve the number of chronically under nurished people on the Earth by the year 2015. The plan of action sets a number of targets for governmental and non-governmental organisations for achieving food security at the individual, household, national, regional and global levels. Another *World Summit on Food Security* took place in Rome between November 16 and 18, 2009. The decision to convene the Summit was taken by the Council of FAO in June 2009, at the proposal of FAO Director-General Dr Jacques Diouf. Heads of State and Government attended the Summit, which, took place at the FAO's Headquarters in Rome. The problem of securing 'food for all' looms large due to a large number of social factors. In many developed nations situated in the Northern Hemisphere which, saw an astonishing spate of urbanisation leading to a gradual decimation of farmland.

In many countries of this part of the world, the availability of rural space is even less than 10 per cent of the total land space of the nation. For a very long time, countries belonging to Asia, Africa and South America had been able to maintain a steady food supply to feed the global population including their countrymen. But a relative increase of income in the countries of these continents had led to a steady rise of domestic food supply demand, which, had led to a sharp fall in food exports making the cost of food dear. This had also heavily impacted the food price in domestic markets. For example, Arhar, a very popular variety of pulse consumed by the Indians had been sold at a premium price of Rs 200 per kg. for a number of months in 2015 despite repeated intervention by the government. Not only varieties of pulses, food price in general had been on the rise very steeply very the years in India and several countires of the devoloping parts of the world. Therefore, the Food Security Act was enacted by the government to ensure the challenge of human survival while addressing the basic nutritional requirements of the people, in general and the mothers and children (MCH) in particular. In India, the severity of crisis relating to the supply of food to abate the danger of hunger and mal-nutrition is very depressing. India is abode to 50 per cent of the world's infants and children suffering from chronic mal-nutrition (the Report of the UNICEF, 2014). Moreover, many adults suffer from perennial diseases emerging from severe mal-nutrition and starvation leading to a sharp fall of human productivity of the gross Indian labour force coupled with incessant absentecism and a disappointing form of work culture. Thus, the provision of necessary volume and quality per capita of food intake to meet the crisis of starvation or semi-starvation and address the basic nutritional and calorific requirement of every adult and child especially, pregnant, lactating mothers is a 'sine-qua-non' of the growth and development of India by any standard.

The problem of food crisis has beseised many countries leading to the general agreement to formulate a national policy to ensure food security to every individual.

Universal Access to Food

The World Health Organisation (WHO) states that there are three pillars that determine (1) food security, (2) food availability, (3) food access and (4) food use. The FAO adds a fourth pillar, the stability of the first three dimensions of food security overtime. In 2009, the World Summit on Food Security stated that the four pillars of food security are 'availability, universal, access, utilisation and stability.' In 2014, The Government of India introduced the ambitious Food Security Act in order to meet the food requirement of the less fortunate sections of our society. The estimated cost of Food Security in India is indeed stupendous –

Rs 1.3 lakh crore is likely to be spent every year to ensure Food for All to every countryman. The Act was originally conceived by the National Advisory Council headed by Congress President Sonia Gandhi, who on 27 October, 2010, forwarded the basic framework of the proposed National Food Security Bill (NFSB) to Prime Minister Manmohan Singh. The Bill envisaged covering 75 per cent of the country's population, 90 per cent in rural areas and 50 per cent in urban areas.

Food Security Act, 2013

The National Food Security Act, 2013 (also Right to Food Act) is an Act of the Parliament of India which aims of provide subsidised food grains to approximately 75 per cent of India's 85 crore people. It was signed into Law on 12 September 2013, retroactive to 5 July 2013. The National Food Security Act, 2013 (NFSA, 2013) converts into legal entitlements for existing food security and food security programmes of the Government of India. It includes the Midday Meal Scheme, Integrated Child Development Services Schemes and the Public Distribution System. Further, the NFSA 2013 recognises maternity entitlements. The Midday Meal Scheme and the Integrated Child Development Services Scheme (ICDS) are universal in nature whereas the PDS will reach about 75 per cent in rural areas and 50 per cent in urban areas.

The avowed objectives of the Food Security Act deserve mention Some of these are :

1. The Act seeks to offer rice at Rs 3 per kg., wheat at Rs 2 per kg. and coarse cereals at Re 1 a kg. to the intended beneficiaries. Upto 75 per cent of the rural population and 50 per cent of the urban population will get 5 kg. of foodgrain monthly. The poorest who fall under the *Antyodaya Anna Yojana* will continue with their present monthly entitlement of 35 kg. of food grains.
2. The Act will entitle around 80 crore of India's net population to subsidised foodgrains under the Targeted Public Distribution System.
3. States are given the responsibility to decide on eligibility criteria based on socio-economic and Caste Census (SECC) data.
4. Pregnant women and lactating mothers would receive a one-time maternity benefit of at least Rs 6,000.
5. Children aged 6 months to 14 years will get take-home rations or hot cooked food.

6. The Central Government will also provide money to states and union territories if it runs low on grain as well as providing them with 'assistance' towards the cost of intra-state trransportation and handling of grains.
7. In a bid to give women more authority in running their household, the oldest adult woman in each house would be considered the head of that household for the issuing of ration cards.
8. At the coverage and entitlement now proposed, the total estimated annual foodgrains requirement was 612.3 lakh tonnes and the corresponding estimated food subsidy for implementation of NFSB at 2013-2014 costs, is about Rs 1,245,747 crore that is nearly Rs 1.30 lakh crore.
9. There will be state and district level redressal mechanism with designated nodal officers. Redressal mechanism may also include call centres, helpline etc.
10. The Act provides for penalty to be imposed on public servants or authority, if found guilty or failing to comply with the relief recommended by the District Grievance Redressal Officer.

Endemic Deprivation

There cannot be any debate regarding the justification of the enactment of the FSA considering the dismal plight of the majority of the Indians. The Planning Commission (nee NITI Ayog) had been constantly changing the definition and the parametres of estimates to determine the extent of poverty and identify the yardstick of poverty line from time to time. This had led to several criticism to ascertain the number and percentage of people falling under the purview of poverty line. However, a perusal of the Commission headed by Arjun Sen Gupta to assess the features of Indian Economy especially with regard to unbelievable low per capita income and the extent of poverty in India may indeed prove instructive to comprehend the veracity of the FSA. The Report said, an overwhelming 83.60 crore people in India live on a per capita consumption of less than Rs 20/- a day. The study finding was a sequeal to the 'Arjun Sengupta Report' on the conditions of Work and Promotion of Livelihood in the Unorganised Sector. The Report is based on government data for the period between 1993-94 and 2004-05. While the numbers rose by a staggering 10 crore, the numbers of the new rich has also grown by 93 crore. "Our Survey is very scientific". The other poverty estimates looked at the absolute poor only but we look at different categories of poor." *Chairman, National Commission of Enterprises in Unorganised Sector, Arjun Sengupta* said. So, who are the ones who have actually benefitted from the boom in the economic growth of the country? The middle class and the rich grew from 16.2 crore to 25.3 crore while the neo-rich of 9.1 crore. The middle class grew from 15.5 per cent to 19.3 per cent but the extreme poor have also benefited (27.4 crore to 23.7 crore) – 4.3 crore of them to be precise. Their per capita consumption has gone up from Rs 9 to Rs 12 per day. The rich 'tend to hide their consumption. So if you account for that, they are actually richer than the Report reflects.' "This again reflects the fact that the gap between the rich and poor is even wider," Sengupta explained. One is classified as absolutely poor if the per capita consumption is less than Rs 9 a day. However, if the per capita consumption is Rs 13 a day, then the individual is above the poverty line. So, the definitions of poverty are sometimes difficult to understand. The justification for economic reforms was supposed to be the *trickle down* effect but for those who live in trying conditions 10 years of economic reforms seem to have made little difference. Is it any wonder that those leaders who are seen to be reforming can never with the popular vote? Thus, there is hardly any doubt that the majority of the people of our country strive with dire endemic deprivation.

Harsh Realities

The most important revealation of the Arjun Sengupta Report was less than per capita consumption of Rs 20 a day of 86.30 crore population in India. On the other hand, the gradual withdrawal of farm subsidies as a major condition of the WTO and International Donor Agencies like the World Bank, the IMF and the Asian Development Bank had worsened the quality of life of the rural population who mostly earn their living from the agricultural sector. According to the Reports of the *National Crime Records Bureau (NCRB),* New Delhi it is stated that in 2014, 56,060 farmers committed suicide in India. The highest number of farmer suicides were recorded in 2004 when 18,241 farmers committed suicide. The farmers' suicide rate in India has ranged between 1.4 to 1.8 per 1,00,000 total population over a 10-year period through 2005. India is an agrarian country with around 70 per cent of its people depending directly or indirectly upon agriculture. Farmers' suicides account for 11.2 per cent of all suicides in India. Activists and scholars have offered a number of apparently conflicing reasons for farmers' suicides such as monsoon failure, high debt burdens, Genetically Modified Crops (GMCs), Government Policies, public mental health, personal issues and family problems. There are also accusations of states fudging the data on farmers' suicide. Between 2004 and 2014, the number of farmers' suicide had touched an astronomical figure of more than 2,00,000. Most of the suicides had happened in States like Vidharva, Maharashtra, Andhra Pradesh, Tamil Nadu, Karnataka and Kerala. The escalating cost of cultivation and the relatively low profitability from the sale of farm produces in the aftermath of the beginning of the era of liberalisation had been the major reason of the sad plight of the Indian farmers. But the government authority had consistently denied the high incidence of farmer's suicide and instead explained many of these deaths as deaths due to common ailments.

In West Bengal, over 200 deaths were reported among the tea plantation workers working in the districts of North Bengal, especially in the district of Jalpaiguri. All these deaths occurred due to perennial starvation, severe mal-nutrition, tuberculosis etc. as the workers were unable to get the bare minimum calorific and nutritional intake in their daily diet as they were forced to become paupers for long closure of the tea-gardens. The tea-industry in India is now under severe duress since the disintegration of socialism in Soviet Union and other east European countries as these were the countries, which, used to import a large volume of tea from India. Since then, the tea-plantation workers had been the worse victims. However, they had little option to move out from the tea industry due to absence of alternative job opportunity in North Bengal due to total arbsence of industrialisation and urbanisation. But the authorities had repeatedly denied the deaths of the tea-garden workers due to starvation and mal-nutrition and instead referred these cases as normal deaths happening due to common types of ailments. Similarly, the government had been consistently denying the staggering figures of suicide deaths of farmers due to rising cost of cultivation rendering many of them severely pauperised and highly indebted. (The speech of the Union Minister for Agriculture, GoI in the Parliament on 19 April 2013). Therefore, in this alarming socio-economic scenario of our country there cannot be any question regarding the nationale of the FSA to ensure food for all.

The World Hunger Report

Amidst the wide-ranging debate regarding the veracity of the FSA in India, a recent Report of the United Nations may prove worthy of consideration. According to recently released *United Nations (UN) Annual World Hunger Report* titled *The State of Food Insecurity in the World*

2015, India was placed at top in the World Hunger list. The Report has mentioned that India is home to the highest number of hungry people in the world with around 19.4 crore people, surprassing China. The Report was published by UN sibsidy body Food and Agriculture Organisation (FAO). Some of the Key facts from the Reportre :

Top 10 countries : (1) India (19.46), (2) China (13.38), (3) Pakistan (4.14), (4) Ethiopia (3.16), (5) Bangladesh (2.63), (6) Indonesia (1.94), (7) Tanzania (1.68), (8) Phillipines (1.37), (9) Nigeria (1.29) and (10) North Korea (1.05) *(population in crores).*

At the Global Level : The corresponding figures have dropped to 7.95 crore in 2014-2015 compared to 100 crore in 1990-1992. In this case with East Asia led by China accounted for most of the reductions.

India has shown reduction between 15 years time span from 1990-2015. In 1990-1992 starved of food were numbered around 21 crore. It came down to 19.46 crore in 2014-2015. India's numerous social programmes and schemes have made great strides in reducing the proportion of food insecure persons in the overall population. These schemes are expected to continue to fight hunger and poverty.

China was able to achieve reduction in the number of hungry people which was once much higher than India. China's figures came down to 13.38 crore in 2014-2015 compared to 2.89 crore in 1990-1992.

Millennium Development Goal (MDG) target 72 out of 129 countries mentioned by FAO have achieved the MDG target of halving the prevalence of undernourishment by 2015. The overall analysis of the Report had suggested that inclusive economic growth, social protection and adequate agricultural investments along with political stability has played an important role in eradication of hunger. But the very high incidence of malnutrition and under-nourishment of pregnant and lactating mothers and children had made the condition in India very alarming. This could well be understood from the Report of the UNICEF, 2014 that more than 50 per cent of the World's total mal-nourished children live in India. On the other hand, in the absence of Free Press, Media, Democracy and Multi-party system in China under the Communist regime, the truthfulness of the data relating to development and progress of the country can never be accepted without doubt. But the prevalence of the highest number of hungry people in India does justify why the implementation of the FSA is so important in India.

However, despite the prevalence of many agonising ground realities in India, the history of ensuring Food Security by way of provision of vital foodgrains at an abysmally cheap rate at the expense of tax payers' hard cared money was incessantly tainted by the legacy of political consideration. Instead of abject poverty, starvation, semi-starvation and inadequate purchasing power of the majority of the Indians to have two square quality meals a day, the political calculability of the Indian politicians had always played a crucial role in this regard. As a result, the consideration to enable food secuirty was always weighed prior to elections either in Assembly or Parliament. The timing of the Enactment of the FSA prior to the 2014 Parliament Election by the Congress Party does religiously follow the prevailing legacy of the country – the flag off of the same was perhaps made by NT Rama Rao (NTR), when he declared to provide rice to all in Andhra Pradesh in the mid 1980's prior to the State Assembly Election, which, he could fight successfully. Thereafter several political parties had repeatedly adhered to the policy of appeasement of the voters while providing rice and other cereals and food grains at a price as low as Rs 2 a kg. Still, considering the deplorable socio-economic condition of the majority of the Indians, the policy was never challenged or opposed by the opposition parties fearing erosion of mass popularity, prior to elections.

Strengths and Weakness

The contention of FSA Act is no doubt laudable given the socio-economic condition of the people in our country in general. But scholars and researchers, as well as, several Expert Groups had been candid to express their thought giving positive and negative reactions to the effort.

1. *Crisil* Research believes the proper implementation of the Act will lower spending on foodgrains by below poverty line households and free up resources for spending on other goods and services, in particular health, education and nutritious food.
2. It sees the enabling of an additional savings of around Rs 4,400 each year for each BPL household that begins to purchase subsidised food. The savings equal around eight per cent and five per cent of the annual expenditure of a rural and urban household, respectively.
3. For rural households the savings amount exceeds their current annual medical and educational expenditure. Higher disposable income would allow BPL households to spend more on protein rich food thereby improving their nutritional intake *Crisil* said.

4. The Research House had said key to accruing all these benefits is the proper implementation. "While the benefits of the Act could go well beyond just the provision of food the success of the scheme and its welfare impact lies in identifying the poor and making sure that they are able to avail the food subsidy." – it said.
5. Many critics of the scheme converge on this point. They say beneficiaries do not stand to gain as about 40 per cent of rice and wheat earmarked for the poor gets siphnored off due to corruption irrespensible handling of the distribution of the grains to the public. An efficient distribution channel also leads to waste.
6. Implementing the Act in fair, equitable and transparent manner is going to be a big challenge for the government.
7. Many agriculture experts believe that Food Act which proposes to provide grains to people at very cheap rates may discourage the agriculture production in the country. Hence it must make sure that farmers should not be burdened with the cost of subsidising the supply.
8. Economists have raised concerns about the cost to the exchequer at a time when the government is struggling to bridge the fiscal and current account deficits. *Fitch Ratings* said it was getting more challenging for India to meet its fiscal deficit target in the coming fiscal year due to the gradual the slowing down of the revenues.
9. Economists of the Government's Commission for Agricultural Costs and Prices (CACP), who define the roadmap of agriculture policies, have calculated 'additional' subsidy burden of Rs 1.20 lakh crore per annum from the existing Rs 90,000 crore.
10. The Centre intends to delegate the task of construction of additional storage to the States, which may not be practically feasible given the constrained centre-state relations among the diverse political parties.

The government does not even have enough storage capacity to store the amount of grain that it currently procures and will have to procure from the farmers in the years to come. So more grains could be dumped in the open and may not as a result.

Pauperisation of Peasantry

Utsa Patnaiks offers a lucid comment on the state of economics as a discipline today, as on the economic policies that are running the lives and livelihood of millions of people in the Third World. The unifying theme of her essays is the impact on the Third World consisting Asia, Africa and Latin America of the new imperialism in the present era, which takes the form of deflationary non-liberal 'economic reforms, a thrust towards, free trade and subservient agriculture. She shows how these policies are causing unprecedented rural distress and universal hunger in the developing countries including India. Here is a voice of sanity, conscience and true scholarship. In this book, the author stresses on the grave impact of globalisation, Privatisation and Liberalisation in the aftermath of the debacle of socialism since the 1980s leading to severe form of income differentials in various countries in sub-Saharan region in Africa, in particular and the countries of Asia, Africa and South America in general. The rapid spurt of increasing mass poverty in the post-liberal regime had led to pauparisation of the peasantry on the one hand and the appearance of grave insecurity to avail two-square quality meals each day. Thus, Patnaik with a missionary zeal urged for a *peasant rennaisance* as the peasantry happens to be the most deprived and exploited social category in the wake of rapid increase in the cost of cultivation due to gradual withdrawal of farm subsidies at the behest of the WTO and other international donor agencies who had been able to make these countries critically debt trapped with huge burden of the so-called 'foreign aid'. Therefore, there is hardly any option left but for the government to intervene discretely to ensure Food Security to allay the alarming and emerging socio-economic harsh reality which she aptly calls *the republic of hunger*. Therefore, despite the history of political calculations to provide food at a highly subsidised price prior to various elections in India, the justification of the provision of foodgrain at an incredibly low rate can never be questioned.

Alluring sops by draining out the state exchequer by the ruling parties, especially prior to the elections had been a very discouraging experience in our country. But earlier the sops were in the form of distribution of hard cash, liquor arnd even colour television, laptops to students and lowering of price of various essential items needed in daily life. In comparison, the distribution of food grains at a heavily subsidised price by the government is no doubt indeed commendable to allay the fear of endemic- hunger, starvation or semi-starvation making India a haven of mal-nourished and under-productive population. This could be easily understood from the fact that India had always been a failure in sports, especially in body-contact events requiring physical power to a considerable extent. In the Olympics, Asian Games and events like football, hockey etc. India's performance at the international level is simply dismal. This is one of the unquestionable social indicators of inadequate physical strength and stamina due to the intake of sub-standard quality of daily diet by an average Indian. The number of deaths due to abject poverty and starvation might be less now compared to the past. But many deaths due to common ailments might have been occuring because of perennial low quality food intake having insufficient nutritional and calorific supplements.

According to the health experts, an individual residing in a village who need to exert more physical labour has to have food of minimum 2400 calorie whereas an inhabitant of a city has to have food with at least 2100 calorie. But in reality this could hardly be met by more than 50 per cent of the Indians. In this prevailing social scenario the FSA promises to provide the bare minimum. But whether the lofty ideal of the government may be able to meet the requirement at the ground level is indeed now a million dollar question. As the FSA is yet to take-off across the country is full swing, it may sound immature to speculate about the worthy future of the programme despite its immense relevance in India.

Hunger and Public Action

Jean Dreze, Amartya Sen and Athar Hussain in their companion volume titled 'The Political Economy of Hunger' (1993) said, Poverty is not only a condition that prevents underprivileged individuals and families from satisfying their basic needs or participating fully in society. It is a socio-economic phenomenon, which on a large scale has wide-ranging effects on society as a whole : the growth and composition of the population; its health and level of culture; patterns of settlement and migration, economic development, political stability and environmental issues. Poverty is a plague affecting all parts of the world in the 1990s and it has many faces and dimensions. Empirical studies on the causes and consequences of poverty have revealed its characteristics in both urban and rural environments in developing and industrialised countries. The political, social, economic and cultural dimensions of poverty all have their own roots. There are differences between countries regarding the factors that cause poverty and deprivation: the stagnation and decline of economic growth; low productivity; a poor level of public services; marginalisation of sectors of society because of limited access to information and education; gross inequalities in income distribution; exclusion from gainful employment because of discrimination, etc.

One of the most important and most common manifestations of poverty is the denial of access to the basic necessities of human existence.

The *UNU/WIDER Research Programme* 'Hunger and Poverty : The Poorest Billion', from which the papers were selected was concluded at the end of 1993. It was a comprehensive multi-dimensional, policy-oriented project that ran over several years, with the participation of almost one hundred experts. Various books and pamphlets have been published as country monographs and comparative, issue-oriented studies, which have revealed the global dimensions of hunger and poverty. In the 1990s the number of poor people included close to 30 per cent of the population of the developing world. The number of under-nourished people was estimated at between 73 crore and 78 crore – about 20 per cent of the population of the developing world, and about half of these people were suffering from chronic mal-nutrition. Asia is still home to most of these people, despite the fact that the numbers of malnourished have been in decline for some time. However, in sub-Saharan Africa and Latin America poverty ahnd hunger have been on the increase since the 1980s. The experience in India might be better than what is in vogue in vairous sub-Saharan countries. But the situation is not very encouraging either.

Cerebralisation of 'Human Face'

Considering the noble mission of the FSA there can hardly be any debate regarding the huge relevance of the FSA. However, the bigest stumbling block remains the sluggish economy of our country in the wake of discouraging figures made available by the Central Statistical Office (CSO) under the Ministry of Statistics and Programme Evaluation, GoI. *The Economic Times,* New Delhi, 12 March 2016. The Report of the CSO stated, Industrial production contracted for the third consecutive month in January 2016 dragged down by a sharp decline in manufacturing and capital goods sectors, posing fresh challenges for policy-makers against the backdrop of a sluggish global economy. Data released by the CSO on 11 March 2016 showed industrial production shrank an annual 1.5 per cent in January 2016 compared by 28 per cent growth and the decline of 1.2 per cent in December 2014. The manufacturing sector which accounts for 76 per cent of the index, fell to 2.8 per cent year–on-year in January 2016 compared to a growth of 3.4 per cent in December 2014.

The capital goods sector, which is seen as a guage of industrial activity fell 20.4 per cent year-on-year basis in January 2016 compared to an expansion of 12.4 per cent in December 2015. The data on capital goods sector has remained volatile for a significant period and economists say it makes it difficult to derive a trend, added the Report. These figures offered by the CSO are quite disturbing amidst the policy of the GoI regarding *Make in India* now doing the rounds at the instance of Narendra Modi. The main redeeming feature of Indian economy is the sharp decline of price of fossil fuel reducing the huge pressure on the Current Account Deficit (CAD) in the Union coffure. Therefore, if the economy of the Nation continues to remain sluggish, how can the mammoth expenditure required to implement the FSA be made to run perennially? This remains an important question surrounding the avowed mission of the lofty ideal of the policy.

Moreover, the stiff challenge with regard to global water scarcity, climate change, rapidly decreasing space required for farmland, agriculture emerging as a perennial non-remunerative livelihood, deplorable socio-economic status of the peasantry, rapid rural-urban migration, depleting rural population to carry on agricultural practices, amongst others might prove to be the emerging difficulties to provide *Food for All* due to constant lowering in the volume of food production and the incredible rise of cost of food of all varieties in order to meet the crucial demand to ensure FSA in letter and spirit in India as well as the entire world in the days ahead. There is a growing danger that the Third World War if it is ever fought may be in want of severe food and water for the bare minimum survival of an individual being. Replying to the discussion of the members in the Parliament in the Budget Session subsequent to the presentation of the Union Budget by the then Finance Minister Manmohan Singh in July 1991, the Prime Minister Narasinma Rao supporting the inevitability of the newly-introduced Globalisation said, we need to follow the same to remain tied to the global economy, which, is getting fast integrated. But we need to pursue the policy of 'Globalisation with Human Face'. The humanitarian face of Globalisation remains the pressing agenda in our country and the cerebralisation of guaranteeing *Food For All* is indeed a vital prerequisite to what was then declared as an avowed mission of the government way back in July 1991.

Notes and References

1. The World Hunger Report, 2015 – Food and Agricultural Organisation (FAO), United Nations, Rome, 2015.
2. The Report of the Ministry of Agriculture – Government of India, New Delhi, 2013.
3. The Report on the World Food Security – UNFAO, Rome, 1996.

4. The Report on 'The World Food Summit Plan of Action' – UNFAO, Rome, 1996.
5. The Report of the UNICEF – United Nations, New York, 2014.
6. The Food Security Act – Ministry of Food and Consumer Affairs, GoI, New Delhi, 2013.
7. Despair in Rural India – Samit Kar, K P Bagchi and Company, Kolkata, 2015.
8. The Report on 'Conditions of Work and Promotion of Livelihood in the Unorganised Sector' – Arjun K. Sengupta, New Delhi.
9. The Report of the National Crime Records Bureau (NCRB) – Ministry of Home Affairs, GoI, New Delhi, 2014.
10. The Report on the State of Food – United Nations FAO, Rome, 2015.
11. The Political Economy of Hunger – Jean Dreze, Amartya Sen and Athar Hussain (edited), Oxford University Press, New Delhi, 1993.
12. India : Economic Development and Social Opportunity – Jean Dreze and Amartya Sen, Oxford University Press, New Delhi, 1995.
13. Chirosthayee Bondobosto O Bangladesh-er Krishak (in Bengali) – Badruddin Umar, Chiratya Prakashan, Kolkata, 1982.
14. The Speech Sharad Pawar Union Agricultural Minister on Farmers' Suicide made in the Parliament – Economic Times, New Delhi, 1 April 2013.
15. Factory Output Dips 1.5 per cent in January 2016 – A Press Report, the Times of India, New Delhi, 12 March 2016.
16. Republic of Hunger and Other Essays Utsa Patnaik, Merlin Press, Gurgaon, 2007.
17. The Text of the Union Budget of 2016-2017 presented by Arun Jaitley – The Economic Times, New Delhi, 1 March 2016.
18. Rural Development : Policies and Principles, Katar Singh, Sage Publishers, New Delhi, 1987.

21

Impact of Climate Change on Food Security: A Conceptual Analysis

Bijayalaxmi Mohanta and Amit Kumar Jena

The past half-century has seen marked growth in food production, allowing for a dramatic decrease in the proportion of the world's people that are hungry, despite a doubling of the total population. Nevertheless, more than one in seven people today still do not have access to sufficient protein and energy from their diet, and even more suffer from some form of micronutrient malnourishment.

The global population will continue to grow, yet it is likely to plateau at some nine billion people by roughly the middle of this century. A major correlate of this deceleration in population growth is increased wealth, and with higher purchasing power comes higher consumption and a greater demand for processed food, meat, dairy, and fish, all of which add pressure to the food supply system. At the same time, food producers are experiencing greater competition for land, water, and energy, and the need to curb the many negative effects of food production on the environment is becoming increasingly clear.

Food security is a broad term, which is defined in different ways by a number of organisations around the world. The basic definition of food security is that it refers to the ability of individuals to obtain sufficient food on a day-to-day basis. Internationally food security is defined as the ability of people to secure adequate food. More especially it has been defined by researchers as the access by all people at all times to enough food for an active healthy life (Anderson, 1990).

During 1950 to 1960, Food security was equated with self-sufficiency in major staples. During FAO World Food Conference of 1974, Food Security is defined as access to sufficient food.

Food security is achieved when all people, at all times, have physical, social and economic access to sufficient, safe and nutritious food to meet their dietary needs and food preferences for an active and healthy life (FAO World Food Summit, 1996).

According to the World Food Summit organised in Rome in 1996, food security exists when all people, at all times, have physical and economic access to sufficient, safe, nutritious food to meet their dietary needs and food preferences for an active life.

Food Security within the Department of Agriculture, Forestry and Fisheries, Food and Agriculture Organisation of the United Nations (FAO), as well as the Centre for Poverty, Employment and Growth (CPEG) of the Human Sciences Research Council (HSRC) acknowledged that food security has three dimensions namely, food availability, food access and food use. Food availability in the definition implies that a country must have sufficient quantities of food available on a consistent basis at both national and household level. Food access implies the ability of a nation and its households to acquire sufficient food on a sustainable basis. Food use refers to the appropriate use based on knowledge of basic nutrition and care, as well as adequate water and sanitation.

Food security at national level refers to the condition whereby the nation is able to manufacture, import, retain and sustain food needed to support its population with minimum per capita nutritional standards. At community level food security is defined as the condition whereby the residents in a community can obtain safe, culturally accepted, nutritionally adequate diets through a sustainable system that maximises community self reliance. At household level food security refers to the availability of food in one's home which one has access to. In this case, a household is regarded as food secure when the members of the family do not live in hunger or fear of starvation.

The concept of food (in)security is closely linked with the poverty in the country. The two concepts are interrelated and to some extent have an influence on one another. In any food security discourse, it is also essential to highlight in a nutshell the plight of poverty in the country. Poverty refers to the condition of not having the means to afford basic human needs such as clean water, nutrition, healthcare, education, clothing and shelter.

United Nations Development Programme (UNDP) report of 2006 pointed out that food insecurity is closely linked to poverty, income and unemployment. The report reveals that poverty and unemployment have strong relationship with food insecurity and in most cases food insecurity manifest in multiple deprivations. Food insecurity begins with the loss of employment, which in turns leads to a significant degradation in living standard. Living in poverty creates additional challenges which limit the ability for people to search for employment and that contribute to a long-term unemployment trap. Lack of income due to unemployment, contribute to food insecurity and leads to socials exclusion problems.

Positive Impacts of Food Safety on Food Security

Improved food safety along the food chain reduces food losses, resulting in increased food availability, stability, and utilisation, access to safe food reduces foodborne illnesses with their associated social and economic implications. Improved safety and quality of food contributes to improved nutrition and health.

Food Security depends on

- Climate change
- Growing use of food crops as a source of fuel
- Soaring food prices
- Inefficient food safety systems

FAO estimates that 1.02 billion people are undernourished worldwide in 2009. Two billion people suffer from different forms of starvation, malnutrition and related health implications.

The three deficiencies of greatest public health significance worldwide concern the following micronutrients:

- Vitamin A (deficiency is most common in young children. Untreated it leads to less resistance to respiratory infections, blindness and death).
- Iron (most common dietary deficiency globally, affecting mostly children and women of childbearing age. It leads to anemia, which contributes significantly to maternal and neonatal deaths).

- Iodine (deficiency disorder occurs in mountaineous and flood plain areas, where iodine has been washed away from soils. It is the most common cause of preventable mental retardation, including low Intelligence

The success of food-based programmes to overcome micronutrient deficiencies will depend both by community acceptance and political support. Nutrition objectives must be incorporated into agricultural and other sectors development policies and programmes.

Improved efforts in nutrition assessment, food-based nutrition programmes, nutrition education and policy advice, agricultural R and D and extension, horticulture, fishery and small livestock ventures to increase crops and dietary diversity are keys for improved nutrition.

Government policies and regulations in the agricultural, trade and food processing sectors greatly influence the availability and price of micronutrient rich foods, as well as the profitability of producing, processing and marketing such foods.

According to WHO, every year there are about four billion cases of water-and food-borne diarrhoeal diseases globally. These illnesses exacerbate problems of malnutrition and reportedly account for 1.8 million deaths annually. Unacceptable standards of food safety render food unfit for human consumption and thus impair food security and public health. Food safety and nutritional quality are essential elements and integral part of food security. Effective efforts to improve food security must occur in conjunction with efforts to improve nutrition security.

Food safety implies the absence or acceptable and safe levels of contaminants, adulterants, naturally occurring toxins or any other substance that make food injurious to health on an acute or chronic basis.

The four dimensions of food security are as follows:

Food availability

Availability of sufficient quantities of food of appropriate quality, supplied through domestic production or imports.

- Domestic production
- Import capacity
- Food stocks
- Food aid

Physical and economic access to food

Access by individuals to adequate resources (entitlements) for acquiring appropriate foods for a nutritious diet.

- Purchasing power
- Income of population
- Transport and market
- Infrastructure

Stability of supply and access

To be food secure, a population, household or individual must have access to adequate food at all times.

- Weather variability
- Price fluctuations
- Political factors
- Economic factors

Food utilisation

Utilisation of food through adequate diet, clean water, sanitation and healthcare to reach a state of nutritional well-being where all physiological needs are met.

- Food safety.
- Hygiene and manufacturing practices applied in primary agricultural production, harvesting and storage; food processing, transportation, retail, households.
- Diet quality and diversity: meeting needs in terms of energy, macro- and micronutrients.

At national level Food security refers to the condition whereby the nation is able to manufacture, import, retain and sustain food needed to support its population with minimum per capita nutritional standards. At community level food security is the condition whereby the residents in a community can obtain safe, culturally accepted, nutritionally adequate diets through a sustainable system that maximises community self reliance. At household level food security refers to the availability of food at home level and they have access to. In this case, a household is regarded as food secure when the members of the family do not live in hunger or fear of starvation.

The concept of food (in)security is closely linked with the poverty in country. The two concepts are interrelated and to some extent have an influence on one another. In any food security discourse, it is also essential to highlight in a nutshell the plight of poverty in the country. Poverty refers to the condition of not having the means to afford basic human needs such as clean water, nutrition, health care, education, clothing and shelter.

United Nations Development Programme (UNDP) report of 2006 pointed out that food insecurity is closely linked to poverty, income and unemployment. The report reveals that poverty and unemployment have strong relationship with food insecurity and in most cases food insecurity manifest in multiple deprivations. Food insecurity begins with the loss of employment, which in turns leads to a significant degradation in living standard. Living in poverty creates additional challenges which limit the ability for people to search for employment and that contribute to a long-term unemployment trap. Lack of income due to unemployment, contribute to food insecurity and leads to socials exclusion problems.

Significant effort to assess the potential impacts of climate change on agriculture began in 1978 when the National Defense University assembled an international group of climate experts to predict the probabilities of various climate change events and the resulting impacts on agriculture. Since then, more structured scientific studies have resulted in a growing consensus on the interactions between climate change and agriculture, culminating in the 2007 Fourth Assessment Report of the Intergovernmental Panel on Climate Change (IPCC).

According to (www. Climate Impacts on Food Security _ WFP _ United Nations World Food Programme - Fighting Hunger Worldwide.html) the climate change affects all dimensions of food security and nutrition.

- **Food availability:** Changes in climatic conditions have already affected the production of some staple crops, and future climate change threatens to exacerbate this. Higher temperatures will have an impact on yields while changes in rainfall could affect both crop quality and quantity.
- **Food access:** Climate change could increase the prices of major crops in some regions. For the most vulnerable people, lower agricultural output means lower incomes. Under these conditions, the poorest people — who already use most of their income on

food — sacrifice additional income and other assets to meet their nutritional requirements, or resort to poor coping strategies.

- **Food utilisation:** Climate-related risks affect calorie intake, particularly in areas where chronic food insecurity is already a significant problem. Changing climatic conditions could also create a vicious cycle of disease and hunger. Nutrition is likely to be affected by climate change through related impacts on food security, dietary diversity, care practices and health.
- **Food stability:** The climatic variability produced by more frequent and intense weather events can upset the stability of individuals' and government food security strategies, creating fluctuations in food availability, access and utilisation.

Horticultural crops are likely to be more sensitive to climate change than grains and oilseeds. Climate change is likely to lead to the northern migration of weeds. Weeds respond positively to CO_2 and the commonly used herbicide glyphosate loses its ability in to kill weeds in a higher CO_2 environment. This is particularly troublesome because the use of continuous no-till, which necessitates high applications of glyphosate, is seen as a means to offset GHG emissions. With increased CO_2 and temperature rises there may be an initial expansion of grain and oilseed production. With continued rising temperatures this initial expansion may be short lived, particularly if precipitation patterns become more variable.

With the expected earlier springs and warmer winters, disease pressure from livestock pests, parasites and pathogens on cropland, pastureland and rangeland may increase and livestock producers may need to deal with increased parasites and pathogens as climate change results in increased survivability and expansion of the pests' range. Expected higher temperatures may increase livestock deaths in some regions unless some kind of shelter is made available. Forage production may be expanded as growing seasons lengthen, but this benefit will depend on water availability. Shifts in plant species in rangelands, particularly an increase in perennial herbaceous species, will create greater spring water demands.

Climate change poses a serious threat to our environment, our rural communities and our farmers who rely on them for food and fiber. Shifting to a more resilient, sustainable agricultural system will mitigate climate change while building an agri-food system that is better for our planet and its people. Failing to do so will result in devastating consequences for agriculture and the environment.

Climate change affects agriculture and food production in complex ways. It affects food production directly through changes in agro-ecological conditions and indirectly by affecting growth and distribution of incomes, and thus demand for agricultural produce.

Global and regional weather conditions are also expected to become more variable than at present, with increases in the frequency and severity of extreme events such as cyclones, floods, hailstorms, and droughts. By bringing greater fluctuations in crop yields and local food supplies and higher risks of landslides and erosion damage, they can adversely affect the stability of food supplies and thus food security. Climate fluctuations has become more pronounced and more widespread, droughts and floods, the dominant causes of short-term fluctuations in food production in semi-arid and sub-humid areas, will become more severe and more frequent. In semi-arid areas, droughts can dramatically reduce crop yields and livestock numbers and productivity (Schmidhuber and Tubiello, 2007).

The main concern about climate change and food security is that changing climatic conditions can initiate a vicious circle where infectious disease causes or compounds hunger, which, in turn, makes the affected populations more susceptible to infectious disease. The result can be a substantial decline in labour productivity and an increase in poverty and even mortality. Essentially all manifestations of climate change, be they drought, higher temperatures, or heavy rainfalls have an impact on the disease pressure, and there is growing evidence that these changes affect food safety and food security.

The recent IPCC report also emphasises that increases in daily temperatures will increase the frequency of food poisoning, particularly in temperate regions. Warmer seas may contribute to increased cases of human shellfish and reef-fish poisoning (ciguatera) in tropical regions and a poleward expansion of the disease (Hall *et al.,* 2002; Hunter, 2003; Korenberg, 2004).

Growing population and consumption growth mean that the global demand for food will increase for at least another 40 years (www.food security\Climate Change Impacts on Global Food Security _ Science.html.). Growing competition for land, water, and energy, in addition to the overexploitation of fisheries, will affect our ability to produce food, as will the urgent requirement to reduce the impact of the food system on the environment. The effects of climate change are a further threat. But the world can produce more food and can ensure that it is used more efficiently and equitably. A multifaceted and linked global strategy is needed to ensure sustainable and equitable food security, different components of which are explored here.

Climate change could potentially interrupt progress toward a world without hunger. A robust and coherent global pattern is discernible of the impacts of climate change on crop productivity that could have consequences for food availability. The stability of whole food systems may be at risk under climate change because of short-term variability in supply. However, the potential impact is less clear at regional scales, but it is likely that climate variability and change will exacerbate food insecurity in areas currently vulnerable to hunger and undernutrition. Likewise, it can be anticipated that food access and utilisation will be affected indirectly via collateral effects on household and individual incomes, and food utilisation could be impaired by loss of access to drinking water and damage to health. The evidence supports the need for considerable investment in adaptation and mitigation actions toward a "climate-smart food system" that is more resilient to climate change influences on food security.

References

1. D. C. du Toit (2011). Food Security. Directorate Economic Services.
2. Food security and its determinant factors. Ministry of health, ministry of food and agriculture and consumer protection.
3. Hall, GV, D'Souza, RM, Kirk, MD (2002). Med J Austral 177:614–618.
4. Hunter, PR (2003). Journal of Applied Microbiology. 94:37–46.
5. Intergovernmental Panel on Climate Change. 2007. Climate Change 2007: Synthesis Report.Contribution of Working Groups I, II and III to the Fourth Assessment Report of the Intergovernmental Panel on Climate Change (Core Writing Team, R. K. Pachauri and A. Reisinger (eds.).
6. Josef Schmidhuber and Francesco N. Tubiello (2007). Global food security under climate change. Sustainability science. Vol. 104(50).
7. Korenberg, E (2004). In Climate Change and Public Health in Russia in the XXI Century, Proceedings of a Workshop, eds Izmerov NF, Revich BA, Korenberg EI (Adamant, Moscow), pp. 54–67.

8. National Defense University. 1978. Climate Change to the Year 2000: A Survey of Expert Opinion.
9. National sustainable agriculture coalition. Agriculture and climate change: impacts and opportunities at the farm level. A policy position paper. pp. 1-39.
10. www.Climate Impacts on Food Security _ WFP _ United Nations World Food Programme - Fighting Hunger Worldwide.html.
11. www.food security\Climate Change Impacts on Global Food Security_Science.html.

22

Empowering Small Farmers for Their Food Security Accelerating Flow of Institutional Credit

Mahendra Patel

The FAO of the United Nations had declared the year 2014 as the "*International Year of Family Farming" (IYFF*) to create awareness among all stakeholders, review the current status of family farms, evolve policy and programmes and strengthen institutional infrastructure, among others, that enable family farms to become food-secure and viable. This declaration presented opportunities to the rural financial institutions of India to accelerate the flow of credit to small and marginal farmers (S and MFs) accompanied by improving the effectiveness of the government's role in creating enabling environment, *inter alia,* to make S and MFs in India food-secure and viable by 2020. According to the FAO Director-General, Graziano da Silva, "*a family farm ismanaged and operated by a family and predominantly reliant on family labour, including that of both women and men*". In the Indian context,marginal farmers (owning less than one hectare) who share 67 per cent in total number of holdings and 22 per cent of cultivated area aptly fit in the definition of family farms. The small-holder families, who constitute about 50 per cent of the national population, comprise almost 60 per cent of nation's hungry and poor. Notwithstanding S and MFs best efforts to increase crop-productivity and incomes, most families that operate holdings below 1.0 hectare are *net purchasers* of almost all food items. As banking system in India since country's independence has been supporting the development of agriculture in general and small farmers in particular, this article briefly highlights the changing rural scenario, credit policy and programs, status and implications of small farms, policy initiatives and programmes incorporated in country's Twelfth Five Year Plan (2012-17) and suggests enabling measures to make S and MFs food-secure and viable.

Predominance of S and MFs

Agricultural Census (2010–11) reveals that out of 138.35 million operational holdings, 85 per cent (accounting for 44.6 per cent of the total cultivated area) are less than two hectares characterising India's agriculture a small-scale-farming. Average size of small-holding is only 0.61 hectare whereas overall average size of holdings declined from 1.33 hectare in 2000–01 to 1.15 hectare in 2010–11.

Table 22.1: Percentage of Size-distribution of Operational Land Holdings

Holding category	*1960-61*	*1970-71*	*1981-82*	*1991-92*	*2002-03*
Marginal < 1 hectare	39.1 [6.9]	45.8 [9.2]	56.0 [11.5]	62.8 [15.6]	69.8 [22.2]
Small 1- 2 hectares	22.6 [12.3]	22.4 [14.8]	19.3 [16.5]	17.8 [18.7]	16.1 [20.6]
Semi-medium 2-4 hectares	19.8 [20.7]	17.7 [22.6]	14.2 [23.6]	12.0 [24.1]	9.0 [22.4]
Medium 4-10 hectares	14.0 [31.2]	11.1 [30.5]	8.6 [30.1]	6.1 [26.4]	4.3 [22.7]
Large > 10 hectares	4.5 [29.0]	3.1 [23.0]	1.9 [18.2]	1.3 [15.2]	0.8 [12.1]
All categories	**100 [100]**	**100 [100]**	**100 [100]**	**100 [100]**	**100 [100]**

Figures in parentheses indicate per cent share in operated holdings.

S and MFs account for 70 per cent, 69 per cent, 55 per cent and 52 per cent in total production of vegetables, milk, fruits and cereals respectively against their 44.46 per cent share in area whereas they have lower share in pulses and oilseeds than that of large farmers. Despite S and MFs have potential to diversify cropping system and attain food security, holding size of 0.61 hectare is too inadequate to generate income enough for the family.This is because S and MFs have inherent disadvantages both in the input and output markets. Following Table exhibits average monthly income from different sources, the total consumption expenditure and net income per agricultural household during the agricultural year 2012-13 (July–June) for each size class of land possessed. The share of income from non-farm business in the average monthly income declined with the increase in land size. Further, the net monthly income (farm and non-farm) in respect of size classes up to 1.00 hectare was negative and it increased steadily with the increase in size classes. This demonstrates the need to significantly enhance income of S and MFs through improving productivity of crops per hectare, diversification and providing additional sources of income which can make small-scale farming efficient and financially sustainable.

Table 22.2: Income, Percentage of Sources of income, Total Consumption and Surplus/Deficit per Month

Holding Size	*Total income [Rs.]*	*Sources of income [%]*				*Consumption Expenditure [Rs.]*	*Surplus/ Deficit [Rs.]*
		Wages	*Cultivation*	*Livestock*	*Nonfarm*		
0-0.01	4561	63.6	00.7	25.9	9.8	5108	-547
0.01-0.4	4152	57.5	16.5	15.0	11.1	5401	-1249
0.4-1.0	5247	38.3	40.9	12.0	8.8	6020	-773
1.01-2.0	7348	23.5	57.3	11.1	8.1	6457	+891
2.01-4.0	10730	15.4	68.6	10.8	5.2	7786	+2944
4.01-10	19637	10.3	77.6	7.6	4.4	10104	+9533
<10	41388	03.2	86.2	6.3	4.3	14447	+26941
Up to 1.0	4718	48.1	28.2	13.9	9.9	5701	-983
Average	6426	32.2	47.9	11.9	8.0	6223	+203

India has relatively much higher global hunger index than that in China. In last 25 years India could improve it from 31.2 in 1990 to 17.8 in 2014 as against 13.6 to 5.4 in China. Most hungry in India belong to small, marginal and tenant farmers, oral lessees, share croppers, agricultural labourers and those residing in desert, drought-prone, hilly and tribal areas in particular.

Table 22.3: Global Hunger Index of India and China (1990, 1995, 2000, 2005 and 2014)

Country	*1990*	*1995*	*2000*	*2005*	*2014*
India	31.2	26.9	25.5	24.2	17.8
China	13.6	10.7	08.5	06.8	05.4
Pakistan	26.7	23.3	22.1	21.0	19.9

Changing Rural Scenario

With the progressive institutionalisation of agricultural credit system since 1970s, total credit(short and long-term) disbursed to agriculture during 45 years (1970-2015) amounts to about Rs 59.99 trillion with target of Rs 9.0 trillion for 2015-16. The government programmes and agricultural credit disbursed, among others, helped India to be the number one in the worldin the production of milk, pulses, jute and jute-like fibres and two in rice, wheat, sugarcane, groundnut, vegetables, fruits and cotton production and a leading producer of spices, plantation crops, livestock, fisheries and poultry products. Agriculture has been witnessing a shift in the production from food grains to high-value produce, especially fruits and vegetables. For S and MFs, crop diversification into high value produce is a healthy sign of optimum utilisation of resources, diversifying sources of income, mitigating risks and meeting changing market needs. Share of fruits, vegetables, meat and fibre in total production increased from 38 per cent in 2000 to 45 per cent in 2010. Perception of *'rural'* and *'agriculture'* signifying once as if they were two sides of the same coin is now changing rapidly. This is evident from the fact that the share of income from agriculture in the rural incomes has declined to 30 per cent in 2010 from 74 per cent in 1970s. Over 42 per cent of rural households earn their income from non-farm sources. Rural income and consumption expenditure are witnessing an upward trend. According to NSSO data of mid-2012, the average monthly per capita consumer expenditure in rural areas shot up at a faster rate than urban areas between 2009 and 2012. Another survey by CRISIL in August 2012 revealed that rural spending outpaced urban spending between 2009-10 and 2011-12 for the first time in nearly 25 years. Discretionary spending of an average rural household rose to Rs 24,000 in 2009-10 from Rs 14,000 in 2004-05, growing at about 11 per cent per annum, which is faster than the inflation rate of nearly 6 per cent per annum over the same period.

Credit policy and programs

- Government appointed All-India Rural Credit Survey Committee which made far reaching recommendations in 1954 to strengthen agricultural credit cooperatives and expand the role of the State Bank and its seven Associate Banks to finance agriculture. Government policy in early 1950s till mid-1960s was to increase food output in order to avoid substantial import of food. In this process, government developed seed-fertiliser-irrigation technology and did usher in Green Revolution. Of course, this increased food output but did not benefit S and MFs.Therefore, the government started as pilot projects by establishing two development agencies, viz. Small Farmers' Development Agency (SFDA) and Marginal Farmers and Agricultural Laborers' Development Agency (MFALDA) in late 1960s to improve their farm productivity substantially when technology was already available and 14 private commercial banks were nationalised with a mandate to provide institutional credit to agriculture on priority basis in 1969.

- Government, also, directed nationalised banks to finance Primary Agricultural Credit Societies in rural areas where cooperative credit institutions (which were financing agriculture assigning priority to S and MFs) were financially, managerially and administratively weak.
- In 1973-74, government established Farmers' Service Societies (FSS) for S and MFs in SFDA areas to facilitate and provide linkage between credit and services for production inputs and for investment in land development, sinking irrigation wells, installation of diesel/electric pump-sets, purchase of modern farm equipment and marketing of produce.
- On 2nd October 1975, the government by an Act of Parliament established the Regional Rural Banks (in addition to existing cooperatives and commercial banks) to finance S and MFs, among other rural households, to improve agriculture and rural economy and since mid-2000s RRBs have been amalgamated as a part of reform process.
- Till October 1980, SFDA was the premiere organisation to improve the productivity of small farms. The policy was to support them to exploit their production potential and improve levels of income by adopting improved agricultural practices through government and institutional interventions. The programme was to make small farms viable with irrigation wherever possible and with adoption of modern technology and easy access to inputs and credit. The SFDA provided capital subsidy for investment in agriculture and animal husbandry activities to the extent of 25 per cent to small farmers and 33.33 per cent to marginal farmers of the total cost of the asset acquired/created to motivate S and MFs and meet the margin money required for sourcing institutional credit. While out of 1818 SFDAs, many made appreciable progress, the limiting factors inhibiting the targeted achievements included (i) ineffective inter-institutional coordination and lack of involvement/participation of beneficiaries for planning and implementing the program. (ii) inadequate training and capacity building of implementing personnel. (iii) S and MFs were more tempted in availing subsidy

(misusing subsidy) rather than actually creating and maintaining assets to generate employment and income. Consequent upon this, well-off farmers got the subsidy and non-repayment of bank credit by beneficiaries resulted in larger defaults.(iv) government measured progress in terms of number of beneficiaries assisted (irrespective of their eligibility) and amount of subsidy released rather than number and quality of assets created, employment and income generated. (v) absence of monitoring, review and mid-term correction mechanism. (vi) lack of field studies, detailed planning and integration with other supporting programmes resulted in low level of achievements. (vii) planning devoid of backward and forward linkages, viz. absence of linking credit and subsidy with supply of quality assets, production inputs, technology and marketing, among others. Subsequently, from 2nd October, 1980 these SFDAs and MFALDAs were merged in the newly created District Rural Development Agency to plan and implement Integrated Rural Development Program aimed at removing the rural poverty and unemployment. Thus, the focus of assisting S and MFs was considerably diluted as the IRDP targeted a wide range of beneficiaries and activities. From April 1989, RBI introduced the concept of Service Area Approach and formulation of Potential Link Credit Plans district-wise to substantially enhance quality and productivity of lending.

Institutional credit

Institutional credit is a *sine qua non* to augment working capital required for seasonal agricultural operations and more importantly for investment on farms. Institutional credit, to replace informal credit obtained by S and MFs at exorbitant rates of interest, progressively improved its share in outstanding credit of cultivator households from 10.2 per cent in 1950 to 66.3 per cent in 1990 but declined to 56.0 per cent in 2012, mainly because of increase in the share of professional moneylenders from 19.6 per cent to 28.2 per cent. This is, indeed, alarming.

Table 22.4: Percentage Share of Institutional and Non-institutional Sources of Agricultural Credit

Year	*Institutional*	*Non-institutional*	*Year*	*Institutional*	*Non-institutional*
1950	10.2	89.8	1990	66.3	33.2
1960	20.9	79.1	2000	61.1	38.9
1970	32.0	68.0	2010	64.0	36.0
1980	56.2	43.8	2012	56.0	44.0

Credit to S and MFs

Following Table reveal that inability of S and MFs to access hassle-free institutional credit has benefitted farmers with larger holdings from the credit expansion policy and programmes.

Table 22.5: Percentage of Agricultural Households Indebted According to Farm Size

Farm Size [hectare]	*2003*	*2013*	*Farm Size[hectare]*	*2003*	*2013*
<0 to 0.01	45.3	41.9	2.01 to 4.0	58.2	66.5
0.01 to 0.4	44.3	47.3	4.01 to 10	65.1	76.3
0.4 to 1.0	45.6	48.3	<10	66.4	75.7
1.01 to 2.00	51.0	55.7			

In 2011, out of the 74.97 million S and MFs only about 46.3 per cent (34.70 million) S and MFs had access to credit, either from formal or informal sources. Banks, as major sources of loan for all farmer-households, accounted for 36 per cent outstanding loan amount. During 2007-11, public sector banks increased their share of S and MF credit in Adjusted Net Bank Credit (ANBC) from 4.57 per cent to 6.32 per cent as compared with 0.64 per cent to 2.82 per cent by private banks. In aggregate, banks' share increased from 3.77 per cent to 5.71 per cent. Despite credit to S and MFs is increasing over the years, the number of S and MFs financed had not proportionately increased. As of March 2011, the total numbers of S and MF loan accounts with Scheduled Commercial Banks (SCB) were approximately 23 million. Considering that a farmer, on an average, may have more than one account with bank(s), only around 15 per cent to 20 per cent of S and MFs were availing loans from SCBs.

Table 22.6: Outstanding Agricultural Credit to S and MFs and their percentage share in ANBC (Rs Billion)

Year	*Public Sector Banks*	*Private Banks*	*Total*
2007	602.73 [4.57]	21.40 [0.64]	624.13 [3.77]
2008	753.81 [5.75]	55.60 [1.62]	839.40 [4.92]
2009	1038.75 [6.13]	85.56 [2.10]	1124.31 [5.35]
2010	1308.30 [6.31]	133.43 [2.85]	1441.74 [5.67]
2011	1576.98 [6.32]	150.29 [2.82]	1727.27 [5.71]

Figures in parentheses indicate percentage share of S and MF in ANBC.

Between 2009-10 and 2013-14 total numbers of borrower-accounts financed increased by 65.80 per cent from 48.23 million to 79.968 million of which share of S and MFs in the total increased from 59 per cent to 63 per cent respectively. During the same period, credit disbursed shot up by 85.07 per cent from Rs 3845.1 billion to Rs 7116,2 billion. Share of S and MFs at 63 per cent is significantly less than their share in the total number of operational holdings (85 per cent), whereas the share of S and MF credit (45 per cent) in the total credit disbursed matches with their share in the total area operated (44.6 per cent) in the country. RRBs have performed better in financing S and MFs followed by Cooperatives than commercial banks.

Table 22.7: Number of A/Cs financed and Amount of Credit disbursed with share of S and /MFs

Banks	*Percentage share of A/Cs financed*		*Percentage Share in credit disbursed*	
	2009-10	2013-14	2009-10	2013-14
Commercial	42.57 [52]	47.40[62]	74.33[24]	71.53[40]
Cooperatives	42.28[63]	40.18[64]	16.51[46]	16.86 [58]
RRBs	15.15[68]	12.41[67]	09.16[60]	11.61[62]
Total	48.23 million [59]	79.968 million [63]	3845.1billion [31]	7116.2billion [45]

Figures in parenthesis indicate per cent share of S and MFs in total by respective banks.

Current status and implications of small farms

- Small farmers owning land between one and two hectares and marginal farmers less than one hectare constitute the backbone of Indian agriculture. Policy interventionists need to recognise the significant degree of inequality in land ownership and operation. Medium (4-10 ha) and large farmers (above 10 ha) together accounting for only 5.1 per cent of farmer households operate 34.8 per cent of total operated area, while large farmers (0.8 per cent of the total) still operate 12.1 per cent of total operated area.. Small farms use less capital, higher labour and other owned inputs and reflect a higher index of cropping intensity and diversification.
- According to Agricultural Census 2010-11, out of 138 million farm holdings in the country, 117 million are small and marginal holdings which shot up from 61.7 per cent of total in 1960-61 to 85 per cent in 2010-11 and own nearly 44 per cent of the cultivated area. Interestingly, marginal farmers who share 67 per cent in total

number of holdings and 22 per cent of cultivated area can be considered as a distinct class by itself since farming for them becomes a significant source of livelihood often much more than that of small farmer households.

- Fragmentation of land presents serious problems for all components of agricultural growth and development, viz. production, storage, transportation, processing, marketing and more importantly, generating incomes and making farms economically viable. Fragmentation to owners of small and marginal farms means higher costs for adopting modern technology, purchasing production inputs and accessing extension, credit, insurance and marketing services. Continuous decline in average size of land holding has implications for financial institutions since financial investment to create assets is often not viable on marginal farms.
- At national level, S and MFs account for an estimated two-thirds of national vegetables and milk production and more than half of cereals and fruits produced. The National Sample Survey Organisation (NSSO) has empirically established that small farms produce more per hectare than their larger counterparts in most parts of the country. However, with very little marketable surplus even policy interventions like Minimum Support Price and increased procurement prices do not help these farmers and individual farming is hardly commercially feasible and financially viable.S and MFs may be *'efficient'* but smaller volumes of produce, higher transport cost, inability to store and negotiate for remunerative prices impact on their lower incomes, bankability and financial viability.
- Declining incomes just due to reducing farm sizes have become a serious disincentive for farmers to continue farming. The NSSO in 2003 revealed that 40 per cent of farmers did not wish to continue cultivation if sustainable employment outside agriculture was available.
- Despite the small piece of land not providing enough employment and adequate income, most S and MFs are unwilling to sell their land because land is the last precious asset of their life insurance.
- S and MFs need cash to purchase food and long-term institutional credit at affordable rate to acquire income-generating assets to attain livelihood and pay for family's healthcare and children's education.
- The present constraints of Indian agriculture relate to the declining public investment in agricultural research and development and

small farmers' inaccessibility to institutional credit, technology, extension and marketing services in particular.

- During the 1990s, rates of increase in total factor productivity for crops were appreciably less than in preceding decades. This has been attributed to substantially lower public investment in agriculture and its support to research and extension services. This has adversely impacted on the productivity, production and profitability of S and MFs.
- With the liberalisation, privatisation and globalisation of Indian economy since early 1990s the much needed government's support to agriculture gradually declined. Since then farmers have to depend more on private agencies for their needs, viz. production inputs, extension, markets and credit services. Increasing costs of cultivation leading to higher indebtedness, crop failures and inability to face price shocks with greater liberalisation of the agricultural sector have driven farmers to the extreme. Unfortunately, in the last decade farmers suicides have become widespread and the victims have largely been S and MFs.
- The latest "Situation Assessment of Farmers Survey" showed that among the various inputs of production and services only organic manure was most readily available within the village, whereas in most cases, inputs were available in the nearest large village at more than 2-5 km away. Access to public extension services was very weak which often resulted in farmer's inappropriate choice of crops, their varieties and use of inputs. While these farmers are at disadvantages to deal with the markets, the government interventions also tend to be less effective in this respect.
- A stark reality of India's farm situation today is that while land hunger continues unabated amongst the poor and women, the educated youths are leaving agriculture. Many large and absentee owners are leaving land under-cultivated which could be leased out if they are guaranteed of retaining ownership of land by country's law.

Policy in Twelfth FYP

Based on the lessons learnt from the successes/failures of the earlier programmes and recommendations of several expert committees to enhance productivity per unit of resources of small farms, the Twelfth Five Year Plan (2012-17) provides new directions to the planning process that include, among others (i) formation of farmer-producer organisations (ii) access of landless and women farmers to land (iii) provision of quality seeds and passing Seeds Bill pending in the parliament since 2004 (iv) reforms in agricultural marketing (v) institutional development including expeditiously reforming agricultural credit cooperatives (vi) strengthening community-managed agricultural extension system (vii) National Food Security Mission is being implemented from 2014-15 in 619 districts of 28 States.

Need for Enabling Measures: Followingenabling measures are necessary to increase the share of S and MFs in agricultural credit from 5.71 per cent to 8 per cent as mandated by the RBI within the existing 18 per cent credit to agriculture by 2017 accompanied by the government's policy to create facilitating environment so as to help improve the credit absorption capacity of S and MFs.

- **Bridging yield gaps:** The strategy to bridge the existing 30 per cent gap between the potential and actual yields needs to focus replacing the use of 75 per cent of home-preserved seeds by the quality seeds of high-yielding varieties accompanied by integrated nutrient and pest management technology and water-saving devices.The managerial capability and competence of S and MFs must be improved as the major yield gaps are due to management practices. Whileproductivity of wheat, rice, pulses and oilseeds can be enhanced by 30 per cent at current level of technology, the focus should, also, be the diversification of the cropping pattern to include coarse cereals, vegetables, fruit trees, fodder and farming system to raise output of milk, meat, eggs and fish.
- **Utilisation of irrigation facilities:** During 2007-12, irrigation potential of 9.5 million hectares (59.37 per cent) was created as against targets of 16 million hectares and utilisation is expected to be only 2.7 million hectares (28.42 per cent). Both potential created and likely utilisation during five years are abysmally low. While irrigation potential already created must be fully utilised for obvious reasons, S and MFs access to irrigation has to be improved substantially through their effective participation, capacity building training to efficiently use water saving devices, Participatory Irrigation Management and forming Water Users Associations.
- **Value Chains involving S and MFs:** Linking S and MFs to integrated market systems can improve economic viability of small holdings. Participation of S and MFs makesvalue chains more

sustainable and more conducive to enhance their income. Innovative business models viz. Amul, Nestlé, Safal, Namdhari, among others, have successfully demonstrated that S and MFs who account for 85 per cent of agricultural households along with other resource-poor households pursuing allied activities (dairy, poultry, sheep, goat, fish farming) and non-farm activities, can be brought together to participate in an established value chain. The promotion of farmer producers' organisations (FPO), particularly by organising smallholder producers, has the potential to reduce the costs of marketing of inputs and outputs, and provide a forum for members to share information, coordinate activities and make collective decisions. The Small Farmers' Agribusiness Consortium has already mobilised 6.79 lakh farmers and promoted about 700 FPOs, of which 243 have already been registered and the rest are under process of registration. NABARD is also supporting producer organisations out of its Producers Organisations Development Fund, adopting a flexible approach to meet the needs of producers.

- **Public Investment:** Compared to the overall capital formation in the country's economy (38.9 per cent in 2011-12 and 32.5 per cent in 2013-14 of GDP) capital formation in agriculture and allied activities is very low. Public investment in irrigation, rural roads, power, telecommunication, market information, research and extension services reassures high growth of agricultural sector and reduction in poverty. Large investment in supply chain, R&D, logistic processing and organised retailing is required. A comprehensive value chain model covering innovations in farming, storage, processing, transport, value addition and marketing can help S&MFs earn profit in a sustainable manner.
- **Access to finance:** A road map needs to be drawn to open S&MFs bank accounts in villages by 2016-17 under the Pradhan Mantri Jan Dhan Yojana which can facilitate S&MFs to avail overdraft facility, life and accident insurance cover and to receive money directly credited to their bank accounts under all government schemes. Besides, other enabling measures, *inter alia,* include (i) to complete long pending Cooperative Credit Reforms in next two years. Primary Agricultural Co-operative Societies having the widest geographical coverage must be made more member-driven and less dependent on higher tiers. The recent development of financing PACS through commercial banks needs to be reviewed, strengthened, widened and deepened especially in all villages where

higher tiers of the Short-Term Credit Structure are weak and not in a position to fund them. (ii) scope of Joint Liability Groups can be expanded to cover S&MFs and livestock owners who have productive assets but cannot access credit because they have no land records and are located too far from banks. (iii) Self-Help-Group-Bank Linkage programme can be the appropriate financial mechanism to extend credit to marginal and dry land farmers as this allows better income smoothing since SHGs provide space for diversity in loan purposes and sizes, enabling financing of a variety of activities that such families select as part of livelihood strategies when income from agriculture is low. (iv) there is need for more objective assessment of credit requirements for direct and indirect financing of agriculture by commercial banks specifically in relation to S&MFs (v) exploring further scope to make Kisan Credit Cards small farmer-friendly and make intensive use of ICT applications to track the flow of credit and coverage of S&MFs (vi) government can put in place effective Management Information System to ensure that financing banks strictly comply with mandated RBI's policy interventions, viz. (a) increase in the limit of collateral- free farm loan from Rs 50,000 to Rs 1,00,000 (b) benefit of interest subvention scheme extended to S&MFs having KCC for a further period up to six months after harvest, against negotiable warehouse receipt for keeping their produce in warehouses to avoid any distress sale (c) promoting systematically farm-debt-swapping scheme and capacity building through financial literacy and debt counseling.

- **Insurance products:** S&MFs must be appropriately guided/counseled and assisted to buy recently launched Pradhan Mantri Fasal Bima Yojana policy and help settlement of claims when warranted.
- **Extension:** Agriculture Technology Management Agencies numbering 604 already established across the country in each State at strategic district and block levels to improve extension services accompanied by Krishi Vigyan Kendra should encourage/motivate S&MFs to commercialise their farms by adopting agricultural technologies which have been developed, demonstrated and proven ones in last five years.
- **Others:** While subsidies often benefit the better-off and politically well-connected farmers more than S&MFs, past experience shows

that well targeted subsidies to small farmers play motivating role to help them adopt new technologies and make them viable. S&MFs can benefit considerably by forming multi-purpose service co-operatives and acting collectively when accessing institutional credit and input and output markets. S&MFs have the potentials to enhance income/profit through contract farming and value chain system with agribusiness enterprises. This necessitates a structured legal framework. Political economy can facilitate S&MFs to form Small Farmers Associations to voice their concern. This is essential to remove the widespread political bias against agriculture in country's overall economic development policy and to make small farms engine of agricultural growth, rural prosperity and poverty alleviation.

During 2016-17, the government, academics and media can create awareness among S&MFs about their potentials and their rights to demand implementation of policy and programmes incorporated in the Twelfth FYP document. Success of making S&MFs food secure lies in the demonstration of political will of elected legislators, administrative skill, commitment and accountability of implementing agencies and timely delivery of services by the institutions viz. suppliers of production inputs, technology, credit, insurance and marketing. A road map indicating the timely completion of all activities by 2018-19 should be prepared accompanied by effective Monitoring and Management Information System and quarterly progress displayed on the website of the Union Ministry of Agriculture.

References

1. Government of India (2014). Annual Report. Department of Agriculture and Cooperation, New Delhi.
2. Joshi, P.K.(2015)Has Indian Agriculture Become Crowded and Risky? Status, implications and the way forward. Joshi, *Indian Journal of Agricultural Economics*, 70(1) 1-41.
3. National Bank for Agriculture and Rural Development (2014). *Annual Report*. Mumbai.
4. Reserve Bank of India (2014). *Annual Report*. Mumbai.

23

Food Security in India: Challenges and New Initiatives Ahead

P. Srivatsa

Achieving Food Security is a significant and growing challenge in developing countries like India. Global food security will remain a worldwide concern for the next 50 years and beyond. Food security, in general, is increasingly affected by global economic and environmental phenomena. India's initiatives to ensure food security for its citizens ranges from concerted efforts of government and public to boost agricultural production to far-ranging market interventions aimed at price stabilisation. Many challenges pose en route achieving full-fledged food security in India and we need to propose many initiatives to encounter such challenges and relieve them of problems. The challenges may range from agriculture slow performance to climate change to globalisation and urbanisation. It is, by now, well known that the question of food security has a number of dimensions that extend beyond the production, availability, and demand for food.There has been a paradigmatic shift in the concept of food security, from food availability and stability to household food insecurity, and from assessment of input measures like energy intake to output indicators such as anthropometric measures and clinical signs of malnutrition to eventual political interventions in policy-making and enforcing. This paper tries to throw light on some challenges of achieving food security and ponder on new initiatives to be taken to march forward.

Introduction

Food security exists when all people, at all times, have physical and economic access to sufficient, safe, and nutritious food to meet their dietary needs and food preferences for an active and healthy life (Food and Agriculture Organisation, FAO, 1996). Food security is defined as access to nutritionally adequate, safe, and personally acceptable foods and the ability to acquire them in a socially acceptable way at all states of lifespan (Parnell and Smith, 2008: Cook and Frank, 2008). Ensuring food security ought to be an issue of great importance for a country like India where more than one-third of the population is estimated to be absolutely poor and one-half of all children malnourished in one way or another. Food security has three important components, viz., availability, access, and absorption (nutrition). The three are interconnected.Food security is closely related to limited household resources, low disposable income and poor socioeconomic status (Cook and Frank, 2008; Press, 2004; Rush and Rusk, 2009). Many studies have shown that improvement in nutrition is important, even for increase in productivity of workers. Thus, food security has intrinsic (for its own sake) as well as instrumental (for increasing productivity) value. Food security implies nutritional security and further acknowledges that in its attainment, it supports the actualisation of individual capabilities. This talks of food security in health perspective. But before that there are many other national and global issues that pose challenge to food security. Ways to enhance the availability and access to food will definitely play a major role in achieving and sustaining food security for all. It has become interestingly clear that food security is strongly interlinked with other issues, such as food prices, global environment change, water, energy and agriculture growth (Gustafson, 2013; Hanumankar, 2014; Henningsson *et al*, 2004). Access to food can be increased through employment due to growth in labour intensive sectors and/or through social protection programmes. Added to these are the impacts of global population growth and climate change. Food availability is a necessary condition for food security. India is more or less self-sufficient in cereals but deficit in pulses and oilseeds. Due to changes in consumption patterns, demand for fruits, vegetables, dairy, meat, poultry, and fisheries has been increasing. There is need to increase crop diversification and improve allied activities. It may be noted that the slowdown in agriculture growth could be attributed to structural factors on the supply side, such as public investment, credit, technology, land and water management, etc., rather than globalisation and trade reforms *per se*.

The problem of malnutrition in India is alarming and it needs a multi-disciplinary approach covering diet diversification including micronutrients, women's empowerment, education, health, safe drinking water, sanitation, and hygiene. Some programmes were introduced by Government of India such as TPDS including AAY, nutrition programmes like mid-day meals, and ICDS to improve food and nutrition security. NREGS and self-employment programmes can also increase access to food and nutrition. Social protection programmes in India helped in improving incomes and providing protection from shocks for the population, particularly the poor. Now the NDA Government in its third budget (2016-17), focussed more on farmers welfare and emphasised more on development and sustainability of agriculture and allied sectors effectively ever since independence. The concept of the food, water, and energy nexus is extremely relevant to Asia as the region has to feed two-thirds of the world's population (4.14 billion people) and accounts for 59 per cent of the planet's water consumption. Ensuring food security and providing access to safe drinking water and modern energy for all remains a key challenge for Asia's sustainable development (Rasul, 2015).

Food Security- Definitions, concepts and issues

At various national and international forums many definitions have arrived at about food security, in which one can study transition of the word food security as real as that of the concept itself

At the World Food Summit 1974 food security is defined as, "*Availability at all times of adequate world food supplies of basic foodstuffs to sustain a steady expansion of food consumption and to offset fluctuations in production and prices*".

In 1983, FAO - "*Ensuring that all people at all times have both physical and economic access to the basic food that they need.*" World Bank in 1986 – "*The access by all people at all times to enough food for an active and healthy life.*"

In 1996, World Food Summit redefined the definition of food security as, "*food security exists when all people, at all times, have physical and economic access to sufficient, safe and nutritious food to meet their dietary needs and food preferences for an active and healthy lifestyle*".

In 2002 again, FAO Expert Consultation on Food Security gave a working definition of food security as, "*Food security exists when all people, at all times, have physical, social and economic access to sufficient, safe and nutritious food which meets their dietary needs and food preferences for an active and healthy life.*"

Since then, several definitions have been provided by different organisations such as the World Bank, Food and Agriculture Organisation (FAO) and UNDP's Human Development Report. In general, food security is defined as, *"economic access to food along with food production and food availability."* Food availability alone, therefore, does not ensure food security; access to food is equally important.

An FAO report, August 2008, defines food security in terms of the following four key aspects:

- **Food Availability –** Sufficient availability of food with the nation through domestic production, net imports (commercial or food aid) and carry-over of stocks.
- **Food Access –** Individual's capability to purchase food and to be able to procure food through safety nets or availability.
- **Food Utilisation -** Consumption of food by the household in a proper form. It also takes into account food preparation, storage and utilisation, food safety, nutritional safety and dietary balance.
- **Food Vulnerability-** Vulnerability of the population to food insecurity due to physiological, economic, social or political reasons.

Taking this into consideration we are now in a position to understand the concern of food security with its historical perspective and the realities associated with it. The case of food security is as important to India as it is for the rest of the world.

Programmes and Policies on Food Security in India:

India's basic initiatives to ensure food security ranges from concerted efforts to boost agricultural production to far-ranging market interventions aimed at both income and price stabilisation. One of the first interventions by the Indian government was the passing of the Essential Commodities Act in 1955 to protect the poor from the vagaries of the market. The Act conferred on the government the power to control production, supply and distribution of essential commodities to ensure equitable distribution of food grains at fair prices.With this there are measures introduced to improve the access to food of the poor through public distribution (PD) and income generating schemes with the objective of making basic food grains available to all at affordable prices. The government has set up the Food Corporation of India (FCI). The basic task of the FCI was a twofold activity. The *first* fold was to procure food grains at Minimum

Support Prices (MSP) and the *second* fold was to regulate supply so that prices can be kept constant over a period by building a buffer stock.

Table 23.1: Glimpse on Government's Schemes/ Policies/ Programmes/ Acts designed to ensure Food Security in India

Government's Scheme/ Policy/ Programme/ Act	*Beneficiary Targeted and Policy approach*	*Year of Launching and Prospects*
Essential Commodities Act,1955	General public and the same is Extended to the Whole of India	1955, Availability
Integrated Child Development Scheme	Children and Pregnant Women from 33 Community Development Blocks out of 6118 blocks in the country; including 4790 in rural areas, 805 in tribal areas as well 523 in urban slums.	1975, Utilisation
Scheme for Supply of Food grains for SC/ST/OBC Hostels	Providing 15 kg per month per resident of Hostel.	1994, Vulnerability
Mid-day Meal Scheme	Students in Govt. Primary schools and run by local bodies, covers the students of Class I-VIII of Government and Government Aided schools.	1995, Utilisation
Targeted Public Distribution System (TPDS)	Intended to benefit about 6 Cr. Poor families in the country for whom 35 kg of food grains per family per month is provided with Central Issue price (CIP) for BPL families is Rs 4.15 per kg for wheat and Rs 5.65 per kg for rice	1997, Accessibility and Utilisation
National Food for Work Programme (NFFWP)	Rural poor in need of employment and desire to do manual and unskilled work from the most backward districts (150).	2000, Accessibility
Antyodaya Anna Yojana	5 per cent of the population [@ 1 Cr. of families covered under TPDS-providing them Rs 2 per kg for wheat and Rs 3 per kg for rice] in the country who sleep without two square meals a day.	2000, Accessibility and Vulnerability
Annapurna Scheme	Indigent senior citizens of 65 years of age or above are provided with 10 kg of food grains per person per month free of cost.	2000-01, Utilization
Sampoorna Grameen Rozgar Yojana (SGRY)	Women, Scheduled Castes, Scheduled Tribes and Parents of Children withdrawn from hazardous occupations of all the States and Union Territories.	2001, Accessibility

contd...

Government's Scheme/ Policy/ Programme/ Act	*Beneficiary Targeted and Policy approach*	*Year of Launching and Prospects*
Mahatma Gandhi National Rural Employment Guarantee Act (MNREGA)	Rural Households primarily semi-skilled or unskilled workers living below the poverty line in rural India.	2005, Accessibility and Vulnerability
SABLA Scheme	Implementing in 200 selected districts of the country aiming at empowering adolescent girls of 11-18 years by improving their nutritional and health status.	2010, Utilisation
National Food Security Act	The Act provides for food and nutritional security in human life cycle approach, by ensuring access to adequate quantity of quality food at affordable prices to people to live a life with dignity.	2013, Accessibility and Utilisation

Key Challenges to Food Security

There are some key issues and challenges which come *en route* while achieving food security. Some challenges creates good possibilities to ensure food security while some try to pose hindrance in the way. Thus, caution is alerted while dealing with the challenges and make sure to reap the fruitful results. Some key challenges to food security include Performance of agriculture sector and climate change, Food Inflation, Food Management and Nutrition, Globalisation, Rapid Urbanisation, Massive Out-Migration from rural areas to Urban cities, lack of technical knowledge in mechanising agriculture, fertiliser and seed problems etc.

Performance of Agriculture Sector

Indian agriculture has come a long way since independence, with chronic food scarcity giving way to grain self-sufficiency despite a two-and-a-half fold increase in population. In 1966-67, just before India's Green and White Revolutions, Indian wheat and milk production were just about one-third of US output.The performance of the overall agriculture sector and the factors responsible for the slowdown provide an explanation for the decline in the growth of food production. It may be noted that food grains, pulses, oilseeds, sugar, fruits and vegetables, poultry, dairy, meat, fish, etc. constitute the bulk of the output in the agriculture sector. The performance of agriculture is important for availability and access to food as more than 65 per cent people in the country are dependent on this sector. India achieved near self-sufficiency in the availability of food grains by the mid-seventies. Agricultural growth in India was high from the Fifth Plan period to the Ninth Plan period –

highest being in the Sixth Plan period, at around 5.7 per cent. If we consider longer periods, growth of agriculture decelerated from 3.5 per cent between 1981-82 and 1996-97 to around two per cent between 1997-98 and 2004-05, although there have been signs of improvement in recent years. By 2013-14, Indian wheat output was 60 per cent higher than America's, while Indian milk output was 50 per cent higher. These tremendous increases in aggregate output do, however, mask some disquieting trends.There are both short run and long run problems in Agriculture. Farmers' suicides continue unabated, even increasing in some states, as growth rate in yield is on the decline.

Farming is fast becoming a non-viable activity. Further scope for increase in net sown area is limited. Land degradation in the form of depletion of soil fertility, erosion, and water logging has increased. There has been decline in the surface irrigation expansion rate and a fall in the level of the ground water table. Exposure of domestic agriculture to international competition has resulted in a high order of volatility in prices. Disparities in productivity across regions and crops, and between rain fed and irrigated areas has increased. Long-term factors like steeper decline in per capita land availability and shrinking of farm size are also responsible for the agrarian crisis. Land issues such as SEZs, land going to non-agriculture, alienation of tribal land etc. are becoming important key challenges to agrarian sector in turn affecting food security.

The central challenge of Indian agriculture is low productivity, evident in modest average yields, especially in pulses. First, consider the main food grains – wheat and rice. These two cereals are grown on the most fertile and irrigated areas in the country. Andthey use a large part of the resources that the government channels to agriculture, whether water, fertiliser, power, credit or procurement under the MSP program. Even then, average yields of wheat and rice in India are much below that of China's – 46 per cent below in the case of rice and 39 per cent in the case of wheat. India happens to be the major producer and consumer of pulses, which is one of the major sources of protein for the population. India has low yields comparable to most countries. On an average, countries like Brazil, Nigeria, and Myanmar have higher yields. Given that India is the major producer and consumer of pulses, imports cannot be the main source for meeting domestic demand. Therefore, policy must incentivise movement of resources towards production of pulses. Revolutionary reforms have to be taken up by the government to channelise and streamline the agriculture sector and ensure food safety and security to the bottommost citizen of the nation and relieve them from hunger and food insecurity.

Climate Change

Food security is severely influenced by climate change. The changing climate will influence the food grain production in different ways. For example, the temporal and spatial variations in precipitation including rainfall may result in deficit moisture stress, i.e. drought or excess moisture stress condition, i.e. flooding. Similarly, extreme high or low temperatures result in variations in the length of crop growing season. These factors would also affect the crop productivity and farm net income and hence climate resilient agricultural practices have to be promoted. This is applicable to all the nations, including India. Understanding the impact of climate change on Indian agriculture is quite complex as several factors are involved in this phenomenon. For example, the negative effect of global warming on crop productivity in India may be compensated by carbon fertilisation to some extent. Several researchers conducted studies on the interrelationship between climate change and food security in relation to impacts of climate change on crop productivity, food production and socio-economic aspects. Gregory *et al.,* based on their experiments conducted on wheat and rice reported that global warming would result in decreased crop duration. It is already established that some factors of climate such as increased carbon dioxide level would play a positive role in enhancing crop productivity. However, the crop productivity would be negatively influenced by changes caused by extreme variation in temperature and nutrient interactions and higher rate of natural disasters such as floods and drought.There is an urgent need to address the food security concerns that are central to economic and sustainable development issues in both India and the other nations which is possible by integrating bio-physical and socio-economic aspects of food systems. However, in the present scenario the picture is changing in favour of India in this regard.

According to the World Meteorological Organisation, 2015 was the warmest year, with temperature 1°C above the preindustrial era. This was owing to El Nino and warming caused by greenhouse gases (GHG). Anthropogenic emissions have been increasing at an unprecedented rate since the industrial revolution. According to an International Energy Agency (IEA) report (2015), concentration of CO_2 in 2014 was 40 per cent higher than in the mid-1800s. The energy sector is the largest contributor to GHG emissions and, within this, CO_2 emissions from combustion of fuels have the largest share. The global emissions profile shows that emissions have been distributed very unequally among different countries. If historical CO_2 emissions from 1970 to 2014 are considered, India with 39.0 Gt is way behind the top three emitters – the USA, the EU and China. The USA's emissions, for example, were around six times India's. Even if historical levels are discounted and only present levels considered, both in terms of absolute and per capita emissions, India is way behind the three major CO_2 emitters. Although India seems to be a better performer as far as climate change is concerned, but global climate variations show some significant impact on Indian climate, hence at times resulting in either drought or massive floods causing losses to agricultural harvest at the time of reaping the crop. This shows some countable effect on food safety and security and measures have to be taken in this regard. As a great relieving measure India was a party to The Paris Agreement in 2015 and presented its views and commitments to the conference. The adoption of a new climate change agreement at the 21st Conference of Parties (COP 21) by 195 nations in Paris in December 2015 represents another milestone in the climate change front. India continued to take ambitious targets in its actions against climate change. As a part of its contributions to the global climate change mitigation efforts, India announced its intended nationally determined contribution (INDC) which set ambitious targets for domestic efforts against climate change. India houses 30 per cent of the global poor, 24 per cent of global population without access to electricity, and 92 million people without access to safe drinking water (Economic Survey 2015-16) Coupled with its vulnerability in terms of the impact of climate change, this entails that India faces formidable and complex challenges in terms of balancing the sustainable development agenda. Given the challenges it faces, it has prepared an ambitious plan in terms of clean energy, energy efficiency and lower emission intensity while addressing the critical issue of poverty and food security.

Food Management and Nutrition

The main aim of food management policy is to provide food security to the population. Providing food security entails making food available at affordable prices at all times, without interruptions. In order to provide food security, in the current agriculture scenario, India has to focus on supplies which are timely and uninterrupted and affordable for the poor. Though India's GDP growth has been impressive and the agricultural production has also increased over the past few decades, hunger and starvation still persist among the poorer sections of the population.Nutritionists argue that the energy intake is a poor measure of nutritional status, which depends not only on the nutrient intake but also on non-nutrient food attributes, privately and publicly provided inputs and health status (Martorell and Ho, 1984). There is a strong correlation between stability in agricultural production and food security. Volatility in agricultural production impacts food supplies and can result in spikes in food prices, which adversely affect the lowest income groups of the population. Level of malnutrition and hunger in India seriously raise debates about the fact that for a country like India market system cannot reduce level of hunger and malnourishment. However, data also shows that there is huge gap between demand for food and supply of food through PDS. It means markets still plays a major role in food distribution in India. Success of Food Security Bill significantly depends on present PDS network that is a major critique of this Bill. And this cannot be possible without improving storage capacity in different states and removing the bottleneck in PDS and identifying the role of market in food distribution in India. According to the data of the 66th round of the National Sample Survey (2009-10), the average dietary energy intake per person per day was 2147 Kcal for rural India and 2123 Kcal for urban India. As per the Report of Nutritional Intake in India, 2011-12 (NSSO, 68th round), among the bottom five per cent of rural population ranked by Monthly Per Capita Expenditure (MPCE), 57 per cent of households had calorie intake below 2160 Kcal/consumer unit/day. The average protein intake per capita per day rises steadily with MPCE level in rural India from 43 gm for the bottom five per cent of population ranked by MPCE to 91gm for the top five per cent, and in urban India from 44 gm for the bottom five per cent to about 87gm for the top five per cent. India has the second highest number of undernourished people at 194.6 million persons (FAO, State of Food Insecurity in the World, 2015), which warrants immediate attention. Moreover, with 27 per cent of the population below the poverty line, the rise in prices of food impacts the poor adversely, with a greater proportion of their household incomes being spent on food. Therefore, along with provision of food subsidy, stability in agricultural commodity prices is essential for making the poorer sections food secure.

Table 23.2: Levels of Undernourishment in India

Year	*Number of persons undernourished (in millions)*	*Proportion of undernourished in total population (in per cent)*
1990-92	210.1	23.7
2000-02	185.5	17.5
2005-07	233.8	20.5
2010-12	189.9	15.6
2014-16*	194.6	15.2

Source: FAO, 2015. *Note:* *Provisional Estimates.

With a large number of people who remain undernourished and the issues of volatility in agricultural prices, India has one of the largest number of food schemes in the World to ensure food security. There is entitlement feeding programmes like the Integrated Child Development Scheme (ICDS) (All Children under six, pregnant and lactating mothers) and MDMS (Mid-Day Meal Schemes), food subsidy programmes like the Targeted Public Distribution System, Annapurna (10 kg of free food grain for destitute poor) and the Employment Programmes like Mahatma Gandhi National Rural Employment Guarantee Scheme (100 days of employment at minimum wages) to ensure food security.

Public Distribution System and Food Subsidy

Keeping in view that poverty percentage is very high and benefits of growth cannot reach quickly in the hands of poor, the role of PDS in India cannot be ignored. "A large public distribution system, supplemented by arrangements for moderating prices in the open market and concerted efforts for achieving self-sufficiency in food grains, coupled with measures for maximising procurement from surplus areas, have been the twin objectives of food policy in modern India, ever since the Bengal famine of 1943. These objectives have held sway over the last 55 years, though with changes in emphasis and varying degrees of rigidity, from total control to total decontrol, depending upon the prevailing situation and assessment at each point of time" (GoI, 2000). Currently, the food security system and price policy, basically consist of three instruments: procurement prices/minimum support prices, buffer stocks, and the public distribution system (PDS). Adequate purchasing power for the poor to buy food can be ensured in two ways. One is to have an employment intensive pattern of growth which can provide remunerative work to the poor and enhance their power to purchase the food. Another way is to increase incomes and subsidise food through social protection programmes like PDS and employment programmes.The Public Distribution System (PDS) is one of the instruments for improving food security at the household level in India. The PDS ensures availability of essential commodities like rice, wheat, edible oils, and kerosene to the consumers through a network of outlets or fair price shops. These commodities are supplied at below market prices to consumers. With a network of more than 462,000 fair price shops (FPS) distributing commodities worth more than Rs 300 billion annually to about 160 million families, the PDS in India is perhaps the largest distribution network of its kind in the world. The PDS evolved as an important instrument of government policy for management of scarcity and for distribution of food grains at affordable prices. Supplemental in nature, the scheme is not intended to make available the entire requirements of food grains of the households. This involves procurement of food grain at Minimum Support Price (MSP) by the government, building up and maintenance of food stocks, their storage, and timely distribution, making food grains accessible at reasonable prices to the vulnerable sections of the population. However, the system of PDS has many weaknesses leading to leakages and targeted beneficiaries being left out of the system. The PDS incurs high costs for procurement, storage and distribution of food grains. There is scope to increase efficiency of the PDS operations and reduce costs. Only a small proportion of the public expenditure/subsidy on PDS reaches the beneficiary. There is a case for introducing DBT for consumers of food and kerosene as is under way in Andhra Pradesh.There is a case for replacing the present system of MSP/procurement based PDS with DBT and freeing the market of all controls on domestic movement and import. The entire activity of changes in the policy parameters vitiates the concept of a market and needs to be discontinued to enhance productivity in agriculture.

Initiatives towards enhanced food security:

There is need to increase agricultural output through productivity increases by investing in water-efficient irrigation to achieve more crop yield, along with effective use of other inputs like fertilisers, quality seeds and pesticides. Mechanisation of agriculture by using sprinkler systems, drip irrigation, water guns and farm ponds prove fruitful in making agriculture profitable with low investment and high productivity. There is tremendous potential to increase availability of agricultural produce by reducing wastages. Increasing the share of processing can be done by increasing reliance on markets, rationalising and targeting subsidy, as well as disbursing it through DBT. There is a need to rationalize fertiliser subsidy in an input, crop and region neutral format and to minimize diversions. The disbursal of subsidy on fertilisers should shift to DBT (direct benefit transfer), benefits of which (DBT) will be maximised, if all controls (including on imports) on the fertiliser industry/outputs are lifted simultaneously. There is a case for replacing the present system of MSP/procurement based PDS with DBT and freeing the market of all controls on domestic movement and import. The entire activity of changes in the policy parameters vitiates the concept of a market and needs to be discontinued to enhance productivity in agriculture. Science and technology innovations have been key factors in achieving advances in agriculture. Plant breeding efforts, combined with improvements in agronomic practices have allowed us to keep pace with population growth in terms of providing an adequate level of food supply. Still, agriculture has to face tremendous challenges on many fronts and will have to play a critical role in the improvement process with Bio-technology for sustainable agricultural progress. Technology is going to play a major role to take the grain production from about 210 million tonnes today to 300 million tonnes by 2020 (i.e. 6 per cent increase per year). This much food supply is needed to feed the population which by then will be around 1.4 billion mark. Hence technology has to become essential part to deliver higher food grain supply needs.Local knowledge and local seeds can be used for biodiversity. Organic farming can also be encouraged to protect the environment and generate higher incomes for small farmers. Urban agriculture can improve food security in urban areas. Home-grown food can also be encouraged as it would contribute to food security and nutrition as well as freeing incomes for non-food expenses such as health and education. Various other areas related to allied sectors of agriculture has to be improved alongside farm produces to enhance and sustain food safety and security.

Conclusion

The concept of food security has undergone considerable changes in recent years. Food availability and stability were considered good measures of food security till recent years and the achievement of self-sufficiency was accorded high priority in the food policies of developing countries particularly of India. This necessitated a change in approach and as a result, food energy intake at household level is now given prominence in assessing food security. Though India was successful in achieving self-sufficiency by increasing its food production and also improved its capacity to cope with year-to-year fluctuations in food production, it also need to focus on above discussed challenges. Overall, it may be concluded that food security in India can be achieved by paying higher attention to issues such as climate change, integrated water management, agricultural pricing, crop insurance, performance of agriculture and allied sectors, food management and nutrition, food inflation, procurement and distribution of food grains and effective implementation of PDS and if possible revolutionary changes are needed to enhance food security even to the bottommost citizen of our nation.

References

Bhalla, G.S. and Gurmail Singh (2001), *Indian Agriculture: Four Decades of Development,* Sage Publications, N. Delhi.

Bhalla, G.S.(1994), *"Policies for Food Security in India"*, in Bhalla, G.S. (ed.) *Economic Liberalisation and Indian Agriculture,* Institute for Studies in Industrial Development, New Delhi.

Cook, JT, Frank, DA (2008). *Food security, Poverty and Human Development in the United States*. Annals of the New York Academy of Sciences. 1136, 193- 209.

Economic Survey. (2015-16).

Food and Agriculture Organisation. (2015) Report.

Food First. (2008) July, Yojana.

Global Food Security Index Report. (2015).

Gustafson, DJ (2013). *Rising Food Costs and Global Food Security: Key Issues and Relevance for India*. Indian J Med. 138(3):398–410.

International Energy Agency IEA (2015) Report.

Mortorell, R. and T.J. Ho (1984), *"Malnutrition, Morbidity and Mortality",* Population and Development Review, A Supplement to Vol. 10, pp. 49-68.

National Sample Survey Organisation 68th Round (2011-12) Report.

Parnell, WR, Smith, C (2008). *Food Security: Current Research Initiatives, Globally and in New Zealand.* Nutrition Society of New Zealand Conference. Christchurch.

Press, V (2004). *Nutrition and Food Poverty: A Toolkit for Those Involved in Developing a Local Nutrition and Food Poverty Strategy*. London:

Right to Food. (2013) December, Yojana.

Rush, E, Rusk, I (2009). *Food security for Pacific Peoples in New Zealand: A Report for the Obesity Action.*

24

From Food Crisis to Food Security: A Critical Perspective

Subhash Sharma

Introduction

In different parts of the world there has been and also remains today some sort of food crisis in different ways. For instance, India's National Commission on Farmers, in its first report (2004), pointed out five basic factors of the agrarian crisis: unfinished agenda in land reforms, lack of quantity and quality of water, technology fatigue, lack of access, adequacy and timeliness of institutional credit, and lack of opportunities for assured and remunerative marketing. The worst affected in the agrarian crisis are small and marginal farmers, landless labourers and women. That is why, long back in 1946 at Noakhali, Mahatma Gandhi had remarked perceptively: 'To the hungry, God is bread'. After the World War II, US President F. Roosevelt talked of four types of freedom: freedom of expression, freedom of worship, freedom from fear, and *freedom from hunger*. Even Jawaharlal Nehru had announced in 1947: 'Everything else can wait, but not the agriculture'. However, India did not accord the top priority to agriculture (especially in terms of investment) which it deserved. Needless to say that hunger and starvation are violations of fundamental human rights enshrined in the Universal Declaration of Human Rights (UDHR) (1948). Right to food is a birthright of every individual, group, family or community. Article 25 of UDHR clearly says, 'everyone has the right to a standard of living adequate for the health and well-being of himself and his family, including food'. Further Article 11 of UN's International Covenant on Economic, Social and Cultural Rights (1966) emphasises not only the right to adequate food but also 'the fundamental right of everyone to be *free from hunger*'. Thus, the latter is more radical and fundamental as it is directly linked to right to life, hence it is mandatory for the State to ensure its fulfilment. The Supreme Court of India has deliberated in several judicial decisions that right to food is an integral part of right to life enshrined in Article 21 of the Indian Constitution. Further Article 47 of Indian Constitution states 'the State shall regard the raising of the level of nutrition and the standard of living of its people and the improvement of public health as among its primary duties'. Article 38 of Indian Constitution also states that State shall strive to minimise inequalities in income, status facilities and opportunities amongst individuals and groups. Further, its Article 39 mentions that State shall direct its policy towards security that the citizens (men and women) equally have the right to an adequate means of livelihood.

In fact, massive food production at the macro level (national) is a necessary but not a sufficient condition for ensuring actual food security at micro level. Food security connotes adequate nutritious food entitlement of every person at any given time and place, from local to global levels, not only for his or her mere physical survival but also the complete well-being, just distribution of food (intra-household) with minimum nutrition, and absorption by the body for a health life. United Nations' Food and Agriculture Organisation (FAO) defines food security as 'all people at all times have access to safe and nutritious food to maintain a healthy and active life'. The World Bank has defined food security as 'access by all people at all times to sufficient food for active and healthy life' (Guha – Khasnobis *et al.,* 2008) but we require a 'sustainable food security'. According to M.S. Swaminathan (2008), 'Sustainable food security involves physical, economic and social access to a balanced diet and clean drinking water to every child, woman and man in the country. For achieving physical access, production and productivity of major crops should go up, so that there is a proper match between demand and supply. For economic access, there is a need for ensuring adequate purchasing power, which, in turn, can be achieved through work and income security. Social access involves attention to the gender, class and caste dimensions of food security'. Sociologically speaking, a critical holistic conception of food security comprises of the following aspects:

(a) Physical access to food (food grains, pulses, edible oils, milk etc.)

(b) Economic capability to have (buy) food.

(c) Social inclusivity of entitlement to food.

(d) Cultural acceptability of food.

(e) Environmental sustainability of food.

However, the experience of the Green Revolution in agriculture shows that India's focus only on major crops like wheat and paddy led to the neglect of common people's food crops (considered minor crops) like jowar, bajra, ragi (mandua), sawan, kodo, maize and barley that require less irrigation but mature faster than wheat and paddy. Further these food grains are more nutritious. Needless to emphasise that the food security paradigm has changed on four scores since the first World Food Conference (in 1974) in Rome: first, from the availability of food at the global level to the national, sub-national, household and finally to the individual level;

Second, a change from 'food first' perspective to 'livelihood' perspective;

Third, a change from physical access to economic and social access as well;

Fourth, a change from objective indicators (rising income leading to increase in purchasing power, lower prices of food grains leading to better consumption of food grains) to subjective perceptions (changing attitudes, food habits, gender and age equity in the household), etc.

It declared that every man, woman and child has the inalienable right to be free from hunger and malnutrition. Further the eradication of hunger is a common objective of all countries and all governments' responsibility is to work together to higher food production and a more equitable and efficient distribution of food between and within countries. In 1996, at Rome, World Food Summit made Rome declaration on World Food Security calling international community to reduce the number of hungry people to 400 million (half) by 2015. Among 182 nations US alone opposed the right to food as a human right. World Food Summit 2012 (Rome) was also opposed by the US that supported the cause of bio-technology (in seeds and crops). In fact, the question of food security, in totality, involves various aspects at various levels of a human society with corresponding necessary conditions at a given time: viz., individual, intra-household, household, sub-national and national levels. It is vividly shown in the Table 24.1 below :

Table 24.1: Aspects, Levels of Availability and Necessary Conditions of Food Security

Aspects	*Levels of Availability*	*Necessary Conditions*
1. Food production and productivity (general physical access)	National, State and Sub-national Levels	Right to agri-inputs-Inputs' availability like seeds, fertilisers, pesticides, electricity for irrigation, institutional credit, minimum support price, delivery and storage agencies, pucca rural roads and adequate transport, and market linkage.
2. Food availability (specific physical access)	Gram Sabha/ Panchayat level	Availability of food grains in local market or public distribution system shops or cooperatives or panchayat stores (grain bank).
3. Cultural acceptability of Food	Local Community level	Taking local community into confidence and people's participation in adaptation of new technology and change in eating habits (from rice to wheat in North Bihar, use of mushroom in North India).
4. Food accessibility (economic access – purchasing power)	Household level	Right to work and income – Minimum wages for increasing purchasing power of the labourers, better remunerative prices for agricultural produce to farmers, food grains at cheaper rates
5. Food consumption for well-being (social access)	Intra-household (age, gender, sickness, disability) level	Right to food to all – gender consciousness, sound healthcare for growing children, working adults, lactating/ pregnant women, aged, infirm and ill persons – just distribution of food.
6. Food absorption (healthy life/well-being)	Individual level (Physiological)	Safe drinking water, hygiene, clean environment, primary healthcare.
7. Environmental Sustainability of food	Local, sub-national, national	Protecting the interests of future generations and environment.

Source : Revised version of S. Sharma (2015) 'Development and Its Discontents; p. 74.

However, in the present globalised or globalising era, the problem of food security crosses the national boundaries. Sometimes domestic compulsions affect the global food situation, and at other times the adverse global food situation affects the domestic food situation.

Global Scenario

If we look at the global scenario of food security, the following facts are notable (Guha-Khasnobis *et al.,* 2008; Streitfeld and Bradsher, 2008; Brown, 2008; Sachs, 2008; Varma, 2008):

(a)`q 1 A large number of people in the world are food – insecure, especially in Sub-Saharan Africa and South Asia – about 840 million people worldwide were malnourished or chronically food-insecure earlier which only marginally declined to 795 million in 2015 as per FAO (2015).

(b) About 2.8 million children and 3 lakh women die annually in developing countries, especially in Sub-Saharan Africa and South Asia.

(c) The World Food Summit and the Millennium Development Goals of halving the number/ share of the undernourished people by 2015 could not be achieved.

(d) Though food production increased to 2.3 billion tonnes in 2007 and world cereal output has tripled since 1961, grain stocks are at the lowest levels in three decades (due to the hoarding of food grains by some governments in countries like the US, the Philippines, India, Japan or more consumption due to population growth and better purchasing power) and price rise has continuously been high, leading to global food crisis.

(e) Climate change is showing negative consequences for food security; e.g. droughts and floods recur in some countries leading to loss of agricultural areas; if the Antarctica ice melts, the sea level will rise by 7 metres and Bangladesh would lose 40 per cent of its rice land; two-thirds of the Chinese glaciers will disappear by 2060; Gangotri glacier in India is also melting; Bangladesh and West Bengal would lose Sunderbans and marine bio-diversity. In the last 2800 years there has been substantial rise in sea level.

(f) Rapid exploitation of natural resources and a six-fold rise in population during 1830-2005 (6.5 billion then and now 7 billion) have also negative consequences for food security – further increase in per capita income from 2,000 dollars in 1950 to 6000 dollars in 2000, in some way or the other, led to more food consumption due to better purchasing power and more demand for food.

(g) Trans-National Companies (TNCs) are doing a highly profitable business. Monsanto (US) and Syngenta (Europe) have pushed in their genetically modified (GM) seeds, which usually have crop failures and pest attacks in developing countries like India. Syngenta earned a net profit of1.1 billion dollars in 2007. Similarly, fertiliser TNCs like Potash Corp (of Canada) and Yara (of Norway) made a huge profit of one billion dollars each in 2007. Other fertiliser TNCs like Mosaic and Agrium (of US) and TCL (of Israel) made a profit of half a billion dollars in 2007.

(h) In 2005, according to the FAO, due to food shortage at domestic level, 207 out of 216 countries in the world had to import wheat and 170 had to import rice from international markets; at the global level, FAO estimates, each year hunger robs 46 million year of productive disability-free life from people valued at over 16 billion dollars.

(i) On 3 June 2008, at FAO Summit in Rome, UN Secretary General Ban Ki-Moon highlighted that the world food production needs to be increased by 50 per cent by 2030 to meet the rising food demand. He called for a support of 1.7 billion dollars to low-income countries with seeds and other agricultural support but also warned against food export restrictions imposed by some countries leading to distortion of market prices.

(j) World's farmers will have to double food production by 2050 to feed about nine billion world population then. Unfortunately most of this population growth will occur in food-insecure developing countries – up to 126 per cent in Sub-Saharan Africa, 56 per cent in North Africa and West Asia, and 34 per cent in South Central Asia.

(k) By 2050, 60 per cent of world population will live in cities – fewer farmers but more demand for food.

(l). 1/3rd of food production is lost between farm and actual use.

(m) High food inflation is caused by diversion of food grains for bio-fuel, adverse weather conditions and climate change, dietary shifts in large developing countries like China and India due to better living standards and income, and lack of public investment in agriculture, especially irrigation.

In fact, the processes of liberalisation, privatisation and globalisation for more than three decades have worked against food security in following ways:

(a) State has, to a large extent, retreated from its responsibility to adequately provide food security to the people by making them dependent on 'free market'-thus globalisation is in essence 'global marketisation'.

(b) Now agriculture is very much capital- intensive, that is, costs of agricultural production (mechanical cultivation, fertilisers, pesticides, irrigation, seeds) has increased manifold and the small farmers are unable to cope up with this situation. Many of such inputs depend on petroleum as source of energy.

(c) Many transnational corporations and agribusiness houses (Monsanto, Kargil, Syngenta, Potash Corp, Yara, Mosaic, Agrium) indulge in monopoly control of chemical fertilisers, seeds, pesticides etc. and earn huge profit, now terminator seeds are costlier and by nature cannot be preserved by local farmers as seeds from the harvested produces- this is restricting the freedom of farmers, on the one hand, and looting their pockets on the other.

(d) Many farmers are shifting from food crops to cash crops for exports, thus resulting into diverting of scarce land and water resources for export crops. It is some sort of colonial syndrome (as the British rule in India compelled the farmers of Champaran (Bihar) for indigo cultivation in one-third of their lands under Tinkathia system). This is the essence of World Banks' export-led strategies. Even today in many developing countries a huge tract of productive lands is devoted to cash crops; e.g. jute in Bangladesh and West Bengal, tea in Assam, cotton in Egypt, peanuts in Senegal, 'qaat' in Yemen, coffee in Angola and tobacco in Zimbabwe (and in some parts of India). Further foreign exchange earned by export of cash crops is not correspondingly spent on purchase of food grains, pulses, edibles, milk, fruits etc.

(e) Many developing countries like US, UK etc. themselves provide huge agricultural subsidy but pressure the developing countries like India to reduce or fully remove subsidy (as it is alleged to distort market prices) due to inegalitarian WTO Agreement on Agriculture.

National Scenario

Though a huge population in India is dependent on agriculture, its contribution to Gross Domestic Product has been declining to 14-15 per cent of GDP over the years because of less public investment and under-employment. As per FAO, the population depending on agriculture in India was around 57.84 crores in 2010 and then started declining slowly to reach 57.47 crores in 2020 from around 55.74 crores in 2000. Further, the employment in agriculture, being 60 per cent of the economically active population in 2000, declined to 55 per cent in 2010 and further will decline to 50 per cent in 2020. Thus, FAO projects India's population to 127.22 crores in 2020 (Chakrabarti and Dutta, 2000). As per Census of 2011, India's population was 121 crores then. Naturally, it will have implications on food security in India though India produced over 290 million MT of cereals in 2014 and it became the third largest cereal producer in the world.

Various studies have pointed out that in India even if the total food production of a small/ marginal farmer is not sufficient for family consumption for a year, he has to sell a part of it in the market due to the distress in a monetised economy in order to meet his various needs like purchase of utensils, clothes, social obligations, health and education – that is, there exists a 'compulsive involvement', to use Krishna Bhardwaj's term (1974), with market. Thus, almost all the landholders, while sowing their crops, take into account this very factor. Second, they also grow cash crops like mustard, rapeseed, sugarcane, spices, peas and potato which are more remunerative than the food grains. Third, while sowing crops they also consider that they have to pay wages to the labourers on time. Earlier, for the purpose of wage payment, coarse grains used to be sown, but nowadays the trend has changed as the labourers are not willing to accept coarse grains; rather cash is paid by selling food grains or cash crops. Further, food habits of the farmers themselves have also changed substantially and, therefore, they do not like to grow coarse grains like barley, maize, sawan, kodo and ragi/madua, (though these are nutritious). Fourth, most of the farmers also take into account expected social obligations like festivals, religious ceremonies, marriage and birth ceremonies and debt repayment schedule while planning their cropping pattern. Due to crop failure because of vagaries of monsoon, many of farmers are compelled to take looms on higher interest rates and the vicious cycle of 'crop failure – loan- crop failure again – suicide' goes on.

The difference in the attitude of the 'net sellers' and that of the petty farmers at the time of sale of food grains is that while the former keep most of their produce in store after the harvest and sell 90 per cent of the marketable surplus later in lean season (Paush – Magh, i.e. December – January) when the prices rise due to more demand and less supply, the latter have to sell most of the surplus or, out of necessity, even the annual stock just after the harvest, in order to meet their non-food requirements like medicine, education, clothing, house repair and social functions at cheaper rates due to more supply of food grains than the demand in Chaitra (April-May). During the lean season, there is no adequate employment opportunity in agriculture and the petty farmers purchase food grains at the higher rate – i.e. they become 'net buyers'. Then even the public distribution system shops do not come up with the demand more because of corruption and malfunctioning than because of non-availability of food grains in the government stock. Govt. of India revised Minimum Buffer Norms with effect from 22nd January, 2015 for stocking of food grains in Central Pool as follows (Table 24.2):

Table 24.2 : Minimum Buffer Norms (2015) (Lakh MT)

Date of Effect	*Wheat*	*Rice*	*Total*
1 April	74.6.	135.8	210.8
1 July	275.8	135.4	411.2
1 October	205.2	102.5	307.7
1 January	138.0	76.1	214.1

Source: Department of Food and Public Distribution, Ministry of Consumer Affairs, Food and Public Distribution, Annual Report 2014-15.
N.B: These norms include strategic reserve of 30 Lakh MT of Wheat and 20 Lakh MT of Rice.

Consequently, either the area under food crops ('acreage response') or the yield of food crops per acre ('yield response') is to be increased to cope up with demand of the high population growth. In order to ensure adequate food production, the necessary condition is ensuring adequate inputs to farmers' in time. It transpires from discussions with many villagers in UP and Bihar that subsidy in seeds, fertilisers, pesticides, irrigation and credit contributes to about 50 per cent of the increase in production (but partly siphoned off) and, on the other hand, better remunerative prices contribute to 30 per cent of the increase, while an increase in the wages of the labour will affect the production about 20 per cent. Most farmers cannot afford costly inputs and high wages; hence agriculture has become a loss-making mode of production. India has been providing subsidies on seeds, fertilisers, irrigation (electricity charges), crop loans, etc. But the government has, under pressure from the World Trade Organisation's Agreement on Agriculture, reduced the subsidy on fertilisers, though in comparison with the developed countries, the subsidy on Indian agriculture is very low. Though the western nations pressure developing countries like India to reduce such subsidy, they provide huge agricultural subsidies to their own farmers. For instance, total subsidy provided to Indian agricultural sector by the government was only Rs 4,500 crores or about one billion dollars while the same in the Organisation of Economic Cooperation and Development (OECD) countries was 362 billion dollars (Sharma, 2002). A comparison of India and some developed countries regarding agricultural subsidy per hectare is shown in Table 24.3

Table 24.3: A Comparison of Agricultural Subsidy in Different Countries

Country	*Amount of Subsidy (per ha) ($)*
European Union	1,016
Japan	6,915
New Zealand	317
US	184
Canada	167
India	17.8

Source: S. Sharma (2002).

In order to encourage farmers to increase production the Government of India fixes minimum support prices (MSP) of various food grains, pulses, oilseeds and cash crops. Minimum support/ procurement price works as a safety valve, or rather 'security mechanism', for the farmers. Punjab and Haryana States buy about 90 per cent of the total wheat to the market and crowd out private traders.

One may adjudge the performance of Indian agriculture in food grains in three ways: (a) comparing India's average yield per hectare with the world's average yield per hectare, (b) India's percentage share in world food production, and (c) comparing India's per capita annual average availability of food grains with the world's per capita annual average availability of food grains.

Regarding yield, India lags far behind the world average and other countries. First, against the world average yield of wheat being 2,624 kg per ha, India produces only 2,578 kg per ha, whereas France's yield is 7,603 kg per ha (1998). Second, against the world average yield of rice being 3,747 kg per ha, India produces only 2,890 kg per ha, while Egypt produces 8,527 kg per ha (1998). Third, against the world average yield of maize being 4,395 kg per ha (1998) India produces only 1613 kg maize per ha while Italy produces 9322 kg per ha. Further, in wheat, India shares 11.1 per cent of total world wheat production, and ranks third, while in rice it shares 21.6 per cent of total world rice production and ranks second, but in maize it shares just 1.7 per cent of total world maize production and ranks seventh (with Romania). Thus, it is not a satisfactory situation in view of its huge population being 17 per cent of that of the world. Finally, in per capita availability, India had only 176.3 kg of food-grains per year in 1999-2001, which increased to 290kg per head in 2014-15 (stock of 368.56 lakh tonnes for 125 crore people). For properly implementing National Food Security Act 2013, 612 lakh tonnes of food grains are needed in India.

However, the moot point is that the availability of food grains at the national level is only a necessary condition for ensuring food availability, not a sufficient one. Until and unless food grains are made available at the local level at village/panchayat stores, local market, public distribution system (PDS) shops or cooperative stores, the poor farmers and labourers will not be able to have even a 'specific physical access' because due to hoarding or black-marketing an artificial shortage is created. The PDS in most of the rural areas (except in Kerala, Chhattisgarh and Tamil Nadu) is in a deplorable condition characterised by non-lifting by State government or non-lifting by PDS dealers who are compelled to pay bribes to the officials concerned. In fact, during 1996-97 to 2002-03, there was a massive increase in food subsidy from Rs 6,066 crores to Rs 2,400 crores. Hence N.C. Saxena (2004) rightly remarks: 'The centre is spending more on food subsidy than what it spends on Agriculture, Rural Development, and Irrigation and Flood Control taken together, but benefits to the poor are hardly satisfying.' As a public hearing at Shankargarh (Allahabad) revealed that a bribe of Rs 38 per quintal is given by the PDS dealer to many officials ranging from the godown in-charge to the SDM.

Next important aspect of food security is specific economic food accessibility at the household level. The purchasing power of the agricultural labourers and farmers reflects the economic access to food. Though India had 30 per cent of its grain production in public stock (over 60 million tonnes) by 2000, about 25 per cent Indians were under-nourished and food-insecure. The situation has improved only to some extent as stock has increased to 368.56 MT at national level but affordability is quite less. The farmers have a feeling that the minimum support prices for paddy and wheat remain more theoretical than practical, being meagre in comparison to the rising costs of production. Many farmers rightly argue that actual costs of their labour (family and outside wage labour) is not taken into account while calculating costs of agricultural production by 'urban experts'! Besides, there are not sufficient purchase centres. Further, the government employees posted at the block purchase centre indulge in all sorts of corrupt practices by dilly-dallying and wrongly declaring more than the permissible level of moisture in the paddy and hence they give the farmers lower prices than due. They do not pay in cash and the bank cheques issued are delayed by the banks in their encashment. Again, due to the long distance between the village and the block, most farmers cannot take their paddy to the block purchase centre. The farmers are, therefore, compelled to sell paddy to local traders or local 'net buyers' of villages at less than remunerative rates.

Thus, as far as economic accessibility is concerned, people living below the income poverty line (20.4 per cent in 2005-06 as per the Planning Commission of India) cannot afford to buy food. According to Arjun Sengupta Commission on unorganised labour (2004-05) 77 per cent people in India spend merely Rs 20 per day, hence not able to meet both ends' meet. As per Global Hunger Index (GHI), 2014, that combines undernourishment, child underweight and child mortality with equal weightage, India ranks 120th among 128 countries on GHI. In rural areas, despite the Mahatma Gandhi National Rural Employment Guarantee (MNREG) scheme of giving 100 days' work to all needy adults in a year, in practice, people do not get work for 100 days-actually less than five per cent labourers engaged there get 100 days work in a year. They do not get unemployment allowance either and often get less than the minimum wages in some parts of India as pointed out by the CAG in sample checking. However, it is also a fact that the MNREG schemes have, to some extent, contributed to check starvation deaths and the huge migration from the poor pockets of Andhra Pradesh, Bihar, Odisha, UP, MP, Chhattisgarh, Uttarakhand and Jharkhand to the urban areas but no durable assets have been created in MNREG schemes. To be more specific, in 2005, three lakh persons had migrated from Mahabubnagar district (AP) alone to Mumbai, Pune, Surat, etc. as unskilled labour, but in 2008, the number of such migrants reduced to 53,000 due to the Mahatma Gandhi National Rural Employment Guarantee schemes (Jansatta, 25 June 2008).

Another aspect of food security is the food consumption pattern for the well-being at the intra-household level. There is often a visible discrimination against the females, children, the aged, the disabled, widows, and the unemployed male adults and their wives and children either because of scarcity of food in the family or because of discriminatory social practices or individual biases of the head of the family. Hence, even a large annual family income is not always sufficient for food security to all members in real sense.

Finally, food absorption is another aspect of food security at the individual level. Medically, it has been proved that holistic nourishment and a sound health also require safe drinking water, hygiene and clean environment as much as the staple diet. Unfortunately, about 19 per cent of the Indians do not have access to sanitation services. Since some family members often do not get nutritious food in terms of required calories (1800), there is an increase in the number of underweight children, children with stunted growth, and those infected with diseases due to malnourishment; infirmity as well as weakness results into early mortality. In India, 47 per cent of children below five years are undernourished; 80 per cent of children in India suffer from water-borne diseases; and over seven lakh of these children die every year. In 1996, 65,000 villages in India became waterless (Pant, 2003). The situation has improved only to some extent. As per International norms a person with body mass index (BMI) between 16 and 16.9 is chronically malnourished and a person between 17 and 18 BMI is malnourished. In India 35.6 per cent women and 34.2 per cent men have less than 18.5 BMI. About 50 per cent Indian women are anaemic.

Causes and Consequences of Food Crisis

Though food production has been increasing globally and nationally, its prices have been spiralling for the following reasons:

(a) Rising long-term demand in hugely populated developing countries like China and India, where rising prosperity has led to eating more quantity of food. The US Department of Agriculture estimates that the worldwide rice consumption increased 0.9 per cent in 2007 (about 424 million tonnes) but the rice production increased less than 0.7 per cent.

(b) Short-term supply shocks due to unusually cold weather (due to climate change) and pest infestation in Vietnam, the second largest rice supplier in the world have affected the food situation. The aggregate production of maize, rice and soybean stagnated in 2006 and 2007 due to drought, while the drought in Australia led to a decrease in wheat production. India's many states suffered droughts in recent past. Further Sahel region of Africa and Ethiopia have faced severe droughts due to climate change. This resulted into starvation deaths there.

(c) Diversion of a huge chunk of America's corn crop to ethanol production boosting demand for other staples like rice (Wolf, 2008; Ritter, 2008).

(d) Eating habits due to cultural and religious reasons too have an impact on food security, e.g. many Hindus not preferring non-vegetarian foods including beef and Muslims proscribe pork and so on.

(e) There are less technological innovations and far less investment in agriculture as well as lack of initiatives in extension works to make 'from lab to land' a success.

There seems to be a grand linkage between the prices of energy, industrial raw materials and foodstuffs. The social consequence of such food price hikes is tremendous - food riots have taken place in the Philippines, Bangladesh, Egypt, Haiti and even in Murshidabad in West Bengal. Second, one of the ecological consequences is in terms of more pressure on water and soil. Third, the price hike has led to hoarding locally and nationally. For instance, India, China, Cambodia and Vietnam banned rice exports in order to ease domestic pressure, ultimately depriving the poor in food-deficit countries like Sub-Saharan Africa. This has an inflationary effect at the global level. On the other hand, the world food crisis is also giving us an opportunity to rethink about the entire 'development paradigm', especially to question the WTO Agreement on Agriculture and the so-called Green Revolution ('How green is the Green Revolution?' is the moot question), to adjust to climate change and to practice 'evergreen revolution' (sustainable agriculture through bio-fertilisers, efficient use of water through drip irrigation, short-term early varieties of seeds, dry land farming, integrated pest management and improving indigenous seeds).

Policy Implications: What is to be Done?

Peter Mandelson (2008), European Union Trade Commissioner, suggests two ways to overcome world food crisis: First, 'greater production capacity' through better land use and crop practices, e.g. better/more fertilisers, improved technology and better infrastructure. For this, the developed world should provide development aid to the developing countries. Second, a dynamic farm market to encourage farmers to improve productivity in order 'to feed a growing world market' must be created. To quote him, 'One country's temporary food security can be another's food scarcity.' In order to turn this crisis into a political opportunity, both developed and developing worlds should invest more in agriculture and reform global farm trade. This line of thought has been shared by many western and Indian scholars of neo-liberal perspective. Sunil Kewalramani (2008), a consultant with multinational companies, is of a similar view that the US in the 1970s changed its policy to encourage output rather than to support prices by limiting production and imposing export curbs. Boosting research on improving farm yields, investing more in irrigation and rural transportation and powering farms with solar and wind energy seem necessary to him to tackle the impending food crisis. He thinks even GM food is essential for the developing countries.

On the other side, two views have emerged, mostly in developing countries, with an eco-sustainability and social equity perspective. First, the diversion of agricultural lands from food grains' production to bio-fuel (ethanol) should be reversed immediately, especially in United States of America. This practice is taking deep roots and even in some developing countries like Brazil and India, the cultivation of 'jatropha' (bio-fuel) is slowly picking up. As a report by Oxfam (2008) points out, rich countries' demand for more bio-fuels in their transport is causing food price inflation. Grain reserves are now at an all-time low: Rich countries spent up to 15 billion dollars in 2007 supporting bio-fuels while blocking cheaper Brazilian ethanol, which is far less damaging for global food security. Consequently, bio-fuels are responsible for 30 per cent of increase in global food prices, pushing 30 million people worldwide into poverty. Hence, developed countries should scrap bio-fuels' targets, including the EU plan to get 10 per cent of its transport fuel from renewable sources like bio-fuels by 2020. Global bio-fuel production is projected to rise from 1.3 million barrels per day in 2010 to 2.7 million barrels per day in 2030 with the US accounting for almost half of that growth.

Further, a study by US scientists led by Jennifer Burney (University of California) analysed 30 years of data in India and found that air pollution caused wheat yields in densely populated States to be 50 per cent lower than what could have been in 2010-up to 90 per cent of the decrease in potential food production is linked to smog (mix of black carbon and other pollutants) and the rest 10 per cent decrease is linked to global warming and precipitation level. Obviously tackling global warming requires international action while the problem of smog can be tackled at national level. Kyoto protocol is yet to be implemented by developed countries like US, Canada etc. because there is 'common but differentiated responsibility' at global level.

Again in many developed countries, animals are fed food-grains for getting more meat though animals are very inefficient converters of food-grains to meat- a cow eats 16 kg of food grains to develop only one kg of beef! But unfortunately, as Arun Firodia rightly points out, over 70 per cent of food grains produced in the US are consumed by cows and pigs for producing more meat. An average American eats 125 kg of meat annually (against Indian average of just 3 kg) and all Americans eat 35 million tonnes of meat every year (against just 3 million tonnes in India). In China, annual per capita meat consumption is 70 kg (total 100 million tonnes in a year). World meat consumption increased five-fold in the last five decades, leading to diversion of food grains to animal feed. So, for countries like the US and China, meat is the actual food and not food grains, hence they don't bother much for the price rise of food grains. Again, Arun Firodia rightly points out that for producing just one kg of beef, 10,000 litres of water are needed. But an animal generates 100 times more waste than a human being-so how to dispose off such a huge waste of these 50,000 million animals? And the processing and storage of meat require a huge amount of energy. Hence, if humans consume grains directly, rather than cycle them through animals to eat their meat, there would be enough food to feed the entire world.

M.S. Swaminathan (2004) has rightly suggested the following nine-point State Action Plan for food security:

(a) To identify who are hungry-about 10-15 per cent of villagers (as found in Tamil Nadu).

(b) People should be made aware of the development and welfare programmes schemes of central and State governments through 'entitlement cards' (disaggregated by gender, age, caste and class, giving details of each family, its entitlement and how to access it).

(c) To eliminate energy deprivation and under-nutrition, to have a lifecycle approach of horizontal linkages among vertically structured programmes.

(d) Integrated food-based approach to hidden hunger through chemical and bio-fortification.

(e) To ensure safe drinking water-Jal Swaraj is doing good work for water security.

(f) To provide opportunities for sustainable livelihood-microfinance-led self-help groups should be organised with market linkages, otherwise it would remain a 'numbers game', further, a 'paradigm shift' from unskilled to skilled work is needed to overcome poverty.

(g) Special attention to pregnant mothers and infants (as low-weight baby at birth-2.2 kg or below-is prevalent) is necessary and also to the adverse female-male sex ratio in many States in India. So maternal and foetal under-nutrition is to be accorded priority, as malnutrition is reducing national GDP by more than three per cent.

(h) Capacity-building programmes should be organised in such a way that all able-bodied persons are ultimately able to earn their livelihood. While the deprived people may be helped under State support, training and empowerment should be combined so that even after the discontinuing of the State support, this lateral learning may provide food with freedom and human dignity, and not make people 'beneficiaries' of a 'patronage' approach. Actually, according to Swaminathan, people are not the beneficiaries; rather government officers are the 'real beneficiaries' as 85 per cent of the public money in the form of taxes goes to their salary!

(i) The formation of a consultative Group for Freedom from Hunger at State level under the Chairmanship of Chief Minister is imperative in order to coordinate civil society organisations, women's groups, government departments, academic experts, media, and international agencies like FAO, WFP, UNICEF, UNESCO and UNDP.

Swaminathan also suggests employment guarantee schemes with a 'paradigm shift' at national level from "jobless" to "job-led" growth, 'from green to evergreen revolution', and an Employment Impact Audit in all government programmes and mobilisation of one million elected women members of panchayats. To quote him, 'We must establish community Food, Feed and Fodder Banks in every State.... We may consider developing a Job for Indians Act in order to provide guidelines for achieving the goal of work for all. "Work for all" is the only means of ensuring "food for all" in an economically sustainable manner.' We have MNREG scheme since 2005 for providing at least 100 days of employment for adults in rural India.

In fact, we have to give the highest priority to the basic needs of all human beings- food, water, primary health, education, shelter and clothing- in an integrated manner, not merely as a risk management or relief measure. Not only 'development with dignity' (Amit Bhaduri) but also 'food with dignity' is the need of the hour as right to food is an integral part of our fundamental right to life as enshrined in Article 21 of the Indian Constitution as well as in Article 25 of the Universal Declaration of Human Rights (1948). That is, in most of the development programmes/schemes like Mahatma Gandhi National Rural Employment Guarantee Scheme, Mid-day Meals, Integrated Child Development Scheme, 'Swachchh Bharat' etc, the component of nutritious food and safe drinking water should be included through entitlement card so that it may become inclusive real social development. However, to avoid the sole dependency and patronage syndrome, it is imperative that most of the youth working in employment schemes are trained adequately for new or complementary skills, hence upskilling, bi-skilling, multi-skilling and reskilling is very much needed in the whole India. In addition, awareness about requirement of nutrition at the various stages of lifecycle is to be generated, especially about micronutrients, absorption capacity of body and inadequacy of calories. Hence, nutrition-based, food-based and knowledge-based approaches should be adopted simultaneously. But for that there should also be genuine land reforms in States like Bihar, AP, Rajasthan and MP. Again special attention should be given to vulnerable groups, 'hunger pockets', etc. This requires a strong political will as well as administrative will.

Second, to realize such a lofty ideal, we have to adapt the decentralisation of scheme formulation and implementation of minor public works through Panchayats with more transparency, accountability and shared benefits by practising the concept of 'think globally, act locally.' No doubt, in a large number of cases of Panchayat works, there is corruption involved, but it may be eliminated through proactive and regular checks and balances like social audits by both the local supervisory/monitoring authorities and the civil society organisations (CSOs) and NGOs. Further exemplary purishment should be imposed on defaulter panchayats' functionaries but they should be given more funds, functions and functionaries. Panchayats, CSOs and NGOs can easily manage food banks locally. Many self-help groups of women have successfully operated PDS shops in Bihar. This needs scaling up in other parts of India too.

Third, since adequate quantity of foodgrains is always available in government godowns with increasing costs of storage, it would be appropriate to give foodgrains 'Above Poverty Line' (APL) families also. National Advisory Council rightly recommended (on 14 July 2010) to go in for a universalisation of grain entitlement across the country in a phased manner as more coverage ensures less leakage: one-fourth of the poorest blocks (about 2000 blocks) to be brought under the ambit of National Food Security Act (2013) in the first phase and in the remaining 6000 blocks special food distribution scheme to be strengthened with a focus on infants, children, the aged, pregnant women, the homeless, primitive tribes and seriously ill persons. But under the National Food Security Act 2013, only two-thirds of population will get 35 kg of food grains (rice at the rate of Rs 3 and wheat at rate of Rs 2). Further, in all states the allocation and lifting of food grains by PDS dealers should be publicised on websites and new modes of mass media, (twitter, face book etc. and they should use computer for detailed accounting). All class two officers of blocks/tehsils should make transparent and regular inspection and vigilance under camera. Since 1997 Government of India launched Targeted Public Distribution System (TDPS) and now it estimates 6.52 crore families as Below Poverty Line (BPL). Government of India has developed National Transparency Portal for TDPS to provide all relevant data in public domain. All states have been advised by Union Government for fair price shop Automation. But still the fair price shops' dealers need more commission due to increasing costs of transportation etc. Following measures have been taken: 30 States/UTs have eliminated 493.83 lakh bogus ration cards; Panchayats have been involved in vigilance committees to monitor FPS in 29 States/UTs, display of BPL lists at FPS in 32 States/UTs, display of district-wise and FPS wise allocations of food grains on website for public scrutiny in 22 States, door step delivery of food grains to FPS is being made in 20 States/UTs. Yet the fact remains that about one-third of food grains released to states does not reach the actual beneficiary (Khera, 2011) due to being sold in black market (especially to flour mills) or rots in FCI/States' godowns. (In UP, Bihar, West Bengal, Delhi leakage is more). However, Dreze and Khere (2013) estimate that at all India level PDS will reduce the poverty gap index of rural poverty from 18 to 22 per cent. In fact, against the target of two-third population covered by PDS under FS Act, only 44 per cent of total population is covered under PDS so far. But in States, which are less conducive to grow food grains, like J and K, Himachal Pradesh, Sikkim, Arunachal Pradesh, Mizoram, Assam, Tripura, Meghalaya and Uttarakhand, PDS is relatively more effective.

Fourth, there should be more public investment in agriculture especially irrigation, because still about 55 per cent of the Indians are directly engaged in agriculture (though there is 'disguised unemployment' because more than required family members are employed for agricultural tasks). This has to ensure both bringing unused lands under cultivation and increasing yield per acre- production and productivity. Undoubtedly, various case studies (including the one in Sultanpur, UP by this author) have clearly found that public investment in agricultural infrastructure induces private investment in various agricultural activities. Allied agricultural activities like dairy, animal husbandry, goatry, piggery, fisheries, poultry etc. should be promoted on a large scale. Further, agriculture is not merely a means of livelihood but also a social and cultural way of life; hence, attention should be paid to sensitivity, preferences, food habits, and experiential knowledge of the local people while adapting new technologies for production and ecological sustainability at the same time. Most of Indians eat pulses and edible oils of particular varieties but over the years consumption of pulses and edible oils per head is quite less. For instance, per capita consumption of edible oils per year in India is only 16.2 kg against the same being 27 kg as world average (in 2013-14). About 50 per cent of domestic demand of edible oils is met by imports (crude palm oil 50.4 per cent, RBD palmolein 24.2 per cent, sunflower oil 13.7 per cent, soybean oil 10.7 per cent in 2013-14). Similarly per head consumption of pulses is negligible in India (about 35 gram per day per head) both due to non-availability (due to less domestic production because of drought and less import of pulses) and lack of affordability due to high prices (Arhar dal being sold at Rs 120 per kg in 2015-16). though it is the main source of protein for most of rural Indian population.

Fifth, the policy-makers have to ensure that agriculture should continue to get various subsidies in fertilisers, seeds, irrigation, pesticides, etc. However, it should be changed from chemical fertilisers to green and bio-fertilisers, from chemical pesticides/insecticides/weedicides to integrated bio-pest management, from GM seeds to improved indigenous seeds, from flood irrigation to drip irrigation because Green Revolution in Punjab, Haryana and Western UP has also proved detrimental in terms of water table going down fast, increasing salinity in soil, high quantity of residues of pesticide/insecticides/weedicides found in food grains, pulses, fruits and vegetables grown there. These are resulting into serious diseases like cancer. Food security also requires food safety. There should be only one standard for safe drinking water in India like developed countries and the packaged drinking water companies should be penalised for about 35 times more pesticides than the European Union Norms for drinking water and cold drinks (as found by Centre for Science and Environment, New Delhi in 2003). The high potential of traditional indigenous knowledge system should be tapped fully. Thus, a 'paradigm shift' from green revolution to 'Evergreen Revolution', to use M.S. Swaminathan's term, is earnestly called for. In this regard Government of India's 'Act East' (in place of 'Look East') policy is appreciable and needs to be expedited on the ground.

Sixth, minimum support price (MSP) should be fixed one and half times the actual costs of agricultural production as farmers are in loss due to rising costs of production and lower prices for their produce in open market. Hence lakhs of farmers have committed suicides in southern and western States and 40 per cent farmers have left farming and migrated to work as non-farm workers. Agricultural Costs and Prices Commission, headed by an economist, should be replaced by an active and vibrant Kisan Ayog, headed by an actual and well-informed farmer.

Finally, the procurement of food grains should be decentralised by all States as is being done in West Bengal, MP, Chhattisgarh, Uttarakhand, Odisha, Tamil Nadu, Gujarat, Karnataka, Kerala, AP, Bihar, Rajasthan, Punjab and Telengana in order to have savings in food subsidy, more efficiency and extending benefits of MSP to local farmers. In case of less procurement than allocation by central government the latter, through FCI, compensates the concerned state and this should continue further.

These measures are realisable for 'real social development' with genuine political and administrative will. For this, we have to wake up 'here and now' because the food question cannot wait any more in the present context of severe mass poverty and partial hunger in many parts of India like Bihar, Odisha (KBK), Eastern UP, Bundelkhand, Rajasthan, Uttarakhand, Chhattisgarh, West Bengal, Assam, Jharkhand and Andhra Pradesh. We have to ensure food sufficiency and availability, economic capability, social equity, cultural acceptability and ecological sustainability of agriculture in an integrated way so that there is an intra-generational and inter-generational equity for an inclusive society. To conclude, there has been no famine in India in post-independence period (as it took place in 1943 in Bengal leading to 1.5 million deaths)- this shows better production and food security to poor people, yet full food security in a critical holistic perspective has not been achieved so far. In fact, we have to ensure eradication of poverty and stabilisation of prices of food grains, pulses, edible oils etc. in the long run. The declared vision of Government of India is to ensure food security for citizens of India, hence we have several miles to go to realise this goal.

References

Bhardwaj, Krishna (1974), *'Production Conditions in Indian Agriculture'*, Cambridge University Press, Cambridge.

Brown, Lester R. (2008), 'Business as Usual is No Longer a Viable Option', *The Indian Express*, 13 June.

Chakrabarti, M. and S.K. Datta (2000), 'Agriculture', in *Alternative Economic Survey* 1998-2000, Rainbow Publishers Ltd, Delhi.

Dreze, Jean and R. Khera (2013), 'Rural Poverty and the Public Distribution System', '*Economic and Political Weekly*', Vol. 48, Nos. 45-46, 16 November.

Firodia, Arun (2008), 'Rising Food Prices: The Blame Game', *The Economic Times,* 9 June.

Government of India (2004), 'Serving Farmers and Saving Farming', National Commission on Farmers, Ministry of Agriculture, New Delhi.

Government of India (2015), "Annual Report 2014-15", Department of Food and Public Distribution, Ministry of Consumer Affairs, Food and Public Distribution, New Delhi.

Guha-Khasnobis, Basudeb, S.S. Acharya and B. Davis (eds) (2008), 'Food Security', Oxford University Press, Oxford.

Kewalramani, S. (2008), 'Green Revolution II Needed, and Not Export Curbs', *The Hindu, Business Line,* 7 June.

Khera, R (2011), 'Trends in Diversion of Grains from the Public Distribution system', *'Economic and Political Weekly',* Vol 47, No.21, 21 May.

Oxfam (2008), 'Bio-fuels Pushing Thirty Million into Poverty', *The Times of India,* 26 June.

Pant, Ruchi (2003), 'From Communities' Hands to MNCs' BOOTS: A Case Study from India on Right to Water', Paper submitted to Rights and Humanity, UK.

Ritter, Peter (2008), 'No Grain, Big Pain', *Time,* 21 April.

Sachs, J. (2008), 'Common Wealth', Penguin, Allen Lane, London.

Saxena, N C (2004), 'Synergising Government Efforts for Food Security', in M.S. Swaminathan and Pedro Medrano (eds), Towards Hunger free India, East-West Book Pvt Ltd, Chennai.

Sharma, Subhash (2002), 'Dialectics of Agrarian Development: A Sociological Study in North India', Yash Publications, Delhi.

Sharma, Subhash (2015), 'Development and Its Discontents', Rawat Publications, New Delhi/Jaipur.

Streitfeld, D. and K. Bradsher (2008), 'Weather Adds to Challenge of Food Shortages', *The Hindu,* 11 June.

Swaminathan, M.S. (2004), 'Vision for a Hunger Free India', in M.S.Swaminathan and Varma, Subodh (2008), 'As Food Crisis Worsens, Firms Push GM Seeds', *The Times of India,* 4 June.

Wolf, Martin (2008), 'The Food Crisis is a Chance to Reform Global Agriculture', *Financial Times* (London), 30 May.

Index

T